D0084873

ECONOMIC REFORM AND STABILIZATION IN LATIN AMERICA

Edited by

Michael Connolly
Claudio González-Vega

PRAEGER

New York
Westport, Connecticut
London

Acknowledgments

We are grateful to numerous universities, agencies, and institutes whose collective support contributed to the success of the Second Dominican Republic Conference on Trade and Financial Liberalization in Latin America held in Santo Domingo, March 22–24, 1985. We are particularly indebted to the United States Agency for International Development (USAID), especially Dr. James Fox; the Interamerican Institute of Capital Markets in Caracas, especially Licenciado José París Coronel; the Banco Central de la República Dominicana, especially Governor Hugo Guiliani Cury; the Universidad Católica Madre y Maestra, especially Rector Monseigneur Agripino Núñez; the University of South Carolina, especially Dean James Kane; the University of Miami, especially Dean Jack Borsting and Al Holtmann; and The Ohio State University.

We also wish to acknowledge the efforts of all the participants in the conference. Without the aid of the contributors, discussants, and other participants, this volume would not have been possible.

Library of Congress Cataloging-in-Publication Data

Economic reform and stabilization in Latin America.

Includes Index.
1. Economic stabilization–Latin American.   2. Latin America–Commercial policy.   3. Monetary policy–Latin America.   4. Foreign exchange administration–Latin America.   5. Latin America–Economic conditions–1945-   I. Connolly, Michael B. (Michael Bahaamonde), 1941-   II. González-Vega, Claudio.
HC125.E374   1986   338.98   86-9405
ISBN 0-275-92307-X (alk. paper)

Library of Congress Catalog Card Number: 86-9405
ISBN: 0-275-92307-X

First published in 1987

Praeger Publishers, 521 Fifth Avenue, New York, NY 10175
A division of Greenwood Press, Inc.

Printed in the United States of America

The paper used in this book complies with the Permanent Paper Standard issued by the National Information Standards Organization (Z39.48-1984).

10   9   8   7   6   5   4   3   2   1

Contents

PART III
THE APPROPRIATE EXCHANGE RATE REGIME

PART V
THE LIBERALIZATION EXPERIENCE
OF CHILE AND URUGUAY

PART VI
TRADE POLICY

PART VII
INTEREST RATE POLICY

PART VIII
THE FINANCIALLY SUPPRESSED ECONOMY

Preface

Governor Hugo Guiliani Cury

Introduction: The Debt Crisis

Since the beginning of the decade of the 1970s, there has been a flow of financial capital, rather than of direct investment, toward developing countries. The foreign debt of those developing countries that are also net importers of oil went approximately from U.S.$130 billion in 1973 to $612 billion in 1982.

In many cases, this indebtedness was directed toward stimulating the development of our countries, but I have no doubt that, in others, a large portion of the resources involved were not adequately channeled.

The indebtedness of developing countries rose five times between 1973 and 1982, which represents an average annual increase of 19%. However, goods and service exports by developing countries had a substantially lower increase.

These circumstances gradually created throughout the world the grave crisis that we face today with respect to the external debt.

The main factors that led our countries toward this situation were:

1. World recession, trade restrictions in industrial countries, and the collapse of prices of certain raw materials.
2. The fiscal policy of the United States.
3. High interest rates.
4. Increases in oil prices.
5. Deficient administration of our economies, since adjustments were not applied at the opportune time, nor were the resources available efficiently used.

All these factors led numerous countries to default on their payments abroad. The cases of Poland, Mexico, Argentina, and Brazil are well known.

Temporary versus Permanent Solutions

What are the solutions that have been proposed for the problems of foreign debt and stabilization of our economies?

Diverse approaches and solutions to these problems have emerged, but in practice the solutions have been temporary. It's like putting a bit of soap on a car radiator to cover the hole in it. These solutions will only give relief to our countries for one or two years. The truth is that there has not been a permanent solution and the crisis has merely been postponed.

Despite Mexico's debt renegotiation, the banks and official creditors still present the historical and market conditions as the main term of reference in negotiations carried out with different countries, rather than taking their payment capacity as the main element in the debt-renegotiation process.

To restructure one or two years of due and undue capital payment on the foreign debt gives merely temporary breathing room and will necessarily oblige creditors and debtors to sit down once again to renegotiate the debt. This is even more true when the level of new financing that is being granted to close the balance-of-payments gap has been insufficient. These have been very timid solutions with which to face such a grievous problem. To restructure the debt in a timid way merely worsens the problem, and, in the future, many countries may be inclined to declare their debt in moratoriums, particularly when they come to realize that the amounts they pay for interest are greater than the income they receive from new loans. The failure to find a permanent solution to the debt problem is leading to a growing feeling in our countries that the only way out is a long-term, political solution.

The Stabilization Process

Not only has the approach to the debt problem been one with such narrow vision—that to the stabilization process is an equally narrow one.

It has been agreed upon at a regional level that the International Monetary Fund and the debtor countries undertake stabilization programs so as to correct external and internal imbalance. Those agreements have been established as a prerequisite to negotiating external debt. In the case of certain small countries, bilateral aid has been made conditional on the existence of a Contingency Program with the IMF.

The characteristics of the IMF's programs are familiar: the basic objective is to reduce the global demand in order to restructure internal and external imbalance.

Many of our countries have confronted serious problems of an economic, political, and social order upon trying to pursue the strategies prescribed by the IMF. This has essentially occurred because those stabilization programs have not yet managed to incorporate a certain degree of correspondence between the adjustments required to correct external imbalance and the need also to stimulate the economic growth process. It is absolutely necessary to find a balance between a restrictive policy and one of growth. Both objectives are not contradictory, as has often been pointed out. In particular, it is possible to achieve a balance between restrictive and economic growth measures if, in the absorption process, upon reducing consumption, which is only one part of the equation, the other component—investment—is protected. Thus, the process of stabilization should focus not only on the demand side, but also on the supply side, making an effort to restructure the productive apparatus of our economies. Eliminating deficits and restructuring debts is not the final solution.

What worries us is not only that this problem is present in the IMF programs but that there is a lack of an overall program at the international level to provide a timely flow of funds which could permit a coherent approach to soften the transition between short-term and long-term solutions. Consequently, more and greater short-term adjustment measures are demanded without solutions on a medium- and long-term basis. In turn, this short-term approach generates political discontent and instability in our fragile economies and incipient democracies.

In order to face this situation, we must look for and support solutions aimed at:

1. Increasing the volume of resources provided by the IMF stabilization programs.
2. Effecting a true coordination between the IMF programs, the World Bank, and other multilateral organizations in order that the economic contraction carried out in the adjustment process can be compensated with loans at the proper time and directed to the productive sectors that will generate the foreign exchange required to correct the external imbalance.
3. Effecting a restructuring of foreign debt in more realistic terms. There is no sense in restructuring what has matured and what will mature in the next two years. It is also absolutely necessary that the commercial banks provide a volume of resources that will permit covering the balance-of-payments gap over a longer time.
4. Maintaining the official flow of resources at an adequate level and assuring their availability at the opportune moment.

None of these suggestions makes any sense if there is an absence, at a world level, of an overall policy to restrict expansionist tendencies and policies of subsidies and to remove trade restrictions that keep the prices of our export products depressed in the key industrial countries, such as Germany, the United States, the United Kingdom, and Japan.

Nevertheless, this does not prevent us from questioning the policies we have adopted in the past. It is sufficient to mention the excessive protectionism of a fiscal, exchange, and credit nature that we have given to the industrial sector in all of our countries. This we have done to the detriment of the appropriate use of our comparative advantages and of the stimulus to exports.

For example, in the case of Mexico, for many years the peso was overvalued and accompanied by a deficit policy that sought to promote growth but, in fact, encouraged capital flight of approximately U.S.$17 billion between 1981 and 1982.

Argentina is another case where a deficient application of the instruments of economic policy, manifested through a preannounced rate of devaluation lower than domestic inflation, resulted in an overvalued peso and a rapid process of external indebtedness which, in turn, was also accompanied by capital flight.

Those mistaken policies make us question not only the programs of international organizations and how the rich nations focus upon the problem, but also the viability of the economic growth process. We have to question even further the attitude of our own domestic capital, which has taken its resources abroad while our countries became externally indebted.

This implies that Latin American countries need strong and realistic international measure not only to correct the external and internal imbalance that we have, but also to avoid capital flight and the continuation of external indebtedness.

The Case of the Dominican Republic

The Dominican Republic has had to face serious difficulties in recent years which were in part inherited from the 1970s. These difficulties have their origin in high external indebtedness, the issuance of paper money without any real backing, and the maintenance of a ficticious rate of exchange. We Dominicans did not undertake the necessary adjustments at the proper time. Furthermore, we lived for many years in a monetary fiction, having an overvalued peso. In turn, economic growth was accompanied by a rapid urbanization process.

Finally, there came a day when, having exhausted all international reserves and being highly indebted abroad, the "party" had to come to an end. No one abroad was lending money to the country anymore. To continue issuing fiat money under those conditions was also an act of financial irresponsibility.

It is not easy to put in order the economy of a democratic country which has been distorted for over a decade, particularly during periods close to an electoral process. It is a difficult and delicate task, not too well understood by the majority of our citizens. The government that we represent, headed by the lawyer Dr. Salvador Jorge Blanco, has imposed upon itself that difficult task. In terms of political popularity, adjustment is not the most advisable thing to do. But, in the future, Dominicans will recognize the necessity to return the country to a balanced external and internal situation, thus opening the road to true economic development.

To this end, we initiated, as of January 23, 1985, and through 18 initiatives adopted by the Monetary Board on that date, a financial and exchange reform that was accompanied by fiscal and price measures. The main measures adopted were:

- Unification of the exchange rate.
- Establishment of a transitory exchange surcharge on exports.
- Nongranting of credit to the public sector by the central bank.
- Initiation of a flexibilization process with regard to interest rates.
- Introduction of a group of fiscal measures that would make the country less dependent on foreign trade and which, gradually, would cause a change in the productive structure of the country.
- An increase in the price of fuel, certain basic products, and electricity in order to eliminate subsidies.
- Implementation of measures aimed at reorganizing the central bank's finances and others aimed at organizing the present exchange system.

We have not yet finished, and we acknowledge that the task undertaken is a difficult one. We realize further that the results will not be visible in the immediate future. But it is our conviction that we are making the decisions that others would not make and are facing the problems that others did not face, so that, in the future, Dominicans will have a sounder economy, one adjusted to reflect reality and the scarcity of resources.

Introduction

Major liberalization experiments have recently taken place in Latin America. Argentina, Chile, and Uruguay are the best-known cases. Ecuador and Mexico are also now in the process of economic liberalization. In the Southern Cone, the initial success of such experiments was followed by the collapse and abandonment of liberalization. Yet the reasons behind this failure are unclear. It is important that the historical record be correctly analyzed, which this volume attempts to do.

Economic stabilization is nearly always a policy goal in the Latin American context. Stabilization measures are being applied nearly everywhere: the dramatic June 1985 Austral plan of the Argentinian government, the August 1985 austerity program of the Mexican government, and the 1985 stabilization program of the Dominican Republic are only a few among many attempts to bring prices and the exchange rate under control. These stabilization programs typically involve layoffs of government employees, reductions in government spending, and changes in the exchange rate regime—from floating to fixed in the case of Argentina, from fixed to floating in the case of Mexico and the Dominican Republic. Real shocks such as the fall in the price of oil have adversely affected oil exporters such as Ecuador and Mexico, but these have been cushioned somewhat by the recent decline in the real rate of interest on foreign debt and the real depreciation of the dollar. Other real shocks such as the September 1985 earthquake in Mexico City have rendered stabilization more difficult and painful.

Stabilization and adjustment measures are clearly linked to the need to service foreign debt. This debt is rising in many cases, and it is not a problem that is likely to disappear soon. Bolivia is in default officially, others are in default unofficially. Yet others such as Ecuador and Costa Rica have successfully rescheduled their debt and are paying it off. This volume focuses on economic reform and stabilization in Latin America and the Caribbean.

Governor Hugo Guliani Cury's preface to the volume illustrates dramatically the problems of stabilization and reform in the context of large debt service in the Dominican Republic. This small, island economy is in many ways a microcosm of Latin America. The stabilization measures adopted in early 1985 involve a unified, floating exchange rate, a stop in all domestic credit extended to the government by the central bank, the raising of fuel prices and electricity rates, and so on. Such steps are classical adjustment measures taken at great pain to the general public.

Part I focuses on the theory of economic liberalization. In Chapter 1, Guillermo A. Calvo cautions that liberalization and stabilization programs are often pursued only temporarily. Calvo shows that *temporary* trade liberalization always ends up reducing the level of welfare. Furthermore, the resultant current account deficit is greater, the shorter the period of liberalization. In Chapter 2, Philip Brock and Edward Tower discuss the long-run benefits of permanent liberalization. Drawing from Anne Krueger's work, they distinguish between *gross* devaluation, which is the change in the nominal exchange rate, and net devaluation, the change in the effective exchange rate. Changes in the effective rate tend to be substantially smaller since trade restrictions are frequently eased, and the results differ in the presence of quotas rather than tariffs. Brock and Tower also discuss the management of a crawling peg exchange rate during liberalization and the consequences of pegging the real exchange rate. In Chapter 3, Mohsin Khan and Roberto Zahler examine the macroeconomic effects of reductions in tariffs and removal of controls on capital movements. Furthermore, they attempt to assess the impacts of internal and external shocks to the economy, which allows them to ascertain whether it is liberalization per se that is at fault, or whether primary blame can be laid upon foreign shocks or inconsistent domestic policies.

Part II focuses upon the order of trade and financial liberalization. In Chapter 4, Sebastián Edwards and Sweder van Wijnbergen analyze the appropriate order of economic liberalization—whether to open the trade account first and the capital account later, as in the case of Chile, or the capital account first and the trade account later, as in the case of Argentina. They also address the question of how fast the economy should be liberalized, contrasting "cold turkey" versus gradual approaches. In Chapter 5, Mario Blejer and Silvia Sagari make the distinction between external and internal financial liberalization. External liberalization refers to the removal of exchange controls and impediments to international financial flows, while internal liberalization refers to the elimination of domestic credit controls, interest rate ceilings, and differential reserve requirements. Blejer and Sagari argue that internal liberalization should precede the opening up of the domestic financial market to external financial flows.

Part III deals with the appropriate exchange rate regime in the context of liberalization. In Chapter 6, Vittorio Corbo analyzes the active use of the exchange rate for stabilization purposes in Chile, where the rate of crawl was substantially less than the inflation rate, resulting in a real exchange rate appreciation prior to its collapse. Corbo also points out the major role played by compulsory 100% backward wage indexation starting in October 1974, which resulted in unsustainable rises in real wages until June 1982, when wage indexation was suspended as a measure accompanying an 18% peso devaluation. In Chapter 7, Sergio de la Cuadra analyzes five major changes in the exchange rate in Chile between 1933 and 1982. He finds that in some instances exogenous external shocks lead to fiscal and credit policies inconsistent with a fixed exchange rate, whereas, in others, incompatible policies alone are the direct source of the misalignment of the exchange rate and of subsequent devaluations. In Chapter 8, Michael Connolly, Arturo Fernández-Pérez, and the summer 1985 international economics students of ITAM apply a speculative attack model to the preannounced exchange rate crawl in Mexico from January 1983 to July 1985. They argue that a slightly greater rate of domestic credit growth than of devaluation, a large fiscal deficit, and shock to the price of oil were the main factors leading to a series of speculative attacks on the crawling peg exchange rate system in early and mid-1985. They also relate the real exchange rate appreciation during the crawl to too-rapid domestic credit growth relative to the peso price of the U.S. dollar and link, in turn, domestic credit growth to the size of the fiscal deficit of the Mexican Government.

Part IV deals with economic analysis of the Dominican Republic. In Chapter 9, Víctor Canto develops an exchange rate model that accounts for the "dollarization" phenomenon in the Dominican Republic. Individuals hold both Dominican pesos and U.S. dollars in their portfolios, substituting dollars for pesos when the expected rate of inflation rises in the Dominican Republic. When the Dominican authorities expand domestic credit to finance the government deficit, the evidence suggests that they also raise transactions costs in holding dollars in order to prevent the erosion of the inflationary tax base. In general, however, excess domestic money creation induces increasing dollarization and greater exchange rate depreciation. In Chapter 10, Claudio González-Vega and James E. Zinser analyze financial and foreign exchange markets in the Dominican Republic and their relationship with income inequality. González-Vega and Zinser underline the financial repression that has taken place in the Dominican Republic since the mid-1970s, and the consequent growth in unregulated financial intermediaries. This financial repression has effectively crowded small and medium-sized borrowers out of the regulated financial market, adversely affecting income distribution. The nonregulated financial market has, however, at least partially offset the unfavorable impact of financial repression on income distribution. Consequently, in the absence of a general financial reform, increased regulation of the unregulated financial sector would be undesirable.

Part V focuses upon the economic liberalization experiences of Chile and Uruguay. In Chapter 11, Arnold Harberger reviews the Chilean experience from 1973 to 1983. Harberger finds that the proximate cause of Chile's difficulties beginning in 1982 was the sharp reduction in the rate of net capital inflow. He argues that an exchange rate that was viable in the presence of a large capital inflow was no longer viable when the external financing flow virtually dried up. In addition, Chilean law requiring at a minimum 100% wage indexing also led to adjustment in the labor market being mainly through unemployment rather than a fall in the real wage. When this law was modified, the June 1982 peso devaluation and free float of August 1982 led to adjustment. Furthermore, the failure of the monetary authorities to adequately supervise lending practices in the banking sector led to a large stock of bad loans whose losses were "socialized" by the bank bailout of the monetary authorities.

In Chapter 12, Jaime de Melo argues that Uruguay's opening of the capital account was at first successful because exports were promoted and the real exchange rate was not appreciated. Otherwise, large swings in real economic activity would have occurred because of the speed of adjustment of asset markets. In addition, de Melo finds that currency substitution in Uruguay took place, depending mainly on the expected rate of devaluation. Finally, the evidence suggests that private savings and investment rose as a result of the entire economic reform package, including not only financial liberalization but also commodity market deregulation and tax reforms.

Part VI deals with trade policy. In Chapter 13, Edward J. Ray estimates the impact of U.S. trade liberalization on commodity exports to the United States from Latin America and the Caribbean. Ray finds that U.S. imports of manufactured consumer goods, agricultural goods, and textiles from developing countries under the Generalized System of Preferences are either negatively affected or unaffected by trade preferences. The reason for this is that U.S. preferential import programs have systematically biased U.S. imports from developing areas away from those U.S. industries with high protection. Similarly, he finds that the Caribbean Basin Initiative fails to promote U.S. imports of consumer goods and agricultural products from the region, and systematically discourages U.S. imports of textiles.

Part VII turns to interest rate policy. In Chapter 14 Andrés Dauhajre analyzes interest rate liberalization policy with a floating exchange rate in a small, open country. Dauhajre treats specifically the importance of the coexistence of an unregulated financial market when interest rates in the regulated market are freed. His analysis derives the paths of adjustment of output, the exchange rate, and prices following deregulation of the capital market. In Chapter 15, Paul Burkett and Robert Vogel provide a framework for the microfoundations of financial liberalization from the standpoint of mobilizing savings. Their chapter builds upon McKinnon's model of money, capital, and development by replacing his assumption of indivisability of physical capital with the assumption of complementarity of financial assets and physical capital in the portfolios of households and firms. With such complementarity, the benefits to development from financial liberalization become clear.

Part VIII concludes the present volume with three essays on the financially suppressed economy. In Chapter 16, John McDermott considers the impact on unemployment of foreign exchange controls combined with a minimum wage. McDermott finds that the rationing of foreign exchange compounds the employment problems generated by minimum wages. Rationing of foreign exchange constrains the use of imported inputs and, since domestic labor is a complementary input, also constrains the demand for domestic labor. Furthermore, if expected future shortages of the imported input rise, the firm has an incentive to hoard from current stocks of the input and, consequently, reduce current uses not only of the imported input but also of labor. In Chapter 17, Lynn McFadden calculates the government revenue from money creation in Latin America from 1977 to 1981. McFadden finds that for some highly inflationary countries, the flow of new seigniorage as a proportion of gross national production is high: for example, 6% in Argentina, Mexico, and Peru and 4% in Uruguay and Chile. The inflationary finance phenomenon is the main reason for financial repression, as well as attempts to exclude asset substitutes that erode the monetary base upon which the inflationary tax is levied, reinforcing Víctor Canto's argument in Chapter 9.

I

THE THEORY OF ECONOMIC LIBERALIZATION

1

On the Costs of Temporary Liberalization/Stabilization Experiments

Guillermo A. Calvo

1. Introduction

There exists a tendency among well-trained professional economists to advise relatively small countries to adopt trade liberalization policies. This sort of advice has a solid intellectual basis in the "gains-from-trade" literature. In practice, however, when the typical economic advisor is invited to make policy recommendations, he/she usually operates in an environment where there is a set of political personages who are normally subject to a limited tenure in their present posts. After their tenure runs out, a new set of characters takes power, and the chances are that, for just purely political reasons, some of the previous policy measures will suffer a drastic change. Here is where the complications start. For, the gains-from-trade literature argues that free trade is optimal (in the sense of maximizing output at international prices) *if* free trade is going to be the policy followed in the entire future of this economy. There is no assurance that a temporary liberalization policy would be optimal if, for example, we were to know that at some time in the future a new breed of "mercantilists" would take charge of the Ministry of Economy.

I would like to dedicate this paper to the memory of Carlos Federico Díaz-Alejandro: a teacher, and a very dear friend. I am grateful to Sara Guerschanik-Calvo for her useful comments. The research reported in the chapter was funded by a grant from the National Science Foundation.

The text-book proof that free-trade Pareto dominates tariff barriers in a small economy is usually static (for example, Ethier, 1982). A superficial reading of its implications may, therefore, mislead one to conclude that it is optimal to remove tariffs at a given point in time, even when they are bound to be raised in the future. As the well-trained economist knows (or should know), however, an appropriate analytical procedure to extend the gains-from-trade theorem to a dynamic setting is, instead, to make the dynamic scenario look like the static one by the general equilibrium "trick" (see Arrow and Hahn, 1971) of distinguishing goods according to their static qualitative properties, and also—and most importantly for the present discussion—distinguishing goods according to the point in time when they are consumed, delivered, or used in production. With this convention, the static gains-from-trade theorem implies that it is optimal to eliminate all trade barriers on all present *and* future goods. To do it only on present goods may not even be a second-best solution.

In the following section we present a simple model that will help dramatize the above-mentioned point, since it implies that a temporary trade liberalization experiment always ends up reducing the level of welfare. In addition, we will use the model to obtain estimates of the welfare costs of temporary liberalization policy. Furthermore, we will show that a temporary liberalization policy induces a current-account deficit, which gets worse, the shorter is the period of liberalization. Section 3 extends the model to account for durable and nontradable goods and shows that the model can be used to understand some of the puzzling effects of temporary (inflation) stabilization policy when this is based on a preannouncement of the rate of devaluation—like the recent experiments in the Southern Cone of Latin America (see Díaz-Alejandro, 1985; Edwards, 1985; and Calvo, 1986). The chapter is closed by Section 4, which contains a brief recount of the central results.

2. The Model

The basic model and results will be presented in Section 2.1. Section 2.2, on the other hand, will discuss the simulations.

2.1. Basic Model and Results

We assume the existence of two types of (homogeneous) goods: importables and exportables. The economy is composed of a "representative" infinitely lived family whose utility function at time s is given by

$$\underset{\{c_t | t \geq s\}}{\text{Max}} \int_s^\infty u(c_t) e^{-r(t-s)} \, dt \tag{1}$$

where c is consumption of importables[1] and r is the (positive and constant) rate of discount; the function $u(\cdot)$ is strictly concave and exhibits a positive derivative for all $c > 0$. The family is assumed to behave competitively in all markets and to be subject to the following budget constraint at time s:

$$k_s + \int_s^\infty (y + g_t - p_t c_t) e^{-r(t-s)} \, dt = 0 \tag{2}$$

where exportables are the "numeraire," k is the stock of bonds held by the family, y (positive, constant, and exogenous) is the flow of endowments, p is the (domestic) importables/exportables relative price, g is government lump-sum transfers, and r is the rate of interest on bonds (that is, the own-rate of interest on exportables) assumed to be constant and (for convenience) equal to the subjective rate of discount. Notice that we have implicitly inserted the assumption of perfect foresight.

We assume that the international importables/exportables relative price is unity. Therefore, $p - 1$ is the ad-valorem tax on imports. Since we are not interested in the effects of government spending, we will assume that, uncharacteristically, the government consumes nothing, and that it gives back the proceeds of the import tax in the form of lump-sum subsidies, that is, in equilibrium,[2]

$$g_t = (p_t - 1)c_t \tag{3}$$

The economy can, therefore, be described in the following manner. The family receives a constant manna-type endowment per unit of time, in the form of exportable goods, and consumes only importables that have an international relative price in terms of exportables equal to unity. There exists an entity, however, that imposes an ad-valorem tariff on imports, and, therefore, the domestic relative price may possibly differ from unity. The family's savings are invested in a bond that pays a constant interest rate, which, for convenience, is assumed equal to the subjective rate of discount.

At each point in time s, the family is assumed to maximize condition (1) subject to condition (2), given the initial bond holdings, k_s, and the future expected (= actual) paths of p and g. When optimal $c > 0$ (the only case that we will examine in this chapter) we obtain the following first-order condition:

$$u'(c_t) = \lambda p_t \tag{4}$$

where λ is the Lagrange multiplier associated with the budget constraint (2). This is just the familiar text-book equality condition between marginal utility and price multiplied by the marginal utility of wealth, λ.

To sharpen our focus, we will concentrate on the case where, for some parameter π,

$$p_t = 1 \qquad \text{for } 0 \leqslant t \leqslant T \tag{5a}$$

$$p_t = \pi > 1 \qquad \text{for } T < t \tag{5b}$$

In other words, (5) depicts a situation where there is free trade in the period from 0 to time T, and a constant ad-valorem tariff $(\pi - 1)$ afterward. It is, obviously, the simplest possible scenario of "temporary liberalization."

By (4) and (5), there are numbers x and z such that

$$c_t = x \qquad \text{for } 0 \leqslant t \leqslant T \tag{6a}$$

$$c_t = z \qquad \text{for } T < t \tag{6b}$$

that is, optimal consumption will be constant in the periods $[0, T]$ and (T, ∞); during the "liberalization" period consumption will be x, and when the "dark ages" fall back on us again consumption will be z.

Hence, by (2), (3), and (6b), we have

$$z = y + rk_T \tag{7a}$$

that is, from time T on consumption is equal to gross national product (GNP), which, in the present context, is tantamount to saying that the current account is zero over the interval (T, ∞).

Furthermore, by (2), (3), and (6a),

$$y + rk_T = (y + rk_0 - x)e^{rT} + x \tag{7b}$$

Thus, (7) implies the following overall budget-constraint relationship between x and z:

$$z = (y + rk_0 - x)e^{rT} + x \tag{8}$$

giving rise to curve AA in Figure 1.1 (drawn from the perspective of time 0). On the other hand, the first-order conditions (4), (5), and (6) imply

$$u'(z) = u'(x)\pi \tag{9}$$

Guillermo A. Calvo

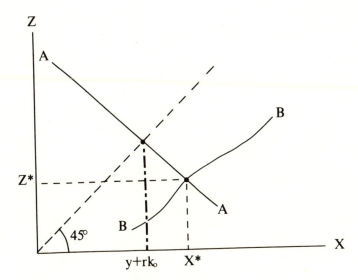

Figure 1.1   Determination of X and Z.

giving rise to curve BB in Figure 1.1. Notice that the concavity of $u(\cdot)$ and the assumption that $\pi > 1$ imply that $x > z$, for all the points on the BB curve. The point where the curves AA and BB intersect corresponds to the situation where the family's optimum is consistent with the overall budget constraint (8)—that is, a budget constraint that takes account of equation (3). Quite conventionally, this intersection point is called an "equilibrium." It is thus clear from Figure 1.1 that there exists only one equilibrium solution.

From Figure 1.1 it follows immediately that in equilibrium $x > z$. In other words, the temporary liberalization policy leads to a current-account deficit during the liberalization period. Does this have any optimality properties? The question has an easy answer. A central planner would face the problem of maximizing (1) subject to (2) with $p \equiv 1$ and $g \equiv 0$. Thus, by (4), the path of c that maximizes utility is constant, and hence, by (2), optimal consumption (from the perspective of time 0) would be equal to y + rk_0. Consequently, the temporary experiment is unambiguously utility-reducing. This is a dramatic illustration of the point made in Section 1, because in our example a policy of temporary trade liberalization— which induces a nonconstant consumption path—is always "bad."[3]

Another relevant question is: What happens to consumption as the temporary liberalization experiment is shortened (that is, as T becomes smaller)? This, again, can be readily answered: curve AA is the only one that shifts when T falls, and it does so in the way depicted in Figure 1.2 (the new curve is denoted A'A'). Consequently, the shorter the period where

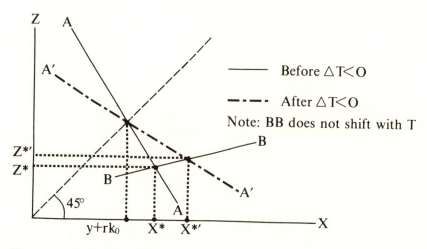

Figure 1.2   Effect of $\Delta T < 0$.

trade is liberalized, the larger the aggregate consumption during the liberalization period—the larger, in other words, the current-account deficit.[4] This is interesting because a more superficial evaluation may lead us to believe that all "real" effects tend to die down as the degree of temporariness goes to zero (that is, as T→0). The intuition is also quite clear; the shorter is T, the smaller is the effect on permanent consumption after T (z) provoked by any given level of consumption before T (x); therefore, the opportunity cost of x in terms of future (after T) utility diminishes as T gets smaller, leading to a higher x.

The impact of a change in T on welfare—an "ordinal"[5] measure of which is equation (1) at s = 0, the beginning of the liberalization experiment—is ambiguous. It is quite intuitive that as T→0 the total welfare cost goes to zero: true, a distortion is always induced on the consumption path, but since welfare is measured by an integral like equation (1), the weight of the distortion in the total goes to zero as T→0. On the other hand, if T is actually equal to infinity, it follows from our previous discussion that consumption will be constant and equal to the level at which a central planner would set it; thus, there would be no welfare costs.[6] It is, thus, plausible to conjecture that as T→∞, welfare costs will tend to vanish (this will be confirmed by the ensuing examples). Consequently, there is some T, denoted by T_*, $0 < T_* < \infty$, such that the welfare cost of temporary liberalization is *maximized*—implying that there is no hope in trying to get an unambiguous sign for the relationship between welfare cost and T. This is, therefore, an appropriate time for us to turn to the examination of more specific examples.

2.2. Simulations

Our simulations are performed on the basis of the class of isoelastic utility indexes, that is,

$$u(c) = c^{1-\alpha}/(1 - \alpha) \qquad \alpha > 0 \tag{10}$$

To calculate costs in terms of output, we will proceed as follows; we denote by $W(T, \theta)$ the equilibrium level of welfare—measured by equation (1) at $s = 0$—when the period of temporary liberalization is of length T and the family's disposable income at time zero—that is, $y + rk_0$—is taxed at the rate θ. By previous considerations, if $T = 0$ (that is, if liberalization lasts for an instant), consumption would be constant and equal to $(y + rk_0)(1 - \theta)$. On the other hand, by our notational convention, if no disposable income tax is imposed (that is, $\theta = 0$), welfare would be $W(T, 0)$. We define the cost of a liberalization policy of length T as the value of θ that solves the following condition:

$$W(0, \theta) = W(T, 0) \tag{11}$$

Therefore, the cost of temporary liberalization, as defined here, is equal to the proportion of permanent consumption that would have to be substracted from first-best consumption in order to attain the level of welfare associated with the temporary liberalization policy.

When (10) holds and $\alpha \neq 1$ we have, recalling equations (6) and (8)–(11),

$$(1 - \theta)^{1-\alpha} = \frac{1 - (1 - q^{1-\alpha})e^{-rT}}{[1 - (1 - q)e^{-rT}]^{1-\alpha}} \tag{12}$$

where

$$q = \pi^{-1/\alpha} < 1 \tag{13}$$

Thus, the value of T that maximizes θ (denoted by T_*) satisfies

$$e^{-rT_*} = \frac{1 - q^{1-\alpha} - (1 - \alpha)(1 - q)}{\alpha(1 - q^{1-\alpha})(1 - q)} \tag{14}$$

By (12) and (14) it follows (remarkably, we believe) that the maximum welfare cost is independent of the rate of interest; it depends only on the price distortion π and the elasticity of marginal utility α.[7]

Our earlier conjectures are easily verified here. By (12), we have that $\theta \to 0$ both as $T \to 0$ and as $T \to \infty$. Furthermore, it follows that $\theta \to 0$ both as $\alpha \to 0$ and as $\alpha \to \infty$. The intuition for the latter is clear. When α converges to zero, we are moving toward a situation where there is perfect intertemporal substitutability of consumption; when the latter prevails (that is, $\alpha = 0$)—at the limit, so to say—the family is indifferent about the time profile of consumption over intervals where p is constant; thus, if p = 1 for all t, the family will be able to attain an optimum by, say, setting c at a constant level during [0, T] and c = 0 afterward. Clearly, the same consumption profile is attainable for the family when a temporary liberalization policy of length T is pursued: so there is no welfare cost. On the other hand, as $\alpha \to \infty$ we are moving toward the case where it is optimal to choose a constant consumption path independently of relative prices; thus, it is to be expected that the price distortion will tend to vanish in the limit.

Table 1.1   Effect of Temporary Liberalization ($\pi = 1.25$)

	$\theta \times 100$		CA/GNP (%)	
α	T = 1	T = 3	T = 1	T = 3
0.064	7.2 (1.75)	8.04 (−0.03)	1,357	613
0.108	2.7 (3.65)	4.75 (1.69)	521	343
0.504	0.22 (2.61)	0.58 (2.25)	52	46
0.9	0.11 (2.42)	0.30 (2.15)	27	24
4.7	0.02 (2.22)	0.05 (2.04)	5	4
10.1	0.01 (2.20)	0.02 (2.02)	2	2

Note: Numbers in parentheses indicate the additional welfare cost incurred when imports are durable goods. CA = Current-account deficit at time zero. GNP = Gross national product.

Table 1.2   Effect of Temporary Liberalization ($\pi = 1.5$)

α	$\theta \times 100$		CA/GNP (%)	
	T = 1	T = 3	T = 1	T = 3
0.064	17.8 (−3.89)	13.13 (−2.04)	2,344	772
0.108	13.00 (1.95)	14.8 (−0.97)	1,520	647
0.504	0.89 (8.11)	2.20 (6.53)	113	96
0.9	0.4 (7.44)	1.03 (6.45)	53	47
4.7	0.06 (6.67)	0.17 (6.12)	9	8
10.1	0.03 (6.57)	0.07 (6.06)	4	4

Note: Numbers in parentheses indicate the additional welfare cost incurred when imports are durable goods. CA = Current-account deficit at time zero.

Table 1.3   Worst Temporary Liberalization

α	T_* (years)		$\theta \times 100$		CA/GNP (%)	
	$\pi = 1.25$	$\pi = 1.5$	$\pi = 1.25$	$\pi = 1.5$	$\pi = 1.25$	$\pi = 1.5$
0.064	2.31	0.28	8.14	20.3	759	7,595
0.108	5.9	2.05	5.33	15.1	222	898
0.504	14.7	12.8	1.22	4.0	25	50
0.9	16.2	15.4	0.70	2.3	13	24
4.7	17.9	18.3	0.13	0.4	2	4
10.1	18.1	18.7	0.06	0.2	1	2

Note: T_* = length of period of temporary policy at which welfare is minimized; CA = current-account deficit at time zero.

To obtain some feeling about the quantitative relevance of these effects, we present some computations in Tables 1.1, 1.2, and 1.3. All the tables assume that the real interest rate equals 4% per year. The values of α cover a wide range; the most plausible ones, in view of the recent literature, are the values comprised of (and including) $\alpha = 0.504$ and $\alpha = 10.1$. The tables are self-explanatory and need no further elaboration. A point that is worth mentioning, however, is that the worst T, T_*, could represent a rather long period of time (see Table 1.3).

3.   Durable Goods, Home Goods, and Money

This section will show that the simple model studied in the previous section is easily extendable to account for relevant aspects of a liberalization process. In addition, we will show that certain key variables can be re-interpreted to make the model applicable to a monetary economy with a cash-in-advance constraint.

3.1.   Durable Goods

The model of Section 2 implicitly assumed that consumption goods could not be stored. If they could, one would have to specify some kind of storage production function. To understand the new complications introduced by storability, however, it is sufficient to focus on the simplest case where consumption goods (importables here) can be stored without cost.[8]

First, notice that if p is constant over time, there are no incentives for the family to hold any inventories given that $r > 0$. Therefore, the equilibrium solution for p constant will be the same as in previous sections. On the other hand, however, if a policy like (5) is being followed, then it is quite intuitive that the economy will stock up on consumption goods before time T. In fact, given that $r > 0$, the family will do all the stocking up exactly at time T, and will steadily consume from the accumulated stocks until they are depleted (at time T', say, where, obviously, $T' > T$); from time T' onwards the stock of importables will be zero since at that point there would be no further incentive to accumulate stocks given that p would be expected to remain constant forever.

Storability does not eliminate the distortionary fluctuations in consumption. It might, in fact, exacerbate them. A case in point is when T $= 0$, that is, when liberalization occurs for an "instant" of time. Without storage, this would be equivalent to no liberalization at all; with storage, however, there are incentives for the family to accumulate stocks at time 0, which induces a welfare cost. Some estimates of this cost are presented in Table 1.4. A fact that clearly emerges from the table is that, as a general rule, the cost is quite significant when compared to the corresponding numbers in previous tables.

The existence of durable goods, however, has a positive side from the point of view of welfare because it allows some optimal "smoothing" of consumption. This is shown in Tables 1.1 and 1.2, where numbers in parentheses reckon the extra cost that would be incurred with (perfectly) durable goods. In Table 1.1, for example, it is shown that if $\alpha = 0.064$ and $T = 3$, the existence of durable goods would reduce the welfare cost by 0.03%. It should be noted, however, that for most of the other entries in those tables—and for all the entries in the relevant range—the possibility of storage increases *substantially* the welfare cost of temporary liberalization.

3.2. Home Goods

Liberalization experiments may have dramatic effects on the "real exchange rate" (Calvo, 1986; Edwards, 1985). To assess this in terms of our model, we have to introduce "home" or "nontradable" goods. This will be our next task.

Let h denote the supply of home goods. We will assume that the latter is the only form of consumption available to the family. Importables and labor (the supply of which is assumed equal to unity) are used to produce the home good according to the following production function:

Table 1.4 Instantaneous Liberalization: Durable Goods

	$\theta \times 100$	
α	$\pi = 1.25$	$\pi = 1.5$
0.064	9.0	16.2
0.108	5.9	16.9
0.504	2.8	9.1
0.9	2.6	8.0
4.7	2.3	7.0
10.1	2.3	6.8

$$h = c^\beta \qquad 0 < \beta < 1 \tag{15}$$

where c denotes the input of importables. Thus, letting e denote the relative price of importables in terms of home goods (which we will call "the real exchange rate"), we have, by (15), that at the profit-maximization point [that is, where $h - ec$ is maximized with respect to c subject to (15)],

$$e = \beta/c^{1-\beta} \tag{16}$$

We assume that the utility index satisfies

$$u(h) = h^{1-\alpha_0}/(1 - \alpha_0) \qquad \alpha_0 > 0 \tag{17}$$

Thus, combining (15) and (17) we obtain

$$u(h) = \gamma c^{1-\alpha}/(1 - \alpha) \tag{18}$$

where

$$\alpha = 1 - \beta(1 - \alpha_0) \tag{19}$$

$$\gamma = (1 - \alpha)/(1 - \alpha_0) > 0 \tag{20}$$

Since the reduced form of the utility function is equivalent to (10), it follows that the equilibrium configuration of c satisfies the same properties as in Section 2.2. In the present case, however, parameter α is given by (19), and thus it involves the elasticities of both the marginal utility and the production functions. In addition, since β is constrained to be between 0 and 1, it follows that

$$\alpha \geq \alpha_0 \quad \textit{if and only if} \quad \alpha_0 \leq 1 \tag{21}$$

Hence, the relevant values of α tend to be further shrunk around 1.

By (16), there exists a negative relation between e and c; thus, compared to the first-best, a temporary liberalization policy like (5) induces an appreciation of the real exchange rate—that is, a fall in e—in the interval [0, T], followed by a permanent depreciation. Furthermore, the smaller is the duration of the liberalization period, the larger will be the initial fall in e. Thus, a message of the model is that a liberalization experiment may provoke gyrations in the real exchange rate; but relatively large movements in the latter may reflect a low degree of credibility (a "small" T).

3.3. A Monetary Economy

Let us imagine that the government imposes no tariff on importables and, hence, that the relative price of importables with respect to exportables is, by hypothesis, permanently equal to unity. Let us assume, however, that this is a monetary economy, with domestic fiat money being issued by the domestic monetary authority. We will assume that consumption is subject to a cash-in-advance constraint by postulating that

$$m \geq \delta c \qquad \delta > 0 \qquad (22)$$

where m is real monetary balances in terms of importables. The economic interpretation is that the family is constrained to hold real monetary balances in an amount no smaller than δc (for related models, see Calvo, 1985).

Furthermore, assuming perfect capital mobility, the nominal interest rate at home is $r + \varepsilon$, where ε is the expected (= actual) rate of devaluation. Therefore, when (22) holds with equality—which would happen at equilibrium if the nominal interest rate is positive, the normal case—we have that the total cost of consuming at rate c, which we denote (as before) by p, satisfies

$$p = 1 + \delta(r + \varepsilon) \qquad (23)$$

where 1 is the direct cost of consumption, and $\delta(r + \varepsilon)$ is the opportunity cost of the money balances held against consumption.

Consider now the case where the monetary authority preannounces the exchange rate (for recent applications of this policy see Calvo, 1986; Edwards, 1985), and, in particular, let us consider a "temporary stabilization policy" by which $\varepsilon = 0$ during the interval [0, T], and $\varepsilon = \pi - 1 > 0$ afterward. Clearly, this generates a time profile of p which is identical to the one postulated in (5). In fact, if we further assume, as in previous sections, that the government consumes nothing, and distributes its revenue in the form of lump-sum subsidies to the family, one can easily show that the reduced form of the economy is similar to the nonmonetary one studied before (for more details and extensions, see Calvo, 1985). One can, therefore, immediately infer that a temporary stabilization experiment will deteriorate the current account and appreciate the real exchange rate—the latter being one of the most outstanding features of the recent Argentinian and Chilean programs (see Calvo, 1986; Edwards, 1985). Another implication is that the shorter is the stabilization period, the larger will be the initial effects on the current account and the real exchange rate.

4. Conclusions

This chapter has demonstrated that temporary liberalization/stabilization policies may be costly, and that the cost could be substantial. Furthermore, it has shown that temporariness may retain its harmful power even when the above-mentioned policies are expected to be maintained for a (surprisingly) long period of time.

For the sake of clarity, we loaded the dice heavily against temporary policies (in this chapter, they are all "bad"). Therefore, a more useful evaluation of these issues will have to allow for realistic ingredients such as, for instance, importables/exportables substitutabilities in consumption and production, which will give some positive value to liberalization or stabilization policies even when they are expected to be temporary.

Notes

[1]Results are essentially the same if exportables and importables are assumed to be perfect complements.

[2]For a definition of equilibrium, see below.

[3]It should be noted, however, that temporary liberalization policy could be welfare-enhancing in less extreme models where, for instance, exportables are arguments in utility or production functions.

[4]Notice that z is also larger.

[5]A measure in terms of output will be defined in Section 2.2.

[6]Recall note 2.

[7]The formulas for the case $\alpha = 1$, or, equivalently, $u(c) = \log c$, are as follows:

$$\log (1 - \theta) = e^{-rT} \log q - \log [1 - (1 - q)e^{-rT}]$$

and

$$e^{-rT*} = (1 - q)^{-1} - (-\log q)^{-1}$$

Thus, once again the maximum welfare cost is independent of r.

[8]See Edwards (1985) for a discussion of the role of durable goods in the recent Chilean liberalization experiment.

References

Arrow, K. J., and F. H. Hahn (1971). *General Competitive Analysis*. San Francisco, Calif.: Holden Day, Inc.

Calvo, S. A. (1986). "Fractured Liberalism: Argentina under Martinez de Hoz." *Economic Development and Cultural Change* (April).

_____ (1985). "Temporary and Permanent Exchange Rate and Banking Policy with and without Capital Mobility" (February).

Díaz-Alejandro, C. F. (1985). "Good-Bye Financial Repression, Hello Financial Crash." *Journal of Development Economics* 19 (September/October): 1–24.

Edwards, S. (1985). "Stabilization with Liberalization: An Evaluation of Ten Years of Chile's Experiment with Free-Market Policies, 1973–1983." *Economic Development and Cultural Change* 33(1): 223–54.

Ethier, W. (1982). *Modern International Economics*. New York: W. W. Norton.

2

Economic Liberalization in Less Developed Countries: Guidelines from the Empirical Evidence and Clarification of the Theory

Philip Brock & Edward Tower

In the last several years a considerable body of empirical evidence has accumulated about the process of economic liberalization in developing countries. This chapter summarizes some of the more important findings and discusses the interpretation of the evidence within the framework of several simple analytical models. The chapter is designed as an introduction to the subject for use by both policy advisors and policymakers.

For the purpose of this chapter liberalization is defined as the reduction of impediments to the efficient functioning of markets—that is, the sweeping away of distortions. Ideally one would wish to know for what countries liberalization is likely to work, how best to time its beginning, how long should be taken from start to finish, and the order in which various markets should be liberalized. Unfortunately, our knowledge of the process is not good enough to specify the ideal set of rules, so we ask the reader to settle for somewhat less. Section 1 begins with a set of observations drawn from Krueger (1978) and other sources in order to model those economic factors most likely to facilitate or frustrate the adjustment process to economic liberalizations. Section 2 discusses the appropriate use of exchange rate policy in response to movements in the real exchange rate and current account during economic liberalizations. Section 3 offers some concluding remarks.

1. Devaluation and Economic Liberalization

The publication of Anne Krueger's *Liberalization Attempts and Consequences* in 1978 provided the first comprehensive survey of attempts by developing countries to relax quantitative and price restrictions on trade. Drawing on the work of investigators in the NBER's Foreign Trade Regimes and Economic Development project, Krueger centered her book around the analysis of 22 devaluations undertaken by the ten NBER countries between 1950 and 1972. Formal devaluations often accompanied attempts by the governments to remove quotas, lower tariffs, and simplify the bureaucratic administration of the trade regime.

Krueger's analysis of the effects of devaluations under regimes characterized by quantitative restrictions on imports (QRs) has sparked further writing on the topic by McKinnon (1979), Aizenman (1981), Blejer and Hillman (1982), Kimbrough (1984), and Daniel, Fried, and Tower (1985). Because there seems to be some confusion regarding the role of devaluation in liberalization attempts, our intention in this section is to put forward a simple framework within which Krueger's evidence can be analyzed. We first review Krueger's conceptual framework for the analysis of liberalization attempts and summarize her findings regarding the outcome of devaluations. We then construct a simple analytical model of the determination of expenditure and relative prices for economies with trade regimes characterized by tariffs and QRs. Next we use the model to offer a consistent explanation for the short-run and long-run consequences of devaluation reported by Krueger. Finally, we use the model to show why trade and financial market distortions may often be the unintentional consequence of policies that restrict the central bank's authority to alter the exchange rate.

1.1. The Process of Liberalization

Two exchange rate definitions play important roles in Krueger's analysis of 22 devaluations. E is the nominal exchange rate, and it is defined as the number of units of local currency which trades for one unit of foreign currency at the official exchange rate. Thus a devaluation consists of an increase in E. EER_i is defined as the effective exchange rate on the ith transaction. It is the amount of local currency actually paid (or received) for imports (or exports) priced on world markets at one unit of foreign currency. If there were no controls, taxes, or subsidies on trade, the EER for all transactions would be identical to E. Since imports are generally made artificially expensive through the use of import tariffs, the EER for imports generally exceeds the nominal exchange rate. To the extent that exports are subsidized, the EER for exports will also exceed the nominal rate. Krueger's measure of the EER does not include the premiums associated with import restrictions.

Table 2.1 summarizes Krueger's data on net and gross devaluations. The net devaluation is defined as the percentage change in the effective

Table 2.1 Percent Changes in Exchange Rates (22-country experience)

| | | Net change | |
	Cross % change	Import EER % change	Export EER % change
Largest	221	201	111
Smallest	6	3	−1
Median	57	47	31

Source: From Krueger (1978), table 5.1.

Note: In this table and in Table 2.2, when there are an even number of observations the value that we report as the median is the mean of the two middle observations. When the calculated median ends in 0.5, we round off by selecting the nearest even whole number.

exchange rate. We see from the table that the magnitudes of the median cases are large. Also, devaluations, along with the policy changes accompanying them, tend to have a larger impact on import EERs than export EERs. Finally, the typical pattern is for the net devaluations to be considerably smaller than the gross devaluations.

Krueger defines four concepts designed to describe the changing character of trade regimes over time. The two most important concepts are liberalization and bias alteration. Departing from the common professional usage, Krueger defines liberalization specifically to mean the relaxation of QRs or the replacement of QRs by tariffs.[1] The relaxation or replacement of QRs eliminates economic rents that are equal in value to the license premiums. As Krueger (1974) and others have demonstrated, the socially wasteful competition for economic rents implies that QRs will generally impose substantially greater welfare losses than tariffs producing the equivalent price distortion. Consequently, it is correct to view the substitution of tariffs for quotas as a liberalization even if relative prices remain unchanged. The package of economic policies that accompanies a devaluation results in a liberalization only if the value of license premiums falls. If imports are subject to tariffs and quotas, Krueger defines the license premium for an importable good to be

$$Pr = \frac{P_m - (1 + t)EP^*_m}{EP^*_m}$$

where P_m is the domestic price of the importable, t is the tariff rate, E is the nominal exchange rate, and P^*_m is the foreign price of the importable.

Bias alteration specifically refers to the alteration of domestic relative prices. Krueger measures bias by the formula $B = (1 + t + Pr)/(1 + s)$,

Table 2.2   Bias of Trade Regimes before and after Devaluation

	Bias		
	Old	New	Two years later
Largest	6.31	3.05	2.26
Smallest	.67	.97	.78
Median	1.94	1.74	1.50

Source: Krueger (1978), table 6.2.

where (as before) t is the premium for tariffs and other price measures charged for imports, Pr is the proportional value of license premiums on imports subject to QRs, and s is the level of export subsidies and other price measures granted to exporters. By noting that $P_m = (1 + t + Pr)EP^{\star}_m$ and that $P_x = (1 + s)EP^{\star}_x$, bias can be expressed equivalently as $B = \mu^{\star}/\mu$, where $\mu^{\star} = P^{\star}_x/P^{\star}_m$ and $\mu = P_x/P_m$ are the world and domestic terms of trade, respectively. Thus bias is the world price of exports relative to that of imports divided by the same ratio at home prices. Whenever $\mu = \mu^{\star}$ (whether by operating at free trade or with offsetting import tariffs and export subsidies) the trade regime's bias equals 1, so that neither the production of exportables nor the production of importables is favored relative to world prices.

Table 2.2 summarizes the extent of bias preceding and following devaluation for the 12-country experiences for which Krueger obtained the appropriate data. Table 2.2 indicates that devaluation is often accompanied by a substantial reduction in the divergence of domestic relative prices from world relative prices. In the median case in Table 2.2 the divergence of relative prices is reduced from 94% to 50% two years after the devaluation. Krueger writes (1978, p. 110), "In general the evidence from the country studies is that bias reduction is usually a major concomitant of net devaluation and that the reduction comes about more through the absorption of preexisting premiums on import licenses than by differential changes in export and import EERs."

The analysis of the interaction between liberalization (the reduction of license premiums) and bias alteration during the 22 devaluations forms the conceptual framework for much of Krueger's book. Our next section examines the role of exchange rate devaluation in altering the bias of a trade regime and in reducing license premiums. By separating the analysis of monetary from real factors we hope to clarify the determination of relative prices in a QR regime and explain the difference between a devaluation that accompanies a large bias reduction and a devaluation that leaves bias unaltered.

1.2. Trade Distortions in a Nonmonetary Economy

To examine the effect of liberalization and bias alteration on the long-run equilibrium of an economy, we first need to construct a simple model that highlights the role of tariffs and QRs in shifting resources away from free-trade equilibrium. We have chosen to begin with the familiar exportable-importable model shown in Figure 2.1.[2] In Figure 2.1 the free-trade equilibrium is shown by the triangle ABC. Production takes place at A, consumption takes place at B, and the economy exports AC of the exportable good in return for BC of the importable good. The relative price of the exportable to importable good is given by $\mu^* = P^*_x/P^*_m$. Since the slope of AB is $-(P^*_m/P^*_x)$, the slope of the ray orthogonal to AB is μ^*. Tariffs or quotas on imports distort the terms of trade by raising P_m relative to EP^*_m and lowering μ relative to μ^*. In Figure 2.1 the triangle DEF describes the equilibrium with tariff and quota distortions. Production moves from A to D as firms move into the protected import-competing sector. Consumption moves from B to E reflecting the consumption loss incurred by moving away from free trade.

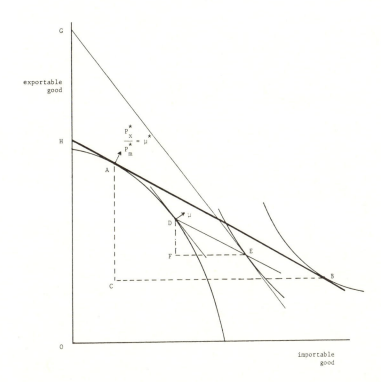

Figure 2.1 Relative price distortions and international trade for a small country.

The equilibrium portrayed in Figure 2.1 can be written as a simple set of equations. Production of the import-substituting good and the exportable good is determined by the internal relative price $\mu = P_x/P_m$. Consequently, we can write production of the two goods as a function of μ:

$$Y_x = Y_x(\mu) \qquad Y_m = Y_m(\mu)$$

Expenditure in Figure 2.1 is determined by the point of tangency of the community indifference curve with the economy's budget constraint. In simple analytical terms, expenditure on each of the two goods is a function of relative prices and real expenditure (A):

$$D_x = D_x(\mu, A) \qquad D_m = D_m(\mu, A)$$

We will assume that exports are neither taxed nor subsidized so that $P_x = EP_x^*$, where E is the nominal exchange rate. Imports will be subject to tariffs or quotas so that μ will be less than μ^* for any positive level of protection.

The equilibrium conditions for the economy are given by equations (1) through (5). Equation (1) says that the market value of exportable production (P_xY_x) must equal the market value of domestic consumption (P_xD_x) plus the market value of exports (P_xX):

$$P_xY_x(\mu) = P_xD_x(\mu, A) + P_xX \tag{1}$$

Equation (2) is a similar condition for importables:

$$P_mY_m(\mu) = P_mD_m(\mu, A) - P_mM \tag{2}$$

Equation (3) is the economy's budget constraint. P is the implicit GDP deflator and will be represented by the approximation $P \approx P_m^\alpha P_x^{1-\alpha}$ where α is the share of expenditure falling on importables:

$$PA = P_xD_x(\mu, A) + P_mD_m(\mu, A) \tag{3}$$

Equation (4) is the balanced trade constraint, while equation (5) is the goverment budget constraint that constrains transfers to the private sector (V) to be continuously adjusted to equal the sum of the tariff and quota taxes on imports:

$$P_x^*X = P_m^*M \tag{4}$$

$$V = (P_m - EP_m^*)M \tag{5}$$

The transfer payments of tariff revenue are made in lump-sum fashion whereas the allocation of quotas is made by lottery, to avoid any further complication of the model. By dividing equations (1)–(3) by P_m and making use of equation (4), the economy's equilibrium can be expressed in real terms as follows:

$$\mu Y_x(\mu) = \mu D_x(\mu, A) + (\mu/\mu^*)M \tag{6}$$

$$Y_m(\mu) = D_m(\mu, A) - M \tag{7}$$

$$\frac{A}{\mu^\alpha} = D_x(\mu, A) + \frac{D_m(\mu, A)}{\mu} \tag{8}$$

$$\frac{A}{\mu^\alpha} = Y_x(\mu) + \frac{Y_m(\mu)}{\mu} + \frac{M}{\mu} - X \tag{9}$$

Equations (6)–(8) contain two independent equations since (8) is the budget constraint, and equation (9) we store for future reference. There are three unknowns (A, μ, M) so that the model is undetermined. To solve the model we can specify the import restriction as a tariff (t), in which case $\mu = [1/(1 + t)]\mu^*$ and the model determines the levels of A and M. Alternatively we can set M = M̄ via quota restrictions and let the model determine μ and A.

In our model, the long-run level of μ is determined without regard to monetary variables. Therefore bias (μ^*/μ) and the license premium are also invariant to monetary changes. It is easy to show that Krueger's definition of the license premium, $Pr = [P_m - (1 + t)EP^*_m]/EP^*_m$, implies that in our model the premium can be expressed as $Pr = (\mu^*/\mu) - (1 + t)$. The most important message of the nonmonetary model is that relative price distortions are determined by tariff or quota policies and that devaluation will succeed in reducing bias only if tariffs are reduced or quotas relaxed.

1.3. Devaluation and Relative Price Changes

Equations (6)–(8) determine the long-run composition of output and expenditure without reference to the nominal exchange rate or money supply. By adding money to the model, we can examine whether devaluation of the currency has a constructive role in liberalization attempts.

The demand for the monetary base (H^d) is assumed to be proportional to nominal expenditure: $H^d = kPA$, where P is the implicit expenditure deflator defined by equation (3). The supply of the monetary base (H^s) is divided into the domestic credit component (C) and international reserves (ER): $H^s = C + ER$. Equation (10) expresses the money market equilibrium condition ($H = H^s = H^d$) in foreign currency terms after dividing both sides by E:

$$\frac{\dot{H}}{E} = \frac{C}{E} + R = \frac{kPA}{E} \tag{10}$$

Equation (10) can be written equivalently as follows:

$$\frac{\dot{H}}{E} = \frac{C}{E} + R = \frac{kP_x^{\star}A}{\mu^{\alpha}} \tag{11}$$

As can be seen from (11), the long-run demand for money is determined by the values of A and μ generated by equations (6)–(8). Consequently, a devaluation (rise in E) will lower the real supply of the monetary base by decreasing the value of the domestic credit component of the base but will leave the real demand unchanged. When the supply of the base is less than the demand, the economy must accumulate international reserves as long as the central bank leaves C unchanged.

If the economy's capital account is closed, the accumulation of international reserves requires a trade balance surplus. The speed of adjustment to a devalution can be shown to depend on the shadow value of existing money balances to agents in the economy[3] and is represented here by a stock adjustment equation:

$$\frac{\dot{H}}{E} = \dot{R} = \lambda \left[\frac{kP_x^{\star}A}{\mu^{\alpha}} - \left(\frac{C}{E} + R \right) \right] \tag{12}$$

The last two terms of equation (9) sum to the private sector's balance of trade deficit at domestic relative prices measured in units of the exportable. We rewrite it as

$$\frac{A}{\mu^{\alpha}} = Y_x(\mu) + \frac{Y_m(\mu)}{\mu} - \frac{\dot{R}}{P_x^{\star}} + \frac{M}{\mu^{\star}} \{Pr + t\} \tag{13}$$

In the short run, a devaluation under a tariff or quota will lower C/E and Ḣ/E, which reduces A and makes R positive. Under a tariff, μ will not change; while under a quota, μ will rise (P_m will rise less than P_x) since μ is endogenously determined under a quota. Aizenman (1981) and Kimbrough (1984) find, in our terminology, that the gap between $kP^*_x A/\mu^\alpha$ and (C/E) + R following a devaluation is larger under a tariff than under a quota so that the adjustment speed to a devaluation is faster under a tariff than under a quota, whereas Daniel, Fried, and Tower (1985) in their correction of Blejer and Hillman (1983) find that relative adjustment speeds under the tariff and quota are indeterminant. However, as with our simple model, all four papers also demonstrate the invariance of the long-run equilibrium of expenditure and relative prices to devaluation under either tariffs or quotas.

If the capital account is open, even the short-run distinction between tariffs and quota may disappear. With an open capital account, domestic residents—if they so choose—can exactly offset the effects of a devaluation on the real money stock and hence on the economy by lowering their holdings of foreign assets to allow the central bank to raise its holdings of international reserves. In contrast, when the capital account is closed, devaluation must have a long-run effect on the country's net foreign asset position under either tariffs or quotas since domestic residents can only buy international reserves with goods and not with assets. Obstfeld (1984) has explored this long-run non-neutrality of devaluation with a closed capital account that is a special case of a breakdown of Ricardian equivalence.

The addition of money to the model allows us to elaborate on remarks made by Krueger (1978) and McKinnon (1979) regarding devaluation under quotas as opposed to tariffs. Krueger (1978, p. 93) states that "Liberalization results from devaluation itself because the premium on import (and export) licenses is partially or totally absorbed by the exchange rate change." McKinnon (1979, p. 443), in a review of Krueger's book states that,

> In an inflationary situation with excess demand for goods and services under a pegged exchange rate, the great beneficiaries are producers in non-tradables and in import substitution industries protected by QRs; whereas the losers are exporters (who do not receive offsetting subsidies) and import-competing industries protected only by tariffs or by nothing at all. Hence, the beneficiaries can be counted on to resist the pressure to undertake an offsetting devaluation or deflation that would hurt producers of the pseudo non-tradables, while benefiting importers and exporters in "open" tradable activities.

Our analysis shows that the real effects of devaluation under QRs described by Krueger and McKinnon can only occur in the short run and are strongest in countries with closed capital accounts. In those countries a devaluation will produce a short-run expenditure reduction and rise in μ (fall in P_m relative to P_x) as domestic residents acquire real balances by producing a trade balance surplus that increases the central bank's international reserves. Whenever the capital account plays an important part in the monetary adjustment process—whether by official capital inflows or by increased foreign trade credit that results in short-term capital inflows—a change in the nominal parity of the exchange rate should only have slight transitory effects on license premiums or on the bias of a regime.

Krueger makes clear throughout her book that sustained liberalization involves real policy changes to eliminate quotas and to lower tariffs. Our model in this section is intended to clarify the purely monetary nature of changes in the exchange rate under either tariff or QR regimes. As equation (13) shows, a nominal devaluation will reduce A and raise μ in the very short run under a QR regime, but without changes in the level of quotas ($\bar{M}$) or tariffs (t), the equilibrium values of A and μ in equations (6)–(8) must remain unchanged.

Equation (12) shows that one outcome of a devaluation in developing countries is the accumulation of international reserves. If tariffs and quotas are left untouched, the accumulation of reserves will be the *only* long-run outcome of a devaluation. However, if policymakers are seriously attempting to liberalize and to reduce the bias of a regime, devaluation can play a very constructive role in the change of policies. Equation (11) shows that money market clearing requires $(C/E) + R = kP_x^*A/\mu^\alpha$. Since the lowering of tariffs and relaxation of quotas raise μ (by lowering P_m), the demand for money in foreign currency terms will fall during a bias reduction.[4] If a country wishes to avoid losing international reserves, a devaluation will serve to lower the value of C/E to maintain the equality between money supply and money demand.

Our simple model of the liberalization process therefore predicts that devaluations will be accompanied by an improvement of the trade balance and an accumulation of international reserves in those cases where no serious attempt is made to alter the bias of the regime. In cases where bias is actively reduced by policy measures in conjunction with the devaluation, our model predicts that devaluation will be accompanied by relatively stable levels of international reserves, or perhaps falling reserves if the devaluation is not large enough to offset the reduction in bias.

Consequently, we have made an attempt to re-examine the 12 devaluations for which Krueger obtained data on bias alteration in order to provide insights into the monetary nature of the adjustment process. Table 2.3 provides data on the changes in the trade balance and in international reserves in the year of each devaluation. The changes in the trade balance

Table 2.3   Devaluation, Bias Alteration, and the Balance of Payments

	$\dfrac{\Delta\text{Bias}}{\text{bias}}$	$\dfrac{\Delta E}{E}$	$\Delta(X-M)$ (U.S.$ mill.)	$\dfrac{\Delta(X-M)}{X+M}$	ΔR (U.S.$ mill.)
Korea 1964	+0.18	0.65	165	0.315	5
Korea 1961	+0.16	1.04	31	0.087	50
Chile 1959	+0.03	0.47	37	0.046	65
Brazil 1964	−0.05	1.98	232	0.086	36
Brazil 1956	−0.08	0.38	117	0.043	120
Chile 1965	−0.08	0.34	97	0.075	49
Philippines 1970	−0.15	0.64	250	0.110	130
Brazil 1961	−0.21	0.55	136	0.047	125
Philippines 1960–62	−0.32	0.48	−68	−0.061	−5
Turkey 1970	−0.40	0.67	−73	−0.089	186
Chile 1956	−0.47	0.94	+4	0.004	−3
Turkey 1959	−0.75	2.21	−23	−0.028	−21

Source: Figures for bias are taken from Krueger (1978), table 6.2. ΔBias/bias is calculated from the figures in the columns marked "old" and "two years later" under the bias heading. ΔE/E is taken from Krueger (1978), table 5.1. Figures for the trade balance and international reserves are taken from various issues of *International Financial Statistics.* $\Delta(X-M)$ is the trade balance in the year of the devaluation minus the trade balance in the year preceding the devaluation. ΔR is calculated in the same manner as $\Delta(X-M)$.

and international reserves are calculated based on the trade balance and level of international reserves in the year preceding the devaluation.

The 12 devaluations are ranked by the measured change in bias two years after the devaluation in order to separate permanent bias alterations from short-run alterations caused by the transitory soaking up of license premiums. For the first 8 devaluations, the trade account improved and international reserves increased as predicted by our model for cases in which bias alteration is negligible compared to the size of the devaluation. The 4 devaluations that accompanied substantial long-run alterations in bias—the Philippines 1960–62 (−.32), Turkey 1970 (−.40), Chile 1956 (−.47), and Turkey 1959 (−.75)—exhibited substantially different movements in the trade balance and international reserves. In all four cases the trade account either remained unchanged (Chile 1956) or worsened. More importantly, the level of international reserves *fell* in the year of the devaluation for all cases except Turkey 1970.[5]

Consequently, our interpretation of devaluation under a QR regime distinguishes between passive policies accompanying the devaluation and active policies that alter tariffs and quotas. Devaluation under either a tariff or a QR regime will produce a balance-of-payments surplus if tariffs and quotas are left untouched. Any short-run soaking up of license premiums that occurs after a devaluation in a QR regime will quickly be eroded by the accumulation of international reserves. If a serious attempt is made to eliminate quotas and lower tariffs, then a devaluation will permit the reduction of the trade regime's bias to take place without the loss of international reserves. In the long run, the bias of a regime is determined only by relative price distortions and quantitative restrictions, not by the level of the nominal exchange rate.

1.4. Monetary Causes of Trade and Financial Restrictions

The preceding analysis of the role of devaluations in an economic liberalization implies that changes in nominal variables, such as the exchange rate and money supply, by themselves have no long-lasting effect on relative prices and the allocation of resources within an economy. However, as Krueger repeatedly emphasizes, tariff and quota distortions frequently arise in response to disturbances when nominal variables are not allowed to adjust. Although economists often analyze inward-looking trade regimes as if policymakers had consciously decided to reject free trade, trade restrictions in fact often occur in response to external shocks, given the desire to defend the established parity of the nominal exchange rate. Krueger (1978, p. 24) herself identifies a sharp drop in major export prices, such as occurred in the Great Depression or 1952/53, as a major cause of the imposition of across-the-board controls on trade.

To see why an external shock may lead to trade controls, notice from the money market clearing condition given by equation (11) that the demand for money is affected by the international price of a country's export good as well as by the internal terms of trade (μ):

$$\frac{C}{E} + R = \frac{kP_x^* A}{\mu^\alpha}$$

A fall in P_x^* will also cause A to fall, so that both changes will lower the demand for money. Either a devaluation or loss of international reserves will restore money market equilibrium. If, however, a country decides to defend the value of the nominal exchange rate and lacks enough international reserves to allow price-level deflation to take place, the government can raise tariffs or impose quotas in order to lower μ. In addition, the government can take steps to raise k = H/PA. In simple theories of the demand for money, k is treated as a constant or as a function of the nominal interest rate. In fact, a government can take a number of the following steps to raise k: (1) close the capital account to eliminate foreign assets as substitutes for money; (2) raise reserve requirements and impose prior import deposits to increase the demand for the monetary base; and (3) impose interest rate ceilings on bank deposits to raise the demand for currency by lowering the opportunity cost of holding cash.

If a government is committed to a fixed exchange rate and cannot afford the loss of international reserves, then policies to lower μ and raise k must inevitably follow. So although most analyses of the monetary response to a terms-of-trade shock center on the adjustment of the exchange rate and international reserves, policy interventions in the goods and financial markets also represent an adjustment to terms-of-trade shocks. Unlike changes in E and R, policies to lower μ distort relative prices in the real side of the economy whereas policies to raise k distort relative prices in the financial side of the economy.

Terms-of-trade shocks often exacerbate existing fiscal deficits, so that over time the extension of domestic credit must cause trade and financial controls to become more binding. By logarithmically differentiating equation (11), it is straightforward to show that

$$\hat{C} - \hat{E} = \frac{k - \alpha\hat{\mu} + \hat{P}^*_x + \hat{A} - (1 - \beta)\hat{R}}{\beta} \tag{14}$$

where $\beta = C/(C + ER)$ is the share of the domestic credit component in the monetary base. According to (14), an extension of domestic credit ($\hat{C} > 0$) under fixed exchange rates ($\hat{E} = 0$) must be met either by the loss of international reserves or by some combination of a fall in μ and a rise in k.[6] If a government wishes to prevent the loss of international reserves under fixed exchange rates, it must increase its intervention in goods and financial markets as long as $\hat{C}$ is greater than zero.

Ortiz and Solís (1979) and Gil Díaz (1984) document a case for which equation (14) with $\hat{C} > 0$ and $\hat{E} = \hat{R} = 0$ must imply $\hat{k} > 0$ or $\mu < 0$. In Mexico during 1972–76, the federal government ran large fiscal deficits that averaged 4.1% of GDP each year compared to the 1967–71 average of 1.7%. With no domestic bond market, the government was forced to borrow overseas to cover part of the deficit and to monetize the remaining part. Under fixed exchange rates, extension of domestic credit to the government by the central bank will cause a loss of international reserves *unless* k is raised by financial market interventions or μ is lowered by tariffs

Table 2.4   Financial and Trade Distortions in Mexico, 1971–77

	Mid-year reserve ratios (%)	Percentage value of imports subject to quantitative restrictions
1971	20.5	67.7
1972	35.1	66.3
1973	48.7	69.6
1974	63.6	82.0
1975	80.8	68.4
1976	71.5	90.4
1977	50.6	67.7

Source: Reserve Ratios are taken from *International Financial Statistics* by calculating the ratio $(14 - 14a)/(34 + 35 - 14a)$, where 14, 14a, 34, and 35 refer to the *IFS* line numbers for reserve money, currency outside of banks, money, and quasi-money. The figures for import value subject to QRs were taken from Gil Díaz (1984), table A-7.

and quotas. Table 2.4 shows mid-year reserve ratios and the percentage of imports subject to quantitative restrictions during 1971–77 in Mexico. Although neither the reserve ratio nor the import value subject to QRs rose monotonically during 1971–76, the two measures taken together reached their peak in mid-1976. In August 1976 the peso was devalued from the parity of 12.5 pesos/dollar it had held since 1954. It is clear from Table 2.4 and from the discussions by Ortiz and Solís and by Gil Díaz that the refusal to allow E to adjust in the face of central bank monetization of fiscal deficits was the motivating force behind the increased use of QRs on imports and higher reserve requirements on bank deposits during 1972–76. Devaluation in 1976 permitted a relaxation of QRs and reduction of reserve requirements, although reserve requirements remained substantially higher than in 1971.

Our analysis in this section has focused on the commitment to a fixed exchange rate in the face of external shocks and government deficits as two underlying determinants of trade and financial market distortions.[7] Equation (14) shows that an alternative to manipulating μ (through tariffs and quotas) and k (through reserve requirements and interest rate restrictions) is to change E, the nominal exchange rate. In particular, if the central bank is allowed to set $\hat{E} = \hat{C}$, fiscal deficits will not require the loss of international reserves or intervention into the real and financial sides of the economy. When the economy does suffer an adverse terms-of-trade shock ($P_x^* \downarrow$), then a discrete devaluation ($E \uparrow$) will allow the economy to adjust without losing international reserves.

Krueger (1978, chapter 10) cites the willingness to allow upward adjustments in E as a major factor in the extended liberalizations enjoyed by Colombia after 1967, Brazil after 1964, and Korea after 1964. By setting Ê roughly equal to Ĉ, a central bank can separate the financing arrangements of fiscal deficits from explicit policy decisions to intervene in goods markets and financial markets. The experiences of Colombia, Brazil, and Korea suggest that the elimination of balance-of-payments pressures allows a more rational decision-making process to determine the level of tariffs and quotas in an economy. The experiences also suggest that trade and financial restrictions are generally relaxed once the commitment to a fixed parity is eliminated.

2. Management of the Crawling Peg During a Liberalization

2.1. The Determination of the Relative Price of Tradables to Nontradables

The preceding section discussed the determination of expenditure (A) and the relative price of exportables to importables (μ) in the context of trade and financial market distortions. Moving to a crawling-peg exchange rate regime allows a government to monetize fiscal deficits without distorting relative prices that guide resource allocation within the economy. Consequently, once a crawling-peg regime is put into place, the removal of balance-of-payments pressures permits rationalization and liberalization of the trade and financial regimes.[8]

Successful liberalization attempts are often characterized by a tendency for the rate of domestic inflation to exceed the rate of exchange rate crawl, thus permitting an appreciation of the "real" exchange rate and an enlarging of trade account deficits. Our purpose in this section is to develop a simple model to explain the origin of the capital inflows and the trade account deficits and to discuss the appropriate intervention to prevent appreciation of the real exchange rate if policymakers so desire. The model we use is a variant of the small, open economy, traded/ nontraded goods model as developed by Salter (1959) and Dornbusch (1974), among others. The model looks essentially like equations (6), (7), and (8) of the previous section except that exportables and importables are aggregated into a composite tradable good, and nontradable goods are added as a second good. The choice of production is now guided by the relative price of tradables to nontradables, $\rho = P_T/P_N$, while expenditure on each good depends on ρ and A. The market-clearing condition for the tradables sector is given by equation (15), where $P_T = EP_T^*$:

$$\rho Y_T(\rho) = \rho D_T(\rho, A) + \rho(X - M) \tag{15}$$

In equation (15) the trade balance $(X - M)$ is equal to the output of tradables $[Y_T(\rho, A)]$ minus domestic expenditure on tradables $[D_T(\rho, A)]$. The market-clearing condition for the nontradables sector is given by equation (16):

$$Y_N(\rho) = D_N(\rho, A) \tag{16}$$

Finally, the economy's expenditure constraint is given by (17):

$$\frac{A}{\rho^\alpha} = D_T(\rho, A) + \frac{D_N(\rho, A)}{\rho} \tag{17}$$

where $\rho^\alpha = P_T/P$ and P is the expenditure deflator that is approximated by $P_N^\alpha P_T^{1-\alpha}$ where α is the share of expenditure that falls on nontraded goods.

As was the case of the model described by equations (6)–(8), equations (15)–(17) contain three unknowns (ρ, A, and X − M) but have only two independent equations. Consequently, one of the three unknowns must be specified outside the model. If trade must be balanced, X = M, and the model determines ρ and A. However, successful economic liberalizations often result in large trade deficits, so that it is helpful to specify A and let the model determine ρ and X − M.

Before discussing the determinants of A, it is important to note that we make the usual assumption that tradable and nontradable goods are both normal goods. Consequently, a rise in A will raise the demands for both goods. Since the supply of nontradable goods is not perfectly elastic, the increased demand for nontradables will raise P_N and cause ρ to fall. Since the economy is a price taker in world markets, the increased demand for tradable goods will show up as a trade deficit.[9]

We typically think of A as composed of consumption, investment, and government expenditure. A successful economic liberalization will generally raise the real rate of return on investment projects above the world rate of return. The divergence of the domestic real rate of interest from the world real rate implies that there are gains from intertemporal trade: the economy's comparative advantage is in growth today, and foreign sources of financing permit the use of that comparative advantage. Consequently, a successful liberalization will cause A to rise by an increase in investment. In addition, if agents perceive the liberalization process to result in a higher trajectory of income over time, consumption will rise as forecasts of permanent income are raised.

The government can keep the capital account closed in order to prevent domestic agents from borrowing to finance investment and consumption. With a closed capital account, the domestic real rate of interest will be kept high just as with tariffs the price of importables is kept high. A closed capital account imposes welfare costs on domestic residents, so most liberalization efforts, including those most recently in the Southern Cone, permit a relaxation of capital controls. Once capital controls are relaxed, our model shows that the rise in A will cause ρ to fall and X − M to turn negative. The fall in ρ (appreciation of the "real" exchange rate) is a natural outcome of an economic liberalization that is accompanied by a relaxation of capital controls.[10]

As in the model of Section 2, our purpose here has been to emphasize that the real exchange rate is a relative price, just as $p_x/P_m = \mu$ is a relative price. In Section 2 we showed why simple devaluations do not produce a change in μ *unless* real policy changes are made to reduce the bias of the trade regime. Likewise, it is the case that $P_T/P_N = \rho$ is a relative price whose movements will depend fundamentally on real variables, such as variations in expenditure relative to output.

2.2. On Pegging the "Real" Exchange Rate

It is instructive to examine whether indexing the rate of exchange rate crawl to the difference between domestic and international inflation is advisable policy during a liberalization. It is easy to see that $P = P_N^\alpha P_T^{1-\alpha} = EP_T^\star/\rho^\alpha$ implies that setting $\hat{E} = \hat{P} - \hat{P}_T^\star$ also implies $\hat{\rho} = 0$, where the "^" symbol denotes a percentage change. However, our model, as defined by equations (15)–(17), states that ρ is determined once A or X − M is determined. Consequently, allowing A to rise during a liberalization is not compatible in the long run with an exchange rate policy that attempts to set $\hat{\rho} = 0$.

As long as there are adjustment costs, indexing the exchange rate to a purchasing power parity rule may be desirable in the short run. As in equation (12), it is possible to write a stock-adjustment mechanism for international reserves that captures the response of the balance of payments to monetary disequilibria:

$$R = \lambda \left[\frac{kA}{\rho^\alpha} - \left(\frac{C}{E} + R \right) \right] \tag{18}$$

In equation (18) a rise in A will set up a gap between the demand for the monetary base and the supply, producing a rise in international reserves. The rise in R causes ρ to start falling, so P_N is allowed to rise. Eventually the gap between supply and demand is closed so that $A/\rho^\alpha = [(C/E) + R]/k$ and the real side of the model (A/ρ^α) determines the real supply of the monetary base $[(C/E) + R]$.

However, a crawling peg indexed to $\hat{E} = \hat{P} - \hat{P}^*_T$ can, in fact, keep $\varrho = 0$ in the short run. Suppose that A rises so that ϱ must fall in the long run. Then, under an indexed crawling peg, the domestic price rise that results from the increase in R will cause the central bank to increase the rate of crawl of the exchange rate. In essence, the central bank is attempting to keep the supply of the monetary base constant in real terms by keeping $\hat{E}$ large relative to $\hat{R}$. That is, the growth rate of the monetary base ($\hat{H}$) is equal to $\beta(\hat{C} - \hat{E}) + (1 - \beta)\hat{R}$, where $\beta = C/(C + ER)$. If $\hat{R}$ is greater than zero, then setting $\hat{E} > \hat{C}$ will temporarily prevent H from rising and ϱ from falling. Of course, the indexed policy will only work as long as the domestic credit component of the base can be reduced in real terms. It should be noted that policies that raise k (such as increases in reserve requirements) will also temporarily prevent ϱ from falling. However, we stress once again that, for a given level of output, ϱ is a function of the level of expenditure so that only measures that directly affect expenditure can affect ϱ.

Colombia during the period 1975–79 provides a good example of the futility of using exchange rate policy to prevent a change in relative prices dictated by real factors. Since 1967, Colombia had used a crawling-peg exchange rate to keep $\hat{E}$ about equal to $\hat{C}$ and in the process was able to reduce the trade regime's bias and to promote the rapid growth of minor exports. However, a series of Brazilian coffee freezes beginning in 1975 raised world coffee prices and placed downward pressure on ϱ via an increase in A. The monetary mechanism by which ϱ appreciated was a large increase in international reserves that raised the domestic price level. The Colombian government wished to protect the minor export sector and took steps to prevent ϱ from falling. According to Urrutia (1981, p. 217):

> by 1976 all conceivable measures were being taken to restrict money supply growth and to compensate for the growth in the monetary base caused by the growth of international reserves. Reserve requirements in the banks were put into effect, large retentions of coffee export earnings were established, a government budget surplus was produced, and the public sector paid back external debt. All these measures, however, were insufficient, and money supply increased by 34.7%.

In terms of equation (17), the Colombian government was attempting to prevent A from rising and ϱ from falling by increasing k (via reserve requirements and retained export earnings) and lowering C/E by setting $\hat{C}$ < 0. However, the policies to raise k and lower C/E only delayed the inevitable monetization of the accumulating international reserves and establishment of money market equilibrium at the higher level of A and lower level of ϱ consistent with higher coffee prices.[11]

2.3. *Transitory versus Permanent Shocks and the Trade Account*

By focusing special attention on equation (15), we can emphasize more strongly the role of movements in the trade account as responses to transitory macroeconomic changes, such as those brought on by economic liberalization. Recall from (15) that $Y^T - D^T = X - M$, where from now on we write the Ts as superscripts rather than subscripts. We divide D^T into its consumption component (S^T), investment component (I^T), and government purchases component (G^T). We further make the assumption that consumers try to smooth consumption over time in the manner suggested by theories of permanent income. Consequently, we assume that, at time t, consumption is determined as follows:

$$S_t^T = \frac{r}{1 + r} \sum_{i=0}^{\infty} \frac{Y_{t+i}^T - I_{t+i}^T - G_{t+i}^T}{(1 + r)^i} \qquad (19)$$

although any variant of (19) that permits smoothing of consumption will work. In (19) notice that if Y^T, I^T, and G^T are constant over all time, then $S^T = Y^T - I^T - G^T$ and trade is balanced since $Y^T = D^T$. We can now write a more general specification for the determination of the trade balance that makes use of (19):

$$Y_t^T - I_t^T - G_t^T - \frac{r}{1 + r} \sum_{i=0}^{\infty} \frac{Y_{t+i}^T - I_{t+i}^T - G_{t+i}^T}{(1 + r)^i} = X_t - M_t \qquad (20)$$

Equation (20) indicates that trade balance deficits are due to transitory declines in Y or to transitory increases in I and G. Our hypothesis regarding the Southern Cone is that I or G was perceived by the public to be transitorily high relative to long-run levels. An alternative hypothesis has been put forward by Vittorio Corbo (1985) for Chile. Corbo maintains that the legally mandated system of backward indexing of nominal wages led to a rising real wage after 1979 that caused the real exchange rate to appreciate and the trade deficit to grow. In terms of equation (20), if Corbo's thesis is correct and the minimum real wage was a binding constraint that raised P_N relative to P_T, then Y_t^T would fall as ρ fell. However, to produce a trade deficit, agents would have had to view the real wage policy as transitory. If the decline in Y^T were viewed as a permanent fall of, say, 100 units, then (18) shows that S^T would fall by

$$\left(\frac{r}{1 + r}\right)\left(\frac{1 + r}{r}\right)100 = 100$$

Table 2.5 Colombia's Balance of Trade (in U.S.$ millions)

	Exports f.o.b.	Imports f.o.b.	Trade balance
1974	1,495	1,511	−16
1975	1,717	1,424	293
1976	2,243	1,665	578
1977	2,713	1,979	734
1979	3,506	2,996	510
1980	4,062	4,300	−238
1981	3,219	4,763	−1,544
1982	3,230	5,176	−1,946

Source: International Financial Statistics, various issues.

In the context of our analytical model one cannot say whether in Chile's case the trade deficit was due to the rise in investment and consumption due to a higher perceived permanent income or whether the deficit was due to the real wage policy. It is clear, however, that in this nonmonetary model only transitory changes in macroeconomic variables can cause fluctuations in the trade deficit.

To finish this section, it is worthwhile to examine the behavior of the trade balance for Colombia during the 1970s. As noted earlier, after 1975 a series of coffee freezes in Brazil raised world coffee prices and Colombia's export earnings. Our model predicts that a transitory increase in Y will improve the trade account as consumption rises by less than the amount of the change in Y. In fact, during the years 1975–79 Colombia ran a trade surplus, as shown by Table 2.5. When the world recession began in 1981, Colombia began to run large trade deficits as output fell by more than consumption. Colombia's trade account surplus during 1975–79 and its trade account deficit during 1981–82 are both consistent with equation (19) and, more generally, with any specification of consumption that permits smoothing behavior in response to transitory output shocks.

3. Conclusion

In this chapter we have emphasized that movements in relative prices during an economic liberalization are determined by *real* policy changes and not by the time path of the *nominal* exchange rate. Changes in the nominal exchange rate, however, may permit a government to undertake reforms that would be difficult without a change. For example, Section 2 demonstrated that a reduction in bias—caused either by a relaxation of quotas or by the lowering of tariffs—will cause a country to lose international reserves unless accompanied by a discrete devaluation. The four largest alterations of bias in Table 2.3 exemplify liberalizations in which a devaluation kept international reserves from falling very much as P_x/P_m was allowed to rise. However, devaluation by itself—under either a tariff or a QR regime—will not alter relative prices except in the very short run. Without policy changes to relax quotas or to lower tariffs, devaluations produce only transitory improvements in the trade balance and balance of payments and fail to create incentives to move resources out of the import-competing sector and into the export-producing sector.

Section 2 also demonstrated that trade and financial market distortions can result from the failure to adopt a flexible exchange rate in the face of adverse terms-of-trade shocks. Given a fixed exchange rate, a fall in the world price of a country's export good will cause a loss of international reserves unless increases in tariffs, quotas, reserve requirements, or prior import deposits are used to raise the domestic demand for the monetary base. Similarly, monetization of fiscal deficits under fixed exchange rates requires intervention in goods markets and the financial system to prevent the loss of international reserves. Of course, the welfare costs associated with trade and financial market intervention are apt to be high. As our analysis showed, a government can prevent this loss of international reserves and avoid distorting relative prices by adopting a crawling-peg exchange rate regime. From the standpoint of economic liberalization, the most important contribution of a crawling-peg exchange rate regime is the freeing of policy decisions regarding trade and financial controls from balance-of-payments considerations.

Once a country does reduce the bias in its trade regime and moves to a flexible exchange rate policy, such as a crawling peg, historical experience from Korea (1965–70) to Chile (1976–81) has shown that large capital inflows often occur in response to the improved growth prospects for the country.[12] Our model of Section 3 showed that an increase in investment or consumption expenditure following a liberalization must produce a deterioration of the current account and a fall in P_T/P_N. The only way to prevent the fall in P_T/P_N is to impose very strict capital controls that keep the domestic real interest rate above the world real rate and thereby reduce real expenditure. The divergence of the domestic from the world real interest rate imposes a welfare loss on a small country, but if a government has reason to believe that externalities are causing the private sector to increase investment and consumption too quickly—or, equivalently, to borrow too rapidly—then a tax on capital account transactions will permit the government to control the levels of domestic expenditure, the current account, and P_T/P_N.[13]

We do not believe that changes in the nominal exchange rate have much influence on P_T/P_N, especially in cases where the rate of exchange-rate change is consistent with the rate of domestic credit expansion ($\hat{E} = \hat{C}$). In particular, the large appreciations of P_T/P_N that occurred in Chile, Argentina, and Uruguay in the late 1970s could not have taken place without an opening of those countries' capital accounts. In addition, attempts to use the nominal exchange rate to prevent P_T/P_N from falling during favorable terms-of-trade shocks cannot succeed. As discussed in Section 2, Colombia's deliberate attempt to use the crawling-peg and other policies failed to prevent its real exchange rate from appreciating in the late 1970s in response to higher coffee export quotas. Blaming exchange rate policy for the behavior of the relative price of tradables to nontradables serves only to draw attention away from real factors—such as successful liberalizations and terms-of-trade changes—that do affect relative prices.

Notes

[1] "A QR regime is said to be more *restrictive* the higher is the value of premiums as a percentage of the value of trade. Conversely, a regime is more *liberalized* the smaller is the value of premiums as a percentage of the value of trade" (Krueger, 1978, p. 88).

[2] Although this model has a long tradition in international economics, our analysis of the monetary effects of real distortions is most closely related to earlier work by Mussa (1974, 1976).

[3] See Kimbrough (1984) for such a treatment based on a money-in-the-utility-function framework.

[4] More precisely, the demand for money will fall provided that A/μ^α falls. Equation (8) shows that a fall in A/μ^α implies a fall in expenditure measured in terms of the exportable good. Any move to free trade will unambiguously cause A/μ^α to fall, as can be seen in Figure 2.1. For example, in Figure 2.1 a bias reduction that moves consumption from point E to the free trade point B will cause the value of the consumption bundle measured in terms of the exportable good to fall from OG to OH.

[5] Turkey 1970 is a somewhat special case. According to Krueger (1978, p. 126) "In a few instances covered by the NBER project, increases in reserves following devaluation have resulted in important inflationary increases in the money supply. Perhaps the most notable case was the Turkish devaluation of 1970. Turkish reserves rose from a low of $218 million at the end of June 1970 to $443 million in June 1971 and then to $955 million in June 1972. The large change was attributable in major part to the responses of Turkish workers abroad . . . who substantially increased their remittances."

[6] See also note 4.

[7] See Brock (1984) for a discussion of trade and financial distortions in the context of inflationary finance.

[8] See Williamson (1981), McKinnon (1981), McKinnon and Mathieson (1981), and Blejer and Mathieson (1981) for accounts of the proper management of a crawling-peg exchange rate regime.

[9] More specifically, differentiation of (15), holding ρ constant, shows that

$$\frac{d(X - M)}{dA} = -\frac{\partial D_T}{\partial A} < 0$$

[10]McKinnon (1973), Mathieson (1979), and Harberger (1984), among others, also make the same point.

[11]See Edwards (1984) on the close correlation between coffee prices and the "real" exchange rate (ρ) in Colombia in the post-war period.

[12]See Mathieson (1979) for an account of the large capital inflows into Korea following the 1964–65 trade and financial reforms.

[13]See Harberger (1976) for a discussion in favor of a tax on capital inflows based on an externality argument.

References

Aizenman, Joshua (1981). "Devaluation and Liberalization in the Presence of Tariff and Quota Restrictions: An Equilibrium Model." *Journal of International Economics* 11(May): 197–206.

Blejer, Mario I., and Arye L. Hillman (1982). "On the Dynamic Non-Equivalence of Tariffs and Quotas in the Monetary Model of the Balance of Payments." *Journal of International Economics* 13(August): 163–69.

Blejer, Mario I., and Donald J. Mathieson (1981). "The Preannouncement of Exchange Rate Changes as a Stabilization Instrument." *IMF Staff Papers* 28(December): 760–92.

Brock, Philip L. (1984). "Inflationary Finance in an Open Economy." *Journal of Monetary Economics* 14(July): 37–53.

Corbo, Vittorio (1985). "Reforms and Macroeconomic Adjustments in Chile during 1974–1983." *World Development* 13(August).

Daniel, Betty C., Harold O. Fried, and Edward Tower (1985). "On the Dynamic Non-Equivalence of Tariffs and Quotas in the Monetary Model of the Balance of Payments: Comment." *Journal of International Economics* 18.

Dornbusch, Rudiger (1974). "Real and Monetary Aspects of the Effects of Exchange Rate Changes." In *National Monetary Policies and the International Financial System*, edited by R. Z. Aliber. Chicago: University of Chicago Press.

Edwards, Sebastián (1984). "Coffee, Money and Inflation in Colombia." *World Development* 12: 1107–17.

Gil Díaz, Francisco (1984). "Mexico's Path from Stability to Inflation." In *World Economic Growth*, edited by Arnold C. Harberger. San Francisco: Institute for Contemporary Studies Press.

Harberger, Arnold C. (1976). "On Country Risk and the Social Cost of Foreign Borrowing by Developing Countries." Typescript. The University of Chicago.

———— (1984). "La Crisis Cambiaria Chilena de 1982." *Cuadernos de Economia* 63(August): 123–36.

Kimbrough, Kent P. (1984). "Tariffs, Quotas, and Welfare in a Monetary Economy." Typescript. Duke University.

Krueger, Anne O. (1974). "The Political Economy of the Rent-Seeking Society." *American Economic Review* 64(June): 291–303.

———— (1978). *Liberalization Attempts and Consequences.* Cambridge, Mass.: Ballinger Publishing Company.

Mathieson, Donald J. (1979). "Financial Reform and Capital Flows in a Developing Economy." *IMF Staff Papers* 26(September): 450–89.

McKinnon, Ronald I. (1973). *Money and Capital in Economic Development.* Washington, D.C.: The Brookings Institution.

———— (1979). "Foreign Trade Regimes and Economic Development: A Review Article." *Journal of International Economics* 9: 429–52.

———— (1981). "Monetary Control and the Crawling Peg." In *Exchange Rate Rules*, edited by John Williamson. New York: St. Martin's Press.

————, and Donald J. Mathieson (1981). "How to Manage a Repressed Economy." *Essays in International Finance* No. 145, Princeton University (December).

Mussa, Michael (1974). "A Monetary Approach to Balance of Payments Analysis." *Journal of Money, Credit and Banking* 6(August): 333–51.

———— (1976). "Tariffs and the Balance of Payments: A Monetary Approach." In *The Monetary Approach to the Balance of Payments*, edited by Jacob A. Frenkel and Harry G. Johnson. Toronto: University of Toronto Press.

Obstfeld, M. (1984). "Capital Flows, the Current Account, and the Real Exchange Rate: Consequences of Stabilization and Liberalization." Unpublished.

Ortiz, Guillermo, and Leopoldo Solís (1979). "Financial Structure and Exchange Rate Experience: Mexico 1954–1977." *Journal of Development Economics* 6: 515–48.

Salter, W. E. G. (1959). "Internal and External Balance: The Role of Price and Expenditure Effects." *The Economic Record* (August): 226–38.

Urrutia, Miguel (1981)."Experience with the Crawling Peg in Columbia." In *Exchange Rate Rules*, edited by John Williamson. New York: St. Martin's Press.

Williamson, John (1981). "The Crawling Peg in Historical Perspective." In *Exchange Rate Rules*, edited by John Williamson. New York: St. Martin's Press.

3

The Liberalization of Trade and Capital Flows in Developing Countries: Some Theoretical and Empirical Issues

Mohsin S. Khan & Roberto Zahler

1. Introduction

The decade of the 1970s saw several developing countries move toward the elimination of restrictions on foreign trade and capital flows. This process, which has been termed as "liberalization" or "opening up" of economies, attracted considerable interest on the part of policymakers in the developing world, who saw in it a way of improving the standard of living of residents and a recipe for faster development. There were three principal reasons why countries, particularly those in Latin America, adopted such strategies for development.

First, there was the arguments associated with the well-known theory of the "gains from trade." Briefly, according to this theory, international trade is believed to contribute to the development process in the following ways: trade allows a country to follow the route indicated by the theory of comparative advantage; offers greater opportunities to exploit economies of scale; increases the supply capacity of the economy through imports of capital goods, raw materials, and other inputs in the production process; and, finally, by providing competition for tradable goods, is both a source of stimulus for domestic production and, depending on the exchange rate policy being pursued, can set limits to the domestic rate of inflation. In a

This chapter is based to a large extent on previous work by the authors (Khan and Zahler, 1983, 1985). The authors are grateful to Abdel Ismael for providing efficient research assistance. The views expressed are the sole responsibility of the authors and do not necessarily reflect the opinions of their respective institutions.

similar vein, insofar as liberalization of capital movements is concerned, proponents argue that capital flows can increase national savings, in particular financial savings; augment the stock of capital; and induce competition and efficiency in the domestic financial system.

Second, there was the "demonstration effect" imparted by the economic performance of a select group of developing countries, particularly in Southeast Asia, where the growth of trade has played a major role. A number of studies of individual country experiences (Balassa, 1980; Keesing, 1979) have shown that, at the broadest level, the countries adopting "outward-looking" development strategies have fared far better in terms of economic growth, employment, economic efficiency, and adjustment to external shocks than those that have engaged in more "inward-looking" strategies. The outward-oriented strategies have been typically characterized by, inter alia: the provision of incentives for export production; the encouragement of import competition for most domestically produced goods; and the use of the nominal exchange rate for the maintenance of realistic real exchange rates. At the same time, various developing countries have experienced a relative loss of dynamism in import-substitution-based industrialization processes, and thus have had to consider designing new strategies for the external sector along the lines adopted by the "outward-looking" developing economies.

In the third place, the generally increasing integration of the world economy, in both the goods markets and the capital markets, has meant that countries have been drawn into closer international relationships, whether expressly desired or not. This growing interdependence has also contributed to a re-orientation of thinking and policies in these countries so as to be able to adjust to international developments.[1]

For these and other reasons many developing countries, especially the ones located in the Southern Cone of Latin America—Argentina, Chile, and Uruguay—embarked on opening up their economies to international competition. Other countries in the region also emulated the example set by these three countries, albeit in a more restrained fashion. The beneficial results of such policies turned out, however, to be very short-lived, and all the countries that had been at the forefront of liberalization suffered significant reversals in their economic fortunes. What caused these setbacks after such a promising start has become a crucial question for both policymakers and academics alike.

Broadly speaking it is possible to identify four main lines of thought on this issue. First, there is the view that the liberalization policies were themselves misconceived and were not really relevant to developing countries even at the theoretical level. For various reasons, given the institutional and structural characteristics of developing countries, it is argued that opening-up is destined to fail, and therefore it is of no great surprise to find countries that pursued such policies in their present straits.

A second view, which is related to the first, while not condemning liberalization policies per se, holds that it was the implementation of these policies that was at fault. In other words, the proponents of this view, while tending to accept the neoclassical premise that opening-up has long-run advantages, are nevertheless critical of how the policies were in fact executed. Third, it is possible that the countries were the victims of exogenous, specifically external, shocks that coincided with their attempts to liberalize, and it was the deteriorating international economic situation that bears some part of the responsibility for the problems that these countries encountered. It is generally recognized that liberalization involves difficulties even under the most ideal circumstances, and the task for the policymaker is made doubly demanding when the country is faced with external shocks while it is in the process of liberalizing. Finally, there is the argument developed by Edwards (1982), Sjaastad (1983), and Dornbusch (1984), among others, that lays the principal blame on what are referred to as "domestic policy inconsistencies." In essence the position of these authors is that fiscal, wage, credit, and exchange rate policies were not sufficiently coordinated and, furthermore, toward the end, proved to be in basic conflict with the overall strategy of opening-up. The true picture most likely combines elements of the arguments listed above to some degree, and it would be difficult a priori to pick only one as being the predominant cause of the "failure" of the liberalization experiments.

This chapter discusses some of the important issues relating to both the general strategy of liberalization as well as the factors that possibly led to the failure of this policy. The study builds on previous work undertaken at ECLAC and the IMF[2] and first examines the macroeconomic effects of reductions in tariffs and removal of controls on capital movements. We then proceed to assess the impacts of certain external and internal shocks. This type of exercise allows us to ascertain whether it was the liberalization itself that was at fault, or whether primary blame can be attached to foreign shocks and inconsistent domestic policies. The analysis is conducted by simulating a model designed explicitly to examine the liberalization issue, so that the focus is mainly on the quantitative aspects. As such, we purposely exclude from discussion the broader question of whether liberalization is beneficial or not from a welfare standpoint, and which particular type of liberalization strategy is "optimal" for developing countries. Nevertheless, even with the narrower perspective it should be possible to point out the general effects a country pursuing an opening-up policy is likely to face, and what types of supporting policies it should adopt.

In Section 2 we present the basic framework of analysis, including a brief description of the model utilized. The results from the various simulations are presented in Section 3. The concluding section brings together the main results and attempts to provide a judgment on the effects of liberalization and the significance of the role played by external and internal factors in the liberalization experiments, and, furthermore, whether these factors were sufficiently important to unravel the opening-up process.

2. Framework of Analysis

The analysis of the effects of shocks that occur while the foreign sector is being liberalized is conducted within the framework of the dynamic general equilibrium model developed by Khan and Zahler (1983) to examine the transitional macroeconomic effects of changes in barriers to trade and capital flows. The model has its roots in the general equilibrium econometric models, such as the ones designed by Feltenstein (1980) among others, as well as the more monetary-oriented models typically specified to analyze short-term stabilization policies.[3]

A detailed description of the basic model is given in Khan and Zahler (1983), so that here we present only a brief outline of some of its main features. The model contains three composite goods—exportables, importables, and nontradables—for which supply and demand equations are separately defined. The supply equations are derived in a manner outlined by Clements (1980) in the framework of a multiproduct supply model. The supply of each good depends exclusively on the relative prices of the three goods, the technical conditions of transformation of one good into another, and the initial resource endowment.[4] Total output of the economy is simply the aggregate of the outputs of the three goods, and the unemployment of resources is modeled as a linear function of the difference between potential output (equal to the resource endowment) and total output.

The demand system incorporated in the model represents a fairly straightforward application of standard demand theory. The private component of total aggregate expenditures is related to disposable income, the excess supply of money, and the domestic interest rate; government expenditures, as is customary, are assumed to be exogenous.[5] By invoking separability we argue that once total expenditures are determined, the distribution between importable, exportable, and nontradable goods is determined by a process of maximization subject to a budget constraint represented by the (predetermined) level of aggregate expenditures. This yields demand equations for each good, as a proportion of aggregate expenditures, that depend solely on relative prices. The demand system satisfied the properties of homogeneity, symmetry, and additivity.

The domestic price of exportables (Px) is taken to be equal to the product of the international price of tradables (Pf) and the exchange rate

(ε). The domestic price of importable goods, allowing for tariffs, is defined as:

$$Pi = (1 + \tau)\varepsilon Pf \tag{1}$$

where Pi is the domestic price of importable goods and τ is the tariff. As the prices of importable and exportable goods are essentially given from abroad,[6] disequilibrium in the tradable goods markets results in changes in imports and exports. Imports are defined as the difference between domestic demand and domestic supply of importables and, similarly, exports are equal to the domestic excess supply of exportables.

The price of nontradable goods (Pn) is, however, endogenously determined and is assumed to respond positively to excess demand for nontradable goods (and variations in foreign prices). The general price index, constructed as a Divisia index of the three composite goods, with the (endogenous) weights corresponding to the expenditure shares of each of the three goods, is therefore endogenous as well. Expectations of inflation are also incorporated into the model, although in a fairly simple fashion using an adaptive-expectations formulation.

The monetary sector of the model contains three basic relationships: a money demand function, a money supply identity, and an equation that links changes in the domestic interest rate to the excess demand for money. The demand for money is specified in the customary way, that is, relating money holdings to income, inflationary expectations, and the domestic interest rate. The supply of money is made up of net international reserves, credit to the private sector, and credit to the government. It is assumed that all fiscal deficits are financed by government borrowing from the banking system, so that there is a one-to-one correspondence between budget deficits and variations in the money supply brought about by changes in credit to the public sector. For the case of the interest rate, a standard LM mechanism is assumed so that an excess demand (supply) for money leads to an increase (decrease) in the domestic interest rate. In the model, monetary disequilibrium affects aggregate demand both directly through the spillover into private expenditures, which works like a real balance effect, as well as indirectly through changes in the interest rate.

Capital flows, aside from an autonomous component, are assumed to be determined by the differential between domestic and foreign interest rates, adjusted for expected exchange rate changes and a country risk premium. The presence or degree of controls on capital movements is represented by a parameter β which scales the explanatory variables in the following way:

$$DK = \overline{DK} + \beta[\gamma(rd - rf - \dot{\varepsilon} - \rho)] \tag{2}$$

where DK is the flow of capital (with $\overline{DK}$ representing the autonomous component), rd is the domestic interest rate, rf is the corresponding foreign interest rate, $\dot{\varepsilon}$ is the expected change in the exchange rate,[7] and ρ is the risk premium. The parameter γ reflects the response of capital flow to deviations in interest parity. In this formulation, by varying β one can control the extent of capital flows; for example, for $\beta = 0$ the economy is completely closed and for $\beta > 0$ capital flows are assumed to respond to variations in the explanatory variables.

To allow for the possibility of an upward sloping supply curve of foreign credits the risk premium is made a function of the ratio of external debt to income:

$$\rho_t = \rho_0 + \rho_1(Bf/Y)_t \tag{3}$$

where ρ_0 is a constant, Bf is the stock of external debt, and Y is the level of income. The parameter ρ_1 is assumed to be positive, so that as the ratio Bf/Y rises the risk premium will also increase. This will reduce net capital inflows to the country even though domestic and foreign interest rates, and the expected exchange rate, remain unchanged.[8]

Basically, despite its high level of aggregation—as compared, for example, to the computational general equilibrium models—the model is sufficiently detailed to be able to provide meaningful answers relating to the short-run consequences of opening- or closing-up of the economy. The model explicitly incorporates the linkages between the balance of payments, fiscal, and monetary sectors, as well as their relationship to expenditures and output. Moreover, considerable attention is paid to the role of relative prices in the demand and supply functions for the three composite goods. Finally, since it is formulated in dynamic form, the model is able to provide the path of adjustment of the main macroeconomic variables from one equilibrium to another.[9] The analysis of the transition path, which is essential in devising operational liberalization strategies, clearly requires the introduction of some type of dynamics into the system.

The main theoretical characteristics of this model can be shown through some simple experiments relating to trade and financial liberalization. Consider first the case where a country has some positive tariff ($\tau > 0$) on imports, which it then reduces to zero. Following Dornbusch (1974) the relative price effect of this measure can be analyzed through the aid of Figure 3.1. In this figure, assuming that income and expenditures are equal, along the HH schedule there is zero excess demand for tradable goods, and, by Walras' Law, excess demand for nontradable goods is zero as well. Northeast of the HH schedule the relative price of nontradable goods is too low and there is an excess supply of tradable goods (trade

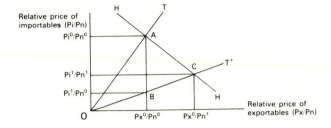

Figure 3.1

balance surplus) and an excess demand for nontradable goods. Similarly, southwest of HH there would be a trade balance deficit and an excess supply of nontradable goods.

Assuming that $\tau > 0$, that the nominal exchange rate is fixed (and for simplicity set equal to unity), and that the economy is closed to capital movements, the initial equilibrium is at point A where the ray OT (the slope of which measures the domestic price of importables in terms of the price of exportables) intersects HH. At A the relative prices of importable and exportable goods in terms of nontradable goods are Pi^0/Pn^0 and Px^0/Pn^0, respectively, and there is equilibrium in both the trade balance and the nontradable goods market.

If τ is reduced to zero, the domestic price of importables falls (to Pi^1) and rotates the ray to OT'. Assuming that Pn is unchanged, the initial effect of the tariff reduction is represented by a movement from A to B,[10] which involves an appreciation of the real exchange rate (defined as the ratio of the price of nontradables to the price of tradables.)[11] Obviously, this is not an equilibrium position since at B there is an excess demand for tradable goods and an excess supply of nontradable goods, requiring a fall in Pn along OT' so as to restore general equilibrium at point C, with $Pn^1 <$ Pn^0. This movement from B to C has been identified in the literature as the real exchange rate depreciation associated with trade liberalization. Although at point C the trade account is in balance with both imports and exports above their respective values in the original equilibrium (A), it should be recognized that the initial effect of opening-up (point B) generates a trade balance deficit. In other words, the depreciation of the real exchange rate associated with the movement from B to C represents a transitory equilibrating movement necessary to close the foreign exchange gap created by the trade deficit.

The changes in relative prices and their effects on demands and supplies that result from tariff removal correspond to a sort of production and expenditure "switching" effect. However, it should be noted that opening-up also creates an expenditure "increasing" effect. Assuming that

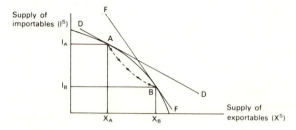

Figure 3.2

inflation is zero initially,[12] the fall in the prices of importable and nontradable goods causes a reduction in the general price level, which in turn creates an excess supply of money and a fall in the domestic interest rate. This stimulates expenditures that reinforce the trade balance effect and, in the short run, dampen the fall in the relative price of nontradable goods.[13]

The effect of trade liberalization on aggregate supply and output can be seen in Figure 3.2, which relates the production possibilities between importables and exportables, assuming that resources utilized by the nontradables sector remain constant.[14] At the initial relative price DD the economy would be at point A, producing X_A of exportables and I_A of importables. When the tariff on imports is reduced to zero, the country will face the new (domestic) terms of trade FF and the new equilibrium will be at B. If adjustment were instantaneous, we would simply move along the transformation curve from A to B, and output of tradables would be unchanged. However, if the reduction in the production of importables is faster than the expansion of exportables, then the path of tradables output would be pushed inside the transformation curve (indicated by the dashed line). In such a case, during the transition period as the economy moves from A to B, it will be operating below its productive potential, creating greater resource unemployment and a larger output-gap, as compared to the respective long-run equilibrium levels of these variables.

In summary, as demonstrated in Figures 3.1 and 3.2, the main theoretical results of a tariff reduction in the short run are a trade balance deficit and consequent loss of international reserves, an increase in both imports and exports, a lowering of the price level, a fall (rise) in the nominal (real) interest rate, and, assuming that the production of importables adjusts faster than the production of exportables, a temporary decline in output and increase in resource unemployment.

To analyze financial opening-up, as in Khan and Zahler (1983), we start from an initial equilibrium in which the domestic interest rate is above the foreign rate plus the risk premium, and capital movements are

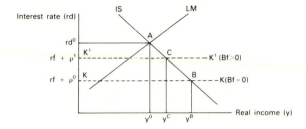

Figure 3.3

completely restricted ($\beta = 0$). Financial liberalization takes the form of increasing the value of β, and capital movements then take place as long as:[15]

$$rd > rf + \rho$$

In the traditional IS–LM framework (Figure 3.3), the initial equilibrium point would be A, with real income at y^0, the domestic interest rate equal to rd^0, and zero foreign debt (Bf = 0).[16]

With a constant risk premium and foreign interest rate, the (small) country faces an infinitely elastic supply of international financial capital which, when monetized, makes the effective LM curve horizontal.[17] The short-run effect of financial opening-up is therefore represented by shifting LM to KK. At point B expenditures (y^B) exceeds income (y^0) and induces a current account deficit.[18] Whether international reserves rise or fall depends obviously on the size of the capital inflows relative to the current account deficit. As a consequence of the capital inflow, the stock of foreign debt would naturally rise.

In Khan and Zahler (1983) it was assumed that the resource endowment (potential output) was fixed, which implies zero net savings and investment.[19] Consequently, as output remains constant and foreign debt increases, the risk premium rises and increases the total cost of financing faced by the country. This shifts KK upwards to K^1K^1, reducing the difference between expenditures (y^C) and income (y^0) and, therefore, the current account deficit. At the point C the inflow of capital is smaller due to the lower interest differential, and the foreign debt rises at a smaller rate. The process continues until a new overall equilibrium is reached at the original values of income and the domestic interest rate (point A), with expenditure equal to income, and current account equilibrium. However, now at A there is a larger stock of foreign debt and higher risk premium, and a lower level of real expenditures on goods and nonfinancial services, as compared to the initial equilibrium.

The main results of financial opening-up are that the domestic nominal interest rate initially declines and then rises back to its original level. The current account deficit is financed by increases in foreign debt rather than by a fall in international reserves, as was the case in the trade liberalization. During the transition period, real expenditures on goods and nonfinancial services increase but would then be lower in the final equilibrium due to the need to service the now larger stock of foreign debt.[20]

The model embodying the characteristics described was simulated in earlier papers for a variety of opening-up strategies—including, among others, the gradual and sudden removal of barriers to trade and capital flows, both simultaneously as well as in different sequences—and was found to yield generally sensible results. Because of the way in which this model is structured, it is quite capable of handling a large variety of shocks aside from those directly related to opening-up. The only change we made to the original model was to introduce a distinction between the price of importables and exportables, which had previously been assumed to be equal to a single international price level. This change was necessary to be able to discuss terms-of-trade variations, and therefore the current version of the model contains two separate foreign prices—one for importables and the other for exportables.

The simulation experiments start with the case of a gradual reduction in trade barriers and restrictions on capital movements. This particular case was studied by Khan and Zahler (1983) as well, and here it is taken as the "control" or base-line simulation to which the other simulations are compared. The specific foreign shocks we consider are a simultaneous temporary increase in the nominal foreign interest rate, and a temporary deterioration in the terms of trade. The change in the terms of trade is taken for purposes of this particular exercise as a decline in the price of exportables relative to the price of importables.[21] The domestic-policy inconsistency scenario analyzed here is represented by a simulation in which there is a temporary increase in the fiscal deficit.[22] Furthermore, as it is assumed in all the simulations that the nominal exchange rate is fixed, this implicitly yields a second inconsistency that has been stressed in the recent literature. Keeping the exchange rate unchanged while opening-up in the presence of external shocks or an expansionary fiscal policy will generally lead to a larger appreciation of the real exchange rate, and thus a more weakened external payments position and increased vulnerability to speculative attacks on the currency. In each of these simulations that are undertaken, we trace the response of the following macroeconomic variables: the general price level, the domestic interest rate, the current account balance, international reserves and foreign debt, the real exchange rate, and real expenditure on goods and nonfinancial services.

These various simulations obviously do not cover all the possible shocks that occurred during the 1970s. For example, we do not explicitly consider the effects of a slowdown in the growth rates in industrial countries. As this effect was not found to be particularly significant in the results reported by Khan and Knight (1983), we felt that we could exclude it from consideration here. Furthermore, we do not attempt to determine the effects of growing protectionist pressures in industrial countries on the exports of developing countries. Neither of these simulations is particularly difficult to perform, but they would require some respecification of the basic model to incorporate a foreign demand function for exports. As the model is currently formulated, it utilizes a small-country assumption and implicitly assumes that foreign demand for exports is infinitely price elastic. Finally, we do not go into the wage-indexation question since the model does not include an explicit wage-determination equation, although it is possible, as discussed in Khan and Zahler (1983), to handle this indirectly. Nevertheless, we feel that the simulations here provide sufficient information to enable one to form a reasonable judgment on the principal effects that specific external shocks and policy changes are likely to have in the course of liberalization.

3. Results

In the initial equilibrium, the economy is assumed to have a uniform tariff of 100% on imports, and capital flows are completely restricted.[23] In other words, the economy is *not* completely closed to trade since imports are allowed, although at a domestic price substantially higher than the world price, and the country does engage in export activities. On the other hand, neither capital inflows nor outflows are permitted. The balance of payments, the current account, and the government budget are all in balance; prices are constant; the economy is assumed to be on its aggregate transformation curve;[24] and the exchange rate is fixed. In specific terms, liberalization involves lowering the tariff rate gradually to zero, over four periods, and the simultaneous elimination of restrictions on capital flows, also over four periods. In the control simulation the foreign interest rate, the terms of trade, and the government budget deficit are kept unchanged (Chart 3.1). For the external-shocks scenario, the nominal foreign interest rate is raised to 15% in period 3 and is then lowered back to its original level of 5% after four periods (Chart 3.1–A). Concurrently with this, the terms of trade are assumed to deteriorate by 5% per period for four periods, and then progressively improve so that by the seventh period they are at their original level (Chart 3.1–B). The domestic shock is represented

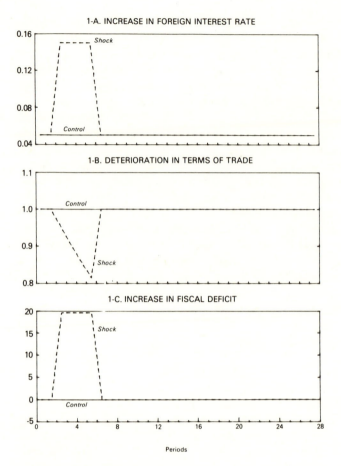

Chart 3.1   Exogenous shocks.

by the emergence of a fiscal deficit (approximately equal to 7–8% of national income) for four periods (Chart 3.1–C), after which the budget is once again assumed to be balanced.

A very important point to note in analyzing the simulations reported here is that the outcomes for the variables under consideration are conditional on the numerical values of the parameters of the underlying model.[25] Clearly, alternative scenarios could be created by changing the parameter values employed. It should also be stressed that the values chosen for the shocks, and the periods over which they extend, are only illustrative and not intended to be necessarily realistic. However, even though these specific shocks are arbitrary, they nevertheless should give a reasonable flavor of what can be expected to happen if one superimposes shocks of certain types on the opening-up process.

3.1. Control Simulation: Simultaneous Removal of Restrictions on Trade and Capital Flows

The liberalization of the trade and capital accounts directly lowers the price of importables (by the amount of the reduction in the tariff rate) and thus initially raises the relative prices of both exportables and nontradable goods in terms of importable goods. The change in the pattern of demand and production resulting from the change in relative prices also tends to exert downward pressure on the price of nontradables. As a consequence,

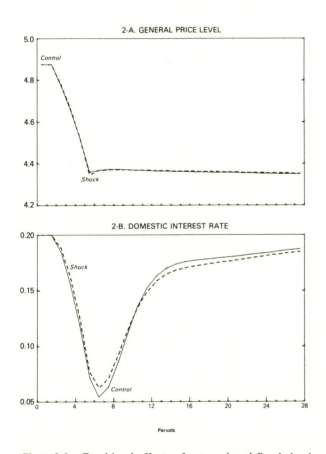

Chart 3.2 Combined effects of external and fiscal shocks.

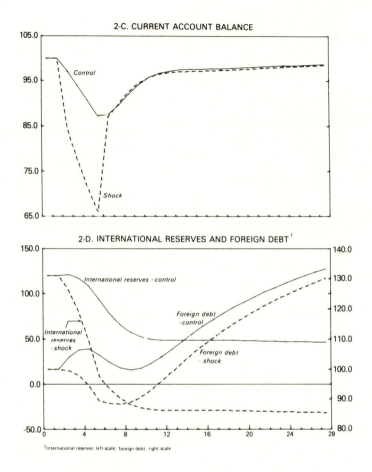

Chart 3.2   *(Continued)*

the general price level falls quite rapidly in the beginning and then, once the effects of the tariff reduction have worked themselves out, stays permanently at the new lower level (Chart 3.2–A).

As expected, the fall in the overall price level lowers the nominal demand for money; furthermore, since initially the domestic interest rate is assumed to be above the corresponding foreign rate, with the removal of capital controls there is a large inflow of capital from abroad which augments domestic liquidity. The resulting excess supply of money causes the domestic interest rate to decline (Chart 3.2–B), and both these factors have an expansionary effect on aggregate demand. The combination of the change in relative prices and the rise in domestic absorption results in a pronounced deficit in the current account (Chart 3.2–C) that persists for a

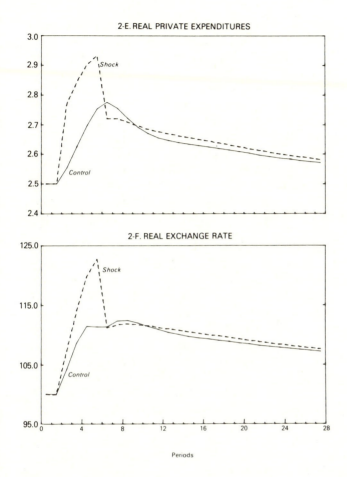

Chart 3.2   *(Continued)*

number of periods.[26] The volume of trade (imports plus exports), however, is larger than in the initial equilibrium, which is a desired result of the liberalization policy. Given the parameters of the model, the capital flows generated by the interest rate differential are not adequate to cover the deficits in the current account, so that the country will continue to lose international reserves until monetary equilibrium is reestablished (Chart 3.2–D). By the end of the transition, the stock of international reserves falls to less than one-half of its original level. In the context of our model this result points to an important precondition for liberalization policies, namely that when starting off the process of opening-up the policymakers should ensure that the country has a comfortable cushion of reserves or the ability to borrow from abroad. The foreign debt of the country rises in a somewhat cyclical fashion, reflecting closely the path taken by domestic interest rates and the resulting capital inflows. Until the risk premium rises by enough to close the differential between domestic and foreign interest rates, the stock of foreign debt will continue to increase. In this particular simulation, equilibrium is reached when the final stock of foreign debt is about 25% of national income (Chart 3.2–D).

Two additional results are worth mentioning. First, real private expenditures on goods and nonfinancial services increase substantially when the domestic price of importable goods falls (Chart 3.2–E). This tendency is then reversed as interest payments on foreign debt absorb an increasing proportion of the income of residents, although, given the model structure and specific parameter values, in the long-run equilibrium real expenditures on goods and nonfinancial services are still higher than their pre-reform level.

Second, as was analyzed in Figure 3.1, during the course of liberalizing the domestic relative price of importable goods with respect to the other goods decreases, and the relative price of exportables tends to rise. With the assumed parameter values, and the initial shares of the three goods in total output, the real exchange rate—defined as the ratio of the price of nontradable goods to the price of tradables—will appreciate (Chart 3.2–F). This real appreciation is a natural consequence of the removal of tariffs on importable goods, and the economy has to move to a new equilibrium real exchange rate. Other things being equal, this appreciation will result in a short-run loss of international competitiveness and a worsening of the current account. Although this movement represents an equilibrium change, the authorities could reduce its impact on the current account through appropriate exchange rate policy.[27] What is important, however, is the prevention of a real appreciation beyond the new equilibrium real exchange rate that is consistent with the elimination of restrictions on trade and capital movements.

3.2.   Effects of External and Domestic Shocks

The effects of a combination of external shocks and the emergence of a budget deficit while the foreign sector is being liberalized are also shown in Chart 3.2. It is quite evident from Chart 3.2–A that the various shocks appear to have little impact on the path of the general price level that results from only opening-up. We would expect the deterioration in the terms of trade to exert additional downward pressure on prices, as the decline initiated by the fall in the domestic price of importables is amplified by the reduction in export prices. However, at the same time the fiscal deficit, by increasing aggregate spending, would tend to push up the price of nontradable goods. The values of the parameters of the underlying model are such that these effects tend to offset each other, and the net impact on the general price level turns out to be negligible.

While the domestic interest rate does fall when the shocks are superimposed, the decline is somewhat smaller than in the control simulation (Chart 3.2–B). Since the foreign interest rate is increased, there is a net capital outflow during the first few periods and a smaller excess supply of money, despite the fact that the financing of the fiscal deficit expands the nominal money supply.[28]

A more striking difference between the two sets of simulations can be observed in the case of the current account position (Chart 3.2–C). Even though there is less excess liquidity in the economy during the initial periods, the combined effect of the deterioration in the terms of trade and the expansionary fiscal policy causes the current account balance to be significantly worse than it would be in the absence of such shocks. Starting from an equilibrium position, the current account deficit, as a proportion of nominal income, reaches around 18% by period 6, as compared to less than 7% in the same period in the control simulation. Once the shocks have worked themselves out, the paths of the current account balance from the two simulations become quite close.

Accompanying this larger current account deficit, there is also an initial outflow of capital because of the increase in the foreign interest rate. As a consequence, international reserves decline much more rapidly in this scenario (Chart 3.2–D); in the final equilibrium, net international reserves actually become negative. In marked contrast to the control simulation, the stock of foreign debt falls for the first 8 periods or so, [29] and rises steadily thereafter, although its level remains permanently smaller than in the control simulation (Chart 3.2–D). This would necessarily mean that debt service payments would be smaller than in the scenario without shocks, despite the temporary increase in the foreign interest rate.

From periods 2 to 6 real expenditures on goods and nonfinancial services increase significantly more than in the control simulation (Chart 3.2–E). This is primarily due to the expansionary effect of the budget deficit, moderated somewhat by the impact of the terms-of-trade deterioration on domestic spending. As the terms of trade and the foreign interest rate return to their respective original levels and the fiscal deficit is eliminated, real expenditures end up being slightly higher than in the control simulation because of the smaller debt-service payments.

The appreciation of the real exchange rate also turns out to be more pronounced when there are external and domestic shocks (Chart 3.2–F). This occurs basically for two reasons: first, the price of tradable goods falls relatively more, with the decline in import prices caused by the tariff reduction now being accompanied by a fall in the price of exportables.

Second, the expansion in aggregate demand caused by the fiscal deficit increases the price of nontradable goods. Eventually, as the foreign price of exportables returns to its original level and the fiscal balance is reestablished, the real exchange rate first depreciates (relative to the control simulation path) and then moves to a slightly higher equilibrium level. This long-run result occurs because less resources from the tradable goods sector—that is, smaller trade balance surpluses—are required to service the now lower stock of foreign debt.

The movements in the real exchange rate clearly highlight the importance of adopting an appropriate exchange rate policy during the liberalization process. Maintaining a fixed nominal exchange rate, or for that matter simply operating a policy that does not permit the exchange rate to move in line with the relative price of tradables to nontradables when there are external shocks or domestic fiscal imbalances, would not appear to be suitable. In particular, budget deficits, and excessive private expenditures financed by foreign borrowing, result in an expansion in aggregate demand that is basically inconsistent with the reduction in the price of nontradable goods that would keep the current account deficit—and consequent loss of international reserves—within reasonable bounds. In such circumstances fixing the nominal exchange rate would exacerbate the situation. This issue of inconsistency between excess domestic expenditures and exchange rate policies has been discussed by a number of authors engaged in analyzing the experience of the Southern Cone countries during the 1970s.[30]

In connection with the exchange rate issue, an interesting question arises as to what the likely effects would be if the country did in fact adopt a more flexible exchange rate policy while it engaged in opening-up. We analyzed this case by repeating the experiment of reducing tariffs and eliminating capital account restrictions, but now instead of maintaining a fixed exchange rate we allowed for a gradual depreciation of about 50% between periods 3 and 6. This policy led to a much smoother evolution of the real exchange rate over time, although, as expected, in the final equilibrium there was still a real appreciation. The decline in the general price level and domestic interest rate was markedly smaller, as was the increase in real expenditures, relative to the control (fixed exchange rate) simulation. There was also an improvement in the current account position even though restrictions on trade and capital flows were removed, and the stock of international reserves initially rose before settling down to a value very close to the original equilibrium level. Although the policy of steady depreciation is not totally without costs, since there is an increase in the foreign debt above that observed in the control simulation, and the price level falls by a smaller amount, nevertheless it can be argued that at least some of the negative aspects of the transition period following liberalization could be moderated if the authorities pursued a more flexible exchange rate policy.[31]

4. Conclusions

The results in this chapter indicate that the liberalization of trade and capital flows is likely to have substantial effects on the domestic economy. Specifically, it was shown that the removal of barriers to trade and capital flows produces the following results in the short run. While the rate of inflation and domestic interest rate (adjusted for changes in risk) tend to approach their respective international values, this is accompanied by a rise in the domestic real rate of interest, worsening of the current account, a loss of international reserves, and a significant build-up of foreign debt. There is, furthermore, an appreciation of the real exchange rate to a new equilibrium level. In the context of this particular exercise, the negative effects of opening-up become magnified if one then further allows for the possibility of domestic policy inconsistencies and adverse international shocks during the liberalization process.

Whether in the long run the liberalization experiments would have been successful in the absence of external shocks, and if the right macroeconomic policies had been in place, is not a question one can answer with certainty. What we can say, however, is that the possibilities of success were greatly diminished once the international picture worsened and countries pursued other domestic policies that apparently worked at cross purposes with the policy of liberalization. Based on the results reported here, if external shocks are large and persist for long enough and inconsistent domestic policies are maintained, then it is quite likely that the economy will suffer serious problems. In reality, limits on external borrowing prevented developing countries from financing their way out of their difficulties, brought about by the various shocks and inappropriate policies, and finally forced them to undertake painful adjustment and even to reverse the overall strategy and reimpose barriers to trade and capital flows.

What, then, is the policy lesson that can be drawn from the analysis conducted here? The conclusion that comes out quite forcefully is that opening-up policies have to be actively supported by domestic macroeconomic management. This becomes even more imperative if the country is subjected to external shocks while it is in the process of liberalizing the foreign sector. While the individual developing country can do little about changes in the international environment, it would seem that a judicious combination of external financing, use of international reserves, and domestic adjustment should be called for at an early stage to offset or minimize the effects of any external shocks that occur. Since there are quantitative limits to the amount of international reserves and foreign financing, it is obvious that eventual adjustment of the basic supply–demand balance in the economy is necessary. Fiscal and monetary restraint to control both public and private spending, coupled with a more flexible exchange rate policy, would seem to be the relevant instruments of adjustment under the circumstances in which a number of developing countries found themselves in the late 1970s and early 1980s. While there were some attempts in this general direction, they can perhaps be characterized as being too little and too late. As a consequence, many developing countries, and particularly those engaged in the process of opening-up, found that they had eventually to undergo more painful adjustment than would have been necessary if action had been taken more promptly.

Notes

[1]For a detailed study on the effects of the changing international environment on developing countries, see Goldstein and Khan (1982).

[2]See Khan and Zahler (1983, 1985).

[3]We can include in this group the models of Blejer and Fernández (1980), and Khan and Knight (1981).

[4]Since the resource endowment is fixed in the short run, we do not allow for any net investment or savings.

[5]Private expenditures on goods and nonfinancial services require that interest payments on foreign debt be subtracted out. It should also be noted that we assume that the pattern of government spending on the three goods is identical to that of the private sector.

[6]Assuming that the exchange rate and the tariff level remain unchanged.

[7]The expected change in the exchange rate is assumed throughout to be equal to the actual change.

[8]The relevance of this particular formulation to the analysis will be made clear below.

[9]This is generally not possible in the larger computational general equilibrium models.

[10]Following Khan and Zahler (1983) it is assumed here that nontradable goods substitute with each of the tradable goods, but for simplicity we rule out cross-price effects between importables and exportables. This assumption does not change the conclusions reached by Kahn and Zahler (1983) in any significant way.

[11]It should be noted that the real exchange rate is defined including tariffs.

[12]Starting with a positive rate of inflation would not alter the analysis.

[13]See Blejer (1978).

[14]In general a change in relative prices would change production of nontradable goods, and the transformation curve between importable and exportable goods would have to shift. We make this restrictive assumption in Figure 3.2 only for expositional purposes.

[15]We assume here that the expected (and actual) nominal exchange rate is constant.

[16]Starting with a positive stock of foreign debt would not change any of the basic results.

[17]In the Khan and Zahler (1983) model it was assumed that the response of foreign capital to interest rate differentials was high, although not instantaneous. The approach adopted here for the graphical analysis, that is, shifting the LM curve, yields qualitatively similar results.

[18]The current account deficit is also created by the increase in the relative price of nontradable goods that results from the excess supply of money created by the inflow of capital.

[19]This would hold, for example, if domestic and foreign savings were perfect substitutes.

[20]It should be stressed that by assuming that net savings are zero the potential benefits of financial opening-up are in a sense being minimized. For an alternative approach where productive capacity grows with foreign savings, see Zahler (1982).

[21]Obviously one could also obtain the same decline in the terms of trade by increasing the price of importables relative to the price of exportables. The outcomes, however, are not symmetrical, so that one has to be careful to note that our results are conditional on how the terms-of-trade change is specified.

[22]A similar set of results are obtained if private sector expenditures are increased through an expansion in domestic credit.

[23]For the reasons for choosing an equilibrium position to begin from, see Khan and Zahler (1983), page 245.

[24]The model assumes a "normal" rate of unemployment of 5%.

[25]For these values see Khan and Zahler (1983), Appendix II.

[26]In equilibrium the current account is set equal to 100; values below 100 therefore imply a current account deficit.

[27]Of course, nominal depreciation of the currency would entail certain costs, particularly with respect to inflation.

[28]One would normally expect an increase in the fiscal deficit to result in a greater excess supply of money, but in this framework there is a larger increase in the demand for money (due to the increase in nominal income resulting from the fiscal deficit); furthermore, the additional monetary expansion created by the deficit leaks out very rapidly through the current account of the balance of payments.

[29]In the model only foreign residents are allowed to acquire domestic debt, and domestic residents (including the government) are restricted from holding foreign debt. As such, an increase in foreign interest rates, by reducing the incentive for foreigners to invest, leads to a smaller (or even negative) inflow of capital and a lower stock of foreign debt.

[30]See, for example, Edwards (1982), Sjaastad (1983), Zahler (1983), and Dornbusch (1984).

[31]This result confirms the argument put forward by Dornbusch (1984) that the exchange rate policies in the Southern Cone countries led to steady overvaluation of their respective currencies, and that this outcome could have been avoided through more flexible exchange rate management.

References

Balassa, Bela (1980). "The Process of Industrial Development and Alternative Development Strategies." *Essays in International Finance* No. 141, International Finance Section, Princeton University (December).

Blejer, Mario (1978). "Nontraded Goods and the Monetary Approach to the Balance of Payments: A Graphical Note." *Quarterly Review of Economics and Business* (Summer): 102–6.

———— , and Roque B. Fernandez (1980). "The Effects of Unanticipated Money Growth on Prices and on Output and Its Composition in a Fixed-Exchange-Rate Open Economy." *Canadian Journal of Economics* (February): 82–95.

Clements, Kenneth W. (1980). "A General Equilibrium Econometric Model of the Open Economy." *International Economic Review* (June): 469–88.

Dornbusch, Rudiger (1974). "Tariffs and Nontraded Goods." *Journal of International Economics* (August): 177–85.

———— (1984). "External Debt, Budget Deficits and Disequilibrium Exchange Rates." M.I.T. Working Paper No. 347 (June).

Edwards, Sebastián (1982). "Economic Policy and the Record of Economic Growth in Chile in the 1970s and 1980s." UCLA Working Paper No. 283 (November).

Feltenstein, Andrew (1980). "A General Equilibrium Approach to the Analysis of Trade Restrictions, with an Application to Argentina." *IMF Staff Papers* (December): 749–84.

Goldstein, Morris, and Mohsin S. Khan (1982). *Effects of Slowdown in Industrial Countries on Growth in Non-Oil Developing Countries.* IMF Occasional Paper No. 12, Washington (August).

Keesing, Donald (1979). "Trade Policy for Developing Countries." World Bank Staff Working Paper No. 353 (August).

Khan, Mohsin S., and Malcolm D. Knight (1981). "Stabilization Programs in Developing Countries: A Formal Framework." *IMF Staff Papers* (March): 1–53.

———— (1983). "Determinants of the Current Account Balances of Non-Oil Developing Countries in the 1970s: An Empirical Analysis." *IMF Staff Papers* (December): 819–42.

Khan, Mohsin S., and Roberto Zahler (1983). "The Macroeconomic Effects of Changes in Barriers to Trade and Capital Flows: A Simulation Analysis." *IMF Staff Papers* (June): 223–82.

———— (1985). "Trade and Financial Liberalization Given External Shocks and Inconsistent Domestic Policies." *IMF Staff Papers* (March): 22–55.

Sjaastad, Larry A. (1983). "Failure of Economic Liberalism in the Cone of Latin America." *The World Economy* (March): 5–26.

Zahler, Roberto (1982). "Estrategias Alternativas de Apertura: Un Modelo de Simulación." *Monetaria* (July–September): 303–58.

———— (1983). "Recent Southern Cone Liberalization Reforms and Stabilization Policies: The Chilean Case, 1974–1982." *Journal of Interamerican Studies and World Affairs* (November): 509--62.

II

THE ORDER OF TRADE AND FINANCIAL LIBERALIZATION

4

On the Appropriate Timing and Speed of Economic Liberalization in Developing Countries

Sebastián Edwards & Sweder van Wijnbergen

1. Introduction

The welfare costs of intervention in international trade are firmly established theoretically and increasingly well-documented empirically. Trading at world prices, both at a point in time in commodity markets and intertemporally via capital markets, maximizes the gains from trade for countries too small to influence the terms at which trade takes place in the world.[1] However, demonstrating the superiority of free-trade equilibrium provides little guidance on the problems likely to be encountered *during* an attempt to liberalize the external sector in a particular country. In practice, many times such attempts have been frustrated at different stages, with the countries involved reverting to inward-looking development strategies. The characteristics of the transition between a repressed and a liberalized economy are not well understood, and serious research efforts in this area have started only recently.[2] Among these dynamic aspects, those related to the speed and order of liberalization are particularly important. With respect to the former, the main question is how fast an economy should be liberalized, that is, "cold turkey" vs. gradual approaches. Regarding the

We thank Ed Tower, Gene Grossman, Jere Behrman, the participants in seminars at the University of Chicago, Stanford University, and the University of Minnesota for helpful comments. The views presented in this chapter are our own and do not necessarily reflect those of the institutions with which we are affiliated. The research reported here is part of the NBER's program in international studies.

order of liberalization, the main question is what the welfare consequences are of alternative sequencing scenarios (that is, trade liberalization while maintaining a closed capital account like Chile in the late 1970s, or capital market liberalization while retaining trade barriers as was the case in Argentina in the same period).

The purpose of the present chapter is to address some aspects of these two problems—speed and order of liberalization. The analysis focuses on the opening-up of a small developing economy to the rest of the world, concentrating on the liberalization of the current and capital accounts of the balance of payments. We investigate the welfare consequences of trade and capital market liberalization processes under alternative sequencing scenarios. The analysis assumes that the simultaneous and instantaneous opening of both accounts of the balance of payments is not considered as a policy option. The recent experience of a group of countries in Latin America is in fact one of partial (that is, one market only) liberalization. In Argentina, for example, only the capital account was liberalized. In Chile, on the other hand, the trade account was fully liberalized, while a number of controls affecting capital transactions with the rest of the world were maintained. Moreover, historically trade liberalization has often been implemented during periods of severe constraints on external borrowing (for example, the IMF routinely pushes for trade liberalization as part of its "rescue programs").[3]

In this chapter, we draw on standard trade theory to show that the opening of the capital account in the presence of trade distortions may be welfare reducing if foreign borrowing is used to increase investment, and if investment decisions are made using domestic market prices. However, we demonstrate that this welfare-reducing effect of opening the capital account will not occur if shadow prices are used to guide investment decisions. We also demonstrate that the welfare costs of capital market restrictions are larger to the extent that they fall disproportionately on investment relative to consumption.[4] We then show that under such circumstances gradual reduction of tariffs is superior to an abrupt liberalization.

The chapter is organized in the following form: In Section 2, a one-period model is developed and some preliminaries are presented. The analysis in this section is carried out in terms of welfare effects of transfers and factor movements from abroad, and previous results by Johnson (1967), Brecher and Díaz-Alejandro (1977), Grossman (1984), and van Wijnbergen (1983a) are summarized and discussed. This analysis is useful for the investigation presented in Section 3 of the dynamic effects of liberalizing the capital account. The reason for this is that the effects of opening of the capital account can be viewed as the combination of a positive transfer today, plus a (larger) negative transfer tomorrow. In this section we point out that the distinction between transfers in the form of consumption goods and transfers in the form of capital (that is, machinery) is critical for the welfare analysis. The crucial role of shadow prices in the investment process is also discussed. In Section 3, a two-period model is developed and the welfare effects of reducing import tariffs in an economy with capital market distortions are analyzed. Here our argument for a gradual trade liberalization in an economy where the capital market distortions fall disproportionately on investment is fully developed. Finally, in Section 4 some concluding remarks are presented, and the policy implications of our analysis are discussed.

2. Welfare Effects of Transfers and Foreign Investment in a One-Period Framework

In this section, we develop a simple one-period model of a small open economy to analyze the effects of transfers and direct investment on welfare. Regarding transfers, we consider two possible forms in which these can be made: in the form of consumption goods and in the form of capital (that is, machines).[5] Since this analysis is based on a one-period model, it cannot really deal with issues of borrowing in the international capital market. However, most of the issues that arise in a two-period model with foreign borrowing and lending are already present in the single-period analysis with exogenous transfers presented here. The reason for this is that, if the capital market distortion takes the form of a quantity constraint on foreign borrowing, the effect of opening the capital account can be viewed as a positive transfer today (when a foreign loan is obtained), plus a larger negative transfer tomorrow when the foreign loan (plus interest) is repaid.

We first look at the effects of a transfer in the form of capital (that is, the donor ships machines) on the recipient country's welfare. The analysis is developed for the case of a small country with two goods, whose importable is assumed to be capital intensive. The country in question uses convex technology that can be described by a twice differentiable revenue function; consumer preferences are summarized by a twice differentiable concave expenditure function; and it is assumed that the economy is distorted by production subsidies and consumption taxes on the importable good. The model is given by equations (1) through (4):

$$R(1, q; K, L) + G = E(1, p; U) \tag{1}$$

$$G = \beta E_p(1, p, U) - R_q(1, q, K, L) \tag{2}$$

$$p = p^* + \beta \qquad\qquad (3)$$

$$q = p^* + \alpha \qquad\qquad (4)$$

where R is the revenue function; E is the expenditure function; q is the domestic producer's price of commodity 2 relative to commodity 1; K is the stock of capital; L is the total labor available in the economy; p^* is the world price of commodity 2 relative to commodity 1; p is the domestic price of commodity 2 relative to commodity 1; β is the consumption tax on good 2; α is the production subsidy on good 2; $E_p = \partial E/\partial p$ is the compensated demand for good 2; $R_q = \partial R/\partial q$ is the supply function for good 2; and G is the government (*net*) revenue from taxation.

Equation (1) is the budget constraint for a distorted economy, where G equals net government revenue. Good 1 is taken to be the numeraire commodity, and it is assumed that this country imports good 2, so that E_p is the consumption of good 2 and $E_p - R_q > 0$. Notice that in the case of a tariff, $\alpha = \beta$. The effect of a transfer in the form of capital on welfare can be found by totally differentiating (1), and using (2) through (4):

$$\frac{dU}{dK} = \frac{R_K - \alpha R_{qK}}{E_U(1 - \beta C_E)} \qquad\qquad (5)$$

where the subindex refers to a partial derivative with respect to that particular variable. C_E is the pure income effect of a change in expenditure on good 2; $0 < pC_E < 1$ if both goods are normal. Therefore, $1 - \beta C_E$ is positive but smaller than 1.[6] R_K is the marginal productivity of capital, and R_{qK} is the Rybczynski term, which will be positive if good 2 (the importable) is capital intensive as we have assumed. The denominator of this expression is positive; however, the numerator can be either positive or negative, depending on whether $R_K \gtreqless \alpha R_{qK}$. It follows that a transfer in the form of capital will be welfare worsening in a distorted small economy if $R_K < \alpha R_{qK}$. This result, of course, is the one obtained by Johnson in his classical 1967 article on capital accumulation in the presence of tariffs. If the transfer results in an intensification of the preexisting distortion, welfare will be reduced.

The above discussion assumes that the transfer is made in the form of machines, and that as a result capital is accumulated in the country in question. Brecher and Díaz-Alejandro (1977) have analyzed an alternative case where capital accumulation occurs due to foreign investment. This case differs from the previous one in that foreign investors will now take their profits out of the domestic country. In this case the budget constraint [equation (1)], is written in the following form:

$$R(1, q, K + dK, L) + G - H = E(1, p, U) \qquad\qquad (6)$$

where H are profits remitted to the foreign country, given by $H = \rho dK$ where ρ is the rate of profit obtained by the foreign investor. The change in welfare is now equal to:

$$\frac{dU}{dK} = \frac{R_K - \alpha R_{qK} - \rho}{E_U(1 - \beta C_E)} \tag{7}$$

If the rate of profits obtained by foreign investors is equal to the marginal productivity of capital in the domestic country (that is, $\rho = R_K$), expression (7) becomes:

$$\frac{dU}{dK} = \frac{-\alpha R_{qK}}{E_U(1 - \beta C_E)} < 0 \tag{8}$$

This means that if foreign investors repatriate the full rental rate, under the assumption that the importable good is capital-intensive (that is, $R_{qK} > 0$) *welfare will always decrease* as a result of foreign investment. This result is independent of the relationship between αR_{qK} and R_K. If, however, the return to foreign investment is taxed, it is possible that foreign investment will be welfare improving. The tax required for this to be accomplished has to exceed αR_{qK} and could conceivable drive the after-tax rate of return to foreigners below their alternative rate of return r^*, and so become prohibitive (Grossman, 1984; van Wijnbergen, 1983a).

Consider now the opposite case, where the country uses the proceeds from the transfer to increase consumption.[7] In this case the change in welfare will be equal to (where T represents the transfer):

$$\frac{dU}{dT} = \frac{1}{E_U(1 - \beta C_E)} \geqslant 0 \tag{9}$$

which is always greater than zero: a transfer made in the form of consumption goods can never be welfare worsening. [We are ignoring "induced" distortions à la Brecher and Bhagwati (1982) and transfer-induced changes in the world relative-price vector.]

In the presence of distorted trade, then, a transfer in the form of capital (that is, machines) may be welfare worsening; while a consumption transfer will always be welfare improving. This suggests that if a transfer is given partially in terms of consumption goods and partially in terms of capital, a reduction in welfare in the recipient country could result, even under stability (which is assured by the small country assumption). This kind of immiserizing transfer is similar to the distortion-induced transfers analyzed by Brecher and Bhagwati (1982). The relevance of this case—where the transfer is made in capital and consumption goods—stems from the fact that in the real world it is common to find aid which is given on the condition that part of the resources are used for investment (that is, to increase the capital stock).

Should we therefore conclude that foreign aid channeled into investment (typical World Bank practice) has dubious welfare effects in distorted economies, while consumption out of aid is to be encouraged? Clearly, this is much too sweeping a statement to be true. In fact, we will show that the immiserizing effects of capital transfers can be eliminated completely by using *shadow prices* to guide the sectoral allocation of, and technology choice incorporated in, the influx of capital goods.

Consider again our two-sector economy. To simplify the exposition we now assume that $\alpha = \beta = \tau$, so that $p = q = p^* + \tau$. We have already shown that introducing a gift (that is, transfer) of machines could be welfare deteriorating if allocation and technology choice are governed by the relative price vector $(1, q)$. However, deciding on allocation and technology choice using *world prices* $(1, p^*)$, which clearly are the appropriate shadow prices in this context, leads to different results. This can be modeled by introducing a separate revenue function based on the optimal allocation of labor $(\bar{L})$ to the new machines by the Shadow Pricing Agency (note that we have constant returns to scale technology), where $\bar{R}$ is revenue from government production measured at shadow prices. Of course, labor use on new machines means less labor available for old machines: the shadow wage rate is positive. Choosing $\bar{L}$ is clearly equivalent to setting a shadow wage rate. The equilibrium condition can be summarized by the following structure:

$$R(1, q; K, L - \bar{L}) + \tau(E_q - R_q) + \bar{R}(1, p^*; K^*, \bar{L}) = E(1, q, U) \quad (10)$$

where K^* is the capital transfer. We assume that output is actually sold at market prices so that if protected goods were to be produced with the new capital goods, the tariff revenue replacement effect exactly cancels that part of total revenues represented by the excess of market price q of over p^*, justifying our use of $\bar{R}(1, p^*)$ which omits that component, and the absence of $\tau\bar{R}_p$. in the tariff revenue term. It is possible, moreover, that $\bar{R}_{p^*} = 0$, since we do not impose incomplete specialization on the Shadow Pricing Agency.

Differentiating (10) we obtain:

$$(-R_L + \bar{R}_L + \tau R_{qL}) \, d\bar{L} + \bar{R}_K \, dK^* = E_U(1 - \tau C_e) \, dU \quad (11)$$

Optimally choosing $\bar{L}$ implies setting $dU/d\bar{L} = 0$ which yields the intuitively appealing formula for the shadow wage rate $\bar{R}_L$:

$$\bar{R}_L = R_L - \tau R_{qL} \qquad (12)$$

This means that the shadow wage rate $\bar{R}_L$ is above or below the market wage (R_L) depending on whether the Rybczynski term R_{qL} is negative or positive. In our example q is the price of the capital-intensive good, so $R_{qL} < 0$ and the shadow wage is *above* the market wage. This makes sense: protecting the capital-intensive sector leads to overproduction of the capital-intensive good; to reconcile that with a fixed aggregate capital–labor ratio, overly labor-intensive techniques in any given sector have to be chosen so that the market wage is below the wage that would obtain in the absence of relative price distortions.

Inserting (12) into (11) immediately gives the result that with shadow pricing immiserization is ruled out:

$$\frac{dU}{dK^*} = \frac{\bar{R}_k}{E_U(1 - \tau C_e)} > 0 \qquad (13)$$

3. Trade and Capital Market Liberalization in a Two-Period World

The static framework of the previous section is not really a satisfactory framework for the analysis of capital market distortions. Capital market distortions are in a sense isomorphic to trade distortions, in that they involve barriers to trade between goods today and goods tomorrow, in the same way that trade barriers interfere with trade in different goods at any moment of time. Accordingly, an intertemporal framework is appropriate.

In this section we develop a simple two-period model, similar to the one in van Wijnbergen (1984), and use it to derive expressions for the welfare costs of capital market distortions. In particular we analyze quantity constraints in international capital markets under various rationing mechanisms. In order to organize the discussion we concentrate on two cases. We first look at the general case where the external rationing affects both consumption and investment. That is, when the government imposes a foreign borrowing constraint, the availability of foreign funds for all uses is reduced. This, however, is not a very realistic assumption. A number of studies have shown that governments do not generally act in this way; when borrowing (or spending) constraints are imposed, they usually fall in a disproportionate way on investment.[8] For example, after discussing their empirical findings, Hicks and Kubisch (1984, p. 38) state that "politicians ... find it more acceptable to reduce investment, ... than to make ... reductions in present consumption." For this reason, in this section we also

consider the case where the foreign borrowing constraint falls dispro-
portionally on investment. Furthermore, to simplify the exposition we
assume that the credit rationing takes an extreme form, fully falling on
investment.

We then extend the model to a two-commodity per period setting to
analyze trade liberalization under external balance constraints, empirically
a very important case.

We draw on recent work on the relationship between temporary tariffs
and private savings (that is, Razin and Svensson, 1983; van Wijnbergen
1983b) to analyze the question of cold turkey versus gradualism in trade
liberalization in the case where external rationing falls disproportionately
on investment. We unambiguously establish that under those circumstances gradualism is the optimal strategy.

3.1.   The Welfare Costs
of External Capital Market Constraints

Consider a simple two-period, one-sector open economy with endogenous
investment. Assume first that there are no capital market distortions, so
that the domestic discount factor δ (1 over 1 plus the interest rate) equals
the world discount factor δ^* (that is, $\delta = \delta^*$). The model can be
summarized by the intertemporal budget constraint with savings and
production decisions already solved via the use of revenue and expenditure
functions:

$$R^1(K, L) + \delta^* R^2(K + I, L) - I = E(1, \delta^*; W) \tag{14}$$

where δ^* is the world discount factor $[\delta^* = 1/(1 + r^*)]$, or the price of
future goods in terms of today's goods. R^1 refers to the revenue function in
period 1, while R^2 is the revenue function in period 2. E, on the other
hand, is the intertemporal aggregate expenditure function, and gives the
minimum discounted value of expenditure required to achieve the level of
welfare W, given the discount factor δ^*. Investment (I) is determined by
value maximization of the firm, which leads to an equivalent of "Tobin's q"
being set equal to 1:

$$\delta^* R_K^2(K + I, L) = 1 \tag{15}$$

or

$$I = I(\delta^*) \qquad I_{\delta^*} = -\frac{R_K^2}{\delta^* R_{KK}^2} > 0 \tag{15a}$$

Assume now that a binding external borrowing constraint is imposed. Then the current account deficit in period 1 is equal to the constant $\bar{T}$:

$$CA^1 = -\bar{T} \tag{16}$$

In the absence of such a constraint, the first-period deficit would have been larger ($CA_1 = -\hat{T} < -\bar{T}$, where "$\char`\^$" indicates a variable from the unconstrained solution). The optimal way of dealing with this constraint is to charge a cost of foreign borrowing r, above the world rate of interest r^*, to consumers and investors alike. A convenient way of parametrizing this is to assume that there is a tax on foreign borrowing that pushes the domestic discount factor δ below the foreign one, δ^*:

$$b = \delta^* - \delta > 0 \tag{17}$$

where $b = (r - r^*)/[(1 + r)(1 + r^*)]$, the discounted value of tax payments per unit paid. Equation (14) then becomes

$$R^1(K, L) + \delta R^2(K + I, L) + b(R^2 - E_\delta) - I(\delta) = E(1, \delta, W) \tag{18}$$

where δ is determined by the requirement

$$\delta^*(R^2 - E_\delta) = \bar{T} \tag{19}$$

That is, the second-period current account surplus discounted at the *world* rate of interest should equal the maximum allowable deficit today.

Equation (17) simply says that to satisfy the external balance constraint, future goods should be made cheaper in terms of current goods so that people will willingly shift expenditure toward tomorrow. Expression (19) indicates that this process should continue until the constraint just ceases to be binding. Differentiation of (18) gives us the expression for the welfare effects of a change in δ (because of a change in $\bar{T}$):

$$(\delta^* - \delta)(-E_{\delta\delta} + R_K^2 I_\delta) \, d\delta = E_W \, dW \tag{20}$$

From (20), it follows that an increase in δ toward its optimal δ^* will improve welfare (that is, $W/\partial\delta > 0$). Integration of (20), on the other hand, yields the approximate total welfare gain to be expected from such an increase in $\bar{T}$ that δ will equal δ^*, where the constraint just ceases to be binding:[9]

$$E_W \frac{\Delta W}{\Delta\delta} = \frac{1}{2}(\delta^* - \delta)^2(-E_\delta + R_K^2 I_\delta) \tag{21}$$

where ΔW is the accumulated change in welfare resulting from an increase of δ to δ^*. Since homogeneity of compensated demand functions implies $E_{\delta\delta} = -E_{\delta 1}/\delta$, (21) can be written as

$$E_W \frac{\Delta W}{\Delta \delta} \approx \frac{1}{2}(\delta^* - \delta)^2(E_{1\delta} + I_\delta)R_K^2 \tag{21a}$$

(21a) is an approximation because second-order effects via dependence of $(E_{1\delta} + I_\delta)R_K^2$ on δ are ignored.

So the cost of the distortion, in familiar Harberger fashion, is proportional to (compensated) savings and investment elasticities and to the *square* of the equivalent price wedge $\delta^* - \delta$ introduced by the distortion. An alternative way of writing (21) may be useful for empirical work; note that the first-period current account equals

$$CA^1 = R^1 - I - E_1 \qquad CA_\delta^1 = -I_\delta - E_{1\delta}$$

where $CA_\delta^1 = -\delta^{-2}(\partial CA^1/\partial r)$. Therefore (21a) can be written as

$$E_W \frac{\Delta W}{\Delta \delta} = -\frac{1}{2}\frac{(\delta^* - \delta)^2}{\delta} CA_\delta^1 \tag{21b}$$

where we used $\delta R_k^2 = 1$.

Equation (21) gives the social cost of the externally imposed constraint on the current account *if* the optimal policy response is followed. In practice however, and as discussed above, rationing often falls disproportionately on investment rather than consumption, since governments are less prone to constrain consumption than to "postpone" investment.[10] It is easily demonstrated that in that case the social loss caused by the constraint is larger.

Since we will use below an extreme version of this rationing mechanism, it is useful to elaborate on this point. To simplify the exposition, we will assume without loss of generality that *only* investment is rationed. Assuming further that tax revenues are handed back to the public in the period in which they are levied, the model with only investment rationed becomes

$$R^1(K, L) + \delta^* R^2[K + I(\tilde\delta), L] - I(\tilde\delta) = E(1, \delta^*, W) \tag{22}$$

$$\tilde\delta R_K^2(K + I, L) = 1 \tag{23}$$

$$\delta^*\{R^2[K + I(\tilde\delta)], L] - E_\delta(1, \delta^*, W)\} = \bar{T} \tag{24}$$

where δ is the inverse of 1 plus the "shadow" rate of interest under this rationing mechanism (that is, the interest rate at which unconstrained investment would in fact equal the rationed amount).

Differentiating equation (22), we obtain the welfare loss caused by the imposition of the constraint $CA_1 \leq \bar{T}$ under the rationing scheme used here:

$$E_W \, dW = (\delta^* R_K^2 I_\delta - I_\delta) \, d\tilde{\delta}$$

After some manipulations, using (23), we obtain:

$$E_W \, dW = (\delta^* - \tilde{\delta}) R_K^2 I_\delta \, d\tilde{\delta} \tag{25}$$

(see Appendix I for a more detailed derivation of the results presented in this section). Integration of (25) gives us the equivalent of (21) for this particular rationing scheme:

$$E_W \frac{\Delta \tilde{W}}{\Delta \tilde{\delta}} \approx \frac{1}{2} (\delta^* - \tilde{\delta})^2 R_K^2 \, I_\delta \tag{26}$$

where $\Delta \tilde{W}$ is the welfare gain obtained if $\tilde{\delta}$ is raised until it equals δ^*.

As may be seen, contrary to equation (21), our new welfare change expression (26) does not include an $E_1 \delta$ term. This, however, is not surprising since, under the present rationing scheme, only investment is rationed.

To compare the welfare effects of the two alternative rationing schemes considered here [equations (21) and (26)], we would need expression for $\delta^* - \delta$ and $\delta^* - \tilde{\delta}$. Linearization of (21) and (26) gives, after some manipulation (see Appendix I),

$$\frac{\tilde{\delta} - \delta^*}{\delta - \delta^*} = 1 + E_{1\delta}/I_\delta > 1 \tag{27}$$

where the inequality sign follows from the fact that $E_{1\delta}, I_\delta > 0$.

The insertion of (27) into (21a) and (26) yields a particularly simple expression for the relative welfare costs of the external constraint under different rationing regimes:

$$\frac{\Delta \tilde{W}}{\Delta W} \approx \frac{(\delta^* - \tilde{\delta})^3}{(\delta^* - \delta)^3} \frac{I_\delta}{E_{1\delta} + I_\delta} \tag{28}$$

$$= (1 + E_{1\delta}/I_\delta)^2 \geq 1$$

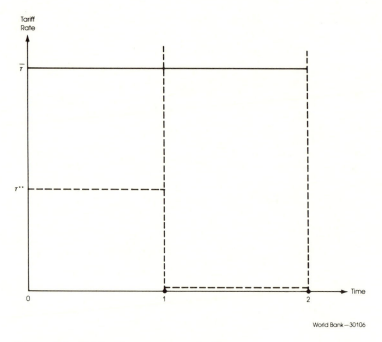

Tariff
Rate

$\bar{\tau}$

$\tau^{\cdot\cdot}$

0   1   2   Time

World Bank—30106

Figure 4.1 Cold turkey versus gradualism.

Equation (28) indicates that the investment rationing scheme leads to larger welfare losses. However, as discussed above, this rationing scheme may be the only feasible one available. In the next section we draw on some recent work on the impact of temporary tariffs on the consumption rate of interest and private savings to construct an argument for gradual trade liberalization under such circumstances.

3.2.   Trade Reform under an External Balance Constraint:
A Second-Best Argument for Gradualism

Consider an extension to two goods of the model of Section 3.1, with an external balance constraint falling on investment only. We will exploit the link between temporary tariffs and private savings via the consumption rate of interest stressed by Razin and Svensson (1983) and van Wijnbergen (1983b) to construct an argument for gradualism in liberalizing trade.[11]

   Cold-turkey liberalization implies that the pre-liberalization tariff τ is lowered to *zero* in both periods. Gradualism implies a zero tariff in period 2 but a lower but positive tariff in period 1 ($\tau^{\star\star}$ in Figure 4.1). The *differential* welfare effect can accordingly be obtained by evaluating the welfare effect of a tariff τ^{**} in period 1 under the assumption of a zero tariff in period 2.

To do so we have, of course, to extend the model to at least two traded goods (x and y) each period. By choice of normalization, assume that good x is the untaxed commodity. The budget constraint then becomes

$$R^1(1, p_y^1; K) = \delta^* R^2(1, p_y^2; K + I) - I(\delta) + \tau(E_{P_y^1} - R_{P_y^1}^1)$$

$$= E[\Pi_1(1, p_y^1), \delta^* \Pi_2(1, p_y^2); W] \qquad (29)$$

where p_y^1, the domestic price of good y in period 1, equals the world price plus tariff rate, $p_y^1 = P_y^* + \tau$. We assume that aggregate utility W is weakly homothetically identically separable, which allows us to write the expenditure function as a function of within-period price indices $\Pi_i(1, P_y^i)$ ($i = 1, 2$), the discount factor δ^*, and welfare W (see Svensson and Razin, 1983).

The capital market constraint is represented by

$$\delta^*\{R^2[1, p_y^2; K + I(\delta)] - \Pi_2 E_{\Pi_2}[\Pi_1(1, P_y^1), \delta^* \Pi_2(1, p_y^2), W]\} = \bar{T} \quad (30)$$

Investment is determined by setting the value of capital (evaluated at the "virtual discount factor" δ, since investment is rationed) equal to its production costs:[12]

$$\delta R_K^2 = 1 \qquad (31)$$

where we made the simplifying assumption that investment goods consist of good 1 only, or, alternatively, that the good-2 components can be imported free of tariffs.

Simple differentiation of (29) and (30) and inserting (31) yields

$$\gamma \frac{d\delta}{d\bar{\tau}} = [(1 - \tau C_{1y})\Pi_2 \Pi_{1(P_y^1)} \delta^* E_{\Pi_2 \Pi_1}] + [C_{2E} \tau(E_{P_y^1 P_y^1} - R_{P_y^1 P_y^1}^1)] \qquad (32)$$

$$\text{(A)} \hspace{4cm} \text{(B)}$$

where γ is a positive constant (see Appendix II for explicit formulas), and

$$C_{2E} = \delta^* \pi_2 E_{\Pi_2 W} E_W^{-1}$$

is the marginal propensity to spend (on all goods) in period two. Equation (32) tells us that a small tariff will *increase* δ, or *lower* the interest rate that has to be charged to investors in order to hit the capital market constraint.

The mechanism is clear: a small tariff in the first period only *decreases* the consumption discount factor $\delta^* \Pi_2 / [\Pi_1(1, P_y^1)]$ or, equivalently, *increases* the consumption rate of interest (CRI). An increase in τ in period 1 only makes consumption in period 1 more expensive in terms of consumption in period 2 (for an extensive elaboration, see Razin and Svensson, 1983, and van Wijnbergen, 1983b). This leads to higher private savings, leaving more room for investment given the external current-account constraint. Accordingly, δ can go up, closer to the world market discount factor δ^*. This effect corresponds to term (A) in equation (32). If, however, the tariff is too large, term (B)—which is proportional to τ—will dominate and reverse the result. The reason is once again clear: a large first-period tariff will inflict a large first-period real income loss; consumption smoothing will then lead to downward pressure on the first-period current account. If the real income loss is large enough, this effect will offset the positive effect via the CRI. Define τ^* as the tariff rate where these two effects will just cancel each other out in the margin.

We are now ready to look at the *welfare* effects of a small first-period tariff under the external balance constraint with investment rationing:

$$\gamma_1 \frac{dW}{d\tau} = \Pi_{1(P_y^1)}\, \Pi_2\, E_{\Pi_2 \Pi_1}(\delta^* - \delta) + \tau(E_{P_y^1 P_y^1} - R^1{}_{P_y^1 P_y^1}) \tag{33}$$

$$(+; C) \qquad\qquad (-; D)$$

where $\gamma_1 > 0$ (see Appendix II for a precise expression). Equation (33) backs up our claim in the introduction to this section: a first-period tariff, if not too large, is welfare improving under the external balance constraint-cum-investment rationing mechanism considered. The first term, C, is proportional to the size of the capital market distortion ($\delta^* - \delta$) and the compensated sensitivity of savings with respect to the rate of interest ($E_{\Pi_2 \Pi_1}$) and is positive. A temporary tariff will raise the consumption rate of interest, increasing private savings, therefore allowing an increase in private investment (which was too low because of the external balance constraint and the rationing mechanism adopted) and so reducing the distortionary costs of the external balance constraint-cum-investment rationing. If the first-period tariff is too large however, the second term, D, will increase since it is proportional to τ. In that case the static welfare losses arising from the first-period relative price distortion may offset the dynamic gains via the CRI. Define τ^{**} as the rate where these effects cancel *on the margin*. It is straightforward to show that $\tau^{**} < \tau^*$, that is, the marginal welfare effect changes sign as τ increases *before* the effect on δ is reversed (see Appendix II).

Setting the marginal net welfare gain of a first-period tariff equal to zero implicitly defines the (second-best) optimal first-period tariff:

$$\tau^{**} = -\Pi_2\Pi_{1(P_y^1)} E_{\Pi_2\Pi_1}(\delta^* - \delta)/(E_{P_y^1 P_y^1} - R^1_{P_y^1 P_y^1}) > 0 \qquad (34)$$

Equation (34) shows that under the investment-rationing scheme adopted in response to the external balance constraint, the first-period (second-best) optimal tariff is strictly positive. This establishes the superiority of gradualism over cold-turkey liberalization under the external balance constraint-cum-investment rationing.

To recapitulate, we start off by analyzing the very realistic (for most LDCs) case where an exogenously imposed external balance constraint falls disproportionately on investment rather than on consumption (in fact, we assumed for analytical convenience that it falls *completely* on investment; this is immaterial however). Under those circumstances *a small first-period tariff was shown to be welfare improving* because of its favorable effects on private savings (via the CRI) and the ensuing relaxation of the rationing of private investment. Since gradual trade liberalization can be considered as complete liberalization with a small tariff reimposed in period 1, this constitutes an argument for gradualism when liberalizing trade under external balance constraints.

It should be emphasized, however, that this is conditional on investment taking a disproportionate share of the adjustment burden to the external constraint; if a market-clearing real interest rate above world levels can be charged to consumers and investors alike, it can be shown that the argument for additional first-period relative price distortions via temporary tariffs disappears, the favorable CRI effects notwithstanding.[13] However, since, as discussed above, in most LDCs such a first-best rationing device is typically unavailable, our argument for gradualism stands.

4. Concluding Remarks

In a first-best world without externalities, without market imperfections, and without constraints on commodity taxation, the issue addressed in this chapter—how to liberalize trade in factors and goods—is of no interest: instantaneous complete liberalization will always be optimal for a country too small to influence the world relative-price vector. However, capital market liberalization may be considered while political, distributional, or revenue considerations bar instantaneous trade liberalization; alternatively, trade liberalization may be chosen (or imposed) while external constraints prevent foreign borrowing. The recent experience of a group of countries in South America is one of partial (that is, one market only) liberalization. While in Argentina the capital account was liberalized, the trade account retained its controls. In Chile, the opposite was the case.

In this chapter we have discussed the consequences of these two alternative sequences of liberalization. We first reviewed the literature on immiserizing transfers, extending it in several respects. We discussed immiserizing capital transfers à la Johnson (1967) and capital inflows à la Brecher and Díaz-Alejandro (1977) and showed that immiserization is possible even if the full rental rate differential is taxed. We then showed that a transfer in the form of consumption goods will never be welfare reducing. An interesting consequence is that foreign aid that stipulates that at least part of the transfer has to be invested can be immiserizing, while aid that is purely consumed cannot (in the small country case). So it is possible to have immiserization, if liberalizing the capital market leads to more investment (as it will if the external balance constraint falls on both consumers and investors alike). It is straightforward to show that the private sector will invest both too much and in the wrong sector if tariffs protect the capital-intensive sector. We demonstrated that shadow pricing of new investment projects would avoid that. If, however, imposing the use of shadow prices on the private sector in evaluating new projects is infeasible, opening-up capital markets while restricting trade could lead to immiserization, cautioning *against* this sequence.

Capital market distortions are, in a sense, isomorphic to trade distortions in that they imply barriers to trade in goods across time rather than between countries at a given moment in time; accordingly, one needs an intertemporal framework for a satisfactory analysis of the welfare cost of capital market constraints. This was provided in Section 3 of this chapter.

We derived a simple expression linking the cost of capital market distortions to the square of the induced interest rate differential and the (compensated) interest elasticity of savings and investment. The same procedure was used to demonstrate the *increase* in distortionary cost if external rationing falls disproportionately on investment, empirically a very important case.

We finally drew on recent work on the relation between temporary tariffs and private savings via the consumption rate of interest to analyze the question of cold turkey versus gradualism in trade liberalization in the case where external rationing falls disproportionately on investment, and we established unambiguously that under those circumstances *gradualism is the optimal strategy*[14] Most examples of trade liberalization took place under external balance constraints, and in most cases of external balance constraints investment takes a disproportionate share of the adjustment burden, so this conclusion is of great policy relevance.

Appendix I

Derivation of Some Results in Section 2

1. Consider the model with investment rationing:

$$R^1(K, L) + \delta^* R^2[K + I(\tilde{\delta}), L] - I(\tilde{\delta}) = E(1, \delta^*, W) \tag{A.1}$$

$$\tilde{\delta} R_K^2(K + I, L) = 1 \tag{A.2}$$

$$\delta^*[R^2(K + I(\tilde{\delta}), L] - E_\delta(1, \delta^*, W) = \bar{T} \tag{A.3}$$

Differentiation of the budget constraint (A.1) gives

$$E_w \, dW = (\delta^* R_K^2 I_\delta - I_\delta) \, d\tilde{\delta} = [(\delta^* - \tilde{\delta})R_K^2 I_\delta + (\tilde{\delta} R_K^2 - 1)I_\delta] \, d\tilde{\delta}$$

$$= (\delta^* - \tilde{\delta})R_K^2 \, d\tilde{\delta} \tag{A.4}$$

via application of (A.2). Integration of (A.4) over $\tilde{\delta}$ between δ^* and the $\tilde{\delta}$ defined by (A.3) gives expression (26) in the text:

$$E_W \, \Delta W = \frac{(\delta^* - \tilde{\delta})^2}{2} R_K^2 I_\delta \, \Delta\tilde{\delta} \tag{A.5}$$

(A.5) is an approximation because dependence of $R_K^2 I_\delta$ on $\tilde{\delta}$ is ignored while integrating (A.4).

2. Compare the external balance constraint in the two rationing regimes:

$$R^2[K + I(\tilde{\delta}), L] - E_\delta(1, \delta^*, \bar{W})$$
$$= R^2[K + I(\delta), L] - E_\delta(1, \delta, W) \tag{A.6}$$

Take a first-order Taylor approximation to (A.6) and rearrange:

$$R_K^2[K + I(\delta^*), L]I_\delta \cdot (\tilde{\delta} - \delta) = -E_{\delta\delta}(\delta - \delta^*) + E_{\delta w}(\bar{W} - W) \tag{A.7}$$

$$\quad\quad\quad\quad (A) \quad\quad\quad\quad\quad\quad (B)$$

Consider first the expression for $\tilde{\delta}/\delta$ ignoring the second-order effect[15] via $\bar{W} - W$:

$$\frac{\bar{\delta} - \delta^\star}{\delta - \delta^\star} = \frac{-E_{\delta\delta} + I_\delta R_K^2}{I_\delta R_K^2} \tag{A.8}$$

$$= 1 + E_{1\delta}/I_\delta > 1$$

using $E_{\delta\delta} = -E_{1\delta}/\delta > 0$.

Substitution of (A.8) in the expression for $E_W \, \Delta W$ and $E_W \, \Delta \tilde{W}$ yields

$$\frac{\Delta \tilde{W}}{\Delta W} = \frac{(\delta^\star - \bar{\delta})^3}{(\delta^\star - \delta)^3} \frac{I_\delta}{I_\delta + E_{1\delta}}$$

$$= (1 + E_{1\delta}/I_\delta)^2$$

This is expression (28) in the text.

Appendix II

Consider the model of Section 3 in differentiated form:

$$\begin{vmatrix} (1 - \tau C_{1y}) & (\delta^\star - \delta)R_K^2 \\ C_{2E} & -\delta^\star R_k^2 \end{vmatrix} \begin{vmatrix} E_W \, dW \\ I_\delta \, d\delta \end{vmatrix} = \begin{vmatrix} \tau(E_{p_y^1 p_y^1} - R_{p_y^1 p_y^1}^1) \, d\tau \\ -\Pi_2 \Pi_{1(p_y^1)} \delta^\star E_{\Pi_2 \Pi_1} \, d\tau \end{vmatrix} \tag{B.1}$$

The determinant of the matrix on the left-hand side equals:

$$\Delta = -(1 - \tau C_{1y}) \delta^\star R_K^2 + C_{2E}(\delta^\star - \delta)R_K^2$$
$$\quad (-) \qquad\qquad\qquad (+)$$

which appears of indeterminate sign. However some manipulation yields

$$\Delta = -(1 - C_{2E})\delta^\star R_K^2 - C_{2E} + \tau C_{1y}\delta^\star R_K^2 \tag{B.2}$$

$$= -(1 - C_{2E})\delta^\star R_K^2 - C_{2E} + P_y^1 C_{1y}\delta^\star R_K^2$$

$$\quad - \left(1 - \frac{\tau}{P_y^1}\right) P_y^1 C_{1y} \delta^\star \, R_K^2$$

$$= -P_x^1 C_{1x}\delta^\star R_K^2 - C_{2E} - \left(1 - \frac{\tau}{P_y^1}\right) P_y^1 C_{1y} \delta^\star R_K^2 < 0$$

where we used $P_x^1 C_{1x} + P_y^1 C_{1y} + C_{2E} = 1$ and $\delta^\star R_K^2 = 1$.

Cramer's rule applied to (B.1) now gives

$$I_\delta \frac{d\delta}{d\tau} = \frac{-1}{\Delta}[(1 - \tau C_{1y}) \Pi_2 \Pi_{1(p_y^1)} \delta^* E_{\Pi_2 \Pi_1} + C_{2E} \tau(E_{p_y^1 p_y^1} - R^1_{p_y^1 p_y^1})] \qquad (B.3)$$

which is expression (29) in the text with $\gamma = -I_\delta \Delta$.

The expression for $DW/d\tau$ becomes

$$E_W \frac{dW}{d\tau} = -\frac{\delta^* R_K^2}{\Delta}[\Pi_2 \Pi_{1(p_y^1)} E_{\Pi_2 \Pi_1}(\delta^* - \delta) + \tau(E_{p_y^1 p_y^1} - R^1_{p_y^1 p_y^1})] (B.4)$$

which is expression (33) in the text with $\gamma_1 = -\Delta E_W/\delta^* R_K^2$.

To show that $\tau^{**} < \tau^*$, it is sufficient to demonstrate that the following holds:

$$\left.\frac{dW}{d\tau}\right|_{\tau^*} < 0$$

To do this, use (B.4) and (B.3) to obtain:

$$\gamma_1 \left.\frac{dW}{d\tau}\right| = [\Pi_2 \Pi_{1(p_y^1)} E_{\Pi_2 \Pi_1}(\delta^* - \delta)$$

$$+ \tau(E_{p_y^1 p_y^1} - R^1_{p_y^1 p_y^1})] + \gamma \frac{d\delta}{d\tau} - \gamma \frac{d\delta}{d\tau} \qquad (B.5)$$

Rearranging terms and evaluating the expression at $\tau = \tau^*$ (where $d\delta/d\tau = 0$ by definition), we obtain

$$\gamma \frac{dW}{d\tau} = \tau_{1y} \Pi_2 \Pi_{1(p_y^1)} E \Pi_2 \Pi_1 \delta^* \qquad (A)$$

$$- \Pi_2 \delta E_{\Pi_2 \Pi_1} \Pi_{1(p_y^1)}$$

$$+ (1 - C_{2E}) \tau(E_{p_y^1 p_y^1} - R^1_{p_y^1 p_y^1}) \qquad (B)$$

(B) is always negative by concavity of E and convexity of R; (A) is negative if

$$1 \frac{\tau_1}{P_y^1} \cdot C_{1(p_y^1)} P_y^1 \frac{\delta^*}{\delta} > 0 \qquad (B.6)$$

(B.6) is a sufficient but not necessary condition for (B.5) to be negative. (B.6) will be negative for all but extreme capital market distortions. Note that $\tau/P_y^1 < 1$ by construction, and that $C_{1(P_y^1)}P_y^1$ is the share of total wealth spent on today's imports, clearly also a number substantially below 1.

Notes

[1]On the advantages of opening the economies in developing countries, see, for example, Little, Scitovsky, and Scott (1970); Krueger (1978, 1982b); Bhagwati and Srinivasan (1979); Little (1982); and Balassa (1982a, 1983). For a summary of the empirical evidence on liberalization experiences in LDCs, see Tower (1984).

[2]On the dynamics of liberalization see the general discussion in Krueger (1984). See also Khan and Zahler (1983), Edwards (1983, 1985b).

[3]On the Chilean and Argentinian experiences see Edwards (1985a) and McKinnon (1982). On the relation between liberalization reforms and stabilization programs, see Krueger (1981).

[4]In practice, restrictive policies in less developed countreis (LDCs) have generally resulted in large reductions of government expenditure on investment, with only small reductions of consumption. This pattern in government behavior has been recently documented by Hicks an Kubisch (1984).

[5]Some of the discussion presented in this section draws on Edwards and van Wijnbergen (1986).

[6]The derivation of (5) uses the identity $E_{pU} = C_E E_U$.

[7]In Section 3 we will endogenize both size and use of the transfer.

[8]See, for example, Hicks and Kubisch (1984).

[9]Approximate because we asssume $E_{\delta\delta}$ and I_δ to be constant when performing the integration, that is, (21) can be interpreted as a second-order Taylor expansion.

[10]See the discussion presented above. See also Hicks and Kubisch (1984).

[11]Some of this discussion draws on Edwards and van Wijnbergen (1986).

[12]The concept of "virtual prices" at which rations are willingly consumed is used, for instance, by Neary and Roberts (1980).

[13]A proof of this statement is available on request from the authors.

[14]Throughout the analysis, however, we have ignored issues related to the degree of credibility of the trade liberalization. On this subject see, for example, Edwards (1985b).

[15](B) gives the effect on $\bar{\delta} - \delta$ via $\bar{W} - W$ which in itself is only nonzero because $\bar{\delta} - \delta$ is. (B) is therefore indeed second-order.

References

Balassa, B. (1982a). "Disequilibrium Analysis in Developing Economies: An Overview." *World Development* 10(12) (December): 1027–38.

――― (1982b). "Exports, Policy Choice and Economic Growth in Developing Countries after the 1973 Oil Shock." DRD Discussion Paper No. 48, The World Bank.

Bhagwati, J., and T. N. Srinivasan (1979). "Trade Policy and Development." In *International Economic Policy: Theory and Evidence*, edited by R. Dornbusch and J. Frenkel. Baltimore: Johns Hopkins Press.

Brecher, R., and J. Bhagwati (1982). "Immiserizing Transfers from Abroad." *Journal of International Economics* (November): 353–64.

Brecher, R., and C. Díaz-Alejandro (1977). "Tariffs, Foreign Capital and Immiserizing Growth." *Journal of International Economics* 7 (November): 317–22.

Dixit, A., and V. Norman (1980). *Theory of International Trade*. Oxford: Nisbets and Welwyn.

Edwards, S. (1983). "The Order of Liberalization of the Current and Capital Accounts of the Balance of Payments: A Survey of the Major Issues." Working Paper, U.C.L.A.

——— (1984). "The Order of Liberalization of the External Sector in Developing Countries." *Essays in International Finance*, No. 156. Princeton University.

——— (1985). "Stabilization with Liberalization: An Evaluation of Ten Years of Chile's Experiment with Free Market Policies." *Economic Development and Cultural Change* (January).

Edwards, S., and S. van Wijnbergen (1986). "The Welfare Effects of Trade and Capital Market Liberalization." *International Economic Review*. Forthcoming.

Grossman, G. (1984). "The Gains from International Factor Movements." *Journal of International Economics*.

Hicks, N., and A. Kubisch (1984). "Cutting Government Expenditure in LDCs." *Finance and Development* 21 (September): 37–39.

Johnson, H. (1967). "The Possibility of Income Losses from Increased Efficiency or Factor Accumulation in the Presence of Tariffs." *Economic Journal* 77 (March): 151–54.

Khan, M., and R. Zahler (1983). "The Macroeconomic Effects of Changes in Barriers to Trade and Capital Flows: A Simulation Analysis." *IMF Staff Papers* 30 (June): 223–82.

Krueger, A. O. (1978). *Foreign Trade Regimes and Economic Development: Liberalization Attempts and Consequences*. Cambridge, Mass.: Ballinger.

——— (1981). "Interaction between Inflation and Trade Objectives in Stabilization Programs." In *Economic Stabilization in Developing Countries*, edited by W. R. Cline and S. Weintraub. Washington, D.C.: Brookings Institution.

———— (1983). *Trade and Employment in Developing Countries*. Chicago: University of Chicago Press.

———— (1984). "The Problems of Liberalization." In *World Economic Growth*, edited by A. C. Harberger. San Francisco: Institute of Contemporary Studies.

Little, I. M. D. (1982). *Economic Development*. New York: Basic Books.

Little, I. M. D., T. Scitovsky, and M. Scott (1970). *Industry and Trade in Some Developing Countries*. Oxford: Oxford University Press.

McKinnon, R. I. (1982). "The Order of Economic Liberalization: Lessons from Chile and Argentina." In *Economic Policy in a World of Change*, edited by K. Brunner and A. Meltzer. Amsterdam: North Holland.

Mussa, M. (1979). "The Two Sector Model in Terms of Its Dual: A Geometric Exposition." *Journal of International Economics* 9 (December): 513–26.

Neary, P., and K. Roberts (1980). "The Theory of Household Behavior under Rationing." *European Economic Review* 13 (January): 25–42.

Razin, A., and L. Svensson (1983). "Trade Taxes and the Current Account." *Economic Letters* 1: 55–57.

Svensson, L., and R. Razin (1983). "The Terms of Trade, Spending and the Current Account: The Harberger–Laursen–Metzler Effect." *Journal of Political Economy* 91 (February): 97–125.

Tower, E. (1984). "Economic Liberalization in Less Developed Countries: Guidelines from the Empirical Evidence." Unpublished manuscript. The World Bank.

van Wijnbergen, S. (1983a). "The Economics of a Duty Free Zone." Mimeo. The World Bank.

———— (1983b). "Tariffs, Employment and the Current Account: Real Wage Resistance and the Macroeconomics of Protectionism." CEPR Discussion Paper No. 30.

———— (1984). "The Dutch Disease: A Disease after All?" *Economic Journal* 94 (March): 41–55.

5

The Structure of the Banking Sector
and the Sequence of Financial Liberalization

Mario Blejer & Silvia Sagari

1. Introduction

After the oil shock of the early 1970s, many Latin American countries—most noticeably, the Southern Cone countries—adopted a new set of policies to deal with their long-standing economic problems. The specifics of the strategies implemented differed among countries; in general, however, those strategies implied an effort to introduce far-reaching trade and financial reforms based on deregulation, on the opening-up of the economy to external forces, and on the adoption of an outward-looking development strategy. Although many of these policies were implemented in conjunction with comprehensive stabilization plans, the specific objective of these so-called liberalization policies was to eliminate distortions in the allocation of resources and to change the basic economic structure of the countries.[1]

A key component of the financial reforms was the elimination of interest rate ceilings and the opening-up of the capital account. The expectation was that the free flow of funds would induce interest arbitrage and reduce the impact of domestic monetary disequilibrium on the cost of credit to the private sector. Interest rates, however, failed, or took a long time, to converge to the world rate adjusted for the expected rate of

We are thankful to Jaime de Melo, Thomas Pugel, and Ingo Walter for comments and suggestions. The views expressed are the sole responsibility of the authors.

devaluation.[2] Several studies have emphasized different reasons for this performance. Yet, within this context, little attention has been given to the structure and organization of the domestic financial markets as a factor affecting interest rate behavior.

The objective of this chapter is to analyze the impact of the adoption of financial liberalization policies on some key variables related to the banking sector, within the framework of a small economy. We argue here that this impact is a function of the characteristics of the domestic banking market or, more specifically, of its competitive structure and of the level of public sector participation.

We start by analyzing the meaning of financial liberalization and discussing the different dimensions of the concept. Then we concentrate on the issue of the competitive structure of the banking sector and study the impact on the domestic loan market of the implementation of different policy sets concerning financial liberalization. In Section 4, we expand on our hypothesis on the optimal sequence in the adoption of financial liberalization measures. Section 5 considers the role of public institutions in the domestic banking market. We end with some general comments and final conclusions.

2. Some Conceptual Issues
Concerning Financial Liberalization

The first issue that needs to be discussed refers to the distinction between external and internal financial liberalization. By external financial liberalization we mean the opening-up of domestic financial markets to international financial flows, the removal of exchange controls, the elimination of barriers to entry of foreign banks, and so on. Internal financial liberalization refers to the set of financial reforms leading to the liberalization of the domestic financial markets—such as the elimination of domestic credit controls relating to credit rationing, interest rate ceilings, differential reserve requirements, and so forth—and also to the elimination of discriminatory practices and/or capital requirements that drastically curtail free entry of local participants into the domestic market.

Theoretical analyses of financial liberalization policies frequently include both internal and external liberalization within a single framework. Furthermore, to a large extent, they were implemented together during the 1970s in the Southern Cone countries—Argentina, Chile, Uruguay. However, and despite the clear interactions existing between them, they imply different processes and therefore produce different results.

Our hypothesis is that there may be an optimal sequence in the implementation of internal and external financial liberalization policies. In general, relaxation of domestic regulation—internal liberalization—should *precede* the opening-up of the domestic financial market to external flows—external liberalization. We will discuss this hypothesis in more detail later.[3]

The second conceptual aspect that needs to be dealt with refers to the distinction between the concept of liberalization and the idea of perfect competition. With regard to this, our analysis shows that banking markets with different competitive structures will tend to react to financial liberalization and deregulation in different fashions.

We will assume an economy with a banking sector characterized by differential levels of regulation and a nonperfectly competitive structure. The issue we will address here is the impact, under those circumstances, of the implementation of financial liberalization on some key macroeconomic variables related to the banking sector. For simplicity, we concentrate on the loan market and analyze changes in the equilibrium level of interest rates and the volume of loans.

3. Financial Liberalization and the Competitive Structure of the Domestic Banking Sector

We have stressed above the distinction between external and internal financial liberalization. In this section, we make use of this distinction to analyze the interaction between the domestic banking sector structure and the results of the implementation of financial liberalization policies.

As discussed before, internal financial liberalization can be broadly associated with the adoption of measures that increase the level of competition in the domestic banking market. Let us associate here external financial liberalization with the elimination of restrictions on foreign lending and borrowing and/or the elimination of barriers to the entry of foreign banks.

At this stage we assume no participation by public institutions in the process of financial intermediation.

3.1. Initial Assumptions

1. Assume a small, less-developed economy. Foreign direct investment in the domestic real sector is allowed, but it is prohibited in the banking and financial sector. Domestic producers and households have no access to foreign borrowing or lending.

2. The economy is sufficiently open to commercial flows to support the assumption that the domestic prices of goods and services are exogenously given.

3. There is only one currency.

4. Barriers to entry in the domestic banking sector give rise to a highly concentrated market structure and a monopolistic behavior.

5. The domestic market is characterized by different types of borrowers from the point of view of the size of their operations, the nature of their investment projects, and their access to financial sources. For simplicity, let us classify borrowers in two groups characterized by the level of interest rates relevant to their respective demand for loans functions. Type-A borrowers have a large variety of investment projects and therefore their range of relevant interest rates $(0, i^A)$ is wide. Type-B borrowers are relatively small and their projects only allow them to pay interest rates within the interval $(0, i^B)$, with i^B lower than i^A.[4]

3.2. The Initial Equilibrium

Given our assumptions, the domestic banks can behave as price discriminators. Pricing decisions in the loan market will be such that

$$\left.\begin{array}{c} i_0^A \\ \\ i_0^B \end{array}\right\} > MC(L_0)$$

where i_0^A is the equilibrium interest rate charged to type-A borrowers; i_0^B is the equilibrium interest rate charged to type-B borrowers; L_0 is the equilibrium loan volume; and $MC(L_0)$ is the marginal cost of production associated to L_0.

Assume further that both i_0^A and i_0^B are higher than i^*, where i^* is the international lending rate (see Figure 5.1).

Given that both i_0^A and i_0^B are higher than $MC(L_0)$, there is a welfare loss since the social value of credit is larger than its private cost. Allocation of resources is therefore inefficient in the sense of satisfying consumer wants with less than maximum effectiveness.

3.3. The Impact of Financial Liberalization Policies

Let us now analyze the impact on the domestic loan market of financial liberalization implemented through different alternative policy sets. We will use comparative statics within a partial equilibrium framework.

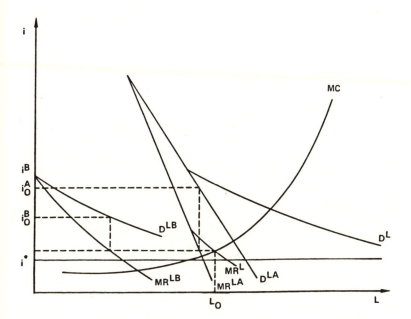

Figure 5.1

Policy Set I: Elimination of Restrictions on Foreign Borrowing and Lending   Liberalization takes here the form of freeing financial flows, but no domestic operation of foreign banks is allowed.[5] Within this framework, let us assume that type-A borrowers have perfect (costless) access to international bank loan markets. They face therefore an infinitely elastic supply at the international lending rate i^*.[6]

For type-B borrowers, given their range of activities and the information set for international lenders, access to international bank loan markets is more costly. They face an infinitely elastic supply at a cost-adjusted international borrowing rate i_I^B, which is higher than i^B. Small borrowers are therefore excluded from the international loan market. The domestic banks can behave as price discriminators.

Figure 5.2 depicts a situation where the domestic monopolistic banking sector produces total loans equal to L_1, and charges small domestic borrowers i_1^B and large domestic borrowers i^*. L_3 is lent to the former and $L_1 - L_3$ is lent to the latter, who additionally borrow $L_2 - L_1$ from abroad.

Again in this case, due to this monopolistic behavior, interest rates on loans to small borrowers are above marginal cost and borrowers able to pay an interest rate within the interval $[i^*, i_1^B)$ are excluded from the market. The average domestic interest rate is above the international interest rate.

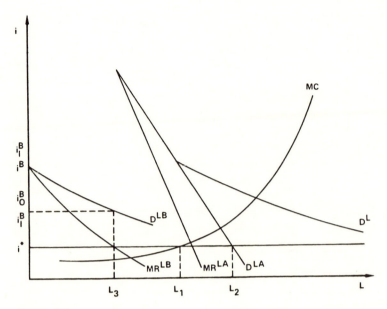

Figure 5.2

The legal restriction on capital movements is substituted here by a market restriction, and the monopolistic domestic banking sector appropriates part of the welfare gains deriving from the access to cheaper sources of funds.

Policy Set II: Elimination of Barriers to Entry for Domestic Banks This policy set may be identified with internal financial liberalization. Policy measures leading to easier domestic bank entry at least weaken the monopolistic structure of the sector. [7] For simplicity, let us make the extreme assumption that the domestic banking sector becomes perfectly competitive.

Equilibrium in the loan market will be determined by the intersection of aggregate supply of and demand for loans. It is possible in this case, depending on demand preferences and domestic bank cost structures, that the domestic equilibrium interest rate be higher than the international rate. Figure 5.3 shows an example of such a case. Yet, the monopolistic distortion observed in the initial equilibrium position is eliminated; namely, the domestic social value of credit now equals its private cost.

The new equilibrium volume of loans is larger, and the equilibrium interest rate is lower, than the corresponding initial equilibrium values. Producers lose part of their surplus to consumers. Deadweight welfare losses are eliminated.

Policy Set III: Policy Set II-cum-Elimination of Restrictions on Foreign Lending and Borrowing   Policy Set III implies first the implementation of internal financial liberalization; then, once the domestic banking sector has become competitive, restrictions on foreign borrowing and lending are eliminated.

Figure 5.4 shows the final effects of the implementation of Policy Set III. The monopolistic position of domestic banks is lost, the domestic equilibrium interest rate tends to fall and eventually will converge to i^*, and the equilibrium volume of loans in the economy increases to L_5. Out of this total L_5^D is supplied by local banks and the rest is borrowed from abroad.

It is clear that if the world interest rate is below the initial equilibrium interest rates (i_0^A and i_0^B), local banks lose part of the local loan market in absolute terms. Total welfare in the economy, however, increases over and above the welfare increase resulting from the implementation of internal financial liberalization.

If we compare equilibrium under Policy Set III with that under Policy Set II, we observe that consumer surplus has increased by area i_4EFi^* (Figure 5.4). Part of this gain, area i_4EGi^*, shows the income redistribution effect, from producers to consumers. The rest, area EFG, is a pure gain deriving from external financial liberalization. Out of it, the area EHG represents a gain resulting from the elimination of deadweight losses corresponding to the inefficient domestic production of loans.

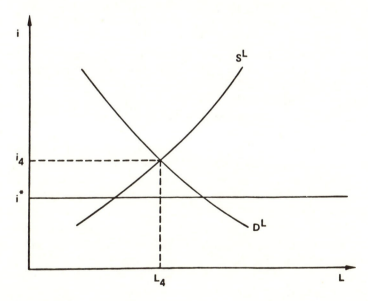

Figure 5.3

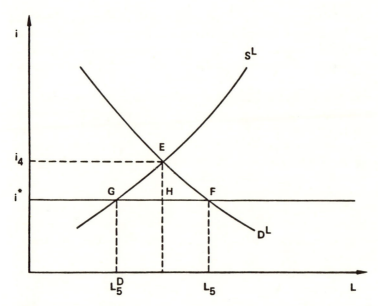

Figure 5.4

Policy Set IV: Elimination of Restrictions on Foreign Bank Entry   So far we have ignored the possibility of allowing foreign bank entry (or eliminating their discriminatory treatment). However, the adoption of this measure deserves some significant comments concerning the domestic banking sector structure.

We have previously assumed that allowing domestic bank entry weakens the monopolistic structure of the sector. This implies both that the firms initially present in the market do not squeeze out the new entrants, and that the new entrants do not collude with existing participants.

Foreign banks may be considered pure competitors in the international market. It seems reasonable to assume therefore that, if foreign banks are allowed to enter the domestic market freely, they will bring into it their international competitive behavior. The weakening of the domestic monopolistic structure does not require, in this case, any additional assumptions.

Furthermore, since foreign bank entry implies the presence in the market of a "new" group of participants, with different competitive strengths and weaknesses, it can be expected to have a larger impact on the level of competition than that resulting from allowing entry to domestic banks exclusively.

A second related aspect refers to the possibility of the existence of a natural monopoly in the domestic banking sector. Assume for instance an economy where the technology available to the domestic banking sector is less advanced than that available in foreign banking sectors. This results in comparatively higher costs of production of domestic banking services, or, for our purposes, of loans. It is possible that a small absolute size of such an economy, in conjunction with the technology available to its banking sector, give rise to a natural monopoly.[8]

Within this context, allowing free entry of domestic banks will not significantly change the competitive structure of the industry, which will continue to be characterized by a natural monopoly. On the other hand, if foreign banks are allowed to enter the market, given their superior technology they may eliminate the natural monopoly. Allowing foreign bank entry could therefore be thought of as a more "powerful" measure to achieve higher levels of competition with the domestic banking sector, both because it is less dependent on domestic banks' behavior and because it could potentially eliminate natural monopoly situations.

The welfare implications of foreign bank entry, with or without the elimination of restrictions on foreign lending and borrowing, could be analyzed within a partial equilibrium framework along the same lines of our previous analyses. The main difference resides in the fact that now we have both local and foreign banks operating in the domestic market. Once foreign bank entry is allowed, local banks will lose part of their share of the local market to their foreign competitors. We come back to this issue later, when we include some brief comments on the process of adjustment to financial liberalization.

4. The Optimal Sequence in the Implementation of Financial Liberalization Policies

We have distinguished here between internal and external financial liberalization. Internal liberalization was associated with the adoption of measures that increase the level of competition in the domestic banking market. External liberalization was associated with the elimination of restrictions on foreign lending and borrowing and/or the elimination of barriers to entry for foreign banks. We have hypothesized that there may be an optimal sequence in the implementation of financial liberalization policies, and that in general internal liberalization should precede external liberalization.

Leaving aside for the moment the impact of foreign bank entry in such a process, and assuming that regulation of the domestic financial market leads to a situation where the banking sector behaves monopolistically, our hypothesis on the optimal sequence of financial liberalization is a direct consequence of the analysis of Policy Sets I, II, and III.

In the case of Policy Set I, where only a form of external financial liberalization is implemented—namely, elimination of restrictions on foreign borrowing and lending—domestic banks behaving monopolistically retain for themselves part of the gains resulting from the availability of lower-cost sources of financing. The monopolistic structure of the banking sector, together with the normal differences in borrowers' characteristics, eliminate a potentially significant share of the welfare gains which could result from external financial liberalization.

On the other hand, Policy Set III—where the opening-up of the capital account to foreign borrowing and lending is implemented only after the monopolistic structure of the banking sector has been at least weakened through the adoption of internal financial liberalization measures—results in a larger gain in consumers' surpluses and less inefficiency in the allocation of resources.

The sequence of internal and then external financial liberalization that is implied by Policy Set III would therefore appear as the most attractive.

Let us now consider the possibility of foreign bank entry, without actually removing other components leading to the monopolistic situation in the domestic market. The elimination of restrictions on both foreign bank entry and foreign borrowing and lending would result in equilibrium values of loans and interest rates identical to those resulting from the implementation of Policy Set III.

However, even within this framework it is possible to argue for the internal–external financial liberalization sequence, mainly from considerations regarding the dynamics of the process of adjustment to a financial reform. Assume that bank regulation in a country has been such that domestic banks have been operating in a highly protective and restrictive environment. Under such circumstances, adjustment to a more competitive setting can be done only gradually. The speed of adjustment will reflect the costs associated with reorganization, marketing, learning, and, in general, the development of new instruments and practices. Within this context, foreign competitors operating locally may be able to capture in the short-run a much larger market share than in the presence of more competitive indigenous banks. A partial equilibrium analysis would reveal in this case the loss of part of the domestic banks' producers surplus to their foreign competitors. Obviously, the evaluation of a "free foreign bank entry" policy versus a gradual opening of the banking sector to foreign competitors will depend on the government's welfare-objective function. However, it appears reasonable that within the framework of a less-developed economy, preference could fall on the latter, namely, internal liberalization should precede external liberalization.

5. State Participation
in the Domestic Banking Sector

So far we have assumed away the presence of public institutions in the process of domestic financial intermediation. However, the case of the Southern Cone countries—Argentina, Chile, Uruguay—shows clear examples of significant levels of participation of the public sector in the domestic financial markets.[9] In those countries, the process of financial liberalization implied, in general, a reduction in the role of the state as a *regulator* of financial activity; that is, interest rate ceilings were made more flexible or were altogether eliminated, reserve requirements were reduced, and so on. However, with the possible exception of Chile, the role of government in directing or subsidizing credit to specific sectors—and, particularly, the role of public institutions in financial intermediation—did not change substantially. In Argentina, for example, even after extensive financial reforms, in 1982 more than 40% of deposits were held by public institutions. In Latin America, therefore, financial liberalization can be largely identified with *deregulation* but not with a decrease in public sector participation in financial intermediation. Without entering into the question of the economic and historical roles of public banking, it is clear that the consequences of financial markets deregulation, in the presence of predominant public-sector activity, constitute an issue that needs close examination.

One possible way of looking at this case might be to consider the public sector as the agent introducing noncompetitive practices in the banking sector. Interesting evidence on this issue has been provided in a recent study by Spiller and Favaro (1982) on the structure of the Uruguayan banking system. In that study, competitive assumptions are empirically rejected and it is found that the larger firms in the sector, and particularly the state-owned Banco de la República with 30% of the market, are the enforcers of a cartel.

Our analysis would indicate that to reduce welfare costs the elimination of these noncompetitive practices should precede the implementation of external financial liberalization policies, namely the opening-up of the capital account.

6. General Comments and Conclusions

It is not our objective here to discuss the need for some kind of bank regulation, which we take for granted, or to analyze the optimal characteristics of such regulation. We are arguing here for an optimal sequence in the implementation of financial liberalization policies. If each specific component of the banking sector regulatory framework could be distinctly labeled either as essential to the "soundness and safety" of the system or as a purely protectionist measure, a concise definition of internal financial liberalization could be easily proposed. In fact, in such context, internal financial liberalization would be fully characterized by the elimination of purely protectionist measures. Obviously, reality does not allow for such a sharp distinction and many measures that hinder free competition may have been designed with the purpose of promoting the banking sector's safety. In Uruguay, for instance, after the banking crisis of 1965, caused among other reasons by the excessive expansion of the banking system, the banking authorities imposed restrictions on the number of branches that banks could have. This measure, originally meant to promote the safety of the banking system, implied, however, some level of protectionism to the extent that free competition in the sector was constrained. Within our very simplistic analytical framework, and if we leave aside the issues related to the dynamics of the process of adjustment to a financial reform, optimal regulation of the banking sector would be that which maximizes the level of competition subject to the constraint that the sector is sound and safe.

We have purposely omitted the introduction into our analysis of uncertainty, moral hazard problems, and imperfect information. In our model there is no default risk, and information is costly but effective, namely type-A and type-B borrowers are unequivocally identified. Stiglitz and Weiss (1981) analyze the case where the interest rate an individual is willing to pay acts as a device for borrowers screening. In their model, borrowers willing to pay high interest rates may be, on average, worse risks. In our model, loans are risk-free, and borrowers' willingness to pay high interest rates rises exclusively from their access to high-return projects. Consideration of different imperfections in the domestic banking market, such as those commented on above, would undoubtedly reinforce the need for an efficient prudential supervision. The point to be stressed once more then is the distinction between internal financial liberalization and surveillance measures necessary to maintain the soundness and safety of the banking sector.

The main objectives of external/internal financial liberalization are the integration of the domestic financial market with the international market and the improvement of the role of the financial markets in the allocation of resources. On the basis of the results of the recent liberalization experiences in the Southern Cone countries, it has frequently been claimed that the financial liberalization measures adopted there, such as the reduction of regulation on bank entry, the elimination of interest rate ceilings, or the relaxation of exchange controls, have failed to attain those main objectives. It is also argued that this failure is reflected in the large spreads existing between foreign and domestic interest rates, after adjusting for changes in exchange rates and in the emergence of very high real interest rates, all in ex-post terms.

These arguments deserve, however, various qualifications. Firstly, large spreads do not necessarily imply an inefficient financial market. Some evidence on this issue is provided by Blejer (1982) on Argentina. It is found that for the period June 1977 to August 1981, during which the exchange rate was preannounced, the observed nominal interest rate differentials—after adjustment for variations in the exchange rate—are white noise, that is, they do not display any pattern of serial correlation, and behave therefore as forecast errors in an efficient market.

Another important aspect that may help to explain the existence of spreads is the set of features associated with different financial instruments. Foreign and domestic financial assets are not perfect substitutes. Furthermore, many domestic financial assets have characteristics that make them nontradables. This implies, in summary, that comparisons of interest rates are not very meaningful unless they reflect differences in rates of return on "equivalent" financial assets.

Finally, and this is the aspect we have tried to emphasize here, spreads may just embody monopolistic profits. For example, as discussed above, the opening-up of the economy to external capital flows does not necessarily imply that all economic agents will have the same direct access to international borrowing. These agents must therefore obtain credit from domestic financial intermediaries that can borrow abroad and lend to domestic agents. If the number of agents with access to foreign markets is limited, the domestic market structure may lead to monopolistic profits which will be reflected in the spread. In their study mentioned above, Spiller and Favaro find that in the case of the Uruguayan banking sector, in recent years, interest arbitrage and a reduction of the spread were achieved only after the central bank actually limited the noncompetitive practices of Banco de la República and required it to reduce its charges for loans and returns on deposits. Clearly, these aspects introduce frictions in the process of integration of the domestic financial markets with the world market. Most of those aspects, such as the limitations in competitive practices or the lack of adequate instruments, should be the target of an internal financial liberalization program.

Internal and external financial liberalization are, undoubtedly, complementary processes. However, our analysis indicates that—given a banking sector characterized by very restrictive regulation, significant government participation, and a noncompetitive structure—external financial liberalization should be implemented only after internal financial liberalization is well under way. If more competitive practices have had time to develop and financial institutions and economic agents have reorganized in line with the less restricted environment, the adjustment costs and disruptive effects of opening the capital account will be considerably reduced.

Notes

[1]For a discussion on the various aspects of the Southern Cone experience, see Ardito Barletta et al. (1984) as well as the special issue of the *Journal of Interamerican Studies and World Affairs* (1983). For a comprehensive study of the Chilean experience, see Edwards (1985).

[2]As part of the reform package, the path to be followed by the exchange rates was preannounced, reducing in this manner the problem of exchange risk.

[3]The question of the optimal sequence of liberalization between trade and financial markets has been discussed in the literature. See Frenkel (1984), McKinnon (1982), and the discussion by G. Calvo, R. Dornbusch, and J. Williamson in Ardito Barletta et al. (1983).

[4]Note that this assumption implies that the elasticity of type-B borrowers' demand curve is larger than that of type-A borrowers' demand curve.

[5]Foreign banks may be legally prevented from operating in the domestic market or, alternatively, differential tax treatment may make their presence in the domestic market uncompetitive.

[6]The underlying assumption for an infinitely elastic supply of foreign funds is that the risk involved in lending to domestic residents does not increase with the volume over the relevant range. The rate i^* could be taken to include all the fees and spreads faced by the country and refers to instruments of similar risk and maturity.

[7]We are assuming away the possibility that the existing participants in the market squeeze out the new entrants through the use of predatory pricing, or that the new entrants collude with the existing participants.

[8]Clearly, relatively high production costs may result from other causes, for instance, regulation. For simplicity, we concentrate here on the technological issue.

[9]This situation is not, however, confined to Latin America. In Greece, for example, the National Bank of Greece, a publicly owned commercial bank, accounts for over 50% of the banking sector assets.

References

Ardito Barletta, N., Blejer M. I., and Landau L., eds. (1984). *Economic Liberalization and Stabilization Policies in Argentina, Chile and Uruguay: Application of the Monetary Approach to the Balance of Payments*. Washington, D.C.: The World Bank.

Blejer, Mario I. (1982). "Interest Rate Differentials and Exchange Risk: Recent Argentine Experience." *IMF Staff Papers* (June).

Edwards, Sebastián (1985). "Stabilization with Liberalization: An Evaluation of Ten Years of Chile's Experiment with Free-Market Policies, 1973–1983." *Economic Development and Cultural Change* (January).

Frenkel, Jacob A. (1984). "Economic Liberalization and Stabilization Programs." In *Economic Liberalization and Stabilization Policies in Argentina, Chile, and Uruguay: Application of the Monetary Approach to the Balance of Payments*, edited by Ardito Barletta, M. I. Blejer, and L. Landau. Washington, D.C.: The World Bank.

Journal of Interamerican Studies and World Affairs 25 (November 1983).

McKinnon, Ronald I. (1982). The Order of Economic Liberalization: Lessons from Chile and Argentina. In *Economic Policy in a Changing World*, edited by Karl Brunner and Allan H. Meltzer. Amsterdam: North-Holland.

Spiller, Pablo T., and Edgardo Favaro (1982). "The Effects of Entry Regulations on Oligopolistic Interaction: The Uruguayan Banking Sector." Department of Economics, University of Pennsylvania (November).

Stiglitz, Joseph E., and Andrew Weiss (1981). "Credit Rationing in Markets with Imperfect Information." *The American Economic Review* (June).

III

THE APPROPRIATE
EXCHANGE RATE REGIME

6

The Use of the Exchange Rate for Stabilization Purposes: The Case of Chile

Vittorio Corbo

1. Introduction

The purpose of this chapter is to evaluate the role of the preannounced exchange rate policy in the recent macroeconomic evolution of Chile. Three effects of the policy are analyzed: that on inflation dynamics and the real exchange rate; that on capital flows and aggregate expenditures; and that on the macroeconomic evolution in the period 1978–82.

The chapter has four main hypotheses. First, the policy of a preannounced exchange rate, with a rate of crawl substantially below previous inflation, is bound to result in a lengthy period of (at least

The author is indebted to Arnold Harberger and Marcelo Selowsky for comments on an earlier draft of this chapter which was presented at the Conference on "The Foreign Exchange Rate in Inflation and Stabilization" organized by the Aron and Michael Chilewich Chair in International Trade, Hebrew University of Jerusalem, Maale Mahamisha, June 3–5, 1985, and to Ricardo Caballero for his very efficient research assistance. Support for this effort was provided by the World Bank ROP 672–85.

The World Bank does not accept responsibility for the views expressed herein, which are those of the author and should not be attributed to the World Bank or its affiliated organizations. The findings, interpretations, and conclusions are the results of research supported by the Bank; they do not necessarily represent official policy of the Bank. The designations employed, the presentation of material, and any maps used in this document are solely for the convenience of the reader and do not imply the expression of any opinion whatsoever on the part of the World Bank or its affiliates concerning the legal status of any country, territory, city, area, or authorities, or concerning the delimitation of its boundaries or national affiliation.

temporal) real peso appreciation. The real appreciation period is even longer for an economy with 100%-plus wage indexation, as was the case in Chile in the period 1979–82. Second, with respect to the asset markets, the preannouncement policy, by causing a substantial drop in the peso cost of foreign borrowing, should result in a drop in domestic interest rates. Third, a wealth effect should result from the decrease in the value of private foreign debt in terms of nontradables and the appreciation of real assets. This wealth effect plus the decrease in the interest rate should result in a large increase in expenditures. Fourth, the deficit on the current account results mostly from the real peso appreciation and the increase in expenditures. Given a deficit in the current account and the evolution of domestic credit, capital inflows will adjust to equilibrate the asset markets. Thus, the capital inflows were endogenous during the period of appreciation in Chile. In this chapter we present strong econometric evidence for hypotheses one and four and some supporting evidence for hypotheses two and three.

The rest of this chapter is organized as follows. Section 2 provides some background on the conditions before the military government took power and the main policies it implemented. Section 3 provides evidence on the effect of the preannounced policy on the real exchange rate and the dynamic of inflation. Section 4 gives evidence on the endogeneity of capital flows, using a model with imperfect assets substitution for a period in which the central bank did not practice stabilization of the monetary effects of capital flows. Section 5 discusses the macroeconomic implications of the preannounced policy. Section 6 presents the main conclusions. An appendix provides information on the chronology of the main reforms.

2. Initial Conditions and Main Policy Reforms

The military government that took power in 1973 had to contend with an economy suffering from widespread distortions and the worst inflation in Chile's history (Table 6.1). The fiscal deficit was close to 25% of GDP, and net foreign reserves were negative. Only by virtue of widespread price controls was inflation kept even moderately in check. Indeed, when the price controls were partially lifted in late 1973, inflation skyrocketed to 1,000% on an annual basis.

Given this situation, the military government spent its first two years in power trying to stabilize the economy. To eradicate the monetization of the fiscal deficit, it introduced a major tax reform in 1974 and implemented large reductions in government expenditures both in 1974 and 1975. The sale of government assets inherited from the Allende years further reduced the need for monetization of the fiscal deficit. Good prices for copper in 1974 and a rollover of 30% of outstanding debt service for 1973 and 1974 also eased the adjustment to the first oil shock.

Still, by late 1974 and early 1975 the external crisis had become increasingly apparent—copper prices dropped almost 50% with respect to their 1974 value, while the price of oil stayed at four times its 1973 value. These exogenous factors forced the government to undertake a major devaluation and a severe austerity program.

After controlling for the emerging external crisis, in the period 1975–79 Chile implemented one of the most sweeping economic reforms in its economic history.[1] In the first two years in office, the government lifted all quantitative restrictions on trade and started a trade reform that reduced the tariffs, which had ranged from 0% to 750% in the Allende years, to a uniform 10% rate by July 1979. It also lifted all commodity price controls, and removed the constraints on domestic interest rates by June 1975. In addition, early in its administration, the military government unified the multiple exchange rate system and instituted a crawling peg targeted to achieve a fairly stable real exchange rate. There was little liberalization in two areas, however. One was labor policy. Although the labor markets were deregulated de facto by the loss of trade union power in the year following the military coup, most of the restrictive labor legislation inherited from previous governments was modified only slowly. One major reform, however, was the introduction of a compulsory 100% backward wage indexation starting in October 1974.[2] Moreover, a new labor code introduced in July 1979 reestablished collective bargaining, albeit for just a fraction of the labor force, and mandated that the lowest offer employers could make had to equal the previous wage adjusted by inflation as measured by the consumer price index. The second area where there was no clear liberalization policy was capital inflows.

In the face of these measures, following the strong recession in 1975, GDP grew at an annual rate of close to 10% in the period 1976–77, while the unemployment rate dropped to 13.2% in 1977, a level that was, however, still substantially above historical levels. The real rate of interest for loans in pesos was 45.4% a year in 1977 (Table 6.2, col. 9). The inflation rate fell substantially below the 1973–74 level but was still close to 100% a year.[3]

In the initial years of its rule, the military government attacked inflation by controlling the growth of money. However, by early 1977, by which time Chile's economy had been opened to trade significantly, a debate developed within the government on the causes of inflation and the most appropriate way to deal with it. As early as June 1976, a 10% revaluation was implemented as a way to decrease inflation and sterilize part of the reserve accumulation. In March 1977, a further 10%

Table 6.1 Annual Macroeconomic Indicators, 1960–82

	GDP[b]			Absorption[c] (% change) (4)	GDP deflator (% change) (5)	CPI (%) (6)	Unemployment[d] rate (%) (7)	Price of copper (cents per pound) (8)	Fiscal deficit (% of GDP) (9)
	Tradables[a] (1)	Nontradables (2)	Total (3)						
1960	—	—	—	—	—	11.6	7.4	30.8	4.6
1961	5.5	2.6	4.8	6.1	7.0	7.7	6.6	28.7	4.5
1962	5.7	5.2	4.7	2.5	12.7	13.9	5.2	29.3	5.8
1963	3.9	8.3	6.3	5.8	44.0	44.3	5.0	29.3	4.9
1964	4.5	0.1	2.2	2.9	48.5	46.0	5.3	44.0	3.9
1965	1.1	1.1	0.8	0.5	39.1	28.8	5.4	58.6	4.1
1966	12.9	8.0	11.2	16.6	28.4	22.9	5.3	69.5	2.5
1967	2.8	4.3	3.2	0.6	25.7	18.1	6.1	51.1	1.3
1968	3.9	3.8	3.6	4.8	34.1	26.6	6.0	56.1	1.5
1969	-0.8	6.6	3.7	5.8	39.5	30.7	6.2	66.5	0.4
1970	1.4	2.9	2.1	1.8	40.9	32.5	7.1	64.1	2.7

Year	(1)	(2)	(3)	(4)	(5)	(6)	(7)	(8)	(9)
1971	9.2	8.8	9.0	9.7	18.4	22.1	5.5	49.3	10.7
1972	−0.8	−1.1	−1.2	1.0	86.9	117.9	3.7	48.6	13.0
1973	−7.3	−3.7	−5.6	−6.2	418.2	487.5	4.7	80.8	21.7
1974	6.6	0.4	1.0	2.4	694.5	497.8	9.7	93.3	10.5
1975	−16.6	−8.4	−12.9	−20.8	342.0	379.2	16.2	55.9	2.6
1976	5.3	1.6	3.5	0.2	250.6	234.5	16.8	63.6	2.3
1977	7.8	9.4	9.9	14.2	103.6	113.8	13.2	59.3	1.8
1978	4.5	9.6	8.2	9.7	56.5	49.8	14.0	61.9	0.8
1979	7.0	9.9	8.3	10.9	46.3	36.6	13.6	89.8	−1.7
1980	5.2	9.7	7.5	9.3	29.8	35.1	11.8	99.2	−3.1
1981	2.9	5.4	5.3	10.9	13.7	19.7	11.1	79.0	−1.6
1982	−12.4	−15.1	−14.1	−23.5	3.6	9.9	22.1	67.1	2.4

Source: Columns (1) and (5), *Cuentas Nacionales de Chile 1960–82*, Central Bank. Column (6) up to 1970 corresponds to the CPI published by the INE; from 1971 on, it corresponds to the revised CPI by Schmidt-Hebbel and Marshall, Feb. 1981. Columns (7), (8), and (9), *Indicadores Economicos 1960-82* and *Monthly Bulletin*, Central Bank.

Note: The rate of change for columns (1) to (4) was computed from raw data at 1977 prices.
[a]Includes agriculture, fishing, mining, and manufacturing.
[b]Includes construction and services.
[c]Includes private consumption, public consumption, and total investment.
[d]Greater Santiago.

Table 6.2 Quarterly Indicators[a]

		Total net[b] capital inflow (1)	Surplus in[c] commercial account (2)	Surplus in current account (3)	Change in reserves (4)	Change in monetary base		Change in money supply		Real interest rate (% in annual base)	
						Domestic credit (5)	Exchange operations (6)	M1 (7)	M2 (8)	Peso loans (9)	Dollar loans (10)
75	I	26.9	−25.7	−209.7	−179.2	101.3	66.7	44.8	38.6	−50.3	53.4
	II	−33.0	−2.5	−220.0	−125.5	54.1	78.2	24.9	38.8	10.1	18.2
	III	−34.6	156.4	−20.5	−10.3	15.9	146.9	45.0	57.1	57.4	11.6
	IV	39.8	85.6	22.9	−28.8	29.1	116.5	38.2	35.2	36.6	3.7
76	I	38.1	115.3	12.0	142.8	−31.3	186.2	37.1	39.8	42.8	−17.1
	II	77.1	186.7	−40.8	117.4	66.1	177.5	22.8	38.9	51.6	−42.9
	III	7.0	108.1	−70.9	64.3	27.5	232.0	34.7	48.2	48.9	−17.1
	IV	79.3	−11.1	−109.1	89.7	9.1	742.5	26.8	29.1	93.5	−8.0
77	I	101.6	105.3	−189.8	113.8	48.7	182.3	45.1	58.3	68.6	−0.3
	II	76.2	−29.8	1.2	28.1	−16.4	219.3	22.9	28.7	31.5	−0.2
	III	115.8	−213.0	−281.7	−20.5	140.4	−54.5	14.4	16.6	26.9	37.8
	IV	73.9	−39.1	−216.4	−8.7	85.5	49.3	11.8	13.7	54.6	22.6
78	I	193.8	84.4	−65.7	358.0	−152.9	350.7	30.2	32.2	41.0	10.2
	II	141.3	−255.5	−128.5	109.8	−87.3	181.2	17.1	18.3	24.3	−4.9
	III III	172.2	−200.5	−405.9	104.4	51.4	44.7	6.6	15.9	27.1	−7.6
	IV	259.8	−223.0	−482.3	136.1	−50.9	216.4	9.6	21.1	46.9	−2.5

79	I	247.9	42.0	−437.3	334.0	−153.6	320.9	21.67	24.19	26.9	−1.5
	II	119.0	−121.8	−328.4	182.3	−72.4	160.6	9.90	8.98	12.4	−2.1
	III	335.8	−144.5	−496.9	352.6	−165.1	292.6	7.22	13.35	9.0	−11.6
	IV	262.5	−230.0	−562.0	218.6	86.4	127.3	11.31	11.15	18.9	−15.3
80	I	251.6	78.3	−537.2	453.4	−352.1	290.5	16.56	13.92	23.0	−11.7
	II	544.9	−84.3	−623.4	216.0	72.9	165.8	13.88	9.79	9.9	−7.1
	III	660.3	−420.1	−666.8	369.8	−138.1	232.8	7.21	12.45	7.7	−15.2
	IV	786.6	−552.6	−971.2	204.5	259.1	121.7	13.74	14.27	13.7	−7.2
81	I	755.6	−415.3	−1,010.9	97.2	−569.7	408.9	11.92	19.18	34.0	2.5
	II	844.1	−614.8	−1,124.5	−13.5	−156.7	39.5	1.31	14.53	36.0	5.9
	III	1,132.3	−754.2	−1,845.9	126.4	−125.6	147.4	−1.15	13.26	39.7	9.8
	IV	489.8	−558.0	−1,431.6	−205.6	209.5	−118.4	5.39	3.95	47.2	9.8
82	I	417.3	−107.3	−700.9	−134.6	−1.3	209.6	0.04	3.86	23.3	22.1
	II	478.5	76.2	−421.9	−181.9	885.5	−1,023.1	−5.15	−0.71	31.9	105.0
	III	−21.3	156.3	−358.9	−754.3	1,201.1	−1,343.2	−6.16	−2.29	17.1	138.5
	IV	53.2	167.8	−700.5	−322.1	962.7	−1,0154.4	−2.24	0.98	38.5	50.7

Source: Columns (2), (3), (4), (5), (9), and (10), Corbo and Matte (1984). Column (2), *International Financial Statistics*, IMF. Column (6), *Monetary Synthesis*, Central Bank, and Corbo and Matte (1984), Columns (7) and (8), *Monetary Synthesis*, Central Bank.
aColumns (1) and (6) in millions of dollars.
bThis column sums up net capital inflow (article 14) plus short-term capital movements through the banking system.
cFOB value.
dThe annualized expected rate of inflation and devaluation were assumed to be equal to

$$[(1 + <_t)(1 + <_{t+1})]^2 \quad \text{and} \quad [(1 + e_t)(1 + e_{t+1})]^2$$

respectively, where $<_t$ = period t inflation and e_t = period t devaluation.

revaluation was undertaken for the same purpose. Toward the end of 1977 the government announced that the rate of devaluation was going to be targeted to exceed the rate of inflation to compensate the import-competing sector for the announced tariff reductions. Surprisingly, however, a preannounced devaluation schedule, with the devaluations to proceed at decreasing rates, was introduced in February 1978. The initial rate of devaluation was substantially below the previous months' inflation. Then in late 1979 the government introduced the aforementioned labor policy of full retroactive compensation for inflation for workers who negotiated collectively, even though less extensive indexation based on full compensation for past inflation had existed since late 1974. The prices of many nontradables, such as housing rent, school fees, mortgage payments, public utility tariffs, and the like, had also been fully indexed backward for some time.

Three goals had been behind the introduction of the preannounced exchange rate system with a decreasing rate of devaluation. First, it was believed this policy would reduce the expected rate of inflation in a small country like Chile, which by then had become an open economy. Second, the new system was supposed to put downward pressure on the rate of increase in the price of tradables and thus help lower the stubborn inflation. Third, this policy was supposed to lead to a further integration of the capital markets and reduce domestic interest rates by reducing the expected rate of devaluation. It was also assumed, when the preannounced policy was formulated, that domestic inflation would converge rapidly with the rate of international inflation (plus the rate of devaluation). Thus, the competitiveness of the tradable-producing sectors would not suffer much (Blejer and Mathieson, 1981; McKinnon, 1980; Direccion de Presupuestos, 1977, 1978).

3. Devaluation, Inflation, and the Real Exchange Rate

Corbo (1985a) studies inflation during this period using a dynamic model. The model contains three groups of goods: homogeneous tradables (agricultural commodities), differentiated tradables (manufacturing goods), and nontradables. For homogeneous tradables, the model assumes that the law of one price applies. For differentiated tradables and nontradables, the price equations include both cost and demand variables. Furthermore, the pricing of the differentiated tradables is also a function of the price of similar imports. As to wages, Phillips curves were augmented by inflation for both the differentiated tradable and nontradable sectors. The model is rounded out with two definitions. The price used for tradables is a geometric average of the price of homogeneous and diffcrentiated tradables, while the CPI is a goemetric average of tradable and nontradable prices.

In the complete model, a devaluation under conditions of full price homogeneity does not affect the relative prices between tradables and nontradables. A test for homogeneity of the whole system found that the null hypothesis was rejected. This rejection originated in the nonhomogeneity of the wage equation for nontradables. Thus, in the Chilean economy of 1982, a devaluation could have improved the real exchange rate.

More important than the rejection of full homogeneity is the finding that inflation adjusts slowly to a change in the rate of devaluation, In particular, even under full (long-run) homogeneity, a stabilization policy based on a preannounced devaluation with a decreasing rate of crawl is bound to generate a lengthy period of (temporal) appreciation of the peso. The dynamic of Chilean inflation can be illustrated by tracing the effects of a 50% devaluation in the first quarter of 1980. Figure 6.1 shows the impact of the devaluation on the relative price between differentiated tradables and nontradables. Even eight quarters after the devaluation, this relative price is 6.5 percentage points above its original value.

The actual trajectories of the real exchange rates are described in Figure 6.2. From this figure, we observe, almost from early 1975, a sharp

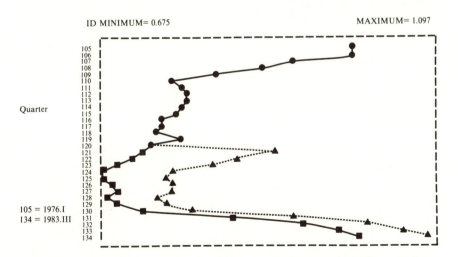

Figure 6.1   The effect on P_M/P_N of a 50% devaluation in the first quarter of 1980.

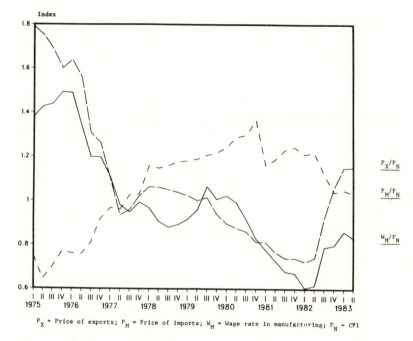

Figure 6.2   Real exchange rate (1977 = 100).

drop in the real exchange rate of imports (P_M/P_N) and in the real exchange rate of exports (P_X/P_N). The lowest value for both series occurs in the first quarter of 1982. In contrast, real wages (W_M/P_N) in manufacturing achieve a peak in the last quarter of 1980.

4.   Exchange Rate Preannouncement, Portfolio Adjustment, and the Endogeneity of Capital Inflows

As to the substitution of assets, when the preannounced formula was introduced, the cost of foreign borrowing decreased substantially. As shown in Table 6.2, it went from 22.6% a year in the fourth quarter of 1977 to 10.2% a year in the first quarter of 1978 and became negative through to the last quarter of 1980. Not surprisingly, even with substantial controls, capital inflows increased from U.S.$73.9 million in the fourth quarter of 1977 to U.S.$194 million in the first quarter of 1978 and U.S.$545 million in the second quarter of 1980[4] (Table 6.2, col. 1). The lifting of the controls on inflows in April 1980 generated a further increase in capital inflows and a drop in peso interest rates (Table 6.2, col. 9).

A contractionary monetary policy (Table 6.2, col. 5) encouraged further capital inflows through portfolio substitution. In addition, the long period of appreciation of the peso that followed the preannounced policy of devaluations increased the current account deficit and triggered additional capital inflows.

The interaction between the current account deficit and the flow of capital is obtained from the estimation of an extension of the Kouri and Porter (1974) and Obstfeldt (1982) model.[5]

The model that we use to look at capital flows consists of demand for money, net domestic demand for domestic bonds, and domestic demand for external bonds, as well as net external demand for domestic bonds. The latter are considered as liabilities of the private sector and consist mainly of medium-term liabilities. The model is completed by a money supply equation, an equation for the change in the central bank's internal credit, the definition of the balance of payments, the restriction of wealth, the equilibrium of the internal bond market, and the equilibrium of the money market.

The reduced form of the model for capital flows is given by the following equation:[6]

$$FCAP_t = \beta_0 + \beta_1 \Delta r_t + \beta_2 \Delta Y_t + \beta_3 \Delta W_t + \beta_4 CAB_t + \beta_5 \Delta CIBC_t \quad (1)$$

where FCAP = net flow of private capital; r = interest rate of foreign bonds in domestic currency; Y = nominal income; W = nominal wealth; CAB = current account surplus; and CIBC = internal credit of the central bank.

The expected signs of the coefficients are as follows:

$$\beta_1 < 0 \quad \beta_2 \lessgtr 0 \quad \beta_3 > 0$$
$$-1 \leq \beta_4 < 0 \quad -1 \leq \beta_5 < 0$$

The principal aim of the model is to explain capital inflows and to determine whether the monetary authority can affect the supply of money. Control over the money supply depends on the compensatory coefficient that measures the drop in the net flow of private capital associated with a rise in the central banks's net internal credit. This effect is measured by the coefficient β_5 of the previous model, denominated as the coefficient of compensation. If $\beta_5 = -1$, we return to the model of perfect mobility of capital, and the monetary authority has no control over the money supply. If $\beta_5 = 0$ and $\beta_1 = 0$, then the monetary policy is completely independent[7] and the central bank can pursue monetary goals without reference to balance-of-payments results. Specifically, it can seek to achieve monetary goals through the expansion of internal credit. In the more general case of $-1 < \beta_5 < 0$, part of the expansion in the central bank's internal credit is lost through a decrease in the net flow of capital.[8]

Equation (1), with quarterly data in constant 1977 pesos from the first quarter of 1975 to the first quarter of 1982, came out as follows:[9]

$$FCAP_t = 888.9 + -14.06\ \Delta r_t^* + 0.25\ \Delta Y_t - 0.32\ CAB_t$$
$$\quad\quad (2.46)\quad (-0.59)\quad\quad (5.66)\quad\quad\quad (-5.64)$$

$$\tag{2}$$

$$- 0.34\ \Delta CIBC_t + 3{,}954.9\ D_t$$
$$\quad (-4.35)\quad\quad\quad\quad (6.66)$$

$$R^2 = 0.93 \quad\quad T = 29 \quad\quad SSR = 23{,}033 \times 10^3 \quad\quad DW = 1.73$$

where $FCAP_t$ = net capital inflow, in 1977 pesos; R_t^* = LIBOR interest rate plus devaluation rate; Y_t = real GDP, in 1977 pesos; CAB_t = current account surplus in 1977 pesos; $CIBC_t$ = net internal credit of the central bank minus the increase in cash reserves, in 1977 pesos; and D_t = dummy variable that takes a value of one from the second quarter of 1980 on, a zero otherwise.

In the preliminary results, the coefficient of the change in internal credit differs significantly from zero but is substantially higher than -1.[10]

In Figure 6.3, we have used this equation to compare the estimated values with the equation versus the true ones for the dependent variable. The figure shows that our model closely follows the observed evolution of the dependent variable. Furthermore, the model identifies most of the break points in the net capital inflow (FCAP).

These results show that both the change in the net internal credit of the central bank ($\Delta CIBC$) and the current account surplus (CAB) coefficients are significantly different from zero and are very similar. Moreover, the compensation coefficient is closer to zero than to -1. In fact, the null hypothesis that the $\Delta CIBC$ and CAB coefficients are not statistically different cannot be rejected (the F computed at 0.039). This condition, which is a restriction in the coefficients of the reduced form, is a rather convincing test of the validity of the model (Kouri and Porter, 1974, p. 450).

The final equation is given by:

$$FCAP_t = 850.7 - 15.18\ \Delta\ r_t^* + 0.25\ \Delta\ Y_t - 0.32\ CAB_t$$
$$\quad\quad (2.84)\quad (-0.66)\quad\quad (5.81)\quad\quad\quad (-7.03)$$

$$- 0.32\ \Delta CIBC_t + 3{,}902.4\ D_t$$
$$\quad (7.03)\quad\quad\quad\quad (7.49)$$

$$T = 29 \quad\quad SSR = 2{,}3072 \times 10^3 \quad\quad DW = 1.74$$

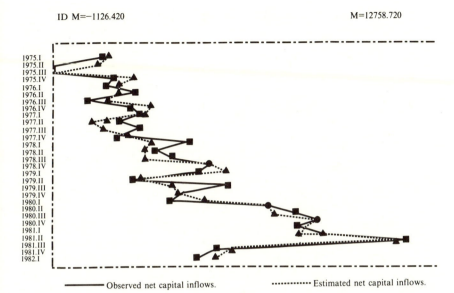

Figure 6.3 Net private quarterly capital flows.

Our results compare well in explanatory terms with those for other countries, especially considering that we are working with real variables. In addition, on the basis of the results of the last equation, we find that the common coefficient of ΔCIBC and CAB is statistically smaller than one using a one-tail test.

Thus, contrary to what has been claimed by other observers of the Chilean economy (Harberger, 1985; S. Edwards, 1984), capital inflows are mostly explained by a portfolio adjustment model, even in periods where controls on capital inflows were present. However, the significance of the dummy variable for the period when the controls on capital inflows were reduced indicates that the lifting of controls gave capital inflows a further push (Corbo, 1983, 1985b).

5. The Macroeconomic Effects of the Preannouncement Policy

The increase in output, the decrease in real interest rates in late 1979 and 1980 (Table 6.2), and the rise in wealth substantially increased domestic expenditures in 1979–80 and 1981. The increase in wealth resulted in part from the increase in the market value of assets without an equivalent increase in the reposition cost (the Tobin's q).

To provide some evidence on the causes of expenditure increases, we estimated an expenditure model. The equation explains expenditures by real GDP, real interest rates, and real wealth (see also Frenkel and Mussa, 1984).

The estimated equation is:[11]

$$E_t = 835.9 + 0.968 \; Q_t - 2{,}112.5 \; r_t - 5{,}888.4 \; r_t^*$$
$$ (0.10) \quad (6.84) \qquad (-0.69) \qquad (-3.97)$$

$$+ \; 0.0011 \; W_t + 0.0022 \; W_{t-1} + 0.0033 \; W_{t-2}$$
$$(2.27) \qquad\quad (2.27) \qquad\qquad (2.27)$$

$$T = 30 \qquad DW = 2.15 \qquad R^2 = 0.978$$

where E = absorption in 1977 prices; Q = GDP in 1977 prices; r = real interest rate of peso loans; r^* = real interest rate of dollar loans; and W = total wealth in 1977 prices, measured as capital stock times Tobin's q, plus the sum of high-power money and net foreign assets.

Real expenditures rose 10.5% in 1979, 9.3% in 1980, and 10.9% in 1981, compared with 8.3%, 7.5%, and 5.3% increases for GDP in the same years. The real expenditures generated demand pressures in the market for both tradable and nontradable goods (see Table 6.1). The interest rate for consumer loans decreased even more, as commercial banks and *financieras* competed in a market that had been the exclusive preserve of retailers and department stores.[12] The decline in real interest rates and increase in wealth also set off booms in the real estate and stock markets.

The increase in domestic expenditures in turn gave rise to a boom in the nontradable sector and required a market-clearing appreciation of the peso (a drop in PT/PN). Thus, although the preannounced exchange rate policy triggered the appreciation of the peso, it did not result in rising unemployment and falling output. Rather, the drop in the real exchange rate was validated by the decrease in the real interest rate and the increase in expenditures that resulted from the portfolio adjustment and the increase in wealth.

In 1981, a large increase in expenditures followed a substantial drop in interest rates. In the relative prices of 1980, excess demand for nontradables developed, and the relative price of tradables fell to clear the market in nontradable goods. The mechanism of adjustment was an expenditure-induced excess demand for nontradables that increased their price, whereas the price for tradables remained almost constant, with international inflation compensated for by the appreciation of the dollar in the international markets.

Concomitantly with these internal developments, Chile was suffering the effects of the international recession. In 1981, it experienced an overall loss in its terms of trade because of a deterioration in the commodity terms of trade and a substantial increase in the international interest rate. This loss—on the order of U.S.$1,200 million in 1981, or 3.4% of GDP—should have dampened the increase in expenditures. However, expenditures continued growing at rates far above the increase in GDP (10.8% versus 5.3%, respectively), a pattern that suggests that Chileans were perceiving a substantial increase in their wealth. Indeed, between December 1977 and December 1981, the Chilean stock market price index septupled. As a result, the deficit in the current account rose to U.S.$4,814 million in 1981 (13.7% of GDP), almost $3,000 million more than the deficit in 1980. Doubts about the sustainability of the exchange rate policy may have accelerated the purchase of durable goods. Furthermore, because of the dynamic of inflation following the fixing of the exchange rate and the appreciation of the dollar in the international markets, the expansion of expenditures took place at very low inflation rates (9.5% in 1981, as against 31.2% in 1980). Indeed, the appreciation of the dollar was equivalent to a decrease in the nominal exchange rate. If, instead, capital inflows had been lower because of a higher rate of crawl or an interest equalization tax or direct controls on foreign borrowing, real interest rates would have been higher in 1980, domestic expenditures lower. In turn, the demand pressures on the market for nontradables would have been correspondingly lower and the current account deficit smaller. In keeping with those conditions, the appreciation of the peso would have been smaller than what was observed (Corbo, 1983; Condon, Corbo, and de Melo, 1985; Harberger, 1985).

The link between an exogenous shock in capital inflows and the real exchange rate can also be studied in a model where capital flows are treated as a transfer (Dornbusch, 1980). Using a five-sector general equilibrium version of this type of model, Condon, Corbo and Melo (1984) found that if capital inflows had been 50% lower in 1980 and 1981, the equilibrium real exchange rate would have been 13% higher. Interestingly enough, the resulting change in the composition of output in favor of labor-intensive sectors would have produced only a marginal drop in employment.

The appreciation of the peso and ensuing loss in competitiveness of the tradable sector between the middle of 1979 and the end of 1981 was about 28% of the mid-1979 value. The profitability of the tradable sector was further weakened by movements in the real interest rate, which started to rise substantially in the beginning of 1981 because of a restrictive monetary policy and doubts about the sustainability of the fixed exchange rate regime. During the second half of 1981, the *ex-post* real interest rate rose to almost 40% a year for peso-denominated loans and 15% a year for dollar-denominated ones.[13] These higher rates also generated a drastic fall in domestic expenditures and a recession toward the end of 1981 that carried over to 1982. When capital inflows started to decline in late 1981, the increase in interest rates and the decline in expenditures became substantial. In early 1982, the fall in expenditures reduced the demand for both tradables and nontradables. In turn, the reduction in the demand for tradables improved the commercial account of the balance of payments, while that for nontradables created an excess supply in the market for those goods and required an increase in the real exchange rate to restore equilibrium with the lower level of domestic expenditures. In fact, given the decline in international prices in nominal terms and the fixed exchange rate, the improvement in the relative price of tradables actually required a substantial decrease in the nominal price of nontradables to restore the real exchange rate to equilibrium. However, with the price of nontradables inflexibly downward, especially in an economy with backward wage indexation, the adjustment to lower expenditures took the form of an increase in unemployment.[14]

Thus, the improvement in the real exchange rate (P_T/P_N) called for by the macroadjustment was slow and costly in terms of output and employment because of the downward inflexibility of the prices of many nontradables. Furthermore, the high real interest rates of 1981 weakened the financial situation of firms considerably, especially those in the tradable sector that had lost an important part of their working capital in the protracted period in which the peso had been appreciating. The appropriate way to move the relative price of tradables back to the equilibrium level called for by the reduction in expenditures would have been a devaluation combined with a suspension of wage indexation, a policy that should have been implemented in late 1981.

On June 14, 1982, the government in fact decided to help the adjustment in relative prices by devaluing the peso against the dollar by 18%. It also adopted a new exchange rate system that pegged the peso to a basket of currencies. This measure was taken to reduce short-term fluctuations in the real exchange rate arising from fluctuations in the value of the dollar in the international markets. In addition, a monthly devaluation of 0.8% with respect to the basket of currencies was announced for the next 12 months. On June 18, 1982, the government announced a further set of measures to accompany the devaluation. Included was the suspension of wage indexation. These measures were aimed at neutralizing the possible effect of the devaluation on the price of nontradables and at reducing the potential fiscal deficit.

As the public judged the initial devaluation—with its associated passive crawl formula—to be inappropriate, substantial pressure was developed in the exchange rate market. In fact, the post-devaluation adjustment of the Chilean economy proved more difficult than policymakers had anticipated. This devaluation—following three years of assurance to the public that the exchange rate policy would not change and that any devaluation would only create inflation—spurred a run on the peso. The central bank lost around U.S.$460 million (13.2% of international reserves) between June 14 and August 6. At that point the government replaced the crawling-peg regime with a flexible exchange rate regime, and simultaneously it also eliminated all restrictions on foreign exchange transactions.[15] Floating the exchange rate did nothing to alleviate the crisis of confidence; instead it became even worse. By then, the foreign debt was U.S.$17 billion, most of it in private hands. A financial crisis started, while the run on the peso continued. As a partial solution, the government introduced a preferential exchange rate for the service of foreign debt contracted on or before August 6, 1982.

After the exchange rate was floated, its value increased substantially, a trend that prompted the central bank to intervene by abandoning the free float in favor of a dirty float. In that attempt to support the peso the central bank lost another U.S.$450 million in reserves between August 6 and September 20, 1982. Meanwhile, the exchange rate fluctuated widely around an upward trend. With capital inflows substantially reduced and with more than half of the export earnings controlled by the government, it became very difficult to implement any type of floating-rate system. Furthermore, the new economic authorities decided it was not proper, in the middle of a major crisis of confidence, to keep a dirty float. Thus, on September 19, 1982, the central bank, to stabilize the exchange rate, announced its intention of supporting an exchange rate band that would allow fluctuations of ±2% around an upward trend for the next 120 days. The trend started at 66 pesos to the dollar and followed a passive crawling-peg system with a monthly rate of crawl equal to the previous month's CPI inflation rate minus 1% (an estimate for world inflation). The band was subsequently extended to 180 days.

The exchange rate adjustment in the second half of 1982 was difficult because of the large capital outflows during the period of unstable exchange rates and the sudden drying up of foreign credit because of the debt problems of Argentina, Mexico, and Brazil. To smooth the adjustment to the sharp drop in capital inflows—net private inflows went from U.S.$4.5 billion in 1981 to −$0.5 billion in 1982—the amount of borrowing by government and state enterprises was increased substantially in the second half of 1982. A long recession and a large devaluation eroded substantially the financial situation of private firms. Furthermore, because of poor banking practices—firms in the nontradable sector were having to deal with large exchange rate risks—the devaluations had unwanted side-effects. As bankruptcies spread, the government decided in early 1983 to take over the two largest private commercial banks to avoid their collapse. Chile has spent the two years since then trying to solve the internal financial crisis as well as its severe balance-of-payments crisis.

6. Conclusions

Three main conclusions can be drawn from Chile's experience. First, the liberalization and stabilization reforms implemented during the early years of the military government, in spite of the unfavorable external shocks of 1975, succeeded until late 1978, except that the rate of unemployment and real interest rate remained stubbornly high. The unemployment rate was largely ignored, while most of the time the high interest rate was attributed mainly to restrictions on capital inflows. The main cause, however, was the lack of adequate supervision of the financial system (Arellano, 1984; Zalher, 1983, 1985; Corbo, Melo and Tybout, 1986; Tybout, 1985).

Second, the second stabilization attempt, undertaken when inflation was down to 35% a year—a level similar to the average for the 1960s—worked at cross purposes with the export-led growth being generated by the liberalization of trade. Indeed, the use of the exchange rate to stabilize the economy not only created a temporal short-term real appreciation of the peso, it also encouraged external borrowing at a time when the restrictions on capital inflows were being lifted and the capital markets were very liquid. The large rise in expenditures that followed the decrease in interest rate and increase in wealth caused the peso to appreciate further. The result was an unsustainable current-account deficit that ran close to 25% of GDP in the first half of 1981. The appreciation squeezed tradables just when exporters were making inroads in the world markets and firms in the import-competing sector had completed a major adjustment to the trade liberalization. Not surprisingly, firms in the tradable sectors suffered a large squeeze on profits (Corbo and Sánchez, 1985; Gálvez and Tybout, 1985).

Third, contrary to what the authorities thought, the large spread between the domestic and foreign interest rates was as much a problem of imperfect asset substitution as it was a problem of control of the inflows of capital. Thus the intensity of the opening-up of the capital account should not have been governed chiefly by the spread in interest rates.

Appendix:[16]
Principal Reforms—
Chronological Synthesis

Commercial Policy[17]

Prereform situation (September 1973): Quotas and quantitative restrictions were widespread. The tariff range was from 0% to 750%, with a mean value (weighted by the number of tariff positions) of 105% and a mode of 90% and a median of 80%. 2,872 tariff positions were subject to an import deposit of 10,000% of the CIF value.

September 1973–July 1975: The highest nominal tariff was reduced from 750% to 140% and then to 120%. The mean weighted tariff (MWT) was reduced from 105% to 57%.

August 1975–November 1977: A tariff goal was defined with six nominal levels between 10% and 35%, to be enacted in the first quarter of 1978. This structure was reached in August 1977 because of an anticipation of the last two stages. During this period the highest nominal tariff (HNT) dropped from 120% to 35% (except for the motorcar industry) and the MWT from 44% to 19.7%.

December 1977 onwards: In December 1977 a target structure was established with a 10% uniform tax to be reached in June 1979. The goal approximation was gradually made by means of small monthly adjustments. In this period the MWT went from 19.7% to 10.1%.

Complementary aspects of the reforms: All tariff exemptions were eliminated, first by requiring the public sector to be subject to the general regime as early as 1974. Consumption surcharge taxes that taxed imports at a higher rate than domestically produced competing goods were eliminated. By September 1976, previous deposits were eliminated except for cars and used or damaged merchandise, and a list of allowed import items was replaced by a short list of forbidden items. Finally, in August 1981 the list of forbidden items was eliminated.

Price Liberalization[18]

Prereform situation (September 1973): More than 3,000 prices were fixed by DIRINCO (Commerce Department, a dependency of the Ministry of the Economy).

October 1973: Law decree 522 defined three groups of goods and services: those whose prices were to be freely determined (the majority); those (33 goods and services) whose price would continue to be fixed by DIRINCO (by means of cost studies); and a group of 18 goods whose prices were to be provided to DIRINCO, even though they were to be freely determined.

October 1973–May 1982: The general tendency was toward price liberalization. In December 1980, law decree 3529 was enacted forbidding items in the informed price category from being reclassified as fixed price goods and those freely priced ones to be put either under the informed price category or the fixed price category.

Labor

Prereform situation (September 1973): The following items were legally included in individual contracts: work hours (normal and overtime pay), work conditions, length of vacation, salary (at least the minimum), and so on. In addition, a lump-sum payment for each year of work made labor dismissal extremely difficult and expensive.

1974 onwards: Discriminatory benefits were slowly eliminated; family allowances and retirement ages were made uniform for blue-collar and white-collar workers. Social security contributions were slowly reduced. Union power was heavily reduced.

In 1978 and 1981: Efforts were made to permit greater bargaining flexibility for vacations, indemnizations, and profit sharing. Furthermore, employers were allowed to lay-off workers without justification. Minimum wage market coverage was reduced.

July 1979: A "Labor Plan" was enacted. This plan reintroduced collective bargaining for a fraction of the labor force. In contract bargaining, the lowest offer that employers could make was equal to the previous wage adjusted by the CPI.

External Capital Markets[19]

The reforms in the capital markets were too numerous and in the initial stage lacked a clear direction. Among the main reforms were the following.

September 1977: Commercial banks were allowed to become indebted under article 14 of the exchange law.[20] A monthly *minimum* limit of 5% of capital and reserves was imposed for the flow of this type of operation.

January 1978: The central bank established a stock limit of 25% of capital and reserves for debt under article 14.

March 1978: The stock limit was raised to 160% of the capital plus reserves of commercial banks.

April 1978: The global limit was raised to 180% and a sublimit of 160% for debts, with a mean amortization of 36 months or lower. Article 14 limits were raised to 45% and 25% for debt of the above types. This credit had to be channeled toward dollar-denominated debt.

For the first time, a limit on external debt was imposed on development banks. This limit was 400% of capital and reserves, or 500% if the excess over the 400% was covered by credits with a maturity of 36 months and over.

December 1978: The global limit and sublimit were raised to 180% and 215% for commercial banks and to 400–600% for development banks. The limit under article 14 was raised from 45% to 60%.

April 1979: The sublimit of 215% was raised to 225% for commercial banks, and the article 14 limit from 60% to 70%. A variable reserve requirement was established for external credits depending on the length of maturity of the loans: 10% for those with a maturity of 48–66 months, 15% for those of 36–48 months, and 25% for those of 24–36 months.

June 1979: The global limits on external borrowing were eliminated. From this moment on the only limitation on bank indebtedness was the lawful internal limit on total debt: 20 times capital and reserves. Debt limits under article 14 were eliminated. The monthly limits under article 14 were maintained, but reduced to 5% of capital and reserves or U.S.$1 million, whichever was greater.

April 1980: All monthly limits under article 14 were lifted.

September 1980: Commercial banks were allowed to lend in external markets using their own resources.

December 1981: For the first time, commercial banks were allowed to lend short term (180 days) with external credit for purposes other than financing commercial operations.

May 1982: Commercial banks were allowed to obtain external credit with a maturity under two years subject to a reserve requirement of 20%.

July 1982: Commercial banks were allowed to use part of their short-run foreign credits to lend in pesos, with a limit of 50% of capital and reserves.

Domestic Financial Markets[21]

(a) Interest rates

Prereform: Nominal interest rates were fixed by the central bank. As the resulting real interest rates were highly negative, most credit was allocated by quotas.

May 1974: Law Decree 455 modified the interest rate concept to the quantity that the creditor received and that exceeded the capital value properly adjusted by inflation. In the same law decree, free bargaining of the interest rate was established, subject to the restriction that it not exceed 50% of the current interest rate for inflation-adjustable operations and nonadjustable operations, whichever the case.

September and October 1974: Commercial banks were allowed by the central bank to determine freely the interest rate for deposits with a maturity longer than 60 days, a maturity that was later lowered to 30 days.

June 1975: The central bank allowed commercial banks and the Banco del Estado to determine freely the interest rate on both inflation adjustable operations and noninflation-adjustable operations.

(b) Operational and institutional aspects

December 1973: New bank establishments were prohibited until December 1974. To relax this limitation, the so-called "operative representation of foreign banks" was created. These entities could not operate in the domestic deposit market nor extend domestic currency credits.

December 1974: Rules were established with respect to the organization and functioning of financial institutions, which were to be corporations with the sole social objective of acting as financial intermediaries. Minimum capital limits were established together with specifications of operations that were allowed or not allowed. Limits on investments and credits to the same natural or legal entity are imposed. The banking law was modified, so that no natural entity could own more than 1½% of the capital of a bank, a limit that was raised to 3% if the entity was a legal one. For new banks, this limit would be enforced five years after operations started. Commercial, development, and mortgage banks were not allowed to have shares of small financial institutions. Foreign banks were permitted to establish branches and offices in Chile.

In January 1976: A law concerning the management of investment funds societies (Fondos Mutuos) was published to regulate which investment instrument could be bought, such as corporation shares, bonds, debentures, IOUs, government debt, and other debt. Minimum capital requirements were raised, regulatory provisions were established, and all types of debt instruments were enlarged.

Foreign Exchange Policy[22]

Pre-reform situation (September 1973): There were multiple exchange rates, parallel exchange markets, and large overvaluation of the peso.

October 1973: There was a maxidevaluation, and the exchange markets were reduced to three.

August 1974: The special exchange rate for copper exports was eliminated. The spot market dollar initially suffered 2 devaluations and later another 15. The mean devaluation rate of the year was 6.1%. Total annual devaluation in this market was 166.7%. In the banking market, 24 devaluations were made during the year; the result was a mean devaluation rate of 6.9%, with an annual rate of 392.1%.

1975: The exchange rate policy consisted of small periodic devaluations.

June 1976: A 10% revaluation was effected.

August 1976: An exchange rate system with one rate was reached.

March 1977: A 10% revaluation was effected.

December 1977: The government accounced that the devaluation rate would exceed the inflation rate to compensate for tariff reductions.

February 1978: A formal *tablita* consisting of devaluations at a decreasing rate was established. This one lasted until June 1979.

June 1979: The exchange rate was fixed at the rate programmed for December 1979 in the later *tablita*, with the concurrent announcement that this fixing would last until February 1980.

December 1979: The fixed rate was extended indefinitely.

June 1979–June 1982: An 18% devaluation ended with the fixed-rate period. The new system consisted of one in which the peso was pegged to a basket of foreign currencies.

August 1982: The floating-rate policy was enforced.

September 1982: A new *tablita*, with monthly devaluations equivalent to the previous month's inflation rate minus 1%, was announced. Access to the exchange market was severely restricted.

Notes

[1]For a chronology of all three reforms, see the appendix.

[2]For a review of the indexation, see Edwards, A. (1985).

[3]Evaluation of the Chilean reforms is provided in Corbo (1983, 1985b), Edwards, S. (1984, 1985), Harberger (1982, 1985), and Zahler (1983).

[4]Foreign trade financing, not included in this figure, increased substantially also.

[5]The model was estimated in Corbo and Matte (1984).

[6]Consideration of a fourth asset does not change the reduced form obtained by Kouri and Porter. The only change from their model is the substitution of J( ) by J( ) − (S( ) where S( ) is the domestic supply of medium-term bonds in the foreign markets.

[7]See Kouri and Porter (1974, pp. 450–51).

[8]Initially we used, following Kouri and Porter, a model in nominal variables. However, as should be expected of an economy with high inflation, heteroskedasticity was detected in the errors, and we therefore reformulated the model in real terms. For this purpose, we assumed first-degree price homogeneity in the demand for assets.

[9]The equations were estimated by ordinary least squares. The coefficients in parentheses are the t statistics. We also included a proxy for real wealth in the estimates. The proxy was obtained by computing permanent income with the autoregressive process used in the specification and estimation of a demand for money, with a value for the autoregressive coefficient of 0.513 obtained in the estimation (for the model used, see Corbo, 1982). The wealth variable thus constructed was never significant, and we therefore ignored it in the remaining estimates. Stability analysis of the original equation, which has no dummy variable, clearly indicated a break in the constant beginning in the second quarter of 1982, when most of the controls on capital inflows were lifted.

[10]We also tested the null hypothesis of homoskedastic disturbances. For this purpose we used the Goldfield and Quandt test. In conducting the test we left out the five central observations. The F was computed to 1.25. At a significance level of 5%, the $F_{(6, 6)}$, is 4.28, and therefore the null hypothesis of homoskedasticity could not be rejected.

[11]The coefficients of wealth were restricted to a polynomial of degree 1 with near restrictions.

[12]I owe this point to Carlos Massad.

[13]The increase in the own real interest rate for the tradable-producing sector was even higher, as its inflation was much lower.

[14]This outcome has been anticipated in Corbo and Edwards (1981).

[15]There was a U.S.$10,000 a month limit on the amount of foreign exchange that any Chilean could buy until August 6, 1982, when this limitation was lifted.

[16]This appendix is from Corbo (1985b).

[17]For a good description of commercial policies during this period, see Torres (1982).

[18]Based on Wisecarver (1985).

[19]Extracted from Gutiérrez (1982) and Rosende (1981).

[20]Article 14 refers to the permission given by the central bank to the borrower for future access to the exchange rate market to serve a foreign debt.

[21]Based on "Evolución de las principales normas que regular el mercado financiero chileno, Septiembre 1973–Junio 1980," Banco Central de Chile, 1981.

[22]Ffrench-Davis (1979) and Meza (1981).

References

Arellano, J. P. (1984). "De la liberación a la intervención: El mercado de capitales en Chile: 1974–1983." *Estudios CIPLAN* (11).

Blejer, M., and D. J. Mathieson (1981). "The preannouncement of exchange rate changes as a stabilization instrument." *IMF Staff Papers* (December): 760–92.

Condon, T., V. Corbo, and J. de Melo (1984). "Capital inflows, the current account, and the real exchange rate: Tradeoffs for Chile, 1977–81." DRD Discussion Paper, No. 108. Washington, D.C.: The World Bank, November.

––––––– (1985). "Productivity growth, external shocks, and capital inflows in Chile during 1977–81: A general equilibrium analysis." Unpublished.

Corbo, V. (1982). "Monetary policy with an overrestricted demand for money equation: Chile in the '60s." *Journal of Development Economics* (February).

––––––– (1983). "Desarrollos recientes en la economía chilena." *Cuadernos de Economía* (April): 5–20.

––––––– (1985a). "International prices, wages and inflation in an open economy: A Chilean model." *Review of Economics and Statistics*.

––––––– (1985b). "Reforms and macroeconomic adjustments in Chile during 1974–1983." *World Development* 13(8).

Corbo, V., and S. Edwards (1981). "El rol de una devaluación en la economía chilena actual." Mimeo (June).

Corbo, V., and R. Matte (1984). "Capital flows and the role of monetary policy: The case of Chile." Unpublished manuscript (May).

Corbo, V., and J. M. Sánchez (1985). "How firms adjusted to the reforms in Chile." In *Scrambling for Survival: How Firms Adjusted to the Recent Reforms in Chile, Uruguay, and Argentina*, edited by V. Corbo and J. de Melo. World Bank Staff Papers No. 764. Washington, D.C.: World Bank.

Corbo, V., J. de Melo and J. Tybout (1986). "What went wrong with the recent reforms in the Southern Cone." *Economic Development and Cultural Change* 34(3): 607–400.

Dirección de Presupuestos (Various years). *Exposition of the Minister of Finance*. Santiago.

Dornbusch, R. (1980). *Open-Economy Macroeconomics*. New York: Basic Books.

Edwards, A. (1985). "Wage indexation and real wages: Chile 1974–1980." Mimeo. Washington, D.C.: The World Bank (December).

Edwards, S. (1984). "Monetarism in Chile 1973–1983: Analytical issues and economic puzzles." Mimeo. University of California at Los Angeles (December).

———— (1985). "Economic policy and the record of economic growth in Chile: 1973–1982." In *National Economic Policies in Chile*, edited by G. Walton. Greenwich, Conn.: JAI Press.

Ffrench-Davis, R. (1979). "Regímenes cambiarios 1965–1979." In *Colleción Estudios CIEPLAN* (2). Santiago: CIEPLAN.

Frenkel, J. A., and M. L. Mussa (1984). "Asset markets, exchange rates and the balance of payments." In *Handbook in International Economics*, edited by R. Jones and P. Kenan. Amsterdam: North-Holland, Vol. 2.

Gálvez, J., and J. Tybout (1985). "Microeconometric adjustments in Chile during 1977–81: The importance of being a grupo." *World Development* (August).

Gutiérrez, M. (1982). "Reflexiones sobre apertura financiera: El caso chileno." *Research Report No. 14* (Central Bank of Chile) (May).

Harberger, A. (1982). "The Chilean economy in the 1970s: Crisis, stabilization, liberalization, reform." In *Economic Policy in a World of Change*, edited by K. Brunner and A. H. Meltzer. Carnegie-Rochester Conference Series on Public Policy, Vol. 17. Amsterdam: North-Holland.

———— (1985). "Lessons for debtor country managers and policymakers." In *International Debt and the Developing Countries*, edited by G. Smith and J. T. Cuddington. Washington, D.C.: The World Bank.

Kouri, P., and M. Porter (1974). "International capital flows and portfolio equilibrium." *Journal of Political Economy* (May/June).

McKinnon, R. (1980). "Monetary control and the crawling peg." In *Exchange Rate Rules*, edited by John Williamson. New York: Macmillan Press.

Meza, W. (1981). "Situación de la política cambiaria en el período 1973–1980." *Research Report No. 5* (Central Bank of Chile) (September).

Obstfeldt, M. (1982). "Can we sterilize? Theory and evidence." *American Economic Review* (May).

Rosende, F. (1981). "Algunas reflexiones acerca del proceso de apertura financiera en Chile." *Research Report No. 2* (Central Bank of Chile) (July).

Torres, C. (1982). "Evolución de la política arancelaria: Período 1973–1981." *Report No. 16* (Central Bank of Chile) (September).

Tybout, J. (1985). "A firm level chronicle of financial crisis in the Southern Cone." Mimeo. World Bank (April).

Wisecarver, D. (1985). "Economic regulation and deregulation in Chile since 1973." In *National Economic Policies in Chile*, edited by G. Walton. Greenwich, Conn.: JAI Press.

Zahler, R. (1983). "Recent Southern Cone liberalization reforms and stabilization policies, the Chilean case, 1974–1982." *Journal of Interamerican Studies and World Affairs* 25(4).

_____ (1985). "Las tasas de interés en Chile: 1975–1982." Mimeo (January).

7

Exchange Rate Policies in Chile: 1933–82

Sergio de la Cuadra

1. Introduction

Generally, in economic analysis attempts are made to explain endogenous variables such as output or the level of prices, depending upon variables of economic policy such as the fiscal deficit, the money supply, and the exchange rate. In this chapter, we shall try instead to explain the policy reactions of the economic authorities in the face of variations in endogenous variables, of external shocks to the economy, and of the administration of other policies. In particular, we will focus upon exchange rate policy responses.

In Section 2 we present the problem from an analytical point of view. Section 3 studies the empirical relationship existing between exchange rate policy and international reserves. Other policies, external factors, and other endogenous variables are introduced to analyze five episodes in which the authorities reacted by strongly readjusting the price of foreign currency. From the analysis of these episodes it is seen that, in some cases, it is external factors that create fiscal and credit policies that are incompatible with the exchange rate policy; in other cases, the incompatibility is independent of external factors that may accelerate or retard the exchange adjustment. These cases are summarized in Section 4.

2. An Analytical Framework

We distinguish three types of variables: policy variables, external factors, and result variables. They are designated as follows:

X_t: policy vector (fiscal, credit, exchange rate, commercial, etc.) in period t;

Y_t: external factor vector (external credit supply, terms of trade, etc.) in period t;

W_t: result vector (output, level of prices, international reserves, etc.) in period t.

Typically, theoretical and empirical analysis deals with the relation:

$$W_t = F[W_{t-1}, W_{t-2}, \ldots, X_t, X_{t-1}, X_{t-2},$$
$$\ldots, Y_t, Y_{t-1}, Y_{t-2}, \ldots] \tag{1}$$

which can be summarily expressed as:

$$W_t = F[W^*_{t-1}, X^*_t, Y^*_t] \tag{2}$$

However, we are interested in the inverse relation, that is

$$X_{t+1} = f[X^*_t, Y^*_t, W^*_t] \tag{3}$$

The latter function tells us that policies in period $t + 1$ are formulated with all the information available at that moment.

Considering functions (2) and (3), we have:

$$X_{t+1} = f[Y^*_t, W^*_t] \tag{4}$$

This functional relation states that the reaction of the authorities, measured by means of policy variables, may be accounted for by external factors and by the results of previous periods. As the time unit in which we measure variables is extended, external factors and the results of the same period in which the policies were adopted should be incorporated.

On linearizing function (4) and introducing a stochastic component (u), we may express this as:

$$X_{t+1} = \beta_0 + \beta_1 Y^*_t + \beta_2 W^*_t + u_t \tag{5}$$

This representation of the formulation of policies implies that there exists a systematic behavior involving β parameters which are stable in time. However, an inspection of variables in the case of Chile, over a long period of time, would lead us to believe that such β parameters are not stable. In other words, the authorities change in time and therefore the manner in which authorities react in the face of external factors and results also changes in time. Thus, we believe that a more appropriate formulation would be:

$$X_t = (\gamma_0 + V_{0t}) + (\gamma_1 + V_{1t})Y_t^* + (\gamma_2 + V_{2t})W_t^* + u_t \tag{6}$$

where V_{1t} is also a stochastic component. Rearranging the terms in (6), we have:

$$X_t = \gamma_0 + \gamma_1 Y_t^* + \gamma_2 W_t^* + E_t \tag{7}$$

$$E_t = V_{1t}Y_t^* + V_{2t}W_t^* + V_{0t} + u_t$$

That is, the stochastic component is a function of the independent variables.

Although we will not estimate the parameters of function (7), the equation constitutes the analytic framework utilized in the explanation of the exchange rate policies in Section 3.

The variables that we consider the most relevant are the following:

Policy vector:
  X_1: Exchange rate policy
  X_2: Fiscal policy
  X_3: Credit policy
  X_4: Commercial policy

External factor vector:
  Y_1: Terms of trade
  Y_2: External credit supply
  Y_3: International inflation

Results vector:
  W_1: International reserves
  W_2: GDP
  W_3: Domestic inflation

3. Exchange Policy and International Reserves

In this framework, exchange rate policy is determined by a system of simultaneous equations. In reduced form, the exchange rate is represented by:

$$X_1 = X_1(W_1, R)$$

where R includes other policies, other results, and external factors. In this section we shall establish whether R is an important variable.

3.1. Definition of Variables

From fifty years of exchange rate policy, we may distinguish, in general, two kinds of exchange rates: a completely controlled rate, and another with a degree of flexibility to fluctuate according to market forces. We shall call the former the official rate, and the latter the quasi-free rate. In view of the fact that during several years the official rate discriminated between different exports and imports, we shall estimate a single rate as a weighted average.

For our analysis we have chosen the official rate because we believe that it represents more faithfully the attitude of the authorities in the face of the necessity to adjust the exchange rate. Even though both rates show a similar trend, the quasi-free rate tends to react prior to the official rate.

We shall measure the "exchange rate policy" variable by means of adjustments in the official rate beyond those which offset inflation (for example, changes in the real exchange rate). We take into account inflation in the period preceding exchange rate changes because the intention of the authorities thus stands out more clearly. In effect, if during one year inflation is low and during the following year there is a strong devaluation, this would represent a clear change of policy, and vice versa.

If P is the price level and ER the official rate of exchange, we measure the exchange rate policy variable as:

$$X_{1t} = \frac{[1 + (dER/ER)_t]}{[1 + (dP/P)_{t-1}]}$$

We shall talk of a real devaluation policy when $X > 1$, and of a real revaluation when $X < 1$.

International reserves are measured as the accumulated change during the past three years, divided by the sum of imports during the same years.

Let RIN be (internal) reserves and IMP imports; then,

$$W_{1t} = \frac{dRIN_t + dRIN_{t-1} + dRIN_{t-2}}{IMP_t + IMP_{t-1} + IMP_{t-2}}$$

The reason to add the change of reserves over three years is that policy reaction is determined to a greater extent by the trend in the change of reserves than by the change of the most recent period.

3.2. A Graphic Representation

In Figure 7.1 we measure X_1 on the vertical axis, and W_1 on the horizontal axis. The 51 annual observations from 1932 to 1982 indicate that there is no correlation between these two variables; that is, R is an important variable.

In accordance with the number of observations in each quadrant from IV, III, II, to I, 37% of the observations correspond to revaluations with accumulation of reserves; 25% to revaluations with reserve losses; 24% to devaluations with reserve losses; and 14% to devaluations with accumulation. Nevertheless, cycles of policies can be distinguished. A possible classification of cycles may be seen in Figures 7.2 to 7.5. These are:

1933–49: Revaluation Cycle, with two exceptions in the years 1935 and 1936.
1950–58: Devaluation Cycle, with two exceptions in the years 1954 and 1956.
1959–66: Revaluation Cycle, with one exception in 1963.
1967–75: Devaluation Cycle, with two exceptions in the years 1970 and 1971.
1976–81: Revaluation Cycle, with no exception.

Such graphs also permit the relationship between devaluation and the loss of reserves to be seen more clearly. In the first place, of the 19 devaluations, 14 are accompanied by accumulated losses of reserves during the current or previous year in which such devaluations are undertaken. In the second place, in the 5 devaluations that exceed 39%, an accumulated loss of reserves occurs in both years.

Finally, for reference purposes, we have calculated the average inflation and growth rates for each of the cycles. These are:

		Inflation (%)	Growth (%)
1933–49	(Revaluation)	13.0	4.65
1950–58	(Devaluation)	39.7	3.80
1959–66	(Revaluation)	23.5	5.42
1967–75	(Devaluation)	134.5	−0.26
1976–81	(Revaluation)	33.6	7.84

It is by no means surprising that, during devaluation cycles, inflation rates should become accelerated. However, it may constitute a surprise that, during the same cycles, the growth rate should decelerate.

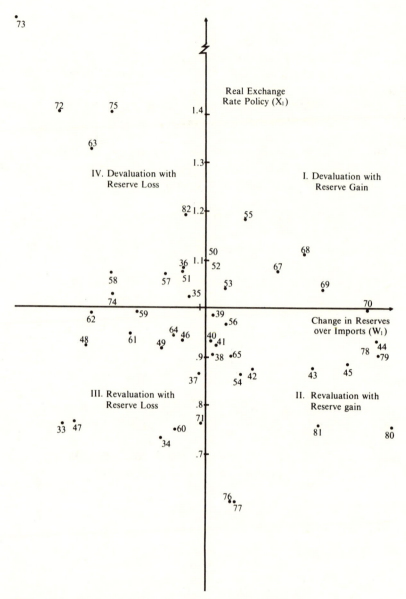

Figure 7.1 Real exchange rate policy in Chile (1933–82).

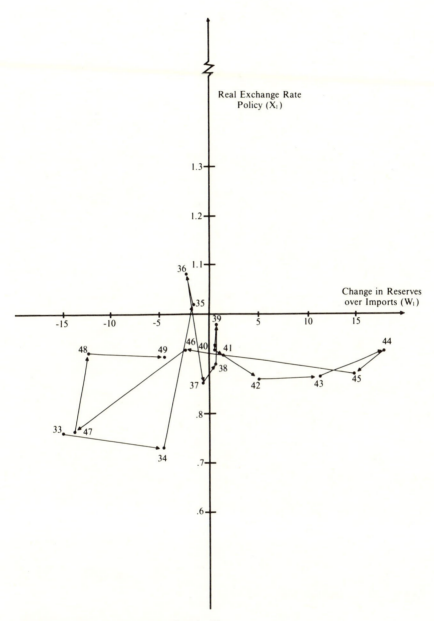

Figure 7.2 Revaluation cycle (1933–49).

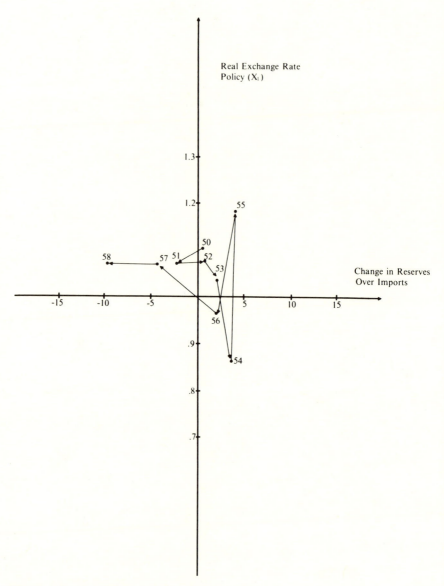

Figure 7.3 Devaluation cycle (1950–58).

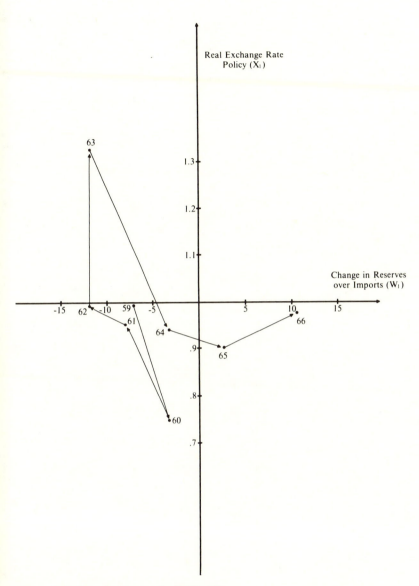

Figure 7.4 Revaluation cycle (1959–66).

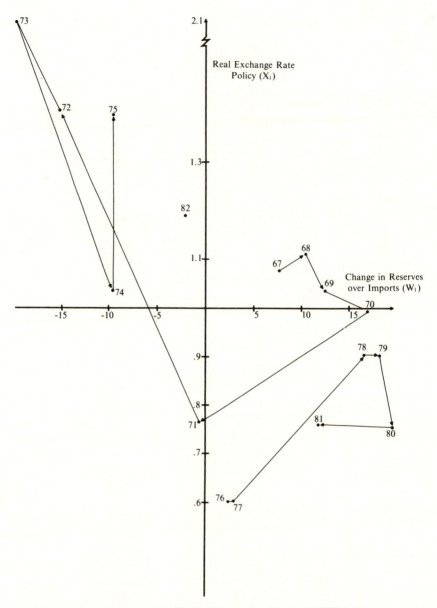

Figure 7.5 Devaluation cycle (1967–75); revaluation cycle (1976–81).

3.3. The Devaluation of 1950

As seen in Table 7.1, from 1933 to 1949 the real exchange rate in Chile appreciated an average of approximately 10% per year. This extraordinary real exchange rate appreciation cycle was the outcome of an exchange rate policy that attempted to maintain a fixed parity devaluation internal inflation relative to the rest of the world. Occasional official devaluations in 1935, 1943, 1948, and 1949 were not sufficient to compensate for the nearly fixed exchange rate period of most of the 1930s and the years 1944–47. In the early 1930s, international reserves declined every year except 1938 and 1939, where they grew slightly. This real exchange rate appreciation was sustained by an overall surplus in the balance of payments in the early 1940s, reserves increasing nearly every year until 1946, as illustrated in Figure 7.2. In 1947, as a result of a business slowdown and a capital outflow of 45 million dollars the year before, the monetary authorities accelerated domestic credit growth at levels that were incompatible with a fixed exchange rate, which was maintained throughout 1947. The 14 and 7% nominal devaluations of 1948 and 1949, respectively, were insufficient to adjust the real exchange rate, and the reserve loss continued so that international reserves continued to decline in 1947, 1948, and 1949.

In 1949 international reserves fell to 1.9 months of imports. In an attempt to resist adjusting the exchange rate, the authorities resorted to imposing controls on imports and tightening quota restrictions. Despite a strongly contractionary fiscal policy in 1949, international reserves continued to decline, probably due to the expectation of devaluation that had grown along with the real exchange rate appreciation. In the face of these circumstances, there was no alternative left but to devalue the currency, which was done in 1950, thereby ending the revaluation cycle of 1933–49.

3.4. The Devaluation of 1955

The major devaluation of 1955 was preceded by a series of small-reach exchange rate depreciations and rising reserves from 1950 to 1953, as depicted in Figure 7.3. In 1954, the failure to adjust the exchange rate sufficiently to compensate for internal inflation led to a substantial real exchange rate appreciation. The same year, the world price of copper fell 11%, and Chilean exports declined. This adverse external shock combined with the real exchange rate appreciation and fiscal deficits in 1953, 1954, and 1955 created an overvalued currency. This overvaluation was corrected by the major devaluation of 1955, in which the real exchange rate was depreciated by nearly 20%. International reserves grew in both 1955

Table 7.1

Policies	1943	1944	1945	1946	1947	1948	1949
Exchange rate							
Official rate (change in %)	10	0	1	1	0	14	7
Deval. rate (+), Reval. (−) (%) (real terms)	12	−7	−12	−6	−23	−7	−8
Fiscal							
Rate of change CBCG[a] (%)	9	15	36	31	4	28	−7
Credit							
Rate of change CBCP[b] (%)	−10	12	−21	72	37	41	43
External factors							
Capital inflows (U.S.$ mill.)	54	5	−8	−45	5	−7	61
Rate of change WPI, U.S.A. (%)	4.7	0.6	1.9	14.1	22.8	8.2	−5.0
Results							
Rate of change in GDP (%)	2.3	1.5	8.7	6.2	−6.3	12.6	−0.4
Change in int. res. (U.S.$ mill.)	24	35	−5	−41	−13	−3	−10
Int. res./av. monthly imports	6.6	9.3	8.9	4.6	2.8	2.6	1.9

Source: Banco Central de Chile, Monthly Bulletins, 1932–83; National Accounts, Corporacion de Fomento de la Produccion (CORFO) and Oficina Nacional de Planificacion (ODEPLAN); Ballesteros y T. Davis, *Cuadernos de Economia*, Universidad Catolica de Chile, No. 7 (September-December 1965); authors' estimates.
[a]CBCG: Central bank credit to the public sector.
[b]CBCP: Central bank credit to the private sector.

and 1956 but fell drastically in 1957 and 1958, as illustrated in Figure 7.3. The causes for the fall in reserves were both external and internal. The world price of copper fell 22% in 1957 and a further 12% in 1958. At the same time, the fiscal deficit grew from a level of 6 million escudos in 1955 to 21 million in 1956, 32 million in 1957, and 44 million in 1958. This large and growing deficit contributed to the loss of international reserves. In short, the 1950–58 devaluation episode resulted from a combination of adverse external shocks and internal fiscal deficits.

3.5. The Devaluation of 1963

The 1963 devaluation episode can easily be analyzed since it represents a textbook case of incompatibility between exchange rate, credit, and fiscal policies. During the years prior to this exchange rate crisis, external factors played no role whatever. The terms of trade remained quite stable between 1957 and 1962. External credit increased as of 1960 and became over-abundant during 1961 and 1962 (see Table 7.2).

The fixing of the rate of exchange in 1959 produced an immediate effect on price levels, the rate of inflation dropping from 33% in 1959 to 5.5% in 1960. An important part of this quick reaction is accounted for by the liberalization of foreign trade, implemented in 1959, beginning to show its effects in 1960.

The causes of the exchange crisis may be understood by inspection of the fiscal and credit policy variables: central bank credit in favor of the public sector grew by 14% and 68% during 1959 and 1960, respectively, and credit to the private sector by 40% during 1961. As a consequence, after two years, the central bank had no reserves left, reserves becoming negative in 1961. The external payments' crisis exploded at the end of this year.

The authorities were reluctant to devalue and, instead, decided to reestablish foreign trade controls, with prohibitions on certain imports, imposition of the prior deposits on imports, and other administrative measures. Instead of restricting public expense in 1962, central bank credit toward this sector was expanded by 115%, which was possible because external credit continued to flow in large amounts. Nontheless, international reserves increased slightly, reaching only 0.4 months of imports during the same year.

Despite the low rate of devaluation in 1962, the inflation rate increased from 9.6% to 27% as a consequence of greater restrictions imposed on imports. These restrictions allowed the devaluation to be postponed only for one year. The official price of foreign exchange was devalued by 70% in 1963.

Table 7.2

Policies	1956	1957	1958	1959	1960	1961	1962
Exchange rate							
Official rate (change in %)	77	46	25	32	0	0	9
Deval. rate (+), Reval. rate (−) (%) (real terms)	−3.7	6.0	6.7	−0.4	−24.9	−5.2	−0.5
Fiscal							
Rate of change CBCG[a] (%)	20	57	44	147	68	29	115
Credit							
Rate of change CBCP[b] (%)	84	55	1	24	2	40	33
External factors							
Change in foreign debt (U.S.$ mill.)	7	64	37	25	76	264	245
Capital inflows/GDP	0.3	2.2	1.4	0.7	1.9	4.1	2.7
Terms of trade (index)	1.54	1.17	1.02	1.14	1.14	1.11	1.12
Rate of change WPI, U.S.A. (%)	3.3	2.9	1.4	0.2	0.1	−0.4	0.3
Results							
Rate of change in GDP (%)	1.2	7.9	2.8	0.5	7.3	5.6	4.0
Change in int. res. (U.S.$ mill.)	−7	−49	3	76	−33	−78	10.2
Int. res./av. monthly imports	2.7	0.8	0.9	3.3	1.8	−0.1	0.4
Rate of change CPI, Chile (%)	37.7	17.2	32.5	33.2	5.5	9.6	27.7

Source: See Table 7.1.
[a]CBCG: Central bank credit to the public sector.
[b]CBCP: Central bank credit to the private sector.

3.6. The Devaluations of 1967, 1968, and 1972

During 1965 and 1966, expansive financial policies were implemented. Credit granted by the central bank to the public sector was expanded by 46% and 41% and, at the same time, credit granted to the private sector increased by 77% and 79%. This credit expansion was not reflected by the rate of inflation, which dropped from 39% in 1964 to 17% in 1966. This was achieved, in part, by the prevailing revaluation policy. The exchange policy was intended to decrease the rhythm of inflation, but without the appropriate credit policy during 1967 reserves were lost despite the strong rise in the terms of trade (see Table 7.3).

The authorities then reversed their policies. During 1967 and 1968, they tightened credit and devalued. Expansion of public credit dropped to 27%, and private credit to 9%, during 1968. Real devaluations amounted to 8% and 11% during 1967 and 1968. Although these policies curbed the rate of growth of GDP, which had jumped 11% in 1966, to approximately 3.5% during the three following years, they succeeded in reversing the decreasing trend in international reserves.

The two following years (1969 and 1970) had highly favorable external factors for the balance of payments. The terms of trade registered the highest values in the history of this index. Also, external credit flowed abundantly, reflected in an increase in foreign debt from U.S.$1,900 million in 1967 to $3,100 million in 1970. The authorities reacted to this by slackening exchange and credit policies in the presence of a substantial increase in international reserves, which reached a level of 5.5 months of imports—the highest value for this variable since 1945.

The combination of policies adopted during 1971 guaranteed an external payments' crisis. Furthermore, external factors worsened the crisis. Credit granted by the central bank to the public sector was expanded by 212%, to the private sector by 60%. As a consequence of the exchange policy of a 24% revaluation, such an expansion did not fully show up in the level of prices; on the contrary, the rate of inflation dropped from 35% to 22%.

In the external sector, the terms of trade dropped by 25% and the capital account had a negative balance equal to 0.3% of GDP. These factors, together with the expansionary credit policies, brought about a drop of international reserves amounting to U.S.$230 million, reducing the reserve level to 2.2 months of imports. Despite all the controls established on foreign trade and on exchange operations, the loss of reserves continued at a growing pace, finally bringing about a devaluation equal to 71% in 1972.

Table 7.3

Policies	1965	1966	1967	1968	1969	1970	1971
Exchange rate							
Official rate (change in %)	25	23	26	35	33	29	3
Dev. rate (+), Reval. rate (−)(%) (real rate in %)	−9.7	−2.2	7.7	10.7	4.0	−0.2	−23.6
Fiscal							
Rate of Change CBCG[a] (%)	46	41	34	27	30	43	212
Credit							
Rate of Change CBCP[b] (%)	77	79	64	9	39	22	60
External factors							
Change in foreign debt (U.S.$ mill.)	146	71	56	293	488	434	73
Capital inflows/GDP (%)	1.1	2.5	1.9	4.2	2.9	3.2	−0.3
Terms of trade (index)	1.27	1.49	1.48	1.52	1.90	1.70	1.35
Rate of change RPI, U.S.A. (%)	2.0	3.3	0.2	2.5	3.9	3.7	3.3
Results							
Rate of change in GDP (%)	0.6	11.0	3.4	3.3	3.9	2.0	9.1
Change in int. res. (U.S.$ mill.)	52	42	−23	71	160	108	−231
Int. res./av. monthly imports	0.8	1.3	1.0	2.1	4.1	5.5	2.2
Rate of change CPI, Chile (%)							

Source: See Table 7.1.
[a] CBCG: Central bank credit to the public sector.
[b] CBCP: Central bank credit to the private sector.

3.7. The Devaluation of 1982

Being the most recent episode, the 1982 devaluation is still full of "noise" which makes it hard to evaluate. Furthermore, its results and policies have not "decanted" sufficiently to be able to appreciate more clearly the events of these past years. However, we shall try to interpret the events that led to this devaluation, pointing out those which in our opinion appear to be the most important.

The fundamental objectives pursued by the governmental authorities were the stabilization of prices and the growth of output. To achieve these, a series of economic measures, policies, and reforms were implemented. Among them were: an extremely disciplined fiscal policy, a trade policy calling for the liberalization of foreign trade, and a credit policy intended to put an end to financing granted by the central bank.

Such policies were strictly applied, and the planned objectives were reached. The rate of growth of GDP for the years 1977–81 reached an average of 7.9%. The inflation rate was reduced from 340% in 1975 to 10% in 1981 (see Table 7.4). Between 1976 and 1978, policy changes involved a reduction of the fiscal deficit from 2.3% of GDP to 0.8%, a reduction in the stock of credit granted by the central bank to the public sector from 4.8 times M1 to 3.6 times, and a reduction of average tariffs on imports from over 100% in 1973 to 14%. During these years, no progress was made with respect to private credit policy, since the stock of credit granted by the central bank to the private sector increased from 21% of M1 in 1976 to 53% in 1978. The cause of this expansion was the failure in 1977 of the Savings and Loans Associations, which obliged the central bank to expand private credit by 363%.

During 1979, all policies were in full application. The fiscal budget began to show a growing surplus. The economic authorities had full confidence that they had central bank credit under control. This was so true that during the following year the stock of central bank credit to the private sector practically disappeared, and the public sector, for the first time during the history of the bank, decreased its stock of credit in nominal terms.

On the other hand, external factors were very favorable. The terms of trade improved by 42%, and the supply of external credit, which had been very restricted during previous years, started to grow strongly as of 1978, a year during which the favorable balance on the capital account reached over 12% of GDP.

As a result of these policies and of external factors, international reserves increased to 12% of GDP during 1979 or to 8 months of imports, levels that had not been observed since 1944. Results in terms of economic

Table 7.4

Policies	1976	1977	1978	1979	1980	1981	1982
Exchange rate							
Official rate (change in %)	168	65	47	18	5	0	31
Dev. rate (+), Reval. rate (−)(%) (real terms)	−40	−40	−10	−9	−25	−14	+19
Fiscal							
Deficit/GDP (%)	2.3	1.8	0.8	−1.7	−3.1	−1.6	2.4
Rate of change CBCG[a] (%)	132	102	26	10	−1	−32	11
CBCG/M1 (%)	479	470	359	246	151	103	111
Credit							
Rate of change CBCP[b] (%)	88	363	90	67	−94	1,224	122
CBCP/M1 (%)	21	46	53	55	3	29	60
Commercial							
Average tariff (%)	33	22	14	10.5	10.1	10.1	10.1

External factors

Private foreign debt (U.S.$ mill.)	1.063	1.361	2.111	3.435	6.031	10.082	10.531
Total foreign debt (U.S.$ mill.)	5.195	5.434	6.911	8.463	10.987	15.564	17.225
Capital inflow GDP (%)	2.4	3.3	12.3	10.7	8.5	13.3	3.7
Terms of trade (index)	1.02	0.92	0.91	1.29	1.18	0.89	0.73
Rate of change GDP, U.S.A. (%)	5.4	5.5	5.0	2.8	−0.4	1.9	−1.8
Rate of change WPI, U.S.A. (%)	4.6	6.1	7.8	12.5	14.1	8.8	2.4

Results

Rate of change GDP, Chile (%)	3.5	9.9	8.4	8.1	7.4	5.5	−13.9
Int. res/GDP (%)	1.1	2.0	12.1	11.2	14.8	11.4	10.2
Int. res/av. monthly imports	0.9	1.5	7.7	6.6	8.9	6.9	8.6
Current account balance/GDP(%)	1.5	−4.1	−7.1	−5.7	−7.1	−14.6	−9.4
Rate of change CPI, Chile (%)	174	64	30	39	31	10	21

Source: See Table 7.1.
[a]CBCG: Central bank credit to the public sector.
[b]CBCP: Central bank credit to the private sector.

growth were also highly successful, with growth rates maintained over 8% during the last three years. With respect to achievement of stabilization, even though important progress had been made, it seemed that an inflationary rate of under 30% was not attainable.

Why had the stabilization process been curbed? In my opinion the fundamental reason rests in the rapid accumulation of international reserves. While it is true that the favorable fiscal position favored reserve growth, the expansion of demand on the part of the private sector did not. In order to accumulate reserves, it is necessary to generate the corresponding savings; if this cannot be accomplished in a voluntary manner, it must be achieved forcefully. One way of obtaining such savings is through higher taxes.

The authorities considered that reserves had reached levels that were more than adequate and were very confident that they would be able to maintain their fiscal and credit policies. In other words, conditions were favorable for fixing the price of foreign exchange, which they did in June 1979.

In 1981, two events occurred that proved to be fundamental in explaining the change in exchange policy brought about in 1982. On the one hand, the terms of trade collapsed; on the other, central bank credit in favor of the private sector increased strongly. The terms-of-trade index registered a fall equal to 25%, and the credit index registered an increase equal to 1,224% (from 3% of M1 to 29%). The terms-of-trade shock is explained by the international recession, and the credit increase by the backing given by the central bank to prevent the collapse of the local banking system.

During 1982, the terms of trade continued to deteriorate, the flow of external credit was reduced, and the central bank lost complete control over credit. In addition, devaluation expectations started to appear during the second quarter of 1981. The 31% devaluation of 1982 can thus be understood.

4. Conclusions

In considering the major devaluation and revaluation episodes in Chile from 1933 to 1982, we can draw the following conclusions:

1. In some instances, external factors induced fiscal and credit policies that were incompatible with a fixed exchange rate policy. This is the case of the 1950 and 1982 devaluations. In the 1950 case, an attempt was made to compensate a drop in external credit through credit and fiscal expansion. In the 1982 case, the terms of trade worsened jointly with a lower rate of

inflow of foreign capital, which lead to an expansion of credit granted by the central bank to the private sector.

2. In other cases, devaluations have been provoked exclusively by incompatibility of policies, without the presence of external factors. In these cases, the effects upon the real sector of economy were minor. That is, when devaluation was accompanied by the inflow of external credit and/or an improvement in the terms of trade, the rate of growth of GDP decreased, but without becoming negative. This is the case of the devaluations of 1963 and from 1967 to 1968.

3. In the 1972 episode, external factors worsened the conditions, but they did not create the policies of expenditure expansion.

4. Controls placed on external trade succeeded in postponing exchange adjustments but not in avoiding them prior to the devaluations that occurred in 1950, 1963, and 1971.

8

Speculation against the Preannounced Exchange Rate in Mexico: January 1983 to June 1985

Michael Connolly, Arturo Fernández-Pérez,
& the Summer 1985
International Economics Students of ITAM:
Alejandra Alvarado-Ham, Miguel Angel Díaz-Ayala, Felipe Gerardo
Figueroa-Muñoz, Gerardo Freire-Alvarado, Eugenio González-Luna, Juan
Antonio Laguna-Guerrero, Ander Legorreta-Molina, Antonio
Martínez-Mendoza, Diana Mier y Concha, José Pacheco-Meyer, Gabriela
Quesada-Lastiri, Antonia Ruíz-Suarez, Jaime Villaseñor-Zertudie, Juan
Salles-Vincourt, Ricardo Weihmann-Illades, and Martín Werner-Wainfeld

1. Introduction

Following the exchange rate crises of 1982, Mexico explicitly overdevalued the peso at the end of the year to assure a rise in reserves during 1983. The "free" peso rate rose from 49 pesos per U.S. dollar at the end of July 1982 to 150 pesos per dollar on December 31, 1982. Similarly, the "controlled" rate rose from 69.5 to 96.5 pesos per dollar from the end of August to the end of December 1982. Consequently, when the preannounced daily depreciation of the peso equal to 13 centavos per dollar began on January 3, 1983, the peso was undervalued and Bank of Mexico reserves rose

A Fulbright grant and the University of South Carolina provided support for this project. We are pleased to acknowledge this support. Also, we are grateful for the helpful suggestions made by Francisco Gil Díaz, Carlos Noriega, Raúl Solís, and Ignacio Triguirez.

steadily from less than U.S.$1 billion at the end of 1982, to nearly $4 billion by the end of 1983. Foreign reserves continued to rise in 1984 to a maximum of $6.6 billion in November but declined precipitously in December to $5.8 billion. The daily rate of devaluation accelerated from 13 to 17 centavos a day in December, but reserves continued to decline in 1985. Despite a further acceleration in the rate of crawl to 21 pesos per day in March, a series of speculative attacks agains the peso took place in May and June, just prior to the national elections on July 7, 1985. In response, the Bank of Mexico reduced sales of dollars at fixed rates, but allowed the peso to depreciate freely at exchange houses, where a substantial premium reaching 30% was paid to obtain dollars.

Finally, on July 11, 1985, just four days after the election, the "free" rate was abolished, effectively devaluing the rate 30% and letting it float. Following a 20% devaluation of the "controlled" peso on July 24, 1985, the authorities adopted a managed float of the controlled peso where the dollar's price would be determined by a fixing-price auction at the Bank of Mexico every working day at 12:30 p.m. beginning August 5. In these auctions, the price fixing would include the net position of the Bank of Mexico acting as the government's agent, principally selling PEMEX dollar receipts from the export of petroleum. In addition to more active peso devaluation, the governments initiated a dramatic cutback in expenditures in an effort to reduce the fiscal deficit, which had grown to over $6.5 billion in the first six months of 1985, just prior to the July 7 election. This unusually large deficit can partly be explained as a result of downward oil-price shocks reducing petroleum exports. Another factor may be a deliberate lack of fiscal discipline to improve the Partido Revolucionario Institucional's standing in the upcoming election. Whatever the case, by early August 1985 the 30-month Mexican experiment with a preannounced crawl in the exchange rate came to a dramatic end.[1] Table 8.1 summarizes Mexican exchange rate policy during the period.

In this chapter, we attempt to identify the causes of the collapse of the system. Briefly, we identify three important factors

1.   Unfavorable oil price shocks.
2.   A rising fiscal deficit, particularly in 1985.
3.   A too-expansionary domestic credit policy, given the rate of devalua-
     tion.

The plan of the chapter is as follows. Section 2 discusses some analytical aspects of a preannounced crawl in the exchange rate, Section 3 presents the empirical evidence, Section 4 discusses real wages and adjustment, and Section 5 makes concluding remarks.

Table 8.1 Selected Exchange and Monetary Policy Actions

Changes during 1982

February 18	The Bank of Mexico stopped intervening on the exchange market. The next day, the peso depreciated from 26.86 to 38.1 per U.S. dollar.
June 5	The Bank of Mexico resumed intervention on the exchange market with a policy of a 4 centavo daily depreciation of the peso in terms of the dollar.
August 5	Dual exchange rates were introduced with a preferential rate of 49 pesos per dollar for exports of petroleum debt service, public borrowing, and priority imports and a freely floating rate for all other transactions. Commercial banks were required to surrender net foreign exchange holdings, and also gold and silver.
August 13	Mexdollars no longer convertible into U.S. dollars but into pesos at the preferential rate of 69.50 per Mexdollar.
September 1	By Presidential decree, generalized exchange controls were established. Transactions in dollars limited to $5,000. Accounts and loans could only be in pesos, with exceptions made for foreign embassies, press correspondents, export in-bond, and tourism industries.
November 3	In the border and free-trade zones, the exchange rate was allowed to be determined freely by supply and demand.
December 13	Controlled and free foreign exchange rates were established. The controlled rate applied to exports, priority imports, and principal and interest payments. Other transactions would take place at the free rate. Individuals could purchase $1,000 maximum per transaction; firms, $5,000 with no limits placed on the number of transactions. The free rate was to be set by supply and demand.
December 17	Forward exchange transactions were banned.
December 20	The Bank of Mexico set controlled rates of 95.1 pesos per dollar, and a selling price of 150 pesos per dollar in the "free" market and a buying price of 148.5.

Changes during 1983

| January 3 | From this day on, the controlled rate was to be devalued by 13 centavos daily, including Saturdays and Sundays, from a base of 96.92, the previous day's rate. |
| September 23 | The "free" rate to be devalued 13 centavos daily from a base of 149.1 per dollar. |

Table 8.1 *(continued)*

Changes during 1984	
December 6	Both the "free" and controlled rates were to be devalued at 17 centavos daily.
Changes during 1985	
March 6	The rate of devaluation was raised from 17 to 21 centavos per day.
July 11	The "free" market was closed, effectively floating the "free" rate at the Exchange Houses, equivalent to a 35% devaluation.
July 24	The controlled rate was devalued 20%, and the rate of crawl left at 21 centavos a day until August 4.
August 4	The controlled rate was to be determined by a daily price fixing auction held at 12:30 p.m. at the Bank of Mexico, with the Bank of Mexico taking a net position in the fixing. The rate of devaluation accelerated.

Source: IMF, *Exchange Arrangements and Exchange Restrictions,* Annual Reports, 1982–84. For 1985, *El Inversionista Mexicano.*

2. Analytical Aspects of a Crawling-Peg Exchange Rate

In a simple model where individuals can hold domestic currency (pesos) and foreign currency (U.S. dollars) the share of pesos held in an individual's portfolio depends largely upon the expected rate of depreciation of the peso in terms of the dollar. With a rise in the price of the dollar equal to γ per period, the crawling-peg rule is given by:

$$r = \bar{r}\, e^{\gamma t} \tag{1}$$

(Crawling-Peg Exchange Rate)

where r is pesos per dollar and $\bar{r}$ the initial exchange rate. Similarly, we may indicate the domestic credit policy by:

$$C = \bar{C}\, e^{(\gamma + \varepsilon)t} \tag{2}$$

(Domestic Credit Policy)

where $\bar{C}$ is the initial level of domestic credit, C, and $\gamma + \varepsilon$ is the rate of growth of domestic credit. If individuals divide their monetary wealth between pesos, M, and dollars, F, according to the expected rate of crawl, we have

$$\frac{W}{r} = \frac{M}{r} + \frac{F}{r} = \omega \tag{3}$$

$$= k\omega + (1 - K)\omega$$

(Wealth Portfolio)

where $K = k(\dot{r})$ and $k'(\dot{r}) < 0$, and ω is a fixed amount of real wealth. During the crawl in the exchange rate, $\dot{r} = \gamma$.

Finally, from the balance sheet of the monetary sector, we have the following identity:

$$M = m(C + R) \tag{4a}$$

(The Money Supply Identity)

where m is the money multiplier, R is the peso value of dollar reserves held by the Bank of Mexico, and C is, once again, domestic credit of the Bank of Mexico. Alternatively, we may use the identity from the consolidated banking system, which aggregates the balance sheets of the central bank and the commercial banking system:

$$M = \hat{C} + \hat{R} \tag{4b}$$

(Consolidated Banking System Identity)

where $\hat{C}$ is domestic credit of the consolidated banking system, and $\hat{R}$ is foreign reserves held by the consolidated banking system.

In light of equation (3)—the portfolio constraint—nominal money demand will be growing at the rate γ during the crawl in the exchange rate. However, from the money supply identities (4a) and/or (4b), if domestic credit is rising at the rate $\gamma + \varepsilon$, and if ε is positive, domestic reserves in dollars will fall at the rate:

$$R/r = (\bar{M}/\bar{r}) - (\bar{C}/\bar{r})e^{\varepsilon t} \tag{5}$$

(Path of Reserves in Dollars
during the Crawl in the Exchange Rate)

(see Connolly and Taylor, 1984, for a detailed analysis). Reserves will decline continuously according to (5) until a point in time where a sudden speculative attack depletes remaining reserves at:

$$t^* = \ln\left[(k_2/k_1)(\bar{R}/\bar{C} + 1)\right]/\varepsilon \qquad (6)$$

(Timing of the Speculative Attack)

where k_2/k_1 equals the ratio of pesos held in the individual's portfolio after and before the collapse into floating exchange rates. Since the rate of devaluation will accelerate to $\gamma + \varepsilon$ after the collapse, $k_2/k_1 < 1$. The ratio $\bar{R}/\bar{C}$ measures initial reserves as a proportion of domestic credit, and ε measures growth in domestic credit minus the rate of depreciation during the crawl in the exchange rate.

Clearly, this simplistic model does not take into account other important factors determining reserve behavior in Mexico such as oil price shocks, but it does highlight domestic monetary considerations.

Another aspect of the crawling-peg model that deserves attention is the behavior of the price of home or nontraded goods relative to the price of traded goods during the crawling-peg experiment. In particular, it can be shown in a Walrasian model that the relative price of nontraded goods will rise during the crawl in the exchange rate if $\varepsilon > 0$, then will fall at the point of collapse into floating exchange rates. Specifically, if we indicate the price in pesos of nontraded goods by p, the path of the relative price of home goods during the crawl is indicated by:

$$p/r = \bar{p}/\bar{r} + \phi e^{\varepsilon t}$$

(Relative Price of Nontraded Goods)

(see Connolly and Taylor, 1984).

Consequently when $\varepsilon < 0$, or domestic credit grows more rapidly than the exchange rate, a rise in the relative price of home goods takes place. In terms of indices, we would expect the ratio of the consumer price index in pesos to rise more than the U.S. CPI converted into pesos by the exchange rate; that is, a rise in P/rP^*. This is also known as the real exchange rate; consequently, with $\varepsilon > 0$ we would expect an appreciation of the real exchange rate in Mexico during the crawl. That is, the peso price of the dollar would rise less than the inflation rate differential between Mexico and the United States. Furthermore, the degree of appreciation would be related to growth in domestic credit less the rate of devaluation.

3. Empirical Results

In December 1982, Mexico devalued the "free" peso from 70 to 150 pesos per dollar, and the controlled peso from 50 to 96.5, just prior to beginning the active crawl of 13 centavos per day. As a result, the peso was undervalued during 1983 and reserves grew rapidly. Table 8.2 illustrates the behavior of net foreign reserves held by the Bank of Mexico. Using the "free" rate as a benchmark, the difference between Bank of Mexico domestic credit growth and the rate of crawl was an average of 0.65% per month, while domestic credit growth of the consolidated banking sector less the rate of crawl was 1.55%. The Bank of Mexico created domestic credit only about ½% greater than the monthly rate of devaluation, while the consolidated banking sector created domestic credit about 1½% per month more rapidly than the rate of crawl. This latter rate, which was particularly high in 1984, may not be consistent with balance-of-payments equilibrium so that a reserve loss would be expected. Furthermore, the real exchange rate would also be expected to rise during the crawl.

Figure 8.1 displays the behavior of net reserves of the Bank of Mexico. Thanks to the overdevaluation of the peso at the end of 1982, reserves grew the first year and a half of the crawl from January 1983 until late 1984 when they began declining in November. The decline in late 1984 was precipitous and continued until February. After a slight recovery in March, reserves continued to be attacked in May, June, and July. It should also be noted that in February 1985 the price of oil fell from $29 to $27.75, representing a negative real shock to Mexican reserves. Over the period November 1984 to June 1985, Mexican reserves fell over $2 billion, that is, the Bank of Mexico sold $2 billion to maintain the crawling-peg rate before adopting a floating exchange rate. The path of reserves started downward later than expected according to the model, but the decline was precipitous when it began, as a result of speculative attacks. However, the Bank of Mexico reduced its sale of reserves and nearly stopped selling dollars

Table 8.2   Epsilon Values, 1 January 1983 to 29 June 1985

ϵ	Bank of Mexico (% per month)	Consolidated banking sector (% per month)
Free	0.65	1.55
Controlled	0.59	1.49

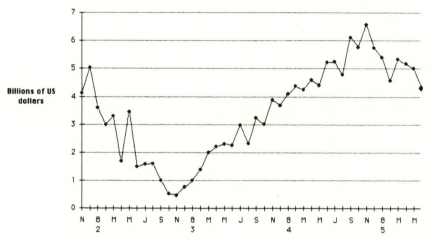

Figure 8.1   Bank of Mexico reserves.

altogether toward the end of the crawl in June and July. Instead, adjustment came about via a rise in the Exchange House Rate where the premium over the "free" rate grew steadily from a 3% premium in November 1984 to a 29% premium in June 1985.

   With a positive ε for the consolidated banking sector, we would also expect to observe a real exchange rate appreciation during the crawling peg, and, further, the real exchange rate should depend upon the level of domestic credit relative to the exchange rate, or C/r. With a positive ε, C/r rises.

   Figure 8.2 charts the real exchange rate, P/rP^*, by month from 1982 to 1985. The preannounced crawl began in January 1983, and we do indeed observe a steady appreciation in the rates—both the "controlled" and the "free" real exchange rates in Figure 8.2. For the floating rate at the Exchange Houses, the collapse shows up as an abrupt real exchange rate depreciation in May and June of 1985. In terms of the set rates, they depreciate also in these months, but to a lesser degree. After June, the "free" rate was abolished, and the "controlled" rate was first devalued 20% and then set by a daily price-fixing auction at the Bank of Mexico beginning August 5, 1985. The auction involved a much more rapid rate of devaluation than with the crawl, perhaps twice the rate of devaluation.

   Finally, the real exchange rate depreciation is indeed related to the ε values, as confirmed by the following monthly regressions during the active crawl. Equation (7) uses domestic credit of the Bank of Mexico and the "free" rate:

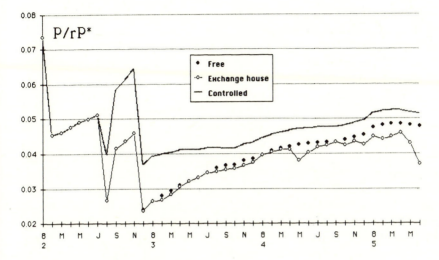

Figure 8.2   The real exchange rate in Mexico

Bank of Mexico

$$\ln(P/rp^*) = -3.02 + 0.85 \ln(C/r) \tag{7}$$
$$(-11.87)\ (5.20)$$

$R^2 = 0.56$ (t statistics in parentheses)   DW = 0.48   d.f. = 22

Equation (8) uses domestic credit of the consolidated banking sector and also the "free" rate:

Consolidated Banking System

$$\ln(P/rP^*) = -7.48 + 1.14 \ln(\hat{C}/\hat{r}) \tag{8}$$
$$(-50.19)\ (28.20)$$

$R^2 = 0.97$ d.f. = 22   DW = 1.66

Both regressions were for the 24-month period January 1983 to December 1984.[2]

The more rapid growth in domestic credit than of the rate of devaluation is clearly associated with the real exchange rate appreciation during the crawling peg. This result is consistent with the speculative attack model.

Reserves began declining gradually in mid-1984, then fell precipitously toward the end of the year and the beginning of 1985. The explanatory factors are (1) slightly more rapid growth in domestic credit than exchange rate devaluation, (2) a decline in the world price of petroleum, and (3) an extremely large ($6.5 billion) fiscal deficit in the first 6 months of 1985. The latter cannot have failed to ignite speculative expectations and behavior.

4. Domestic Credit and the Fiscal Deficit

If domestic credit growth is partly responsible for the collapse in Mexico's crawling peg, it is important to know what causes domestic credit to grow. Firstly, changes in domestic credit of the Bank of Mexico are, in part, closely linked to financing the fiscal deficit of the government. In terms of a linear regression of the monthly change in domestic credit of the Bank of Mexico as the dependent variable, with the fiscal deficit of the same and the previous month as the independent variables, we have:

Bank of Mexico

$$\Delta C = 1.13 + 0.66FD \qquad\qquad (9)$$
$$(0.04)\ \ (4.72)$$

$$R^2 = 0.37 \qquad DW = 2.47 \qquad d.f. = 21$$

where FD represents the fiscal deficit. Consequently, an extra million pesos of this month's deficit increases domestic credit extended by the Bank of Mexico by 660,000 pesos. This is a measure of inflationary finance of the Bank of Mexico.

Domestic credit growth of the consolidated banking sector is even more closely linked to the fiscal deficit, as reported in equation (10):

Consolidated Banking System

$$\Delta\hat{C} = 98.8 + 0.94FD \qquad\qquad (10)$$
$$\phantom{\Delta\hat{C} =}(2.36)\ \ (5.05)$$

$$R^2 = 0.41 \qquad DW = 2.17 \qquad d.f. = 21$$

The current deficit raises total domestic credit nearly by the same amount.

This evidence clearly suggests that a major cause of the problem of excess domestic credit growth is the fiscal deficit. Consequently, to reduce domestic credit growth, the most obvious place to start is by reducing the fiscal deficit. This is indeed the objective of the new austerity program initiated in July 1985. Figure 8.3 shows the rising fiscal deficit prior to the July 7 elections.

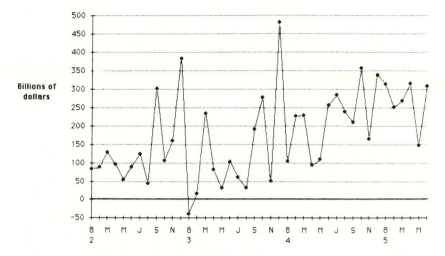

Figure 8.3   Fiscal deficit in Mexico.

5.   Adjustment and Real Wages

In 1982, Mexico experienced an economic crisis and took measures that had permanent repercussions on the economy. In that year real output declined 1%, and in 1983 gross domestic product fell a further 5%. At the end of 1981, the real minimum wage was at a level of 89; by the end of 1982, it had fallen to 76. By the end of 1983, it was even lower, at 61; and at the end of 1984, it was 60. The real minimum wage has since recovered somewhat to a level of 73 in June 1985. While this index is not an ideal measure of real wages, many people are employed at the minimum wage, so that its decline over the past 3 years does suggest a dramatic fall in the standard of living of the Mexican worker. Figure 8.4 documents this decline. The new austerity program clearly cannot reverse this decline. Real wages, rather than the level of employment, have adjusted downward during Mexico's contraction.

6.   Conclusion

In terms of the conduct of monetary policy, domestic credit grew slightly too fast during the sliding exchange rate in Mexico from January 1983 to June 1985. Falling oil prices and the large fiscal deficit in the 6 months prior to the July 7, 1985, election compounded the problem. The failure to

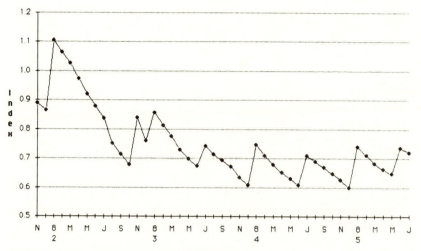

Figure 8.4   Real minimum wage in Mexico.

introduce an adjustment program sooner—in particular, prior to the election—condemned the preannounced system of exchange rates to be attacked by speculators, which led to its collapse into floating. It may well be that a preannounced crawling exchange rate is inevitably unsuccessful because of pressures, on the one hand, to expand credit to finance the fiscal deficit and, on the other, to keep a low rate of devaluation for political purposes. This leads to inconsistency in the management of a crawling peg. For this reason, a floating exchange rate may be easier to manage.

Notes

[1]A brief bibliography containing discussions of Mexico's exchange rate policy is provided at the end of the chapter.

[2]When the regressions are run in terms of differences in logarithms, we have

$$\ln(P/rP^*) = -5.12 + 0.52 \ln C + 0.13 \ln r$$
$$ (-0.49) \quad (4.50) \qquad (0.69)$$

$$R^2 = 0.89 \qquad \rho = 0.37$$

for Bank of Mexico credit, and

$$\ln(P/rP^*) = -7.45 + 1.15 \ln \hat{C} - 1.16 \ln r$$
$$ (-29.13) \, (13.94) \qquad (-6.93)$$

$$R^2 = 0.97 \qquad \rho = 0.16$$

for the consolidated banking sector. In both cases, domestic credit is significant so the result does not hinge upon having the same term, r, on both sides of the equation. With the crawling peg, r is exogenous as is, in principle, C, so the equations are reduced forms.

Bibliography

Blanco, Herminio, and Peter Garber (1986). "Recurrent Devaluation and Speculative Attacks on the Mexican Peso." *Journal of Political Economy* 94(1): 148–66.

Connolly, Michael, and Charles Lackey (1984). "Presiones en el Mercado Cambiario de México: 1955–82." In *México: Una Economía en Transición*, edited by Alejandro Violante and Roberto Dávila. Mexico City: Editorial Limusa.

Connolly, Michael, and Dean Taylor (1984). "The Exact Timing of the Collapse of an Exchange Rate Regime and Its Impact on the Relative Price of Traded Goods." *Journal of Money, Credit and Banking* (May): 194–207.

Gil Díaz, Francisco (1984). "Mexico's Path from Stability to Inflation." In *World Economic Growth*, edited by Arnold Harberger. San Francisco: Institute for Contemporary Economics.

Gómez de Reyes, María Teresa (1985). "Experiencias de Políticas de Estabiliza-ción: Los Casos de Argentina, Chile, México y Uruguay." Serie Cuadernos de Investigación, Centro de Estudios Monetarios Latinoamericanos, Mexico City, No. 3, June.

González, Jesus Cervantes, and Federico Rubli Kaiser (1984). "El Uso de Canastas de Moneda en la Política Cambiaria de las Economías en Desarrollo." Análisis Económico, Universidad Autónoma Metropolitana, No. 2, June–December.

Ortiz-Martínez, Guillermo (1983). "Currency Substitution in Mexico: The Dollar-ization Problem." *Journal of Money, Credit and Banking* 15(2): 174–85.

Pérez-Porrua, Juan Manuel (1983). "El Enfoque Monetario de la Balanza de Pagos Bajo Expectativas Racionales." Research Department, Banco de México, Mexico City.

Rodríguez, Flavia (1984). "Crecimiento Económico en Economías con Problemas de Deuda Externa." Serie Cuadernos de Investigaciones, Centro de Estudios Monetarios Latinoamericanos, Mexico City, No. 1, November.

Solís, José F. (1985). "Factores Explicativos del Tipo de Cambio: el Caso de México." *Monetaria* 8(2) (April–June): 209–226.

Appendix: Data Sources

Consumer Price Index, Mexico: *Indicadores Económicos del Banco de México*.

Consumer Price Index, U.S.A.: *International Financial Statistics*, line 64.

Domestic Credit of the Bank of Mexico: *International Financial Statistics*, line 12a plus line 12e plus line 12f.

Domestic Credit of the Consolidated Banking System: *International Financial Statistics*, line 32.

Exchange Rate (pesos/dollar):
  (a) "Free" and "controlled": Subdirección de Investigación Económica del Banco de México, average of buy and sell rates at end of month.
  (b) Exchange House: Subdirección de Investigación Económica del Banco de México and Secretaría de Hacienda de Crédito Público, average of buy and sell rates at end of month at exchange houses in the north frontier of Mexico.

Fiscal Deficit: *Indicadores Económicos del Banco de México*.

Foreign Reserves in Dollars, Mexico: *International Financial Statistics*, line 11 minus line 16c, and Bank of Mexico.

Interest Rates, Mexico: *Certificados de Bonos del Tesoro* (CETES)

Interest Rates, U.S.A.: *Economic Report of the President*, 1984, and *Survey of Current Business*, Treasury Bill rate.

M1 (Narrow Money): *Indicadores Económicos del Banco de México*.

Minimum Wage, Mexico: Comisión Nacional de Salarios Mínimos.

Petroleum Prices: PEMEX, export price of Itsmo-type petroleum.

IV

THE ECONOMICS OF THE DOMINICAN REPUBLIC

9

Monetary Policy, "Dollarization," and Parallel Market Exchange Rates: The Case of the Dominican Republic

Víctor Canto

The experience of floating rates and dual exchange rate regimes has been characterized by the seemingly positive relationship between government restrictions on foreign exchange markets and the stability of those markets. The apparent instability in the exchange rate market can be attributed in part to currency-substitution effects that result in shifts in domestic money demand resulting from variations in the opportunity costs of holding the various monies. Although the currency-substitution literature is capable of explaining the so-called dollarization phenomenon, it fails to explain and/or account for the degree of government intervention in the foreign exchange market as well as the effect of the government actions in the determination of the level of the exchange rate.

The purpose of this chapter is to develop and estimate an exchange rate model that accounts for the "dollarization " phenomena as well as the domestically imposed transactions costs on the use of the foreign currency.[1]

The theoretical framework views the process of exchange rate determination as a monetary phenomenon. The model developed is sufficiently general to account for various alternative views. In contrast to the standard monetary approach to exchange rate determination, the formulation presented does not explicitly assume a preferred habitat view of money demand, whereby the domestic currency is the only medium of exchange used for domestic transactions. Following Calvo and Rodríguez (1977), Miles (1978), Girton and Roper (1981), the model developed in this chapter allows for the possibility of currency switching.

The chapter is organized as follows. Section 1 discusses some of the institutional arrangements that may exist in a developing nation. More specifically, since the model is estimated using data from the Dominican Republic, this section will stylize the Dominican Republic features. Section 2 develops a theoretical model which determines the currency choice. The effects of monetary policy and of restrictions on the use of the foreign currency for domestic transactions on the "parallel" market exchange rates are established.

In Section 3, following the methodology developed by Box and Jenkins (1976), the model is estimated using monthly data spanning the period June 1969 to April 1979. The estimated coefficients are then used to make inferences about alternative hypotheses developed in the previous section. The empirical results are consistent with the implications of the model developed in this chapter for the case in which both the elasticity of substitution between domestic and foreign monies and the responsiveness of the transaction costs to exchange rate levels are large.

Section 4 presents a summary of the conclusions and policy implications of the chapter.

1. Stylized Institutional Features
of the Dominican Republic Parallel Market

Officially, since the creation of its central bank in 1948, the Dominican Republic has maintained a one-to-one parity with the U.S. dollar. The initial arrangement that prevailed was to allow the peso and the dollar to circulate hand in hand for a few years, at which point the Dominican peso became the legal tender. This period was characterized by the absence of foreign exchange restrictions, and the balance of payments behaved along the lines suggested by the monetary approach to the balance of payments.

However, since the early 1960s the seigniorage has not been sufficiently large to finance the government budget deficits, and as a result the Dominican monetary authorities have increased the money supply growth at a rate faster than the amount required to maintain external balance. To protect the central bank reserves, in 1967 after the civil war and U.S. interventions, the authorities enacted a series of restrictions on foreign deposit ownership.[2] Throughout this period the Dominican monetary authorities had pursued a dual exchange rate system whereby the central bank provided foreign exchange at the official parity rate to activities deemed important to the economic development plans of the country. Importation of all other goods and services (as well as private capital flows) were allowed as long as importers provided their own foreign exchange. Largely as a result of this policy, the Dominican Republic simultaneously experienced fluctuations in the black-market exchange rate, as well as in the balance of payments. The dual exchange rate policy resulted in a weakening of the economy balance-of-payments adjustment mechanism to excessive domestic credit creation while simultaneously strengthening the role of the black market as an equilibrating mechanism to excessive domestic credit creation.

Throughout the period analyzed in this chapter (June 1969 to April 1979), the Dominican authorities did not attempt to directly regulate the black market, nor did they alter the official exchange rate.[3] In this regard, up to 1979, the Dominican experience has been different from that of a crawling peg or managed float experienced by many countries during the last decade.[4] Even though in principle illegal, the black market was allowed to operate freely in order to alleviate the pressures on the central bank. Furthermore, the market was officially renamed the "parallel market" in order to eliminate the connotation implicit in the old name.

There are several institutional features of the parallel market worth noting. First, since there were no "official" exchange rate locations, the market had produced its own conveniently located houses of exchange. Second, since there were no restrictions to entry, individual transactors could be found in major tourist stops, outside hotels, banks, and other centrally located places. Third, the exchange price was subject to negotiation, and as a result the price differed not only across locations but also across transactions in a given location. Fourth, while the monetary authorities allowed dollar deposits in domestic banks, these could not be used to settle domestic transactions. Thus domestic transactions settled in foreign currency had to take the form of cash payments or checks drawn on foreign banks. The central bank was able to collect daily information from the major foreign exchange dealers on the average transaction price.

Interestingly, during the 1969–79 period, many of the institutional features of the Dominican Republic closely resembled those assumed in the rational expectations literature, such as the informationally separated markets, the lack of a forward foreign exchange, and the unweighted market index for the exchange rate.

In the first half of 1979, a new administration instituted import controls and tightened further the foreign exchange restrictions. The import prohibitions greatly reduced the government tax revenues; this combined with the new administration expenditure and employment programs resulted in record deficits. The monetization of the budget deficits created severe balance-of-payment problems; as a result, the Dominican Republic central bank did not meet its international obligations. Largely as a result of the monetization of the deficit during the last couple of years, the exchange rate depreciated at what is considered by

Dominican standards an unprecedented rate. In attempts to control the rate of depreciation the authorities abandoned the previous policy of not interfering directly in the market.[5]

2.   The Model

The model is characterized by the following equations:

$$p^d = e + p^f \tag{1}$$

$$[P^d - E(P^d)] - [P^f - E(P^f)] = e - E(e) \tag{2}$$

$$L^J = aY^J - b[E(P^d) - P] \tag{3}$$

$$L_d^d - L^d = \gamma^d - \phi(1 - \alpha)\{[E(P^d) - P^d] - [E(P^f) - P^f] - \tau\} \tag{4}$$

$$L_f^d - L^d = \gamma^f + \phi\alpha\{[E(P^d) - P^d] - [E(P^f) - P^f] - \tau\} \tag{5}$$

$$\tau = \mu_1 e - \mu_2\{[E(P^d) - P^d] - [E(P^f) - P^f]\} \tag{6}$$

$$M^d - p^d = L_d^d \tag{7}$$

$$M^f - p^f = sL^f + (1 - s)L_f^d \tag{8}$$

$$M^f - p^f = L^f \tag{8'}$$

where p^d and p^f denote the logarithm of the domestic and foreign price level; e the logarithm of the parallel market exchange rate; E the expectation operator; L^J the logarithm of country J's demand for real balances; a the income elasticity of demand for real balances; Y^J the logarithm of country J's real income; b the semi-elasticity of demand for real balances; L_f^d, L_d^d the logarithm of the small country derived demand for foreign and domestic real balances; γ_1^f, γ^d a parameter denoting the efficiency of foreign and domestic money in the production of real balances; ϕ the elasticity of substitution between domestic and foreign money; $1 - \alpha$ the share of foreign money in the production of real balances; τ the transaction costs on the use of foreign money imposed by the domestic monetary authorities; μ_1 the elasticity of transaction cost to changes in the exchange rate; μ_2 the semi-elasticity of transaction cost due to inflation rate differential across countries; M^f, M^d the logarithm of the nominal stock of foreign and domestic money; and s the relative size of the country issuing the international medium.

The economy is characterized as a small open economy. Since we do not allow for the existence of nontraded goods, in the absence of any frictions international commodity arbitrage and capital mobility will result in the law of one price [equations (1) and (2)].[6]

Recently, Thomas (1984) has shown that the composition of an investor's asset portfolio is independent of his currency holding or the transaction services that the currencies provide. He argues that increases in foreign currency holding could be financed entirely by foreign borrowing. His results show that one can separate the transaction motive from the portfolio motive. He also shows that the concept of currency substitution and/or dollarizations can only be explained in the context of transaction cost motives. For this reason we assume that currencies reduce frictional losses from transacting in the goods markets [equation (3)]. Within this framework economic agents hold each currency until the marginal unit of the currency produces transaction services equal in value to its holding costs. For ease of exposition, it is assumed that the real incomes of both the rest of the world and the small country are fixed at their full employment levels.

Throughout the chapter the world supply of a given money is assumed to be noninterest-bearing and under control of the relevant monetary authorities. Two countries are initially assumed; one country's currency is used as the international medium of exchange. Thus in what follows we assume that residents of the countries issuing the international medium of exchange will have no need to diversify their currency holding for transaction purposes.

To allow for switching among the different monies by local residents, the demand for real balances is assumed to be of the constant elasticity of substitution variety. Equations (4) and (5) characterize, in log-linear form, the derived demand for each of the two currencies.

To prevent the displacement of the local currency, the monetary authorities of the small open economy impose restrictions on the use of foreign currency in domestic transaction. In addition, the authorities also attempt to regulate the stock as well as the flow of foreign currency held by domestic residents. Therefore, the government may influence the stock of foreign currency circulating in the economy through the imposition of restrictions (e.g., transaction costs) that reduce the convenience of holding foreign currency. We find it plausible to model such a tax as proportional to the value exchange rate in the parallel market. Similarly, the flow of foreign exchange may be regulated by capital controls. Equation (6) represents our attempt to model the transaction costs imposed by the monetary authorities in order to prevent the erosion of the inflation tax base.

Worldwide equilibrium requires the equality of the world demand for the two real monies with the world money supply. Equation (7) reflects the assumption that the small country currency is held only by domestic residents. On the other hand, equation (8) indicates that the world demand for the other currency depends on the rest-of-the-world demand for that currency as well as the small country demand for the foreign currency. That is, the world demand for the international currency is a weighted average of the individual countries' demands for that currency. To the extent that the open economy in question is small, its effect in the determination of the equilibrium condition for the international currency will be negligible. Thus, the world demand for the international currency may be safely approximated by the rest-of-the-world demand for that currency (i.e., $s = 1$). Hence, the market clearing condition [equation (8)] may be approximated by equation (8′).

A sufficient number of relationships have been accumulated by now to allow one to derive an expression for the derived demand for domestic currency. Substituting the demand for domestic currency [equation (4)] into the market clearing condition [equation (7)], and the rest-of-the-world demand for dollars into equation (8), one obtains (after some manipulations) the following expression for the parallel market exchange rate:

$$e = \frac{(M^d - M^f) - a(Y^d - Y^f) + [\alpha b + (1 - \alpha)\phi(1 + \mu_2)]Ee}{1 + \alpha b + (1 - \alpha)\phi(1 + \mu_1 + \mu_2)} \tag{9}$$

2.1. Solution to the Market Clearing Exchange Rate under Imperfect Information

Prior to considering the formation of expectations, it is first necessary to specify the process generating the growth of the different monies M^f and M^d. In what follows it is posited that M^f and M^d are a function of a constant growth rate (assumed to be zero for simplicity) and of random terms m^f and m^d, respectively. Thus,

$$M^d_t - M^d_{t-1} = m^d \tag{10}$$

$$M^f_t - M^f_{t-1} = m^f \tag{11}$$

where m^d and m^f are normally distributed white-noise processes with zero mean and constant variances σ_d^2 and σ_f^2, respectively.

To model the functioning of the economy under imperfect information, it is a convenient abstraction to think that economic activity in the economy occurs in a continuum of physically and informationally separated market locations. It is assumed that information flows instantaneously across the agents within any location, but it is propagated to the rest of the economy with a one-period lag. In this set-up, unexploited profits' opportunities will not exist when there is only one price for each location. But prices may differ across locations.

The spot exchange rate is viewed here as resulting from the optimizing behavior of the household under imperfect information. The formation of expectations is assumed to be rational in the sense of Muth (1961). Given current available information, participants in each market use the structure of the economy, which is known to everyone, to form the operational forecast of the exchange rate. Furthermore, actions based on these forecasts generate the assumed structure. The equilibrium values of exchange rates can be shown to be[7]

$$e_t(z) = \frac{(M^d_{t-1} - M^f_{t-1}) - K}{1 + \phi(1 - \alpha)\mu_1} + [m_t^d - m_t^f + \varepsilon_t^d(z) - \varepsilon_t^f(z)]$$

$$\times \frac{1 + (\theta_1 - \theta_2)[\alpha b + (1 - \alpha)\phi(1 + \mu_2)}{1 + \alpha b + (1 - \alpha)\phi(1 + \mu_1 + \mu_2)} \tag{12}$$

In turn, an aggregate spot price index, e_t, can be calculated as a (geometric, unweighted) average of the spot price where the relative disturbance terms $\varepsilon_t^d(z)$ and $\varepsilon_t^f(z)$ are averaged out in determining e_t:

$$e_t(z) = \frac{(M^d_{t-1} - M^f_{t-1}) - K}{1 + \phi(1 - \alpha)\mu_1} + (m_t^d - m_t^f)$$

$$\times \frac{1 + (\theta_1 - \theta_2)[\alpha b + (1 - \alpha)\phi(1 + \mu_2)]}{1 + \alpha b + (1 - \alpha)\phi(1 + \mu_1 + \mu_2} \tag{13}$$

The literature in the monetary approach to exchange rate determination suggests that fully anticipated changes in domestic money supply will have a proportionate effect on the exchange rate (see Mussa, 1976; Bilson,

1979). Similarly, due to imperfect information, this literature suggests that unanticipated changes in domestic money supply will have a positive and less than proportionate effect on exchange rates. Upon inspection of equation (13), it is fairly apparent that these results will obtain only if the domestic residents choose to hold only the domestic currency irrespective of market conditions (i.e., $\alpha = 1$ and $\phi = 0$). Equation (13) suggests that the larger are the magnitude of the elasticity of substitution between the two currencies (ϕ) and the responsiveness of transaction rates to the parallel market exchange rate (μ_1), the smaller will be the impact of anticipated money growth in the exchange rate. Similarly, notice that for large values of ϕ and μ_1, the sign of the effect of unanticipated changes in the money supply approaches $\theta_1 - \theta_2$. Hence, if the foreign money contribution to the exchange rate variance, θ_2, exceeds that of the domestic money, θ_1, the effect of unanticipated changes in the domestic money supply could be negative. These results suggest that both currency substitution and government-induced transaction costs could have a significant effect on the determination of the parallel market exchange rate.

3. Empirical Analysis

The model developed in the previous section is estimated using the methodology developed by Box and Jenkins (1976).

The data in this study come from a variety of sources reporting monthly time-series estimates from June 1969 to March 1979. The data on the exchange rate, e, and money supply for the Dominican Republic, DRM1, were made available by the Dominican Republic Central Bank. The data on the U.S. money supply, USM1, were attained from the Federal Reserve monthly bulletin.

3.1.   The Univariable ARIMA Models for the Different Variables

There are alternative techniques for developing estimates of anticipated and unanticipated changes in economic variables. The approach followed in this chapter is to estimate autoregressive integrating moving average (ARIMA) models for the various series. The fitted values are taken to be the anticipated values for the variables in question, and the innovations in the series are taken to be the unanticipated changes in the series.

The estimated ARIMA models are shown in Table 9.1. The U.S. money supply appears to be adequately represented by an ordinary

Table 9.1 Univariate ARIMA Models for the Different Time Series for the Period Including June 1969 to March 1979

Constant term	$\Delta\Delta_{12}$ ln USM1 suppressed	$\Delta\Delta_{12}$ ln DRM1 suppressed	$\Delta\Delta$ ln e suppressed
Moving average parameters			
θ_1	0.172 (0.098)	–	suppressed
θ_2	–	–	0.184 (0.101)
Seasonal moving average parameter			
θ_{12}	0.706 (0.089)	0.884 (0.0447)	–
Seasonal autoregressive parameters			
π_{12}	–	–	−0.742
$Q^*(12)$	8.28	7.53	9.14
d.f.	(10)	(11)	(10)
P value	0.655	0.767	0.593
Summary statistics			
Adjusted R^2	0.229	0.385	0.190
F	16.6	66.7	13.3
d.f.	(2,103)	(1,104)	(2,103)
Standard error of regression	0.00708	0.0392	0.00921

Note: Standard errors in parentheses below parameter estimates; Δ denotes the first difference operator, $\Delta X_t = X_t - X_{t-1}$; d.f. denotes the degrees of freedom.

moving-average parameter and a seasonal moving parameter. In turn, the Dominican money supply is represented by a seasonal moving-average parameter while the exchange rate is represented by a slightly more complicated model, a seasonal autoregressive parameter and a second-order moving-average parameter. The models shown in Table 9.1 perform reasonably well in removing serial correlations from the respective series. For each equation, no single autocorrelation exceeded the two standard-error limit, and the $Q^*(12)$ is below the expected value under the null hypothesis of no autocorrelations. Additional checks for model adequacy included "overfitting" with additional parameters.

3.2. Causal Structure between the Exchange Rate and the Domestic Money Supply

The stylized facts presented in this chapter suggest a parallel market where the exchange rate is determined by the demand and supply for foreign exchange by the private sector. This does not suggest that the domestic authorities have no bearing on the equilibrium value of the exchange rate. In fact, the model developed suggests two possible avenues; one is the domestic money creation, the other is the imposition of transaction costs on the use of the foreign money in order to prevent the erosion of the inflation tax base. However, to the extent that the transaction costs are imposed to accommodate the excess domestic money creation, then one would expect a causal relationship going from the money supply to the exchange rate.

An alternative view of the stylized facts in other developing countries is as follows: the foreign exchange market is not really a market in the sense that the price is determined by private supplies and demands. The central bank/government sector dominates that market by its own reserve demand behavior. In effect it pegs the foreign exchange rate, allowing the domestic money stock to respond endogenously. From time to time it changes the exchange rate (in some cases, more or less continuously) in order to achieve a desired path for reserves and other domestic variables. The stylized facts suggest a causal relationship going from the exchange rate to the money supply.

Evidence in favor of either hypothesis may be obtained by looking at the causal relationship between the Dominican Republic money supply, DRM1, and the exchange rate, e.

While not the only definition of causality, in what follows the cross-correlation between the prewhitened residuals of estimated ARIMA models for the money supply and exchange rate reported in Table 9.2 are utilized to examine the causal relationship between the Dominican money supply and the exchange rate. Haugh (1976) has shown that the asymptotic distribution of these cross-correlations under the hypothesis that the series are named and independent is the same as the asymptotic distribution of cross-correlations of the true innovations of the respective series. In particular, the sample cross-correlations are asymptotically normal and independent across lags, with mean zero and variance $(N - |K|)^{-1/2}$ for lag K and N observations. In the data the cross-correlations between the DRM1 residuals and the e residuals are fairly small for the preceding month and approximately two standard deviations for the subsequent month. Durbin (1970) has shown that the sample cross-correlations of ARIMA residuals at negative lags no longer have the same distribution as would cross-correlation of true ARIMA innovations, essentially because of

Table 9.2   Cross-correlation between the Prewhitened Values of e and DRM1

Lead	12	0.053
	11	−0.106
	10	0.013
	9	0.040
	8	0.026
	7	−0.203
	6	−0.023
	5	0.110
	4	0.202
	3	−0.063
	2	−0.113
	1	0.080
Concurrent lag	0	−0.201
	1	0.189
	2	−0.075
	3	0.180
	4	−0.022
	5	0.057
	6	0.074
	7	0.193
	8	0.079
	9	−0.062
	10	0.145
	11	−0.011
	12	0.068
Standard error		0.098

dependence between the ARIMA parameter estimates and the cross-correlation estimates. The implication, as pointed out by Pierce (1977), Haugh and Pierce (1977), and Sims (1977) is that the standard error for the negative lag cross-correlation may be less than $(N - |K|)^{-1/2}$. One must therefore be cautious about accepting the hypothesis that the basis of ARIMA correlation is due to one-way causation from DRM1 to e when the alternative is two-way causation. However, given the basic premise that predictive power, if present, is likely to be strongest at low lags, and that over the sample period e is much more predictable from DRM1 than DRM1 from e, there seems to be a strong case for rejecting the hypothesis of no relation to causality running at least from DRM1 to e. Furthermore, the magnitude of the Box–Pierce statistic adjusted for downward bias, $S^\star$, is below its expected value for the 12 leads under the null hypothesis of no autocorrelation with a P value of 0.442. In short, the cross-correlation function suggests a one-way causal relationship going from the money supply to the exchange rate.

3.3. The Transfer Function Model

The cross-correlation function between the exchange rates and the two money series is the data analysis tool employed here for the identification of the transfer function model.[8] The estimated cross-correlation function suggested that the impulse response function for DRM1 may be adequately represented by two coefficients, a contemporaneous coefficient and a one-month lag coefficient. Similarly, the cross-correlation suggests that the impulse response function for USM1 may be adequately represented, at most, by a contemporaneous coefficient.

Three transfer function models are reported in Table 9.3. Upon inspection of the model reported in the first column, it is apparent that the coefficient for the USM1 is imprecisely measured. The second model constrains the USM1 coefficient to be equal to zero.[9] The validity of the restriction imposed in the second model can be tested by examining the ratio of the log-likelihood function of the constrained equation to the unconstrained equation.[10] It leads us to accept the second model over the first. Alternatively stated, no significant relationship between the U.S. money supply and the Dominican exchange rate was found. This result is consistent with the currency substitution hypothesis, which explicitly distinguishes between the U.S. money supply and the world supply of dollars. The currency substitution model argues that the U.S. money supply is endogenously determined; hence no systematic relationship is expected. On the other hand, the world supply of dollars may be exogenously determined, in which case a negative relationship is predicted. The result does not support the negative relationship predicted by the nonsubstitution models, which equate the USM1 with the world supply of dollars.

The transfer function model reported in the second column of Table 9.3 yields a number of interesting results. The first is that the steady-state gain is positive and smaller than unity, as predicted under the hypothesis that there is currency substitution ($\phi > 0$) and government intervention that attempts to prevent the use of foreign currency in domestic transactions ($\mu_1 > 0$). Another interesting result is that the contemporaneous relationship between the domestic money supply and the exchange rate is negative and significant. Within the context of the theoretical model developed in this chapter, this result is plausible under the following conditions: (1) the main source of exchange rate variance is the U.S. monetary policy; (2) there is a high degree of substitutability between the

Table 9.3   Transfer Function Model for $\Delta\Delta_{12} \ln e_t$

Constant term $\Delta\Delta_{12}$	Suppressed	Suppressed
ln DRM1		
ω_{10}	−0.0344	−0.0353
	(0.0194)	(0.0193)
ω_{11}	−0.0611	−0.0625
	(0.0196)	(0.0194)
Gain	0.0268	0.0273
	(0.0195)	
S*(12)	10.6	10.1
	(9)	(10)
P value	0.409	0.530
ln USM1		
ω_{20}	−0.0495	suppressed
	(0.123)	−
Gain	−0.0495	
S*(12)	8.88	−
d.f.	(9)	−
P value	0.544	
Noise model		
R^2	0.281	0.281
	(0.107)	(0.107)
Seasonal autoregressive noise parameter		
ϕ	−0.607	−0.589
	(0.125)	(0.122)
Summary statistics		
Adjusted R^2	0.277	0.283
F	7.88	9.91
d.f.	(5,87)	(4,88)
Standard error of regression Autocorrelation of residuals		
Q*(12)	7.8	7.76
d.f.	(10)	(10)
P value	0.690	0.692

two currencies; and (3) domestic monetary authorities deliberately alter the transaction costs of using foreign currency on domestic transactions.

The final estimated transfer function model reported in Table 9.3 performs quite well by conventional standards. Diagnostic checks on model adequacy include the Q^* statistic for autocorrelation of residuals, as well as the S^* statistic for cross-correlation of residuals suggested by Haugh (1976). None of the individual cross-correlations between residual and forcing variables exceeded two standard errors, and the $S^*(12)$ corresponds to a P value of 0.530. Also, no single autocorrelation of residual exceeded two standard errors, and the $Q^*(12)$ corresponds to a P value of 0.692.

4. Summary and Conclusions

The purpose of this chapter has been to develop and estimate an exchange rate model that accounts for currency substitution as well as the domestically imposed transactions costs on the level of the exchange rate.

Monthly data spanning the period from June 1969 to March 1979 were used to study the effects of the U.S. and Dominican Republic money supplies on the Dominican black or parallel market exchange rate. The model was estimated using the methodology developed by Box and Jenkins (1976).

The predictions of the model regarding the sign and magnitude of the different parameters appear to be sustained by the data. Overall, the theoretical framework is consistent with the hypothesis that excess domestic money creation will induce both a dollarization of the economy and an exchange rate depreciation. The results also suggest that the domestic authorities anticipated this and took measures to arrest the dollarization phenomena and the exchange rate depreciation. In particular, the contemporaneous relationship between innovations in the Dominican money supply and the exchange rate is negative and significant. The steady-state gain is positive and significantly smaller than unity.

These two results are supportive of the view of this chapter because they suggest that monetary expansion is planned by the domestic authorities; that is, they will increase the transaction costs of using the U.S. dollar in domestic transactions, in anticipation of the increase in the domestic money supply, thereby inducing a shift toward the Dominican peso. To the extent that they are successful, the depreciation of the currency will be less than proportional to the money growth. Also, the fact that authorities are not able to completely arrest the dollarization suggests that significant costs would be incurred in doing so. The negative contemporaneous coefficient is also easily explained within the model when both the elasticity of substitution and the elasticity of transaction cost with the exchange rate are fairly large. In addition, the fact that the results fail to uncover any relationship between the U.S. money supply and the exchange rate is consistent with the currency substitution hypothesis, which distinguishes between the world supply of U.S. dollars and the U.S. money supply, as opposed to the nonsubstitution hypothesis, which assumes the two measures of dollar-denominated money to be the same and as a consequence predicts a negative relationship between the U.S. money supply and the exchange rate.

The empirical analysis developed above also sheds some light on two alternative views of the parallel (black) exchange rate money supply relationship. The evidence presented suggests a causal relationship going from the money supply to the exchange rate rather than the opposite. This evidence clearly supports the hypothesis developed in this chapter concerning the alternative view that the monetary authorities may be pegging the exchange rate and letting the domestic money stock respond endogenously. Due to the structure of the model, and lack of a continuous (monthly) series on dollar holdings by Dominican Republic residents, no direct measure of the elasticity of substitution between the domestic and foreign currency was estimated. However, the estimated coefficients are consistent with a high degree of substitutability. This has profound implications, for it suggests that, if unchecked, the dollarization of the economy would greatly diminish the inflation tax base. The data also suggest that the monetary authorities are aware of this and have in effect taken steps to avert the dollarization of the economy by increasing the costs of transacting in dollars. To the extent that a significant amount of resources are devoted by the monetary authorities to arrest the dollarization of the economy and the economy gets distorted, the benefits of the inflation tax as a revenue-raising measure are greatly diminished. A final implication of our analysis is that a liberalization scheme that reduces the transaction costs of using the foreign currency will lead to a depreciation of the domestic currency.

Notes

[1] See Ortiz and Solís (1979) for a discussion of the "dollarization" of Mexico.

[2] The restriction had the following components: First, foreign-currency-denominated deposits could be held by banks only with a 100% reserve requirement. Second, Dominicans were required by law to exchange at par 90% of their foreign exchange earnings. Third, import duties were required to be prepaid and import quotas were established.

[3]Official devaluation requires approval of the Dominican Congress.

[4]For an analysis of the monetary approach to the crawling peg, see Blejer and Leiderman (1981).

[5]For an explanation and interpretation of the Dominican Republic currency crisis see Canto and Nickelsburg (1984).

[6]The derivation of equation (2) assumes that either through capital mobility and/or trade in goods the real rates are equalized across countries.

[7]An appendix with a formal derivation is available from the author on request.

[8]The estimated cross-correlation functions are available from the author on request.

[9]Since the derivation of the equilibrium exchange rate explicitly accounts for the U.S. dollar substitution effects, this characterization of the world demand for U.S. dollars amounts to neglecting the impact of the rest-of-the-world substitution effects on the U.S. price level. The magnitude of this effect remains an empirical issue. However, since no attempt is made to estimate the effect of the world supply of dollars on exchange rates, this assumption does not directly affect the empirical analysis performed in this chapter.

[10]The ratio of the log-likelihood function is given by:

$$\lambda = \frac{\sigma_a^n}{\sigma_0}$$

where σ_0 denotes the standard error of the constrained model and σ_a^n denotes the standard error of the unconstrained model. The quantity -2 in λ has a χ^2 distribution in large samples with degrees of freedoms equal to the number of restrictions. The high value of λ (i.e., $\lambda = 1$) leads one to accept the second equation as the final model.

References

Bilson, J. (1979). "Recent Developments in the Monetary Models of Exchange Rate Determination." *International Monetary Fund Staff Papers* 26 (June): 201–23.

Blejer, M., and L. Leiderman (1981). "A Monetary Approach to the Crawling-Peg System: Theory and Evidence." *Journal of Political Economy* 89 (February).

Box, G. E. P., and G. M. Jenkins (1976). *Time Series Analysis: Forecasting and Control*, 2d ed. San Francisco: Halden Day.

Calvo, G. (1983). "Lecciones del Monetarismo: El Cono Sud." Paper presented at the 37th Anniversary of the Dominican Republic Central Bank.

Calvo, G. A., and C. A. Rodríguez (1977). "A Model of Exchange Rate Determination under Currency Substitution and Rational Expectations." *Journal of Political Economy* 85: 617–24.

Canto, V. A., and G. Nickelsburg (1984). "Towards a Theory of Currency Choice and Currency Crises." 4th IFACS conference proceedings volume.

Durbin, J. (1970). "Testing for Serial Correlation in Least-Squares Regression When Some of the Regressors Are Lagged Dependent Variables." *Econometrica* 38 (May): 410–21.

Girton, L., and D. Roper (1981). "The Theory and Implications of Currency Substitution." *Journal of Money, Credit and Banking*.

Granger, C. (1969). "Investigating Causal Relations by Econometric Models and Own Spectral Methods." *Econometrica* 37 (July): 424–28.

Haugh, L. (1976). "Checking Independence of Two Covariance Stationary Time Series: A Univariate Residual Cross-Correlation Approach." *Journal of American Statistical Association* 71 (June).

Haugh, L. D., and D. Pierce (1977). "Causality in the Temporal Systems: Characterizations and a Survey." *Journal of Econometrics* 5 (May): 265–94.

Johnson, H. G. (1972). "The Monetary Approach to the Balance-of-Payments Theory." *Further Essays in Monetary Theory*. London: Allen & Unwin.

—— (1975). "The Monetary Approach to the Balance of Payments: A Nontechnical Guide." *Journal of International Economics* 5 (May): 107–51.

Ljung, G., and G. Box (1976). "A Modification of the Overall χ^2 Test for Lack of Fit in Time Series Models." Department of Statistics, Technical Report No. 477, University of Wisconsin (October).

Magee, S. (1976). "Empirical Evidence on the Monetary Approach to the Balance of Payments and Exchange Rates." *American Economic Review* 66 (May): 163–70.

Miles, M. (1976). "Currency Substitution, Flexible Exchange Rates and Monetary Independence." *American Economic Review* 68 (June): 428–36.

—— (1978). "Currency Substitution: Some Further Results and Conclusions." *Southern Economic Journal* 48(1): 78–86.

Mundell, R. A. (1971). *Monetary Theory: Inflation, Interest and Growth in the World Economy*. Pacific Palisades, California: Goodyear.

Mussa, M. (1976). "The Exchange Rate, The Balance of Payments and Monetary and Fiscal Policy under a Regime of Controlled Floating." *Scandinavian Journal of Economics* 78: 229–48.

Muth, J. (1961). "Rational Expectations and the Theory of Price Movements." *Econometrica* 29: 315–35.

Ortiz, G., and L. Solís (1979). "Financial Structure and Exchange Rate Experience: Mexico 1954–77." *Journal of Development Economics* 6 (December): 515–48.

Pierce, D. A. (1977). "Relationships—and the Lack Thereof—Between Economic Time Series with Special Reference to Money and Interest Rates." *Journal of the American Statistical Association* 72 (March): 11–32.

Salant, S. (1983). "The Vulnerability of Price Stabilization Schemes to Speculative Attacks." *Journal of Political Economy* 91(1) (February): 1–37.

Sims, C. A. (1977). "Comment." *Journal of the American Statistical Association* 72 (March): 23–24.

Sjaastad, L. (1983). "The Failure of Economic Liberalism in the Cone of Latin America." *Foreign Affairs* (January): 5–26.

Thomas, L. R. (1984). "Portfolio Theory and Currency Substitution." Mimeograph.

Whitman, M. V. N. (1975). "Global Monetarism and the Monetary Approach to the Balance of Payments." *Brookings Papers of Economic Activity*: 491–536.

10

Regulated and Nonregulated Financial and Foreign Exchange Markets and Income Inequality in the Dominican Republic

Claudio González-Vega & James E. Zinser

1. Introduction

During the 1960s and early 1970s, institutional or "regulated" financial and, to a lesser extent, foreign exchange markets in the Dominican Republic served as important mechanisms for growth. That is, following traditional measures of financial performance—the number, diversity, and growth of financial institutions, the ratio of monetary aggregates to national income, the proportion of private savings captured by the financial system, and the allocation of financial resources to productive investment—these markets would have been evaluated positively, compared with those in other Latin American countries.[1] Most scholars, of course, would have had little difficulty uncovering areas for improvement—especially with respect to interest rate flexibility, the level of transactions costs, the lack of a viable secondary market for financial instruments, and a strong urban bias in institutional location—but on balance the performance was good.

This chapter builds upon research efforts conducted by the authors and members of the Rural Savings Mobilization Project, coordinated by the Department of Agricultural Economics of the Ohio State University and the Financial Department of the Central Bank of the Dominican Republic, funded by the Agency for International Development (see J. Zinser et al., 1984). The conclusions and recommendations of this chapter, of course, are solely those of the authors and do not necessarily coincide with those of the Central Bank and other institutions or individuals who have participated in this project.

The generally favorable climate associated with the regulated financial markets (RFM) has changed considerably since the mid-1970s. In an inflationary environment, rapid growth of balance-of-payments deficits and considerable public-sector borrowing from both the domestic RFM and abroad—combined with interest rate and foreign exchange restrictions and, more generally, the failure to adopt institutional reform—have imposed severe financial repression on the Dominican economy. These restrictions, salient among determinants of disintermediation, have led to a relative decrease in the real volume of resources captured and efficiently allocated by the RFM. Substantially higher effective interest rates in the nonregulated domestic markets (NRFM) have drawn funds out of the regulated system. Indeed, financial and foreign exchange markets in the Dominican Republic have been marked by growth in the number and relative importance of nonregulated institutions. Nonregulated markets, consisting of more than 600 separate institutions, have taken an increasingly large share of financial and foreign exchange activity.

The development of the nonregulated, primarily urban, institutions raises serious questions about the role and consequences of regulation and about the efficiency with which financial and exchange markets in the Dominican Republic allocate the country's scarce savings and foreign exchange. In addition, despite the presence in the regulated markets of extensive controls concerning the availability and cost of funds for small- and middle-sized companies and for individuals, the regulations and the resulting growth of nonregulated markets have had important distributional consequences. This latter theme is considered here. We are particularly concerned with the net impact that the twin swords of financial and foreign exchange repression have had on income distribution. Specifically, we demonstrate (1) that, consistent with findings of other studies, taken in isolation financial and exchange repression have actually squeezed small- and medium-sized borrowers out of the RFM and, simultaneously, imposed severe restrictions on effective savings opportunities, with a considerable negative net impact on income inequality, (2) that development of the NRFM has partially offset these negative distributional consequences, in the sense of providing credit opportunities that would not have otherwise existed, but has also imposed severe costs on borrowers, and (3) that, while the NRFM provide alternatives for all classes of savers, these markets are highly segmented in terms of both return and risk, thus reinforcing the distributional impact of the RFM. These results have significant implications for the design of policies to confront the nonregulated marketplace, emphasizing the need for a reform of existing controls of RFM. In addition, many of the conclusions with respect to income distribution are not immediately obvious from a cursory review of financial intermediation in the Dominican Republic. Indeed, we find that the effect of NRFM on distribution is mixed, but for the most part favorable. These conclusions raise serious doubts about the desirability of efforts that would "regulate" these institutions in the absence of a more general financial reform.

While the broad outlines of these trends, particularly with respect to the regulated financial and exchange markets, are well known, it remains a useful exercise to explore in some detail the evolution of the nonregulated markets. Section 2 provides a brief overview of the nonregulated institutions in the Dominican Republic. Section 3 reviews the relationships between repression, parallel markets, and distribution. Tangible evidence of these links is analyzed in Section 4. Based, in part, on information obtained in an extensive study of the NRFM conducted jointly by the Ohio State University–Central Bank Rural Savings Mobilization Project, we review differential interest rates, institutional risk, and market segmentation. This information provides several direct clues about the consequences of repression and of parallel markets on income distribution. Finally, income distribution impacts are summarized in Section 5, leading to a discussion of policy implications.

2. Nonregulated Financial Institutions in the Dominican Republic

Despite considerable impediments to financial intermediation—restrictions on nominal yields in the RFM, substantial increases in public-sector deficits, in large part monetized by the central bank, and high rates of inflation—disintermediation in this exceptionally open economy has not exclusively led to capital flight. One explanation derives from the development of the NRFM. In just a few years these institutions have grown from a relatively modest share of total financial activity, focusing mostly on household finance, to a position of considerable importance. Furthermore, these institutions have drawn funds not only out of the RFM, but also from abroad, alleviating capital flight that would have otherwise taken place.

It is, of course, difficult to formulate a complete picture of the companies that compose the NRFM in the Dominican Republic; often they border on "grey" areas of financial activities. Nonetheless, due to the research efforts of the Rural Savings Mobilization Project,[2] we have been able to learn a great deal about the roughly 600 separate companies that make up the bulk of the NRFM (see Table 10.1).

The NRFM may be aggregated into four main groups: (1) household finance companies (sociedades inmobiliarias), (2) commercial finance (financieras comerciales), (3) small personal-loan houses (casas de

Table 10.1 Nonregulated Financial Institutions Registered with the Secretary of State for Industry and Commerce, 1967–83 (capital expressed in millions of RD$)

Year	Exchange houses		Small loan companies		Other companies		Total	
	No.	Capital	No.	Capital	No.	Capital	No.	Capital
1967	–	–	–	–	7	1.8	7	1.8
1968	–	–	–	–	6	2.1	6	2.1
1969	–	–	–	–	12	3.5	12	3.5
1970	–	–	–	–	3	0.2	3	0.2
1971	–	–	1	0.2	10	2.2	11	2.4
1972	1	*	–	–	32	9.0	33	9.0
1973	3	*	3	0.1	26	11.7	32	11.8
1974	–	–	–	–	67	18.5	67	18.5
1975	–	–	4	0.6	3	0.1	7	0.7
1976	–	–	–	–	33	9.5	33	9.5
1977	2	*	1	1.0	16	6.9	19	7.9
1978	2	*	16	1.2	21	10.7	39	11.9
1979	–	–	7	0.7	29	7.4	36	8.1
1980	–	–	7	0.6	26	14.8	33	15.4
1981	–	–	7	0.6	45	10.4	57	11.0
1982	8	1.4	6	0.4	37	9.9	46	11.7
1983	6	0.3	–	–	99	23.8	105	24.1
Totals	22	1.8	52	5.4	472	143.1	546	149.8

Source: Memoria Anual, Secretary of State for Industry and Commerce.
*Negligible.

préstamos de menor cuantía), and (4) other finance companies, including pawn shops, small personal-loan offices, and the like. The first three are the most important and are those for which we have the most information.

Briefly, the characteristics of these companies are:

Household Finance: Accounting for roughly two-thirds of the NRFM and almost 20% of *total* credit in the Dominican Republic, household finance companies specialize in lending associated with housing: loans for new construction, remodelling, furniture, appliances, mortgages, and even mortgage downpayments. In large part, their growth coincided with Dominican development efforts in the early 1970s that emphasized new construction (Dauhajre, 1984). Many of these companies were established as affiliates or subsidiaries of the regulated mortgage banks, all of which have formed relationships with at least one household finance company. This relationship is, of course, far from circumstantial; given the interest and credit restrictions faced by the regulated institutions, they have chosen to channel both internal funds (up to an allowable 30% of total capital and reserves) and potential customers into their nonregulated affiliates.

Commercial Finance: Particularly in the last five years, the commercial finance companies have become increasingly important. For the most part they are well organized and also have formed interlocks with regulated institutions. The sector includes several large companies that have been organized as segments of financial groups, an association of 24 smaller firms (Asociacion Dominicana de Empresas Financieras—ADEFI[3]), and a number of small independent companies. All specialize in loans to business, usually but not exclusively loans that could not be obtained from commercial or development banks. Recently these companies have expanded into co-financing arrangements with regulated firms; nonregulated institutions finance working-capital requirements, complementing fixed-asset loans from commercial and development banks. ADEFI provides an interesting contrast with other nonregulated institutions. Established in 1983 as a vehicle to offset negative publicity that had accompanied rapid NRFM growth, it has taken on a broader role, including the supervision of a "deposit insurance" program, and is a vehicle for interest rate and minimum-capitalization guidelines.

Small Personal Loans: Approximately 100 small loan companies (casas de préstamos de menor cuantía) have been registered and nominally are regulated by the monetary authorities. Officially they are permitted to make personal loans in amounts of up to RD$500 at an interest rate of no more than 3% per month. Lending activities, however, have spread beyond their original charter and most maintain operations in both the small personal-loan and larger commercial-loan markets.

Sources of Funds

The nonregulated companies derive the bulk of their resources (63%) from individual deposits. An additional 31% represents invested capital and 6% is obtained from bank loans. It is estimated that the three main groups of nonregulated firms have received approximately RD$800 million in deposits, an amount that represents 36% of the total deposit and fixed-interest liabilities of the regulated institutions. Deposits principally have short maturities and earn between 1 and 3% per month, depending on term and size, reflecting higher default risk and information costs; in contrast, savings rates in the RFM range from zero to 4% per year for demand savings deposits to almost 12% per year for long-term certificates.

Uses of Funds

Loans made by the NRFM usually support both consumption and capital formation activities of borrowers that have been closed out of the RFM; there is, in addition, increasing competition with the RFM. Interest rates range from 2 to 3% per month for commercial customers and may reach as high as 20% per month, or more, for individual borrowers, reflecting both transactions costs and higher default risk. Terms are generally fairly short, 6 months to a year in most instances, although secured loans may have terms as long as 3 years. It is estimated that the NRFM has outstanding loan balances of approximately RD$730 million, about a third of the outstanding loans of their regulated counterparts and one-fourth of total lending in the Dominican Republic.

3. Financial and Foreign Exchange Markets and Income Distribution

Financial Markets and Income Distribution

Financial markets influence income distribution through the access they provide to savings options and to loans. Access to deposit facilities increases portfolio opportunities for wealth-holders, improving their risk–return combinations, while access to loans makes it possible for them to take advantage of unexploited investment opportunities. Both deposits and loans increase rates of growth of wealth. Moreover, differential access provides differential opportunities for income growth and thus influences distribution. Transaction costs and market imperfections usually bias these distributional consequences against the smaller, poorer, riskier agents in the economy. The instruments of financial repression (interest rate ceilings, reserve requirements, minimum deposit size, etc.) further accentuate the negative income distribution implications of nonperfect markets. In addition, financial repression may considerably reduce and bias economic growth, leading to further redistribution (González-Vega, 1977; Adams et al., 1984; Clotfelter and Lieberman, 1978).

For savers, interest rate and/or minimum-deposit restrictions may lead to low, even substantially negative, real rates of return. This is especially true to the extent that lower- to middle-income savers are constrained to low (negative real) interest-bearing savings accounts in the RFM. In contrast, more affluent savers have access not only to insured higher-yield deposits in the RFM, but also to foreign securities. While one might anticipate some differential between the yields earned by each group, because of transactions costs and differing elasticities of supply, these differentials will be much greater than could reasonably be justified by cost. Restrictive interest rate policies encourage lower-income savers, if possible, to substitute purchases of leveraged housing and durables for financial saving. Substitution by higher-income savers may be mitigated by the creation of special savings instruments, but this is only partial and they too will seek alternative savings mechanisms. In both cases, repression increases portfolio risk, lowers the rate of financial saving, and prompts a redistribution of wealth (Wai, 1957; Kane, 1977; Lawrence and Elliehausen, 1981; Reynolds and Corredor, 1976).

For borrowers, financial restrictions have both price and differential-access, or quantity, effects. In the first place, below-market interest rates convey a direct subsidy to successful borrowers, and the size of that subsidy depends directly on the size of individual loans. Nominal lending rates in Dominican Republic RFMs are fixed at 12% per year. This rate is complemented by a series of charges and fees that can increase the effective cost but are not always sufficient to yield a positive real interest rate. Furthermore, although financial policy may provide special incentives that normally attempt to favor lower- and medium-income borrowers, effectively all but the largest or higher-income borrowers are likely to be precluded from the RFM. In general, financial repression tends to separate borrowers into three classes: nonrationed borrowers, usually large and well known, who receive the amount of credit they demand at the going interest rate; rationed borrowers, usually smaller producers, who receive loans of a smaller size than they demand at the low interest rate; and excluded borrowers, who are willing to borrow but are not accepted (González-Vega, 1984). Consequently, repressive financial systems tend to redistribute available credit toward higher as opposed to lower- and middle-income borrowers, toward the larger as opposed to smaller firms, and toward traditional as opposed to nontraditional producers. Indeed, our surveys showed greater RFM borrowing by the larger companies, who expanded their lines of credit well beyond immediate needs (loan hoarding) not only as an inflation hedge, but also to maintain their share of the financial market in anticipation of increased repression! It is clear that, good intentions notwithstanding, financial restrictions in the Dominican

Republic have exacerbated the distributional consequences of initial factor endowments.

Finally, financial repression reduces the overall volume of financial resources that can be allocated by the financial markets (see, for example, the excellent survey by Fry, 1982). This necessarily retards economic growth and biases the growth process (McKinnon, 1973; Shaw, 1973). In both cases, the consequences for income distribution are perverse. Increases in overall income are the prime source for alleviation of poverty in LDCs; and to the extent that financial resources are a constraint on economic growth, then the bias is substantial. Similarly, financial repression biases factor payments from labor to capital. The low (subsidized) interest signal encourages a capital-intensive technology even though the financial resources are not in fact available.

Foreign Exchange Markets and Income Distribution

A similar analysis may be developed for the foreign exchange market. Fixed, nonmarket-clearing exchange rates, like fixed interest rates, have generated an excess demand, rationing in the official market, and the creation of parallel nonregulated institutions. Although both processes have been present, to some extent, since the mid-1970s, the latter course has dominated foreign exchange activities in the Dominican Republic during the 1980s. The rapid growth of the exchange houses and, more recently, the exchange banks exemplifies that development.

Although an increasing proportion of the country's foreign exchange activity has passed through the parallel markets, the two-tiered system has many of the implications found for the parallel financial markets: in particular, average foreign exchange rates have been higher than those that would have prevailed in a free market, the amount of foreign exchange that enters the markets—reflecting both exports and capital flows—may have been reduced, and many exports have been priced out of the market.

Exchange repression mimics the distributional consequences of financial repression. That is, the official overvalued foreign exchange market, with attendant exchange controls, has created biases in the Dominican economy that adversely redistribute income. The consequences of overvalued exchange rates on development have been extensively discussed in the literature (Pfeffermann, 1985), and it is necessary here to stress only three distributional aspects. Overvalued exchange rates clearly discriminate against traditional exporters, especially agricultural exporters. This directly penalizes rural incomes. Furthermore, in the Dominican Republic, traditional exports have had to pass through official markets, and even the moderate "subsidies" that slightly raise effective prices do not come close to full compensation. Overvalued exchange rates also create an urban bias via the substitution of imported commodities for domestic production: this is especially true, given that the import content of consumption for urban consumers is much higher than for rural consumers. While the development of the parallel markets partially offsets these effects, the benefit is asymmetrical, affecting imports and import prices far more than exports and rural incomes.

4. Repression and Inequality in the Dominican Republic

Three characteristics of the regulated and nonregulated markets can be contrasted, to derive conclusions with respect to the distribution of income: interest rates, institutional risk, and market segmentation.

Interest Rates

The structure of interest rates, both paid on funds attracted into the institutions and charged on their lending activities, provides valuable information about the Dominican financial markets. Here we are interested in the relative structure of interest rates in the regulated and nonregulated markets, and their impact on distribution.

Interest Rates on Savings Instruments   Within the RFM in the Dominican Republic nominal interest rates paid on funds attracted from the public ranged from zero for on-demand deposits issued by the commercial banks, to 15% for 3-year certificates of deposit issued by development banks. There were, of course, considerable institutional differences, in terms of both the ability to utilize savings instruments and the average cost of securing funds. For example, only commercial banks can issue demand deposits, and only the commercial banks and savings and loan associations may receive savings deposits. As of early 1984, demand deposits represented almost 40% of the deposit liabilities carried by commercial banks; an additional 22% was in the form of savings deposits that pay just 5% interest. Only 2% of their liabilities were in the form of high-interest-bearing savings certificates. Thus, the average interest cost to these institutions was just 4.2 to 4.5%.[4] In contrast, mortgage bank deposit liabilities represented just 5% of total liabilities and development banks may issue only fixed-interest savings instruments; both thus have an average interest cost of between 11.5 and 12.0%, depending on the term structure of their liabilities. The savings and loans associations have intermediate interest costs, roughly 10%, based on a 60–40% distribution between deposits and fixed-interest savings instruments.

For savers, interest rate offerings in the RFM, especially after adjustment for inflation, are not particularly attractive. To illustrate, for 1984 it was estimated that consumer prices rose by at least 35%. Thus savings accounts earned roughly −20% and the longest-term certificate of deposit, with a minimum deposit of RD$50,000 and a nominal yield of 15%, earned a real return of −10.5%. In 1983, with a more moderate inflation rate (15.4%), the best real return that could be earned in the RFM was −0.4%.

In contrast, the interest rates paid to attract private savings in the NRFM are much higher, earning positive returns even after adjustment for inflation. Based on our survey of these institutions, interest payments on 1-year certificates vary between 1.5 and 2.5% per month, between 19.6 and 34.5% at annual rates. Differences between these yields derive from the size and, to a lesser extent, the term of the individual placement. To illustrate, one commercial finance company interviewed by the project held approximately 60 accounts. The minimum deposit was RD$100 (one account for the son of a client), but the average size was RD$10,300 and one account totaled RD$100,000. Furthermore, although the minimum interest payment was 1.5% per month, or 19.6% per year, the average account earned 2% per month, 26.8% per year. The largest accounts earned 3% per month. Finally, all certificates were issued for 1 year; informally, however, it was acknowledged that funds placed on deposit could be withdrawn at any time, subject to an interest penalty of 1% per month.

There are several obvious implications of these comparisons. First, it is clear that the NRFM has substantial opportunities to attract funds, both from the RFM and from abroad. Institutions in the NRFM pay more than twice as much for funds than their regulated counterparts, for comparable terms. Second, despite higher yields, savings opportunities for low-income savers remain considerably restricted by minimum-deposit requirements in both markets, by information costs, and by transactions costs. Third, given these interest differentials, the fact that full-scale transfers have not yet taken place suggests that many potential savers still have reservations about safety.

Interest Rates Charged by Financial Intermediaries   Interest rates charged in the RFM and, nominally, by all institutions that make loans in the Dominican Republic, are limited to a maximum of 12% per year.[5] In addition, institutions were legally permitted to charge commissions and closing costs of up to 6% of the value of the loan. Thus in the case of 1-year loans, the effective rate of interest would be 18%. For longer-term loans, the allowable rate of interest is somewhat less than 18%; that is, if the 6% commission can be charged only once over the term of a loan, then the nominal interest cost of the loan will decrease with its term to maturity. Indeed, the interest structure carries a strong internal incentive for short-term maturities. In practice, of course, the effective interest rate could be somewhat higher, depending on the method employed by these institutions to calculate interest charges and amortize their loan port-folios.[6]

Interest costs in the NRFM are considerably higher than those charged by regulated institutions, even after adjustment for commissions. There is, moreover, substantial market segmentation of the NRFM, reflected in the spread between commercial and personal loans. Finance-company loans to preferred commercial customers appear to be fairly competitive with commercial banks and other regulated institutions. Interest rates charged to commercial customers by, for example, members of ADEFI are roughly 3% per month. Officially the nominal interest rate is 12% per year, but commissions range from 12 to 15%. Thus if interest is calculated on the outstanding balance, the minimum effective cost to a borrower for a 1-year loan is roughly 34% to 39%.[7] Still, many customers turn to the NRFM because funding is not available to them in the RFM, and costs reflect this difference. Many commercial customers pay effective interest costs of 5% per month, or more.

A survey of small companies in Santiago yielded similar comparisons. The average interest cost of loans obtained in the RFM was approximately 1.8% per month, or 22 to 26% on an annual basis. In contrast, the average monthly interest rate paid in the NRFM was 5.34%, or on the order of 65 to 70% per year (see Table 10.2).[8]

Rates charged on personal loans by inmobiliarias or personal loan companies may be substantially higher. To illustrate, in Santo Domingo, automobile loans carry a nominal interest charge of 2 to 6% per month and effective costs of 3.6 to 10.5% per month. These loans generally use the automobile as guarantee and may nominally circumvent the interest rate restrictions by officially "renting" the vehicle to the borrower. Under this arrangement the lending institution retains title. Borrowers pay a rent equal to the monthly interest cost plus loan amortization, and at the end of the repayment period receive ownership papers.

Based on our survey of these institutions, it is difficult to establish a precise relationship between term and interest. Virtually all loans made by the NRFM are short term, and the interest rate difference between, say, a 6-month loan and one for a full year does not on the surface appear to be substantial.

Table 10.2 Monthly Interest Rates Paid by Small Companies in Santiago

Interest rate	1980	1981	1982	1983	1984	Total
Regulated financial markets						
1% to 2%	4	2	5	9	8	28
3% to 4%	–	–	1	1	–	2
5% to 10%	1	–	–	–	–	1
Total loans	5	2	6	10	8	31
Average interest	2.7	1.7	1.8	1.7	1.5	1.8
Nonregulated financial markets						
1% to 2%	–	2	4	1	5	12
2% to 3%	12	5	12	7	4	40
3% to 4%	2	1	3	1	–	7
4% to 5%	3	2	2	4	2	13
5% to 10%	3	7	4	6	4	24
15% to 25%	3	2	3	1	–	9
Total loans	23	19	28	20	15	105
Average interest	5.8	6.3	5.2	5.3	3.8	5.3

Source: Zinser et al. (1984).

Extreme examples of interest cost abound in this market:

Pawn shops (negocios de compra y venta) receive real assets such as furniture, clothing, and other household goods, as security for short-term loans. In addition, they discount the appraised value of these assets at very high rates of interest, estimated to be between 15 and 20% per month.

One lender is reported to charge 1% each day. A borrower is obliged to deposit a signed but undated check in the amount of the loan with the borrower; in addition, each day, the borrower must pay the 1% interest cost (2% on Saturday). If the borrower fails to meet a single payment, the check would be cashed. The compounded annual interest cost is 378%.

Lenders (restaurants or nightclubs) near the major waterfronts are reported to discount expected pay checks at the rate of 20% per day. That is, a sailor, for example, expecting to be paid his salary in a day or two, is able to present proof of future payment and discount the expected earnings at a rate of 20% per day. The compounded annual interest cost is 791%.

The extreme cases, reflecting interest costs to those who are excluded from both the RFM and the largest segment of the NRFM, are the lowest-income borrowers, both small companies and poorer families.

Contrasts with respect to loan rates and conditions between the RFM and NRFM are striking. The RFM lends at an interest rate of up to roughly 18%. Nonregulated institutions are able to charge in excess of 30% in the case of the commercial lenders and more than 100% for personal and housing loans, reflecting the costs of funds, the clientel that is forced into this market by the rationing process of the RFM, and the transaction costs of relatively small-scale lending operations. Similarly, the NRFM is primarily a short-term market, with loans of from 180 days to 1 year; the RFM nominally services a full spectrum of lending terms, but access to this market is severely limited.

Interest Rate Spreads   The spread between RFM saving and loan rates is set by the monetary authorities. Spreads range from approximately 14% in the case of the commercial banks (average interest payments of aprox-imately 4% and loan rate of up to 18%) to approximately 6% for the other institutions. This spread must be further adjusted for reserve requirements to determine the net interest spread for these institutions, leading to an adjusted spread of approximately 8% and 4 to 5% for the different groups of institutions.

But the spreads in regulated markets pale in comparison with the nonregulated institutions. Differentials in the NRFM are at least 1% per month (12% per year), for a number of the commercial finance companies, and may be considerably higher, as much as 60 to 70 percentage points for several of the personal and household finance companies. At the extreme, the spread could reach as much as 100 percentage points.

What accounts for the large differences in interest spreads between the regulated and nonregulated markets and for their absolute size? Five factors dominate these conditions: (1) forced investments and reserve requirements in the regulated markets, (2) imperfections and transactions costs generated by the rationing mechanism through which regulated institutions must allocate available credit, (3) inefficiencies in the operations of nonregulated institutions, (4) imperfect competition and market segmentation among the nonregulated institutions, and (5) investor expectations with respect to domestic prices, interest rates, and exchange rates.

Institutional Risk

Managers of individual financial institutions seek to maximize profits; this is their long-run objective. Intermediate goals, however, are necessary to achieve that result, including safety or solvency and liquidity. Institutions "must remain solvent [the realizable value of their assets must be equal to their legal liabilities plus the value of the 'capital stock' account] in the long run and be able to ensure convertibility of deposits into currency in the very short run, if the expectation of profit is to be realized." If there were neither risks nor uncertainties, then these goals would present no problems to financial managers; the behavior of assets would be known and manageable, and withdrawals of funds deposited with the institution would be predictable. Control over the long-run solvency of commercial and development banks generally is maintained through regulations imposed by the monetary authorities. There are prohibitions against investments in certain assets, limits to the amount of exposure, and extensive reserve requirements. But to what extent do institutions in the RFM and NRFM in fact manage their portfolios according to acceptable standards?

Four interrelated measures of institutional solvency indicate the extent to which firms have leveraged their invested capital, attracting private savings for their lending operations: the debt/equity ratio (liabilities/paid in capital), the ratio of total liabilities to total assets, the ratio of assets to paid-in capital, and the ratio of assets to capital (see Table 10.3).

Table 10.3 Indicators of Institutional Solvency in the Regulated and Nonregulated Credit Market

Sample	Liabilities/ paid-in capital	Liabilities/ assets	Assets/ paid-in capital	Assets/ capital
Finance companies	2.32	0.70	3.89	3.32
Large	3.15	0.76	4.70	4.15
Medium	1.43	0.59	3.66	2.44
Small	1.71	0.63	2.64	2.71
Housing companies	3.80	0.79	4.57	4.82
Members of ADEFI	7.00	0.88	n.d.	8.0
Commercial banks	7.90	0.88	9.01	8.33
Mortgage banks	2.20	0.66	3.34	2.94
Development banks	2.10	0.52	4.03	2.08

Source: Information on the regulated institutions is available in Central Bank of the Dominican Republic, *Boletin Mensual.* Information on the nonregulated institutions is taken from Zinser et al. (1984).

Note: Paid-in capital: book value of shares issued to ownership. Capital: paid-in capital plus retained earnings and reserves.

In the RFM, mortgage and development banks have debt/equity ratios of 2.1 to 2.2: they have received deposit or other liabilities at the rate of RD$2.0 for each RD$1.0 of accumulated capital. The debt/equity ratios for the commercial banks are much higher, reflecting their ability to attract demand deposits as well as other short-term deposit liabilities. Other indicators yield consistent results. For example, commercial banks have asset/capital and asset/paid-in capital ratios of 8.33 to 9.01, compared with ratios of 2.1 to 4.0 for the other institutions.

Nonregulated financial institutions exhibit similar but more pronounced diversity. That is, as a group the 65 financieras had debt-equity ratios of 2.32 (1.7 for the smallest firms and 3.2 for the largest) that were roughly consistent with the mortgage and development banks. This ratio is somewhat larger for companies specializing in housing, with a value of 3.8. That is, liabilities financed approximately 70% of total assets for the financieras and 80% for the housing companies; only in the latter instance were these institutions outside the limits found for their regulated counterparts. In contrast, members of ADEFI exhibit a financial structure that is close to that of the commercial banks, probably reflecting the background of ADEFI management. The average debt/equity ratio is 7.0, suggesting that liabilities financed 85% of total assets.

The average values for these ratios mask the variation between institutions. For example, among the largest financieras, liabilities financed approximately 76% of total assets, but values range from 13.5% to over 92%. Similarly, for the smaller financieras, the proportion of assets financed by deposit liabilities varied between 1% and almost 100%, suggesting virtually no invested capital. It is at best an irregular pattern. Stated simply, based on the sample of 65 financieras, the data do not show that the average company is significantly undercapitalized, despite a relatively small size. However, there is considerable variation, and for many firms the proportion of total assets financed by short-term debt is very large. This simultaneously limits the exposure of ownership and increases the default risk for those who have deposited funds with the companies.

There is one further issue with respect to solvency and the safety of deposits. In addition to the exposure that depositors face due to a lack of capitalization and the proportion of total assets financed by deposit liabilities, one necessarily must question the quality of the assets themselves. Again, for the RFM there are limits and prohibitions that enhance the underlying value of individual assets in the institution's portfolio. These restrictions do not apply in the NRFM. The process that has led to the creation of a nonregulated market has increased average risks; institutions closed out of the RFM by the rationing process have higher credit risks. Similarly, a large proportion of the customers handled by the NRFM are individuals rather than corporate borrowers, again with relatively higher default risks. The combination seriously calls into question the overall safety afforded the typical investor!

Adequate liquidity, necessary to meet short-term variations in deposit liabilities and to meet long-term fluctuations in the overall debt structure, is a precondition for successful financial management. At the extreme, failure to meet a single customer's withdrawal request could be sufficient to destroy the credibility of the institution. All institutions strive to meet the liquidity objective. But how close to the margin do they come? How liquid are the assets maintained by these firms? What secondary sources of liquidity are available to the individual concern?

In the regulated market, liquidity needs are partially satisfied by legal reserves (the encaje legal); individual institutions are obliged to maintain marginal reserve requirements of between 10 and 100%, depending on the category of liability and institution. The NRFM, of course, faces no comparable system. Any provision for liquidity rests solely with the individual institution or association. Thus it is interesting to evaluate the extent to which these firms do meet minimum expectations. Several performance ratios can be used to evaluate these institutions, including the ratio of currency and bank deposits to short-term liabilities, and the ratio of short-term assets to short-term liabilities and to total liabilities, respectively (see Table 10.4).

One of the most telling comparisons is indicated by the ratio of cash and bank deposits to short-term obligations. For the regulated institutions, this ratio averaged from 50% for the commercial and development banks to 105% for the mortgage banks. Short-term obligations are defined here to include demand and savings deposit liabilities, deposits by other regulated institutions, and advances and discounts from the central bank. For the nonregulated institutions, this ratio was much smaller: 5.3% for the full sample, 6.8% for the ADEFI membership. Indeed, for the larger finance companies it averaged just 1.9%, for the housing companies just 1.4%! Part of this difference derives from a problem of definition. All financial liabilities of the NRFM are classified as short term, and the liabilities of the RFM exclude long-term central bank credit. Furthermore, mortgage and development banks derive the bulk of their private-sector funding from bond sales that *in fact* may have short maturities. Thus their short-term obligations may be more generally defined. But even if one were to adjust these figures by a factor of three or four, there would remain a significant differential: the nonregulated institutions have a degree of liquidity that is significantly less than their regulated counterparts. Furthermore, for individual institutions in the NRFM available currency and short-term bank deposits approaches zero, suggesting virtually no liquidity.

Table 10.4 Indicators of Institutional Liquidity in the Regulated and Nonregulated Financial Markets

Sample	Cash & dep./ S.T. liab. (%)	S.T. assets/ S.T. liab. (%)	S.T. assets/ total liab. (%)
Finance companies	5.3	117.7	79.7
Large	1.9	106.9	67.8
Medium	8.4	134.0	101.1
Small	19.1	147.2	119.0
Housing companies	1.4	82.6	43.0
Members of ADEFI	6.8	107.0	150.0
Commercial banks	50.8	70.7	37.5
Mortgage banks	105.4	127.7	8.7
Development banks	57.2	208.1	27.1

Source: Information on the regulated institutions is available in Central Bank of the Dominican Republic, *Boletin Mensual.* Information on the nonregulated institutions is taken from Zinser et al. (1984).

Note: Cash & dep.: reserves or deposits in the central bank and vault cash. S. T. liab.: demand deposits, savings deposits, advances and discounts from the central bank, and deposits of other financial institutions. S. T. assets: assets with maturities of one year or less.

On average, nonregulated companies do have considerable capacity in their current (short-term) assets to cover their current liabilities, reflecting the term structure of their loan portfolios. This ratio varies between 0.8 to 1.5, higher, interestingly, for the smallest finance companies. For the regulated institutions the ratio varies from 0.7 for commercial to 2.1 for development banks. Again, however, there is much more intercompany variation for the NRFMs than between the two major groups. Finally, differences between the RFM and NRFM with respect to the ratio of short-term assets to total liabilities reflects loan maturities of the different institutions. Mortgage and development banks hold a long-term loan portfolio and have much lower ratios: 9 and 21%, respectively. For commercial banks the ratio of short-term assets to liabilities is just over 37%, comparable to the nonregulated housing loan companies. For finance companies it approaches 80% and for members of ADEFI, 107%. In part, the short-term maturities partially compensate for the lack of regulation.

In summary, balance-sheet information for the NRFM strongly suggests a relative increase in depositor risk, with respect to both what we broadly refer to as institutional solvency and liquidity.

Market Segmentation

The survey of regulated and nonregulated financial and exchange institutions in the Dominican Republic clearly revealed significant market segmentation. That is, operations of these companies appear to be geared toward distinct groups of customers. In our mind this suggests a taxonomy of four such groups.

In the RFM, members of financial groups and other prime customers readily gain access to subsidized credit. The fixed, low-interest deposit liabilities of the regulated market serve as a source of low-cost funds to these customers. Over the past two to three years, loans have been made to these borrowers at rates of interest that are roughly 10 to 12 points below a reasonable market-clearing interest rate (a real rate of interest of, say, 5%). Furthermore, interviews with these borrowers suggested considerable loan hoarding, resulting in a recent increase in the demand for borrowed funds.

A less-favored group consists of non-preferred customers, who have access to funds in the RFM but at much higher implicit prices. The combination of compensating balances, prepayment of interest costs, and compulsory financial services substantially increases true interest rates above the 18% ceiling imposed by the monetary authorities. Here, interest costs may actually approach the free-market rate and undoubtedly are competitive with rates charged at the commercial end of the NRFM.

A third group consists of preferred borrowers in the NRFM itself. These appear to be clients who cannot gain access to subsidized RFM credit because of the excess demand for funds, but who qualify for loans from, for example, the members of ADEFI and the larger commercial credit companies. Interest rates are high, reflecting both the cost of funds and market inefficiencies, but funds are made available. There is undoubtedly a dead-weight loss due to the imperfections in this market, but the net effect on welfare appears to be positive.

Finally, the fourth group consists of the "other customers," those who borrow from finance companies that specialize in housing, automotive and personal credit needs, and loans to small businesses. Interest rates in this segment of the market are very high. The costs to these borrowers are high and suggest a considerable redistribution of income.

Although less pronounced, market segmentation also exists for savers. Simply put, the quantitative restrictions on access to higher-yield instruments in the RFM also carry over to nonregulated institutions. At the extreme it appears as if the smaller savers provide low-cost funds for favored customers. Higher-income savers in turn provide funds for the lower-income borrowers, but at very high rates of interest. Both patterns redistribute income from the bottom to the top.

5. The Overall Pattern of Income Distribution and Financial Repression in the Dominican Republic

Several distinct patterns emerge from our review of the financial intermediation and exchange market performance of the Dominican Republic. This section reviews our findings and suggests a direction for reform.

First, it is clear that, in the absence of the NRFM, financial repression imposes a severe cost in terms of the overall distribution of income. This cost occurs on both sides of the intermediation process. Financial repression entails a bias against the small saver who is unable to transfer financial holdings into alternative, higher-yield deposits. For loans, the "iron law" of interest rate restrictions provides a subsidy to favored customers, members of industrial groups, and traditional borrowers (González-Vega, 1984). Access is afforded to those at the higher end of the income spectrum. This effect is complemented by "loan hoarding." Other borrowers are either penalized by hidden financial costs or denied access to the regulated market entirely; in both cases the penalty can be severe. Similarly, in the absence of a nonregulated exchange market, repression in the exchange market imposes an income distribution cost. The bias here is against exporters, labor, and, especially, the rural sector. Arbitrary administrative allocations of foreign exchange lead to similar redistributive impacts.

Second, development of the nonregulated institutions partially alleviates the distributional impact, both in terms of the real return to savers and the access to borrowed funds. Nonregulated institutions do offer substantially higher returns for savings and, indeed, evidence suggests increases in the overall rate of financial savings and a reversal of capital flight, in addition to a transfer of funds out of the regulated system. They open up the domestic savings options. But these benefits are not obtained without cost. Minimum-deposit requirements remain in place at the "safer end" of the NRFM, suggesting that access by most households to these higher-yield financial instruments may not be possible; in addition, deposit risks and costs increase substantially along the spectrum that runs from the larger commercial finance to personal finance companies. Access to loans in the NRFM clearly benefits lower-income families and smaller companies, but here too the cost is considerable. As we showed in Section 4, some customers have obtained loans at relatively modest cost through the availability either of a greater volume of funds than would otherwise exist or "financial packages" that include both RFM and NRFM participation. Less-favored customers pay substantially higher rates of interest, reflecting increased transactions costs and greater risk. Thus, the nonregulated financial and exchange markets positively affect income distribution relative to financial repression alone, but they are not perfect substitutes for a fully integrated market.

Third, these findings contradict the popular belief that financial reform would hurt distribution. Although it probably is true that financial liberalization will lead to an increase in the RFM interest-rate structure, this would be more than offset by a reduction in NRFM rates. Indeed, these results suggest that liberalization would lower average loan costs, increase the availability of funds to smaller firms and lower-income borrowers, and reduce the overall financial risk. Trends such as these are usually ignored in cost/benefit analyses of alternative reforms.

Finally, our review of the nonregulated markets suggests guidelines for financial reform, emphasizing the desirability of policies that would eliminate the pricing and allocation constraints that currently exist in the RFM and improve access to the NRFM. Specific reforms in the RFM and the NRFM would focus on: (1) reserve requirements, substituting for the current complex reserve structure a simple, uniform legal reserve requirement that would be applied to all financial institutions; (2) interest rates, eliminating most of the ceilings that currently exist; (3) minimum-deposit restrictions, easing or reducing the restrictions that were placed on, for example, certificates of deposit and other savings instruments; (4) secondary markets, providing an open market for resale of longer-term instruments; (5) publicity, making information about the operations, prices, and costs of all financial institutions available to the public; and (6) risk, seeking to provide minimum operating guidelines for institutions in both markets.

Notes

[1]In 1970 this sector consisted of 21 separate institutions (8 commercial banks, 11 saving and loan institutions, and 2 finance companies, now renamed development banks). By the end of 1984, that number had increased to over 65 separate institutions (16 commercial banks, 17 savings and loan institutions, 19 development banks, and 13 mortgage banks). Similarly, in 1970 total assets of this sector amounted to RD$428.9 million; by the end of 1983 assets had increased to RD$1,141.1 million, a nominal rate of increase of 7.8% per year. The ratio of total private-sector funds captured by these institutions to gross domestic product reflects this growth, increasing from 17.5% in 1970 to 27.9% by the end of 1983.

[2]Detailed financial information on 195 nonregulated institutions was collected by the project. The sample included 77 commercial and household credit companies located in Santo Domingo and Santiago, 18 members of the Asociacion Dominicana de Empresas Financieras (ADEFI), a trade association located in Santo Domingo, and 100 casas de préstamos de menor cuantía. A full description of this sample is given in Zinser et al. (1984).

[3]Most owners of the ADEFI institutions have had banking experience in the Dominican Republic, a connection they undoubtedly have retained.

[4]Average interest costs could substantially increase whenever customers convert deposit holdings in the commercial banks to certificados financieros. Through early 1984 this had not been done, in part due to the very large minimum-deposit requirements. As requirements are eased, a substantial transfer is quite likely.

[5]Casas de préstamos menor cuantía (CMC) are exempted from this restriction on loans of less than RD$500; in this case the maximum rate could be 3% per month, a compounded rate of 42.6% per year.

[6]Simply, the customer pays closing costs first, and thus on net receives an amount equal to 94% of the face value of the loan, for an effective interest cost of 18.8%. If the 1-year loans are in fact made for short periods of time, say 90 or 180 days, commissions could be levied several times per year, substantially raising the true interest cost. Depending on the class of customer, regulated institutions may impose additional costs on their borrowers; it has been suggested, for example, that compensatory balances may run 10 to 15% of the loan size and that clients may be expected to purchase compulsory financial services from the financial group.

[7]If the 1-year loans are in practice made for shorter time periods, say 90 days or 6 months, and must pay the commission costs each roll-over, then true costs would rise proportionately. To illustrate, a 1-year loan that is rolled-over four times in the course of a year would have an effective cost of approximately 120%.

[10]Average interest costs are calculated from the mid-points of the interest intervals.

References

Adams, Dale W, Douglas H. Graham, and J. D. Von Pischke (eds.) (1984). *Undermining Rural Development With Cheap Credit*. Boulder, Colorado: Westview Special Studies in Social, Political and Economic Development.

Clotfelter, C., and C. Lieberman (1978). "On the Distributional Impact of Federal Interest Rate Restrictions." *The Journal of Finance* 33 (March): 199–213.

Dauhajre, Andrés S. (1984). "Two Decades of Economic Policies." Conference on Financial Crisis, Foreign Assistance, and Domestic Resource Mobilization in the Caribbean Basin, Ohio State University, Columbus, Ohio (April).

Fry, Maxwell J. (1982). "Models of Financially Repressed Developing Economies." *World Development* 10 (9): 731–50.

González-Vega, Claudio (1977). "Interest Rate Restrictions and Income Distribution." *American Journal of Agricultural Economics* 59: 973–76.

———— (1984). "Cheap Agricultural Credit: Redistribution in Reverse." In *Undermining Rural Development With Cheap Credit*. edited by Dale W Adams, Douglas H. Graham, and J. D. Von Pischke. Boulder, Colorado: Westview Special Studies in Social, Political and Economic Development.

Kane, Edward J. (1977). "Good Intentions and the Unintended Evil: The Case Against Selective Credit Allocation." *Journal of Money, Credit and Banking* 9 (February): 55–69.

Lawrence, Edward C., and Gregory E. Elliehausen (1981). "The Impact of Federal Interest Rate Regulations on the Small Saver: Further Evidence." *Journal of Finance* 36 (3) (June): 677–84.

McKinnon, Ronald I. *Money and Capital in Economic Development.* Washington, D.C.: Brookings Institution.

Pfeffermann, Guy (1985). "Overvalued Exchange Rates and Development." *Finance and Development* 22 (1) (March): 17–19.

Reynolds, Clark W., and Jaime I. Corredor (1976). "The Effects of the Financial System on the Distribution of Income and Wealth in Mexico." *Food Research Institute Studies* XV: 71–89.

Shaw, Edward S. (1973). *Financial Deepening in Economic Development.* Oxford University Press.

Wai, U. Tun (1957). "Interest Rates Outside the Organized Money Markets." *IMF Staff Papers* 6 (November): 80–125.

Zinser, James E., Zunilda Paniagua, Nieves Mármol de Periche, Agueda Lembert de Checo, and Adriana Martínez (1984). *El Mercado Financiero No Regulado en República Dominicana.* Banco Central de la República Dominicana, Departamento Financiero (Rural Savings Mobilization Project).

V

THE LIBERALIZATION
EXPERIENCE
OF CHILE AND URUGUAY

11

A Primer on the Chilean Economy: 1973–83

Arnold Harberger

The intent of this chapter is to sketch some key facts concerning the behavior of the Chilean economy from the early 1970s to the early 1980s. Emphasis has been placed on matters related to economic fluctuations, unemployment, monetary and exchange-rate policy, and so on. The discussion should provide the reader with the necessary background to understand and interpret the roots of Chile's serious economic crisis during 1982–83.

1. *The Chilean stabilization process that started in 1973–74 did not involve a major monetary shock.* The major monetary magnitudes were still expanding at over 200% per year in 1975 (two years after the military coup), at over 100% per year in 1977, and at over 50% per year in 1980. In 1981 the average excess of month-end money supply above that of the previous year was 25% for M1 and 93% for M2. And although M1 dropped slightly in nominal terms in 1982 as against 1981, M2 continued to grow at a 15% annual rate. Moreover, the rate of price increase did not fall significantly below 30% until 1981. In fact, rates similar to those of the "world inflation" really were achieved only from about June 1980 to June 1982 for wholesale prices and from about January 1981 to June 1982 for consumer prices (see Table 11.1).

2. *There was great variation in real money balances.* The ratio of M2 to GDP averaged about 10% in the 1960s. During the (mostly) repressed inflation of the Allende years it averaged about 12.5%. When the

Table 11.1 Chilean Inflation Rates (in percentages)

	Annual average rates			December to December	
	CPI	WPI	GDP Deflator	CPI	WPI
1980	35.1	39.6	29.3	31.2	28.1
1981	19.7	9.1	13.2	9.5	−3.9
1982	9.9	7.2	11.3	20.7	39.6

Data Source: Banco Central de Chile, Indicadores Económicos y Sociales, 1960-82, pp. 217, 121, 125.

repressed inflation became an open one (1974–76), real cash balances (M2) plummeted to around 5.5% of GDP. From then on they made a dramatic recovery, moving up to over 25% of GDP in 1982. The major part of this increase in the M2/GDP relationship took place under the fixed exchange rate of 39 pesos to the dollar, initiated in July of 1979 and abandoned in June of 1982.[1]

3. International reserves grew dramatically under Chile's fixed exchange rate. Chile had U.S.$273 million of international reserves at the end of 1977, and $1,058 million at the end of 1978. By December 1979 these reserves had risen to $2,313 million, and by December 1980 to $4,074 million. Reserves were not much affected as the crisis began brewing in 1981—falling only by some $300 million during that year. By the first devaluation (June 1982) they had dropped to $3,319 million, and by the second devaluation (August 1982) they were down to $2,947—still amply above their 1978 or 1979 levels. The important message here is that, if Chile had pursued a floating-rate policy starting sometime in 1978 or 1979, with other things remaining more or less the same, her exchange rate would probably have appreciated in nominal as well as real terms.

4. Chile's real exchange rate apreciated dramatically under the fixed rate of 39 pesos = $1. Calculating Chile's real exchange rate with the dollar as the nominal peso price of the dollar times the U.S. GNP deflator divided by the Chilean GDP deflator, and setting the 1960–69 average real rate as 100, we find remarkable stability of the annual (average) real rates from 1960 through 1970. Only once did the average real rate exceed an index of 105 (it was 109 in 1963), and not until 1971 did it fall below an index of 94. But then, in the Allende period, it deteriorated rapidly, reaching an index level of 82 in 1972.

Negative international reserves plus great difficulties in obtaining foreign credits forced the new military government into a policy of explicitly stimulating exports. This brought the real exchange rate to an index of 158 in 1975, followed by 126 in 1976. From there on a steady deterioration occurred, with the index reaching 109 in 1978, 97 in 1979, 85 in 1980, and 83 in 1981.

The degree of appreciation is understated by the above figures in the sense that they deal with the relationship between the peso and the U.S. dollar. Since from 1980 onward the dollar appreciated dramatically against the other major currencies, the Chilean peso did so also, on top of its appreciation vis-à-vis the dollar that we have calculated above.

5. *The great appreciation of the peso was not so bad.* Nonmineral exports grew from around $100 million in 1972 to $477 million in 1975 (when the real exchange rate peaked). They continued to grow as the real exchange rate declined, reaching nearly $1 billion in 1978, $1.5 billion in 1979, and $1.9 billion in 1980 before tailing off to $1.65 billion in 1981 and $1.55 billion in 1982.

Industrial production fell dramatically in 1975, but rose steadily thereafter, reaching peaks in March (119.6) and July (121.2) of 1981.

Unemployment at the national level declined from 14.1% in October–December 1978 to 10.4% in October–December 1980. In greater Santiago, the unemployment rate fell from 14.8% in the first quarter of 1979 (that is, before the exchange rate was fixed) to an almost constant 8.3% during the first three quarters of 1981.

The key reason why things were so good in Chile in 1981 was an inflow of capital, equal (over the whole year) to about 15% of GDP. In short, spending exceeded production by about 15%. This extra force of demand helped support a good level of economic activity and a low level of unemployment, *despite* a highly appreciated exchange rate. Had this voluntary capital inflow continued at its 1981 pace, the Chilean economy would probably have stayed in reasonable shape during 1982 and 1983.[2]

6. *The proximate cause of Chile's current trouble was the sharp reduction in the rate of net capital inflow*, from about 15% of GDP in 1981 to about 5% of GDP in 1982.[3] This dramatic shift created an imperative need for the real exchange rate to rise, especially in the light of the fact that the foreign credits received by Chile in recent years had been mainly used to purchase nontradable goods (especially to finance, directly or indirectly, a construction boom). In short, an exchange rate that appeared to be reasonably viable (in the presence of a very large capital inflow mainly directed toward domestic goods and services) was no longer viable when the external financing flow virtually dried up.

7. Chile's labor law made the necessary adjustment of the real exchange rate impossible. The real exchange rate has many guises—among them, (1) the nominal exchange rate multiplied by a foreign price index and divided by a domestic one; (2) the internal (that is, within the country) price level of tradable goods deflated by the internal price level of nontradables; and (3) the ratio of the nominal exchange rate to an index of wages. Case (2) can be seen to revert to case (1) if the foreign price index is the foreign price level of goods traded (with Chile) and the domestic price level is the price level of nontradables. Case (3) can be seen to approximate case (2) given that the nominal exchange rate is the predominant *local* variable in determining the internal prices of world-marketed goods, and the wage level is the principal input into services, which in turn make up the bulk of nontradables.

The adjustment that was called for by the shutting down of the capital inflow can thus be seen to entail either a reduction in wages (assuming the nominal exchange rate remained fixed) or a rise in the nominal exchange rate (assuming wages remained fixed).

Neither of the above two alternatives ensued (up to June of 1982). The result was that the pressure to raise the real exchange rate made itself felt in a dramatic increase in the rate of unemployment. The unemployment rate in greater Santiago marched ineluctably upward, from 8.1% in the third quarter of 1981 to 11% in the fourth; then from 15% in the first quarter of 1982 to 19.1% in the second.[4]

It was, to my mind, the unconscionable rise in the unemployment rate, rather than anything connected with the loss of foreign reserves, that triggered the devaluation of June 1982. But the devaluation was impossible until the labor law was changed. This law, written when the Chilean economy was at the height of its late-1970s boom, mandated essentially that every new labor contract must provide *at a minimum* a full cost-of-living adjustment from the date of the previous contract. For practical purposes, it made reductions in real wages *illegal* in any covered activity.

Nothing could be accomplished to bring about the required adjustment while this labor law was in effect. Yet something obviously had to be done. According to reliable reports, the preferred alternative of the economic team was a decreed reduction of 15 to 20% in all wages and salaries (perhaps with some exceptions at the lowest levels), so as to be able to maintain the exchange rate at 39. The reports go on to say that this proposal was taken seriously, and discussed at the highest levels of government. The final decision, however, was instead to devalue the peso. Yet even for the devaluation to work, a modification of the labor law was necessary. This modification was finally made—it provided that the real wages pacted in new labor contracts could fall below their previous level, but not below a floor equal to their level at the moment the labor law had taken effect. This left an ample margin for downward real wage adjustment, and indeed, Chile's experience since the June 1982 devaluation attests that a serious modification (devaluation) of the real exchange rate was indeed made possible.

8. *The monetary effects of the Chilean devaluations tended to frustrate their purpose*, at least for some time. A devaluation was declared in June 1982, from 39 to 46 pesos to the dollar. This devaluation was "calibrated" to approximate what would have happened if Chile, rather than pegging to the dollar in July 1979, had instead pegged the peso to a basket of major currencies (roughly on a trade-weighted basis). Although I believe (in retrospect) that the policy of pegging to a basket would have been better for Chile than that of pegging to the dollar, and that with such a policy Chile might have averted a major crisis, the failure of the attempt (ex post, in June 1982) to replicate this scenario is quite clear. The new peg (which was to follow local inflation in a crawling-peg fashion) did not last more than two months. It was replaced by a short period of a free float, in which the upward pressure on the exchange rate proved severe, and finally followed by the reinstitution of serious exchange controls, with a parallel market side-by-side with the official one.

From June 1982 to June 1983 the real exchange rate rose by some 50% as the nominal official rate doubled (from 39 to 78) while consumer prices rose by about a third (with U.S. prices increasing only modestly). The "objective" of an increased real exchange rate (which in my view, given the circumstances of the capital market, was an absolute necessity) was thus achieved, but its intended purpose of reducing unemployment was substantially frustrated. In fact, postdevaluation unemployment exceeded the second quarter level of 19.1%, and reached 23.9% and 21.9% in the third and fourth quarters of 1982 and 21.8% and 19.6% in the first and second quarters of 1983.

9. *These monetary effects entailed a reduction in desired holdings of peso cash balances combined with a dramatic drain on dollar reserves* (see Table 11.2). The fall in real M2 signified a reduction in the banking system's capacity to grant credits to domestic borrowers; the loss of reserves worked in the other direction. The net result was that real domestic credit fell only slightly during the period between the June devaluation and May 1983.

However there was a spate of bank failures, dated in January 1983, that was accompanied by a major bailout operation by the central bank. As a consequence the banking system had far less possibility to grant what I call "good" credits in May 1983 than in June 1982.

10. *On "good" and "bad" credits—the Achilles' heel of the Chilean economic experiment*. It is now becoming very clear that the condition of

Table 11.2

	Real money holdings (M2) (billions of pesos of 1978)	International reserves (millions of U.S. dollars)
June 1982	150.1	3,319
August 1982	147.9	2,947
December 1982	132.0	2,577
March 1983	116.0	1,578
May 1983	107.1	1,518

Source: Banco Central de Chile, *Boletín Mensual,* June 1983, pp. 1323, 1378).

the Chilean banking system played a major role in determining the course of economic events in the period since 1974. Recall that, at the time of the military coup in September 1973, hundreds of Chilean corporations were in government hands, nearly all of them generating substantial losses. Those which had been simply "intervened" by the government (that is, not expropriated) were returned to their owners, but those which had been officially expropriated were (with a few exceptions like the major coper mines) sold at auction to the highest bidder.

Regardless of the category to which they belonged, the firms were in a weak financial position at the time that they passed back from government to private hands. The deep recession of 1974–75 can only have made things worse. While I know of no study which explicitly traces the economic fate of the enterprises in question, there can be little doubt that a significant fraction of them must have reached the borderline of technical bankruptcy at some point during the 1975 recession.

It is probable that starting at that relatively early point the Chilean banks began to accumulate a stock of bad loans. Rather than write off these loans as bad debts, the typical practice appears to have been to roll them over, accumulating interest along the way. The apparent reason for this practice was that, upon recognizing a bad loan as such a bank would have to reduce its capital and surplus so as to reflect the loss. This, in turn, would reduce all sorts of legal limits—on lending, on deposits, on borrowing from abroad, and so on—all of which were typically expressed as multiples of capital and surplus.

As time went on, it appears that the volume of bad loans held by the banking system grew. The consequence was that the supply of credit available for "genuine" loans was progressively squeezed. This superimposition of what in effect was a "false" demand for credit on top of a true or good demand is probably the main reason why Chilean interest rates remained so high throughout most of the 1975–82 period. The high interest rates—which hovered most of the time around 3 or 4% per month in real terms—were in turn partly responsible for putting in peril the financial situation of yet other companies, which may have begun the period in relatively healthy condition but simply could not withstand the steady drain on their resources that the high interest rates entailed.

The beginning of the 1982–83 banking crisis in Chile can probably be dated around May 1981, with the failure of the major private-sector sugar company, CRAV. It was not the failure as such that caused the problem, but rather the laxity of banking practices which was revealed as the evidence unfolded. (Most banks had made their loans to CRAV essentially without collateral, "on the signature only" of its distinguished director, Don Jorge Ross.)

During July–September of 1981 it appeared that the financial system was surmounting the crisis. Interest rates, which had risen sharply in the wake of the CRAV failure, began to drift downward, and calm seemed to have been restored in the Chilean financial community. However, new rumblings appeared in October, and by November 1981 eight financial institutions were "intervened" by the central bank. These eight included four banks (of which the largest was the Banco Español) and four financieras which together accounted for about half the assets of the entire financiera system.

The decision of the government was finally to "bail out" these institutions fully—in the sense of guaranteeing the payment of their obligations both to their depositors and to their other creditors. In doing so, the government followed a precedent set several years earlier when the Banco Osorno had failed in an isolated occurrence. Most qualified observers feel that it was a mistake to bail out failing institutions so fully, especially since there is essentially a complete continuum of possibilities— bailout of principal but no interest, bailout of principal plus part of interest, bailout of 90% of principal but no interest, etc.

It was the precedent set by these earlier bailout operations which served as the ostensible motivation under which the international private banking community virtually insisted on a comparable bailout of practically the entire Chilean banking system when the crisis wave hit once again in January 1983. The end result of a lengthy process of negotiations was that the government effectively extended its own guarantee to all outstanding foreign debts of the Chilean banking system.

11. *The consequence of the progressive bailouts of Chile's banks is a wad of bad or dubious paper in the portfolio of the central bank.* This paper, as long as it is present, limits the capacity of the banking system to make loans

to viable enterprises. To the extent that bank credit serves as a productive input (or lubricant) in the economic process, the constricted amount of resources available for credits to truly viable enterprises will limit the pace of Chile's recovery.

In effect, there was nothing plausible that the policymakers could have done to make real M2 go up—indeed, the weakening of confidence made it fall significantly. International reserves, on the other hand, fell to only a little more than a third of the earlier peak levels. The policymakers did not want to lose more, and agreed not to do so, but what was more important was that even if they were "used," the existing reserves were not big enough to finance a very big dose of stimulatory credit expansion. This pretty much ruled out any major expansion of credit in real terms.

12. *A current view*. The story of the Chilean economy in 1981–82 was grim, and the outlook for the future was somber. It would surely take at least two years for the 1981 level of real output to be regained, and for the unemployment rate in the greater Santiago labor market to drop back to the 10–12% range within which it oscillated during the late 1970s. There seemed to be no policy capable of eliciting a quicker recovery.

Key danger signals would be (1) further efforts on the part of the public to flee from the currency; and (2) further substantial reductions in real money holdings. Such reductions would have as their counterpart a further squeezing of the amount of "good" credit (in real terms) available to the system.

Hopeful signs were:

- The unemployment rate, though high, was significantly below its earlier peak of 23.9%.
- Quarterly GDP was up in the second quarter of 1983 compared with the first. Industrial production was also up from its recent troughs.
- Up to the moment at least, Chile had shown the policy restraint necessary to ensure that the nominal devaluation of the peso also entailed a significant real devaluation. This had given a new stimulus to tradable goods production (particularly of nonmineral exports).
- Quotations in the parallel market, which earlier had reached levels in excess of 130 pesos per dollar, ranged between 85 and 95 (compared with an official rate of around 78).
- Despite a number of government retreats from the liberal, noninterventionist policy system that prevailed between, say, 1975 and 1982, the basic structure of economic policy in Chile continued to be sounder than that in most other Latin American countries. Chile still has a basically uniform tariff (now at a 20% rate), a sound

tax system, expenditure restraint on the part of government which has kept public sector deficits down to manageable (that is, noninflationary) proportions, a reasonably "economic" pricing policy of public sector enterprises, and so on.

These attributes of the policy structure should give Chile a certain edge over other countries in the struggle (universal these days among the Latin American countries) for economic recovery.

Notes

[1]Banco Central de Chile, *Indicadores Económicos y Sociales, 1960–1982*, p. 218.
[2]Ibid., pp. 244, 75, 177, 201.
[3]Ibid., p. 237.
[4]Ibid., p. 182.

12

Financial Reforms, Stabilization, and Growth under High Capital Mobility: Uruguay 1974–83

Jaime de Melo

1. Introduction

Financial reforms are the distinguishing feature of the Uruguayan liberalization of 1973–82. A tightly regulated financial system had developed in response to a banking crisis in 1965 when several banks failed. Following the 1965 bankruptcies, a bill on banking regulations was passed in 1965 which prohibited entry into the banking system and limited the expansion of remaining branches. A remarkable contraction in the size

This chapter is part of research in progress at the World Bank under RPO 672–85, "Liberalization and Stabilization in the Southern Cone." I thank Timothy Condon for helpful comments, also James Tybout for permission to draw on joint research, and Gabriel Castillo and Jorge Miranda for able research assistance.

The World Bank does not accept responsibility for the views expressed herein which are those of the author(s) and should not be attributed to the World Bank or to its affiliated organizations. The findings, interpretations, and conclusions are the results of research supported by the Bank; they do not necessarily represent official policy of the Bank. The designations employed, the presentation of material, and any maps used in this document are solely for the convenience of the reader and do not imply the expression of any opinion whatsoever on the part of the World Bank or its affiliates concerning the legal status of any country, territory, city, area, or of its authorities, or concerning the delimitation of its boundaries, or national affiliation.

of the financial market ensued, and regulation of the banking system was to remain until the military takeover in 1973.

The financial reforms of the post-1973 period were to be far reaching. Early on in 1974, domestic residents were allowed to hold unrestricted dollar-denominated accounts in the Uruguayan Banking System (UBS), and the central bank (BCU) started to pay interest on required bank reserves. Directed credit programs were progressively lifted and, by 1976, interest rate ceilings, which had been progressively lifted, were abolished so that banks became free to quote interest rates on loans and deposits. In 1977, commercial banks were allowed to pay interest on checking accounts, and CBU relaxed the legislation governing the regulatory status of banking houses by allowing de facto entry and expansion. And, in 1979 both the 8.4% banking tax and the obligatory reserve requirements were abolished. Within a five-year span, the UBS was virtually entirely deregulated.

Other reforms in commodity markets were also implemented simultaneously (a chronology of these reforms appears in the appendix). Although commodity market reforms were less extensive than financial reforms, they affected the way the economy adjusted in the short and medium run, as did external shocks relating to events in Argentina.[1] It is therefore necessary to take into account the effects of external shocks and other reforms in any study of the outcome of financial market deregulation.

This chapter addresses three issues raised in the literature on financial market reforms. The first issue has only recently been raised and relates to the order of liberalization of the current and capital accounts of the balance of payments. The issue is linked to the trade-offs between real and financial openness: if both accounts are not liberalized simultaneously, does it matter which one is liberalized first? The second issue, also raised recently, is the implication of currency substitution (that is, the holdings of dollars by Uruguayans) on the effectiveness of monetary (and exchange rate) policy for stabilization. The third issue is the best known. It relates to the implications for financial resource allocation and growth of deregulating a financially repressed economy.

The relevance of the Uruguayan reforms to these issues is examined in the remainder of the chapter. Section 2 uses a short-term macro model to show how increased capital mobility and the real exchange rate with Argentina affected stabilization policy. Section 3 looks at preliminary evidence on the extent and causes of currency substitution in Uruguay. Finally, Section 4 appraises the extent to which financial reforms raised growth by increasing savings and investment. Section 5 presents the conclusions.

2. Short-Run Adjustment with High Capital Mobility under the Passive and Active Crawling Peg

The situation that had to be corrected when the military took over in 1973 is summarized in Table 12.1. Negative growth, falling export volumes, and a rising fiscal deficit (which reached 4.4% of GDP in 1974) characterized the pre-reform period of 1971–74. The situation was further complicated by the sharp fall in the terms of trade that took place following the first oil shock and the closing of the EEC market to Uruguayan beef.

Three phases of adjustment can be distinguished during the reforms. The first phase (1975-78) corresponds to the period when the Uruguayan peso became convertible and interest rate controls were progressively lifted. It is also the period when devaluations were set equal to the difference between domestic and world inflation, that is, a passive crawling peg was pursued. During this period, taxes on traditional exports were removed and nontraditional exporters benefited from strong fiscal and financial incentives as well as from the passive crawling peg which maintained a constant real exchange rate (see Table 12.1). The second phase (1979–81) corresponds to the period of active crawl with preannouncement of future values of the exchange rate (the *tablita*). As in Argentina and Chile, from the start devaluation rates were at less than the difference between domestic and world inflation. Although this phase lasted until November 1982, only the period 1979–81 is included in that phase because in those years there was also a strong real depreciation vis-à-vis Argentina, which was also following the *tablita* with even more vigor. During this phase, export incentives were also removed and the financial reforms completed. Finally, the third phase 1982–83 straddles the end of the *tablita* period and the floating exchange rate period. This phase corresponds to the strong recession following the collapse of Argentine demand as the Argentine peso depreciated sharply vis-à-vis the Uruguayan peso and the sharp rise in the fiscal deficit.

To show how the economy adjusted to the financial reforms, I use a short-run model proposed by Bruno (1983). I modify this model to include the effects of a change in the real exchange rate vis-à-vis Argentina on the current account and on internal demand, to reflect the high substitutability in the commodity market between Argentine and Uruguayan goods because of the proximity of the two markets and the lack of impediments to trade. The key feature of the model that makes it useful to study the adjustment to the opening of the capital account is its assumption that domestic residents hold both domestic and foreign assets which allows one to show the effects of increasing capital mobility and changing expectations on short-run macro equilibrium.

Table 12.1 Macroeconomic Indicators (yearly averages)

Period	GDP growth[a]	Terms of trade[b]	Export volume[a]	Real exchange rate[c]	Argentine CPI corrected for exchange rate change[b,d]	Fiscal deficit (% of GDP)	Inflation[a] (% per year)	Real money supply (M1/P)[a]	Real credit to private sector[b,e]
1971–74	−0.9	135	−6.8	114	91	0.6	69	127	108
1975–78	4.1	59	14.8	122	90	2.4	59	103	148
1979–81	4.7	74	8.9	94	119	0.0	55	110	264
1982–83	−7.2	57	2.4	154	66	6.7	34	101	444

Source: Hanson and de Melo (1985, tables 1, 2); BCU.

[a] Annual growth.

[b] Real exchange rate with Argentina. Index: 1974 = 100.

[c] Nominal exchange rate times the ratio of world inflation (IFS) to the CPI index.

[d] Computed as follows (j = Argentina, u = Uruguay): $(CPI_j/CPI_u) \cdot (ER_u/ER_j)$.

[e] Dollar credit converted to pesos at end of year exchange rate.

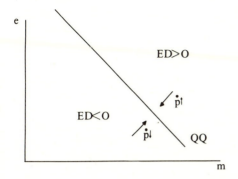

Figure 12.1 Goods market equilibrium.

Goods market equilibrium is described by the QQ schedule in e,m space in Figure 12.1. The schedule is downward sloping because an increase in the real money supply (m) raises absorption and leads to excess demand, which is eliminated by a fall in the real exchange rate (e). A fall in e reduces excess demand in the goods market because imported intermediate inputs enter noncompetitively into the short-run supply function: a real appreciation lowers their relative cost and thus increases supply. Because the price level appears on both axes, price movements take place along a 45° vector toward the QQ curve (inflation falls as one approaches QQ from below).

An increase in government expenditures shifts QQ outwards, and a decline in the terms of trade, which lowers real income, shifts QQ inwards. Because of the high substitutability between Argentine and Uruguayan commodities, demand is a function of the real exchange rate with Argentina. For a given value of e, a fall in competitiveness with Argentina (for example, because of a strong real exchange rate depreciation in Argentina) will decrease demand as Uruguayans shift their expenditures to Argentina. This leads to an inward shift of QQ.

The balance of payments consists of the current account and the short-term capital account. Balance-of-payments equilibrium and the components of the balance of payments are depicted in Figure 12.2. The current account is defined as exports of goods plus net tourist receipts minus noncompetitive imports. The NX schedule depicts current account equilibrium. The current account is in surplus above the NX line. An increase in export subsidies shifts the NX schedule downward. A deterioration in the terms of trade or an increase in net tourist expenditures shifts the schedule downward.

Residents hold a domestic asset (money) and a foreign asset, Z. The relative demand for the foreign asset is an increasing function of the

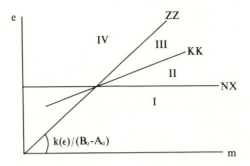

Figure 12.2 Balance-of-payments equilibrium.

expected rate of depreciation as in Miles (1978). Total short-term foreign exchange assets held in the economy, B, include U.S. dollar deposits held by Argentines. They are assumed to be given at any point in time, although they may adjust exogenously. Because the exchange rate was fixed most of the time, central bank reserves, A, are endogenous but are assumed to be given at any point in time. This implies that $Z = B - A$. Different degrees of financial openess are accommodated by assuming that the money market equilibrates while the actual change in the privately held foreign exchange asset, ΔZ, is proportional to the desired change; that is, $\Delta Z = \beta(Z_d - Z_0)$ where Z_0 is the initial level of foreign assets, Z_d is the desired level of foreign assets, and β is a parameter that reflects the speed of adjustment. Relaxing capital controls raises the speed of adjustment in asset markets, and in the limit, when there is instantaneous adjustment, only the capital account matters. Equilibrium in the short-run capital account is given by the ZZ schedule in Figure 12.2. The schedule is upward sloping because a devaluation raises the peso value of the foreign asset which requires a compensating increase in the money supply to reestablish equilibrum in the asset market. Above the ZZ schedule the short-run capital account is in surplus. An increase in the expected rate of depreciation, ε, rotates the ZZ schedule counterclockwise. So does a decrease in total short-term foreign assets, B_0, due for instance to a withdrawal of Argentine deposits. Finally, an increase in central bank reserves, A_0, shifts ZZ clockwise.

Finally, the overall balance schedule, KK, is the sum of the current account and the short-run capital account. It lies between the ZZ and NX schedules. Above the schedule there is an overall surplus, and below a deficit. The model can now be used to show how Uruguay adjusted to the increase in capital mobility that occurred during the passive crawling peg (1974–78), then under the active crawling peg (1979–82).

2.1. Adjustment under the Passive Crawling Peg

Figure 12.3 shows how the economy adjusted to the combination of external shocks and fiscal deficits during the opening of the capital account. Let A be equilibrium around 1972 when the passive crawling peg was instituted and prior to the rise in the fiscal deficit. By the time Uruguayans decided to lift controls on capital flows in September 1974, there was a growing fiscal deficit and deteriorating terms of trade. The net effect of the external shock has been estimated at between 5 and 10% of average GDP during 1974–78 (see Hanson and de Melo, 1985). The net effect of these two shocks was to shift upwards the NX schedule and to shift inwards the QQ schedule. If there had been no relaxation of capital controls and no incentives to exporters, the new short-run equilibrium would have been at a point like B (Figure 12.3) with a much higher real exchange rate and much lower real money supply.

However, the opening of the capital account mitigated the monetary crunch that usually accompanies stabilization packages (see Table 12.1), and the subsidies to exports mitigated the real exchange rate devaluation. Confidence in the passive crawling peg and relaxation of controls on capital flows shifted the ZZ curve clockwise. Furthermore, the export subsidies shifted down the NX schedule so that the net upward shift in the KK schedule was dampened. At the same time falling real wages and increasing investment (see evidence in Section 3) reduced the inward shift of the QQ curve. The resulting equilibrium during 1976–78 was at C in Figure 12.3, which was close to the one prevailing before the external shock and the increase in government spending (see Table 12.1).

In this adjustment, the capital account was opened before the current account, as redundant protection for import-competing sectors remained

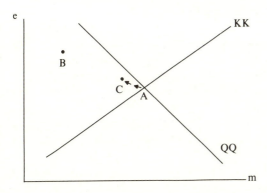

Figure 12.3 Short-run adjustment with the passive crawling peg.

until 1979 (Hanson and de Melo, 1985). Fears that opening the capital account first will lead to a real appreciation that will hurt exporters may be unfounded if exporters are given compensating incentives *and* there is confidence in the exchange rate regime. The Uruguayan experience thus suggests that doubts expressed about this sequencing of liberalization may be unfounded.[2] Table 12.1 indicates that exports responded strongly to these incentives and that the passive crawling peg avoided the predicted real exchange rate appreciation. Also, as mentioned above, opening the capital account helped avoid the monetary crunch by bringing an end to capital flight. Indeed, the net errors and omissions item of the balance of payments, reflecting over- and under-voicing and other forms of capital flight, changed drastically. Prior to the reforms it was always negative (the yearly average was U.S.$40 million or 10% of export earnings over 1970–74). During 1975–78, the average yearly value of net errors and omissions turned to a positive $38 million suggesting an end to capital flight. Also, net credit to the private sector, including dollars, was growing rapidly (see Table 12.1), reflecting the dollarization of the economy, which is discussed further in Section 3. It is indeed remarkable that the increased confidence during the opening of the capital account allowed the fiscal deficit to be eliminated while credit to the private sector grew.

2.2.   Adjustment with High Capital Mobility under the Active Crawl

When the *tablita* was instituted in October 1978, the preannounced rate of crawl was at much less than the differential between internal and external inflation. Since domestic interest rates were deregulated at that time, it became extremely attractive to bring in short-term capital inflows to take advantage of the high peso interest rates under no foreign exchange risk. This shifted the KK schedule to the right to KK' (Figure 12.4), while increased demand from higher than usual Argentine tourist expenditures (because Argentina was appreciating rapidly vis-à-vis Uruguay; see Table 12.1) shifted the QQ schedule outward to QQ'. Loans were issued in pesos because, due to rising inflation, ex post borrowing costs in pesos were negative. The upward dollarization trend was halted (see Figure 12.5). The economy was moving along the path AB in Figure 12.4.[3] As long as the Argentine peso appreciated—that is, until late 1980—the real exchange rate appreciated sharply. Real credit to the private sector also grew rapidly as firms were increasing their indebtedness and consumers were borrowing to purchase importable durables.[4]

When Argentina started depreciating in real terms vis-à-vis Uruguay from March 1981 until Uruguay abandoned the *tablita* in November 1982, expectations that the preannounced exchange rate schedule was unsustain-

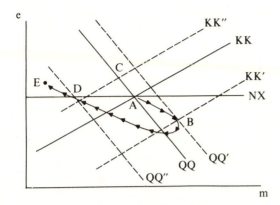

Figure 12.4 Short-run adjustment with the active crawl.

able increased rapidly, rotating the ZZ curve counterclockwise. Temporary equilibrium would have been along KK″ at C (Figure 12.4) if the exchange rate had been allowed to devalue.[5] Since this was not the case, there were heavy foreign exchange reserves losses to finance the ongoing capital flight with money supply falling and the economy moving toward D. Finally, following Argentina's sharp devaluation of July 1982 which shifted the QQ schedule inwards to QQ″ as Uruguayans transferred their demand

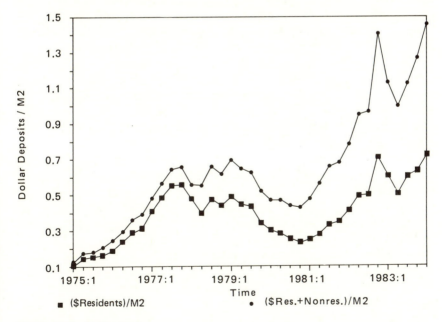

Figure 12.5 Dollarization.

across the border, the *tablita* was abandoned in November and the economy eventually settled at E with 15% unemployment. In the meantime, owing to the high capital mobility, capital flight was large and has been estimated in the neighborhood of $2 billion.[6] Dollarization increased sharply with real M1 falling by 23% between December 1980 and December 1983.

The lesson from the active crawl with high capital mobility is that allowing a sustained real exchange rate appreciation leads to a large current-account deficit that can result in large swings in relative prices prompted by portfolio shifts. An earlier abandonment of the active crawl would have brought the economy to C (Figure 12.4) with less capital flight and less unemployment. While the Uruguayan experience is not sufficient to establish a case against opening the capital account before the current account, it suggests caution in pursuing such a course. Either external shocks or mismanagement of the monetary-exchange rate policy unit is likely to result in short-run swings that lead to costly temporary resource shifts away from tradable sectors.

3.   Currency Substitution and Capital Mobility

The second issue for which the Uruguayan experience with financial market reforms is relevant relates to the effects of liberalizing the capital account on the efficacy of monetary policy. Recall that as early as September 1974 Uruguayan residents could hold unrestricted amounts of foreign currency. The Uruguayan peso became *de facto* a convertible currency. Insofar as Uruguayan holdings of dollars rose beyond what would be needed for international trade transactions and tourism, this would cause a problem for the central bank's conduct of monetary policy. The potential for currency substitution, defined as the ability of domestic residents to switch between domestic and foreign fiat money, becomes an effective way of avoiding the inflation tax on the holdings of domestic cash balances. The escape from domestic to foreign money also results in a loss of seignorage for the government. Below I examine the causes of the increasing dollarization of the Uruguayan economy and attempt to separate the determinants of Uruguayan residents' holdings of dollars; that is, I look for the causes of currency substitution (CS).

The dimensions of the dollarization problem are shown in Figure 12.5. It is immediately apparent that dollarization proceeded very rapidly and that it reached much higher levels than in other countries. For example, in Mexico, the ratio of foreign currency deposits to the total money stock stayed in the 15% range until 1982, when it shot up to 25%. In Argentina the ratio never exceeded 10%.[7] It is also apparent that even though restricted holdings of dollars by domestic residents had been allowed in Uruguay before the reforms, it is only with the lifting of controls toward the end of 1974 that dollar holdings in the domestic financial system started to grow rapidly. Finally, it is also apparent that much of the foreign-currency-denominated deposit growth between 1980 and 1982 was due to deposits held by Argentines. Of course, the rise in Argentinian-held deposits was not due only to the convertibility of the Uruguayan peso. At times it was due to the uncertain conditions in Argentina, but most of the time it was due to the *tablita* which removed exchange rate uncertainty while interest rates paid in pesos remained high in real terms.[8]

It is questionable that an increase in dollarization of the magnitude observed in Figure 12.5 reflected only an increase in the demand for foreign fiat money. Indeed, as suggested by Figure 12.6, it is likely that much of the CS that took place reflected the repatriation of dollars held abroad. Not only did the ratio of dollar deposits in Uruguay to dollar deposits in U.S. banks rise until 1982, but the current dollar value of deposits held in U.S. banks, which had been rising until late 1976, fell until early 1980. Thus much of the CS by Uruguayans was a portfolio adjustment between dollars abroad and dollars held in the Uruguayan financial system. As argued in Section 2, this portfolio shift represented

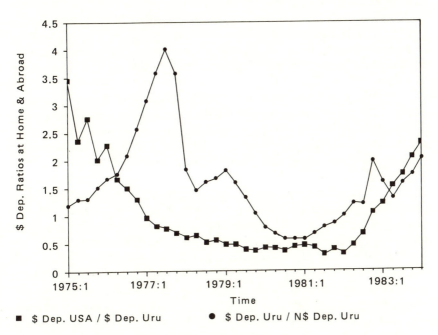

Figure 12.6 Portfolio shifts by Uruguayan residents.

increasing confidence in the economy.[9] It is also clear that when, starting in 1982, confidence in the *tablita* waned, this trend was reversed and dollar-denominated deposits shifted toward U.S. banks. This trend was to continue throughout 1983 after the flotation of the peso because of the internal financial crisis and the growing insolvency of Uruguayan banks.[10]

Starting with Miles (1978), the approach to CS emphasizes the importance of foreign exchange risk among the diverse reasons for holding foreign currency money balances. In the developed country literature this has served as the basis for the argument that monetary authorities lose national monetary independence under floating rates because the elasticity of substitution is likely to increase during periods of floating, reflecting the greater incentive for agents to diversify their portfolios of liquid money assets. In the developing country literature, the emphasis has been on the potential problems for short-run monetary instability that CS can create (Ortiz, 1983; Ramírez-Rojas, 1985), and the crucial variable used to explain the demand for foreign money has been the difference between the real rate of return on domestic and foreign money approximated by the expected rate of depreciation.

As discussed above, in Uruguay the expected rate of depreciation undoubtedly played an important role in determining financial portfolio shifts. However, another potentially important determinant of CS is the rate of return on interest-bearing assets, in particular dollar-denominated bonds which were an important asset in Uruguayan financial portfolios. In the absence of data on these interest-bearing assets, it is not possible to distinguish between capital mobility reflecting portfolio shifts between nonmonetary assets and CS reflecting the substitution of foreign for domestic money.[11]

To test for the presence of currency substitution, I assume that the demand for domestic and foreign money is homogenous in wealth so that the ratio of domestic to foreign money (M_t/F_t) is expressed as a function of the expected rate of depreciation (ε_t) and real income (y_t), the latter variable reflecting the transaction motive for holding foreign money. (The higher the real income, the higher the transactions with foreigners and hence the greater the demand for foreign money).[12] Finally, even though portfolio shifts were rapid in Uruguay during the reforms period, I assume, as in other studies, that the money market does not clear within a quarter, so the lagged dependent variable is included in the specification. Finally, quarterly dummies (not reported) are included in the equation to account for the strong seasonality in income and in the money supply, and the Corchran-Orcutt procedure is applied to correct for autocorrelation.

Selecting a proper proxy for ε_t is crucial, and the proxy used here is very crude so the results must be viewed as preliminary. I select as the proxy, deviations of the exchange rate from the trade-weighted purchasing

Table 12.2 Estimates of Currency Substitution, 1976(I) to 1984(I)

$$\ln \left(\frac{M_t}{F_t}\right) = \begin{array}{cccc} -3.84 & + & 0.54 \ln(y_t) & -0.43 \, (\epsilon_t) & + & 0.55 \ln \left(\frac{M_{t-1}}{F_{t-1}}\right) \\ (-1.59) & & (1.78) & (-3.02) & & (3.95) \end{array}$$

$\bar{R}^2 = 0.62 \qquad F(6, 23) = 9.00 \qquad RHO = 0.80 \qquad H = 1.69$
$$(7.28)$$

Note: t-values in parentheses.

power parity exchange rate. In the definition of M_t/F_t, I exclude dollar deposits held by foreigners but include dollar deposits held by Uruguayans in U.S. banks.[13]

The results are presented in Table 12.2. The sign for y_t does not support the transactions motive for currency substitution, but, as expected, the shift from pesos to dollars is strongly negatively correlated with the exchange rate departure from purchasing power parity. Finally, as is usually the case, the lagged dependent variable is highly significant, but its value suggests that portfolio adjustments were not fully made within a quarter. These results support the stock adjustment specification to asset markets specified in Section 2.[14]

The results in Table 12.2 are very preliminary, but the overall evidence in this section suggests that significant portfolio shifts took place in Uruguay after convertibility of the peso. The evidence also suggests that the degree of confidence in the exchange rate policy was the major determinant of currency substitution by Uruguayans.

4. Financial Liberalization, Savings, and Investment

The Uruguayan experience is also relevant to the issue of the longer-run benefits from financial market deregulation.[15] In their influential works, McKinnon (1973) and Shaw (1973) argued that financial resource allocation is inefficient in "financially repressed" economies. The financial repression syndrome they identify includes one in which fiscal deficits are financed by interest rates ceilings that discourage saving. Fiscal deficits result in financial intermediation between savers and investors being carried out by the government via forced savings mechanisms (including taxation of profits and of the banking system) rather than by the financial system. And because savings which are assumed to be interest-sensitive are low as a result of administratively determined interest rates, nonprice

Table 12.3 Domestic Private Savings Function, 1962–83

$$S^p_t = \begin{array}{l} -0.933 \\ (-0.273) \end{array} + \begin{array}{l} 0.036\ y'_t \\ (1.71) \end{array} \begin{array}{l} -0.020\ r_t \\ (-0.419) \end{array} + \begin{array}{l} 0.048\ e_t \\ (2.20) \end{array}$$

$$\begin{array}{l} +1.75\ D_t \\ (1.43) \end{array} + \begin{array}{l} 0.264\ S^p_{t-1} \\ (1.18) \end{array}$$

$$\bar{R}^2 = 0.30 \qquad F(5,16) = 2.84$$

Source: de Melo and Tybout (1986, table 5).

Note: t-values in parentheses; endogenous variables: r_t, y'_t [see de Melo and Tybout (1986) for the set of instruments used and for structural stability tests].

rationing of investable funds occurs. Interest rate ceilings also discourage risk-taking by financial institutions, who opt for traditional low-yielding investments because they appear the safest to finance.

Financial repression was prevalent in Uruguay before the 1974 reforms.[16] The McKinnon–Shaw hypothesis predicts that the financial reforms would have led to a greater role for the financial system in providing intermediation between savers and investors, as well as to a greater volume of savings and investment. The discussion in Section 3 already indicated that the financial reforms increased the role of the financial system as an intermediary as the financial market deregulation led to financial deepening via dollarization. Here I summarize econometric evidence on the effects of the financial reforms on the volume of savings and investment.

Table 12.3 reports the results of regressions that test whether the financial reforms raised the savings function, and whether private savings in Uruguay responded to interest rates. Note that in contrast with previous empirical studies and in accordance with the financial repression literature, private (S^p_t) rather than total savings is used. The regressors include income growth (y'_t) because it proxies for deviations from "permanent" income which standard theory suggests should induce saving-rate fluctuations. Lagged saving (S^p_{t-1}), is included because adjustment may be spread over multiple periods. The real exchange rate (e_t) is included among the regressors rather than foreign savings because, with the capital account open, agents can borrow abroad and therefore will take into account expectations about future values of the real exchange rate. In particular when the real exchange rate is low and agents do not expect it to remain low in the future, they will dissave to purchase foreign goods while their real price is low. Finally, the ex-post real interest rate on deposits (r_t), and a dummy variable ($D_t = 0$ through 1974 and 1 thereafter), are included, the first to capture the interest elasticity of savings, the second to capture the effects of the reforms on savings.

The results, presented in Table 12.3, show that, after accounting for other factors, there appeared to be a mild upward shift in private savings after the reforms but that no interest rate elasticity of savings could be detected.[17] Interestingly, private savings is inversely related to the real exchange rate, suggesting that low real exchange rates encourage absorption by making traded goods less expensive and perhaps by creating the perception of an increase in wealth.

Turning to the effects of the reforms on investment, one would expect that private investment (i_t) would depend not only on expected profits and accelerator-type mechanisms (proxied by the history of demand growth), but also, if there is financial repression, on the liquidity position of firms, since firms would then have to rely more on internal funds for investment (proxied by current, M'_t and lagged, M'_{t-1}, real money growth). To test the significance of these effects, private investment expressed as a fraction of GDP (i_t), was regressed on the above variables, real interest rates (r_t), and a dummy variable to test the effect of the reforms on the investment level. The results are presented in Table 12.4.

The significance of the coefficients on lagged income and lagged investment suggest that the accelerator mechanism was operating. On the other hand, increase in money stock had only a transitory effect on capital accumulation, so financial repression effects did not appear to be important. Results from further tests, not reported here, suggest that the Uruguayan economy was not savings-constrained in the pre-reform years. Finally, the function clearly shifts upward in the reform period, suggesting that the surge in investment was not wholly due to movements in the

Table 12.4 Private Investment Rate Function, 1962–83

$$
\begin{aligned}
i_t = \ &-0.483 && +0.020\,y'_t && +0.285\,y'_{t-1} && +0.014\,m'_t \\
&(-0.163) && (0.172) && (2.80) && (1.04) \\[6pt]
&-0.021\,m'_{t-1} && +0.024\,e_t && -0.011\,r_t && +2.20\,D_t \\
&(-1.47) && (1.67) && (-0.471) && (3.64) \\[6pt]
&+0.55\,i_{t-1} \\
&(4.83)
\end{aligned}
$$

$R^2 = 0.82 \qquad H = 0.61 \qquad F(8, 13) = 12.68$

Source: de Melo and Tybout (1986, table 6).
Note: t–values in parentheses; endogenous variables: y', e, r.

explanatory variables in the model. Rather, it would appear that the better investment performance was greatly attributable to the other ongoing reforms including the rationalization of the taxation system and the removal of quantitative controls on imports of investment goods (see the appendix for details of the reforms).

In sum, controlling for other factors, the reforms induced an upward shift in private savings and in private investment compared with the pre-reform years. This result is consistent with the improved growth performance during the reform years. Indeed, even if one takes into account the recession year of 1983, trend GDP growth was statistically higher during the post-1974 period (1.4% p.a.) than during 1955–73 (1.0% p.a.). But these upward shifts are attributable to the entire reform package that included commodity market deregulation, not just the financial reforms. In particular, private savings were not responsive to interest rates, and the low private-investment levels of the pre-reform years could not be attributed directly to financial repression effects.

5. Conclusions

This chapter has analyzed the Uruguayan experience to assess several issues in the literature on financial market reforms in developing countries. First, I showed that liberalizing the capital account before the current account can be successful when exporters are provided with incentives and the real exchange rate is kept in line with trading partners. But the Uruguayan experience also shows that rapid financial portfolio adjustments in a financially open economy can be destabilizing for long-run resource allocation. Second, I gave preliminary evidence that currency substitution was mostly determined by foreign exchange risk, a result also found in other Latin American countries. Finally, I gave some evidence that the reform package led to some of the predicted results put forward by proponents of financial liberalization. Controlling for other factors, the reforms induced an upward shift in private savings and private investment compared with the pre-reform years.

Notes

[1]See Hanson and de Melo (1985) and Blejer and Gil-Díaz (1986) for a more extensive interpretation of how the economy adjusted to the reforms and to the external shocks.

[2]See Edwards (1984) for a discussion of the issues raised about alternative sequencing of external account liberalization.

[3]Inflation jumped in 1979, in part because of internal price deregulation. This is not shown in Figure 12.4. For details see Hanson and de Melo (1985).

[4]de Melo, Pascale, and Tybout (1985) study the pattern of adjustments at the firm level and give evidence of increasing dollar exposure.

[5]To simplify the graphical presentation, I omit the inward shift in the QQ schedule due to the growing fiscal deficit.

[6]Capital flight estimates are provided in Corbo, de Melo, and Tybout (1986).

[7]These figures cited in Ramírez-Rojas (1985) include dollar deposits in the definition of the money supply, whereas the ratios in Figure 12.5 exclude dollar deposits from the definition of the money supply. This distinction does not affect the conclusions in the text.

[8]Hanson and de Melo (1985) review alternative explanations of the high peso/dollar interest rate spread.

[9]On an annual basis, the interest rate on dollar deposits in Uruguay was generally constant at one percentage point above the corresponding LIBOR rate so the portfolio shift reflected factors other than changes in relative returns.

[10]For a brief discussion of the factors that led to the internal financial crisis, see Corbo, de Melo, and Tybout (1986).

[11]The distinction between capital mobility and CS was first made by Cuddington (1983). Banda (1982) obtained disappointing results in his estimation of portfolio shifts.

[12]In a portfolio balance model, inclusion of y_t would imply rejecting the usual two-stage budgeting procedure.

[13]Similar results were obtained when dollar deposits held in the U.S. were excluded.

[14]Similar results are obtained by Ramírez-Rojas (1985).

[15]This section is a summary of a more extensive treatment in de Melo and Tybout (1986).

[16]See Hanson and de Melo (1985) and de Melo and Tybout (1986) for a further description of the financial repression syndrome.

[17]Traditional savings functions also gave generally insignificant estimates for the interest rate coefficient.

Appendix: Chronology of Principal Reforms*

A. *Pre-reform Period*: Devaluations in 1959, 1963, 1965(2), 1967, 1968

June 1968   All prices including salaries are fixed and COPRIN, the agency in charge of controlling prices, has to approve all price increases in each industry.

1969   Contralor de Importaciones y Exportaciones abolished.

May 1971   Capital goods imports become subject to prior approval, effectively prohibiting imports.

---

*Source: Hanson and de Milo (1985).

March 1972	New government takes office after November 1971 elections. Beginning of transition period leading to reforms. Recognition that system of price controls established in 1968 must be relaxed; 100% devaluation.
1972	Inauguration of passive crawling peg, pursued until November 1978; creates double foreign exchange market.
1973	Military takeover. Dissolution of parliament and suspension of political activities. Approval of Development Plan.

B. *Reform Period*:

1. *Major Events*

July 1974	Vegh Villegas becomes Minister of Economy and Finance. He is replaced by Arismendi in July 1976.
Sept. 1974	Capital market is opened and foreign exchange holdings by Uruguayans is allowed for the first time. For capital transactions, the exchange rate is determined freely. For transactions in the goods market, the exchange rate is determined by the crawling peg.
Oct. 1978	Commercial and capital markets for foreign exchange are unified. The exchange rate is preannounced 90 days in advance. Treasury bills are guaranteed (buyers of treasury bills can purchase dollars when redeeming treasury bills).
Dec. 1978	Tariff reforms are instituted, with a uniform tariff of 35% to be achieved by 1985 through a linear tariff reduction.

2. *Financial Market Reforms*

Sept. 1974	Uruguayan residents can buy or sell assets denominated in external currencies without restrictions, leading to de facto convertibility of the peso. Ceilings on peso-denominated deposits are raised from 15 to 30%.
May 1975	Foreign investors are allowed to repatriate earnings and capital. Rules dictating allocation of credit begin. Central bank begins to pay interest on reserves required by law.
March–Sept. 1976	Domestic interest rates are effectively freed, with the ceiling raised to 62%. Rediscount facilities for commercial banks are eliminated.
	External currency trade is permitted outside commercial banks. The central bank begins to pay interest on legal reserve requirement.
Mid-1977	The 1965 banking law controlling the number of financial intermediaries is relaxed. The number of casas bancarias rises

from one in 1976 to 23 in 1981. Casas bancarias cannot offer checking account services; they are chiefly engaged in intermediating foreign currency funds obtained abroad (from nonresidents) in the domestic financial market.

Nov. 1977	The dual foreign exchange market is unified. Commercial banks are allowed to pay interest on cash accounts.
Oct. 1978	Three-month treasury bills are sold which could be redeemed in dollars. The central bank thus was effectively preannouncing the exchange rate (official unification of dual foreign exchange market).
	Nil marginal reserve requirement is introduced and legal reserve requirement unified at 20%.
Early 1979	Financial interest subsidies for exports are removed.
May 1979	Subsidized credits to Frigorifios with Banco de la República are eliminated. The legal reserve requirement is eliminated.
	Reserve requirements for commercial banks for deposits in domestic and foreign currency are abolished. The banking tax is abolished (it amounted to 8.4%: 6% lender tax and 2.4% tax on loan to commercial bank).
Feb.–Sept. 1981	To narrow the persistent cross-currency gap in lending rates, the central bank offers implicit exchange guarantees.

3. Commodity and Labor Market Reforms

July 1974	Personal income and inheritance taxes are removed. A uniform 25% tax on corporate net profits is established with exports exonerated for up to 50% of profits reinvested. Export taxes on beef and wool are removed to compensate for the decline in world prices.
July 1974	Internal prices of nonessential goods begin to be liberalized. At this time 94% of CPI still is controlled, as is 75% of value added in agriculture. Some barriers to imports are removed. Compulsory external financing for 180 days and prior permission to import capital goods are abolished.
October 1974	A law is enacted to encourage foreign direct investments: the repatriation of profits and capital is guaranteed.
Jan. 1975	Remaining quantitative restrictions are removed.
July–December	13% of goods in the CPI basket are deregulated.
Feb. 1976	Prices not in the CPI are liberalized, except those deemed to be produced under monopoly. Later in the year, another 25% of prices in CPI are deregulated.

July 1978	A new agency, DINACOPRIN, replaces COPRIN. The major objectives of DINACOPRIN include the promotion of competition of the economy and greater flexibility in setting prices.
Aug. 1978	Another 13% of CPI basket is decontrolled, as is the meat market.
Feb. 1979	Tariff reductions are accelerated to prevent "exaggerated" price increases. There is a return to some price controls (such as clothes and private schooling).
March 1979	The list of goods and services with prices fixed administratively is reduced.
Sept. 1979	To fight inflation, further tariff reduction with price liberalization.
Nov. 1979	Tax reform: —Uniform 18% VAT for nonessential commodities —Reduction of social security charges —Elimination of 8.4% banking tax —Elimination of exoneration of profit tax on exports —Elimination of subsidized credits to exporters.
June 1980	DINACOPRIN fixes car prices because there is no foreign competition. By June 1980, 29% of prices in the CPI are still controlled (16.1% excluding price of public utilities). For agricultural prices, 65% were controlled in December 1973. In December 1979 only 14% are controlled.
June 1982	A 10% surcharge tax is imposed on all imports, and there is a 10 percentage point increase in *reintegros*.

References

Banda, A. (1982). "Una Aproximación Empírica al Estudio de los Substitutos de Dinero en el Uruguay." Paper presented at the Reunion de Tecnicos de Bancos Centrales del Continente Americano, Viña del Mar, Chile.

Blejer, M., and J. Gil-Díaz (1986). "Interest Rate Determination in an Open Economy: the Case of Uruguay." *Economic Development and Cultural Change* 34(3): 589–606.

Bruno, M. (1983). "Real vs. Financial Openness under Alternative Exchange Rates." In *Financial Policies and the World Capital Market: The Problem of*

Latin American Countries, edited by P. Aspe, R. Dornbusch, and M. Obstfeld. Chicago: University of Chicago Press.

Corbo, V., J. de Melo, and J. Tybout (1986). "What Went Wrong with the Southern Cone Reforms." *Economic Development and Cultural Change* 34(3): 607–40.

Cuddington, J. (1983). "Currency Substitution, Capital Mobility and Money Demand." *Journal of International Money and Finance* 2: 111–33.

de Melo, J., R. Pascale and J. Tybout (1985). "Microeconomic Adjustments in Uruguay During 1973–81: The Interplay of Real and Financial Shocks." *World Development* 13 (8).

de Melo, J., and J. Tybout (1986). "The Effects of Financial Liberalization on Savings and Investment in Uruguay." *Economic Development and Cultural Change* 34(3): 561–88.

Edwards, S. (1984). "The Order of Liberalization of the External Sector in Developing Countries." *Essays in International Finance*, no. 156, Princeton.

Hanson, J., and J. de Melo (1985). "External Shocks, Financial Reforms and Stabilization Attempts in Uruguay: 1974–83." *World Development* 13 (8).

McKinnon, R. (1973). *Money and Capital in Economic Development.* Washington, D.C.: The Brookings Institution.

Miles, M. (1978). "Currency Substitution, Flexible Exchange Rates and Monetary Independence." *American Economic Review*: 428–36.

Ortiz, G. (1983). "Currency Substitution in Mexico: The Dollarization Problem." *Journal of Money Credit and Banking* 15 (2).

Protasi, J. C., and C. Graziani (1984). "Determinantes de la Demanda de Dinero en Uruguay." *Banco Central del Uruguay*, Montevideo.

Ramírez-Rojas, C. (1985). "Currency Substitution in Argentina, Mexico and Uruguay." International Monetary Fund. Mimeo.

Shaw, E. (1973). *Financial Deepening in Economic Development.* New York: Oxford University Press.

VI

TRADE POLICY

13

Trade Liberalization, Preferential Agreements, and Their Impact on U.S. Imports from Latin America

Edward J. Ray

1. Introduction

The purpose of this chapter is to extend earlier work by Balassa (1967a, 1967b), Baldwin (1976), Bhagwati (1982), and Ray and Marvel (1984) on the impact of protectionist measures among the industrialized nations on the ability of developing countries to export manufactured goods. The chapter itself is unique in several important respects. First, the data used in this study have not been systematically analyzed in previous work.[1] They include total U.S. imports and exports of manufactured goods in 1983 for 241 four-digit SIC manufacturing industries and, in particular, U.S. imports in 1983 from the Caribbean Basin, South America, Brazil, and Mexico. Second, we provide evidence on the structural determinants of U.S. intra-industry trade that is consistent with and extends previous work by Marvel and Ray (1984). Third, we provide direct evidence on the determinants of U.S. imports in 1983 under the terms of the Generalized System of Preferences (GSP) and predict the commodity characteristics of manufactures declared eligible for duty-free importation into the United States, beginning in 1984, under the terms of the Caribbean Basin

Michael Melvin made a number of useful comments on an earlier draft. The author is particularly grateful to John Suomela, Tom Jennings, and the staff of the International Trade Commission without whose assistance in assembling the data used in this study, this research could not have been undertaken. Joe Denekamp and Mark Summers provided excellent research assistance in developing the empirical analysis for this research project.

Initiative (CBI), adopted in August 1983. Finally, we provide the first systematic empirical investigation of the effectiveness of the GSP program in providing developing countries with increased access to the U.S. market for exports of manufactured goods (especially consumer goods), agricultural products, and textiles.

Our findings include the following striking observations: (1) consistent with earlier work (Marvel and Ray, 1984), we find that any trade-liberalizing effects associated with intra-industry trade are not likely to be biased in favor of developing countries. Intra-industry trade is insignificant in agricultural goods and textiles and negatively and significantly related to manufactured consumer goods and to the capital–labor ratio in production. (2) U.S. imports from developing countries and regions under the terms of the GSP are either negatively or insignificantly associated with manufactured consumer goods, agricultural products, and textiles. Moreover, the relative impact of the GSP is to skew imports away from those three product categories. (3) In Section 4 we explain the apparent paradox just described and provide direct evidence that, contrary to the expressed intent of the GSP program, U.S. preferential import programs have systematically biased U.S. imports from developing areas away from industries with high tariff and/or nontariff trade restrictions in the United States. (4) Finally, we provide direct evidence that the Caribbean Basin Initiative fails to promote U.S. imports of consumer goods or agricultural products from the region and systematically discourages U.S. imports of textiles. Furthermore, CBI duty-free access to U.S. markets appears to be structured to re-enforce the distorting effects of the GSP rather than to moderate the adverse impact of U.S. tariffs and nontariff barriers to trade (NTBs) on Caribbean exports.

These findings have three important policy implications. First, the apparent discrimination against manufactured exports from developing countries to the industrialized nations may be magnified rather than reduced by preferential programs like the GSP, the Lomé Convention, and the CBI. To the extent that efforts to provide preferential access to industrialized country markets for developing countries are blunted by the political process as the current study suggests, North–South relations are not likely to improve substantially as a result of preferential trade agreements. Second, to the extent that Krugman (1983) and others are correct that intra-industry trade serves as a force for further trade liberalization, it is apparent that the force is not with the developing countries. Finally, the failure of preferential trade agreements to stimulate exports of manufactured goods from the developing countries in areas of greatest comparative advantage for them—such as consumer goods, agricultural products, and textiles—undercuts the likelihood that developing nations will be able to deal with their international debt problems in an orderly way through export growth.

Section 2 describes the pattern of U.S. imports and exports in 1983 and the structure of intra-industry trade. The discussion includes a review of the pattern of U.S. imports of manufactured goods from the Caribbean Basin, South America, Brazil, and Mexico. Special attention is given to U.S. imports under the terms of the GSP.

Section 3 reviews critical language in the GSP, Lomé, and CBI documents regarding country and product eligibility and explains how special interests may have undermined the original intent of those initiatives. The underlying model of the political economy of trade restrictions is consistent with earlier work by Baldwin (1976), Marvel and Ray (1983, 1984), Pincus (1975), Ray (1981a, 1981b), Ray and Marvel (1984), and Verreydt and Waelbroeck (1982).

Section 4 reviews our empirical findings regarding the impact of the GSP and CBI on U.S. imports from Latin America. In the process we provide evidence that those preferential agreements were not effectively targeted to reduce the degree of discrimination in U.S. protection against exports from Latin America or, indeed, developing countries in general. Section 5 provides some concluding remarks.

2. U.S. Imports of Manufactured Products from Latin America

Empirical analyses of U.S. trade flows have consistently revealed a tendency for the U.S. to be a net importer of low-skill-intensive and relatively capital-intensive manufactured products. Little direct evidence has been presented on the relative significance of manufactured consumer goods, agricultural products, and textiles in U.S. imports in general or in imports from developing countries. Yet it is generally acknowledged that developing countries have a comparative advantage in exporting those three categories of manufactured goods (Balassa, 1967a; Balassa and Associates, 1971; Bhagwati, 1982; Keesing, 1983; Verrydt and Waelbroeck, 1982). Table 13.1 provides current estimates of the commodity characteristics of U.S. imports of manufactured products in 1983. As indicated, the United States continues to be a net importer of low-skillintensive, capital-intensive products subject to positive scale effects.[2] While net imports of consumer goods are significant, net imports of textiles and agriculture-based manufactures are not significantly different from zero. In short, U.S. net imports are significant in one of three areas in which developing countries are presumed to have a comparative advantage

Table 13.1 U.S. Imports of Manufactured Products in 1983

Independent variables	(1.1) U.S. net imports in 1983	(1.2) U.S. intra-industry trade in 1983	(1.3) U.S. imports from the Caribbean 1983	(1.4) U.S. imports from South America 1983	(1.5) U.S. imports from Brazil 1983	(1.6) U.S. imports from Mexico 1983
				Dependent variables		
Constant	−35.293 (0.08)	0.602 (7.63)	−352.039 (5.16)	−303.813 (4.37)	−23.653 (1.74)	−39.885 (1.97)
Consumer goods	748.054 (2.46)	−0.217 (4.50)	120.850 (2.74)	110.236 (2.41)	14.585 (1.64)	−2.163 (0.16)
Manufactured agricultural goods	−574.171 (1.53)	−0.071 (1.21)	−161.880 (2.99)	−121.099 (2.15)	4.321 (0.36)	−26.362 (1.52)
Manufactured textiles	95.894 (0.20)	−0.062 (0.84)	60.656 (0.92)	66.700 (0.99)	5.380 (0.41)	0.032 (0.00)
Skill intensity of production	−1912.284 (2.02)	0.158 (1.06)	372.274 (2.58)	313.029 (2.13)	−7.273 (0.26)	96.886 (2.28)
Average output/plant	12.006 (8.36)	-2.3×10^{-4} (0.93)	0.599 (2.18)	0.590 (2.76)	0.229 (5.15)	0.322 (5.05)
Capital–labor ratio	161.119 (2.39)	−0.031 (2.78)	95.703 (8.08)	82.951 (7.84)	12.785 (5.96)	7.059 (2.32)
Industrial concentration	–	0.001	–	–	–	–
R^2	0.2824	0.1317	0.3217	0.2722	0.2812	0.1613
Number of observations	241	241	201	228	211	238

Note: The regressions were estimated using OLS. Absolute t-values appear in parentheses.

in production. Equations (1.3) to (1.6) in Table 13.1 are estimates of U.S. imports of manufactured products from several specific areas: the Caribbean Basin, South America, Brazil, and Mexico. With respect to the general pattern of manufactured product imports into the United States in 1983 from each of those developing areas, it is clear that only manufactured consumer goods are significant among imports from the Caribbean and South America. When refined petroleum products are removed from the list of manufactured goods, the consumer goods coefficient is also insignificant.[3]

Intra-Industry Trade and Trade Liberalization

Krugman (1983) has argued that intra-industry trade might serve to promote trade liberalization over time based on the presumption that such trade is dominated by the cross-hauling of differentiated consumer products. Developed and developing countries alike might be expected to embrace freer trade in the Krugman view to jointly capture gains from trade and specialization without being handicapped by the divergent interests of winners and losers that are characteristic of more traditional trade models. Clearly, that possibility is a matter of some importance to developing countries. The question is whether or not commodities involved in intra-industry trade are likely export targets for developing countries.

Equation (1.2) in Table 13.1 provides an estimate of the determinants of U.S. intra-industry trade. In terms of the general nature of intra-industry trade, the results obtained in this study are consistent with an earlier analysis by Marvel and Ray (1984) indicating that intra-industry trade is associated with industries in which output is not subject to scale economies, that do not have high capital–labor ratios or concentration ratios, and that are involved in producer goods rather than consumer goods. These results and the earlier ones are difficult to reconcile with the more popular model by Brander (1981), Helpman (1981), Krugman (1979, 1980, 1981) and Lancaster (1980). However, they are quite consistent with explanations of intra-industry trade offered by Kravis (1971) and by Marvel and Ray (1984).

The results in equation (1.2) are consistent with the view that since intra-industry trade is not positively related to any of the three commodity characteristics associated with potential manufactured exports from developing countries, any impetus it may provide for freer trade is unlikely to benefit developing nations. Stated more simply, if intra-industry trade is a force for freer trade, the force is not with developing countries.

Table 13.2 Leading and Lagging Sectors in U.S. Intra-Industry Trade, 1983

No.	SIC code	Industry	Z
High intra-industry trade industries			
1.	3566	Gear boxes	0.9993
2.	3699	Electrical articles	0.9941
3.	3576	Weighing-machine scales	0.9926
4.	3714	Motor vehicle parts	0.9908
5.	3544	Molds: metals	0.9881
6.	2611	Pulp mill products	0.9868
7.	3542	Metal farming tools	0.9861
8.	3429	Hardware	0.9851
9.	3861	Photo equipment	0.9850
10.	3554	Pulp machinery	0.9837
Low intra-industry trade industries			
233.	2283	Wool and hair yarns	0.0705
234.	3172	Flat goods and leather	0.0689
235.	2046	Corn oil	0.0629
236.	2084	Wines	0.0626
237.	2296	Textile fabrics	0.0557
238.	3171	Womens' handbags	0.0376
239.	3263	Earthenware tableware	0.0264
240.	2044	Rice	0.0263
241	2111	Cigarettes	0.0195
242.	3333	Refined zinc	0.0088

Note: Z is a measure of intra-industry trade equal to [Min (Exports, Imports)]/ (Exports plus Imports) that ranges from 0 to 1.0. The Z-index value increases as intra-industry trade increases.

Before leaving the discussion of intra-industry trade it is perhaps instructive to refer to Table 13.2, which lists the 10 most significant industries and the 10 least significant in terms of intra-industry trade intensity. It is difficult to imagine how one might explain the ranking of industries presented there by appeal to models that explain the phenomenon of intra-industry trade as the consequence of countries specializing in the production of modest variants of differentiated consumer goods in order to capture scale economies and satisfy consumer preferences for variety.

U.S. Import Shares of Manufactures from Latin America

Since the U.S. trades on a substantial scale with both industrialized and developing nations, a more reasonable relationship to look at for evidence of the success of developing countries in exporting consumer goods, agricultural products, and textiles to the United States relative to third parties would be to look at the share of developing country imports into the United States as a share of U.S. imports from all of her trading partners. If trade flows conform to presumed comparative advantage, the developing regions should be relatively important suppliers of U.S. imports of manufactured consumer goods, agricultural products, and textiles.

Table 13.3 contains estimates of the share of U.S. imports of manufactures in 1983 from the Caribbean Basin, South America, Brazil, and Mexico.[4] Relative export strength to the United States for the Caribbean Basin, South America, and Brazil does appear to be positively and significantly associated with agricultural-based manufactured products. However, consumer goods and textiles are not major relative components in U.S. imports of manufactures from our four sample market areas.

The developing countries in general have argued for years that post–World War II trade liberalization has not been as effective in reducing trade barriers to manufactured exports from the developing countries to the industrialized nations as it has been in liberalizing trade among the industrialized nations. Using data from the post–Kennedy Round period for nominal and effective tariffs and nontariff trade barriers in the United States, Canada, Japan, and the EEC, Ray and Marvel (1984) found that:

> As a group, the industrialized countries have continued to employ tariffs to protect producers of consumer goods and textiles. NTBs have been used to bolster tariff protection for consumer goods and textiles, and to increase significantly the protection of agricultural manufactures. While it has been clear for some time that innovations in protectionism have been predominantly in the form of NTBs, this study has been able to demonstrate that those innovations in the industrialized nations have been directed predominantly against consumer goods, agricultural manufactures, and textiles, products of particular significance to the developing countries. (p. 458)

In their study of protectionism in the European Community, Verreydt and Waelbroeck (1982) tried to explain the persistent failure of the developing nations to induce the industrialized countries to end the discriminatory protectionist policies that the developing countries were subjected to throughout the post-war period. They concluded that the LDCs lack any substantial bargaining power: "The Group of 77 is an instrument for the dramatized expression of dreams; apart from OPEC, developing countries have not been able to form groups with enough interests in common and a large enough size to extract trade concessions from the EC, the United States or Japan" (p. 380).

Preferential Trade Agreements

While the evidence is quite clear that the combined effect of tariff and nontariff trade barriers in the United States, Japan, Canada, and the EEC has been to undercut the ability of developing countries to export consumer goods, agricultural products, and textiles to the industrialized nations, important efforts have been undertaken to moderate the bias against developing nations. In 1975, the United States adopted legislation known as the Generalized System of Preferences, and the European Community ratified the Lomé Convention.[5] Both documents established specific beneficiary countries and eligible articles to be imported duty free from developing countries. The Caribbean Basin Initiative (CBI) represents a further effort by the United States to provide a kind of compensatory discrimination in favor of Caribbean Basin exports to the United States.[6] The expressed purpose of each of those preferential trade agreements was to respond directly and substantially to developing country demands that the free-trade movement should include freer access to developed-country markets for manufactured exports from developing countries.

We have already indicated that protectionist measures in the United States and other industrialized nations systematically discriminated against exports of consumer goods, agricultural products, and textiles from developing countries. Therefore, we might naively expect that U.S. imports induced by the GSP program would be biased toward imports of manufactured consumer goods, agricultural products, and textiles.[7] In addition, since the point of the GSP program is to redress distortions in trade flows between the United States and developing countries, we might naively expect the relative importance of GSP imports into the United States from the Caribbean Basin, South America, Brazil, and Mexico to be most significant in newly favored textiles, agricultural products, and manufactured consumer goods. Evidence on both points appears in Tables 13.4 and 13.5.[8]

Before turning to that evidence on the structure of U.S. imports from Latin America, it is important to note that the issue we are exploring is how the GSP affected the composition of imports from Latin America and

Table 13.3 Import Shares from Developing Countries of Manufactured Products in 1983

			Dependent variables	
Independent variables	(2.1) Share of 1983 U.S. imports from the Caribbean	(2.2) Share of 1983 U.S. imports from South America	(2.3) Share of 1983 U.S. imports from Brazil	(2.4) Share of 1983 U.S. imports from Mexico
Constant	0.004 (0.21)	0.0188 (0.81)	0.013 (0.80)	0.108 (3.77)
Consumer goods	0.015 (1.28)	0.002 (0.10)	0.003 (0.27)	−0.024 (1.24)
Manufactured agricultural goods	0.042 (2.91)	0.044 (2.37)	0.050 (3.45)	0.012 (0.51)
Manufactured textiles	0.011 (0.62)	0.027 (1.18)	0.022 (1.38)	−0.050 (1.80)
Skill intensity of production	−0.011 (0.30)	−0.030 (0.61)	−0.015 (0.42)	−0.108 (1.80)
Average output/plant	−2.026 (0.28)	1.458×10^{-5} (0.20)	9.192×10^{-5} (0.02)	-5.341×10^{-5} (0.59)
Capital–labor ratio	0.004 (1.26)	0.011 (3.09)	0.003 (1.24)	0.002 (0.42)
R^2	0.0794	0.0857	0.0829	0.0308
Number of observations	201	228	211	238

Note: Regressions were estimated using OLS. Absolute t-values appear in parentheses.

Table 13.4 U.S. Imports from Developing Countries under the Generalized System of Preferences 1983

Independent variables	Dependent variables			
	(3.1) U.S. preferential imports from the Caribbean 1983	(3.2) U.S. preferential imports from South America 1983	(3.3) U.S. preferential imports from Brazil 1983	(3.4) U.S. preferential imports from Mexico 1983
Constant	0.998 (0.70)	9.131 (2.99)	5.944 (3.28)	3.458 (2.66)
Consumer goods	0.173 (0.19)	-3.821 (1.90)	-2.544 (2.15)	-1.258 (1.45)
Manufactured agricultural goods	1.943 (1.72)	-0.484 (0.20)	-0.688 (0.43)	0.672 (0.60)
Manufactured textiles	-0.837 (0.60)	-5.498 (1.85)	-3.218 (1.85)	-2.812 (2.21)
Skill intensity of production	2.017 (0.67)	-14.408 (2.23)	-7.781 (2.06)	-2.339 (0.86)
Average output/plant	-0.006 (0.99)	0.021 (2.25)	0.019 (3.14)	0.002 (0.50)
Capital-labor ratio	-0.346 (1.40)	0.598 (1.29)	-0.183 (0.64)	0.125 (0.64)
R^2	0.0400	0.0792	0.0892	0.0345
Number of observations	201	228	211	238

Note: Regressions were estimated using OLS. Absolute t-statistics in parentheses.

Table 13.5 The Share of U.S. Imports from Developing Countries That Entered under the Generalized System of Preferences, 1983

		Dependent variables		
Independent variables	(4.1) Share of imports into the U.S. from the Caribbean under GSP 1983	(4.2) Share of imports into the U.S. from South America under GSP 1983	(4.3) Share of imports into the U.S. from Brazil under GSP 1983	(4.4) Share of imports into the U.S. from Mexico under GSP 1983
Constant	0.732 (2.344)	1.867 (6.257)	2.033 (6.385)	0.963 (3.447)
Consumer goods	−0.235 (1.151)	−0.234 (1.278)	−0.575 (3.006)	−0.138 (0.760)
Manufactured agricultural goods	(0.746)	(2.345)	(2.426)	(0.388)
Manufactured textiles	−1.068 (3.201)	−1.949 (6.197)	−2.098 (6.396)	−1.289 (4.212)
Skill intensity of production	0.054 (0.083)	−0.041 (0.068)	−0.382 (0.625)	−0.020 (0.034)
Average output/plant	−0.003 (2.237)	−0.003 (2.875)	−0.003 (2.843)	−0.002 (2.207)
Capital–labor ratio	−0.059 (1.107)	−0.126 (2.870)	−0.121 (2.464)	−0.017 (0.400)
R^2	0.0827	0.2171	0.2441	0.0560
Number of observations	201	228	211	238

Note: The regressions estimated in this table were generated using Tobit to minimize the estimation errors associated with limited dependent variables. Absolute t-statistics are in parentheses.

not simply the magnitude of such imports. Non-OPEC developing country exports to the United States grew from $71.5 billion in 1982 to $98.8 billion in 1984. The United States accounts for 60% of industrialized-country imports of manufactures from developing countries, and GSP imports totaled $10.8 billion in 1983 and $13.0 billion in 1984. Clearly, the GSP expanded U.S. imports of manufactures from developing countries.

Did the GSP also fulfill the compensatory role of encouraging U.S. imports of manufactures from developing countries in product lines in which they would be expected to have a comparative advantage in trade? Again, the naive hypothesis would be that the GSP program was instituted to redress, at least to some extent, any discriminatory bias against imports into the United States from developing countries. Since developing countries have a comparative advantage in the production of manufactured textiles, agricultural products, and consumer goods, we might expect the effectiveness of the program to be reflected by the extent to which GSP imports are found to be predominately in those three product categories. The evidence in Table 13.4 is in sharp contrast with expectations based upon the naive hypothesis. There is no evidence that agricultural imports into the United States from developing areas are encouraged by GSP privileges. Consumer goods exports from South America in general and Brazil in particular and textile exports from South America, Brazil, and Mexico are apparently adversely affected by the GSP program. Given the stated purpose of the GSP program, the evidence in Table 13.4 might seem surprising.

A less stringent test of the effectiveness of the GSP program in promoting exports from developing countries to the United States in specific product lines would involve import shares. While levels of imports from developing areas might not be dominated by targeted product lines, the relative importance of those target commodities in exports to the United States from developing countries as a result of the GSP could be quite significant. Specifically, we can ask whether or not the GSP program had the effect of shifting U.S. imports from specific developing areas toward manufactured consumer goods, agricultural products, and/or textiles relative to overall imports from those same areas.

If the GSP did provide any significant compensatory discrimination in favor of imports of agricultural goods, textiles, and/or consumer goods from the Caribbean, South America, Brazil, and/or Mexico, GSP imports relative to overall imports from those areas should be positively related to some or all of those commodity characteristics. The empirical results summarized in Table 13.5 are even more striking than those presented in Table 13.4.[9] The GSP failed to provide a significant inducement toward consumer goods imports into the United States in any of the regions considered and proved to be negatively related to Brazilian exports to the

United States in 1983. There is also no evidence that the GSP program has stimulated relative exports of manufactured agricultural products from any of the four regions to the United States in 1983. In fact, for both South America in general and Brazil in particular relative export flows in 1983 were systematically biased away from manufactured agricultural products. Finally, the supplemental inducement affect of the GSP program on U.S. commodity imports from the Caribbean, South America, Brazil, and Mexico in 1983 was to reduce the relative importance of manufactured textile imports into the United States.

To summarize the empirical evidence presented so far, we find no evidence from 1983 trade flows to suggest that U.S. implementation of the GSP succeeded in inducing significant imports or even relatively increased imports of manufactured textiles, agricultural goods, or consumer goods from the four areas considered. Furthermore, we found evidence that, if anything, the GSP program has actually diverted exports from Latin American countries away from consumer goods, textiles, and agricultural products. Yet these are precisely those areas of comparative advantage in trade for developing countries that the GSP program was initiated to encourage.

3. The Political Economy of Trade Restrictions

To the extent that trade restrictions can be viewed as evidence of the triumph of special interests over general social welfare (Marvel and Ray, 1983; Pincus, 1975; Ray, 1981a, 1981b; Ray and Marvel, 1984), we would expect special interests to exert the same kind of pressure, with something of the same relative effectiveness across industries, in shaping preferential trade agreements that they affected when general tariff and nontariff trade restrictions were imposed. As outlined earlier, empirical evidence regarding the structure of protection in the industrialized countries indicates that the United States, EEC, Japan, and Canada maintained tariff and NTB regimes that systematically discouraged imports of manufactured agricultural products, textiles, and consumer goods. Regardless of the intent of preferential trade agreements, it would be extraordinary if they succeeded in substantially reducing barriers to U.S. imports in the three targeted areas for LDCs. Again, the same entrenched special interests that succeeded in maintaining substantial tariff and NTB restrictions on textiles, consumer goods, and agricultural products in the post-Kennedy Round period would have invested their energies in preventing the GSP and later the CBI from undercutting their protectionist successes. More generally, we would expect efforts to circumvent U.S. protectionist measures through preferential trade agreements to be frustrated by the same special interest groups that helped to fashion post–Kennedy Round tariffs and NTBs.

In effect, we have two competing hypotheses. The naive hypothesis would be that preferential trade arrangements systematically offset the adverse impact of tariffs and NTBs on manufactured imports. If so, imports under the auspices of the GSP and more recently the CBI should be biased toward generally highly protected sectors. In functional terms the naive hypothesis would lead to the following expectations:

GSP imports from a developing region

$= f_1$(U.S. post–Kennedy Round tariffs, U.S. nontariff barriers to trade)   (1)

with positive first partials of f_1 with respect to each argument, and

GSP share of imports from a developing region

$= f_2$(U.S. post–Kennedy Round tariffs, U.S. nontariff barriers to trade)   (2)

with positive first partials of f_2 for each argument.

With respect to the CBI we would characterize the naive hypothesis as follows:

Probable U.S. approval of CBI imports from the Caribbean Basin

$= f_3$(U.S. post–Kennedy Round tariffs, U.S. nontariff barriers to trade)   (3)

with positive first partials of f_3 for each argument.

In contrast, the special interest–political economy interpretation of how preferential trade agreements are likely to be shaped would lead us to expect the partials of equations (1)–(3) to be zero or negative. Partial derivatives insignificantly different from zero would indicate that with respect to tariffs and/or NTBs, the intended preferential effects have generally been blunted. Negative partial derivatives would suggest that special interests had actually succeeded in providing incentives through preferential agreements that magnify the distortions in trade flows induced by the original protectionist measures. Direct tests of these naive and non-naive hypotheses are presented in the following section. At this point we merely wish to point out that empirical support for the non-naive hypotheses would be consistent with the empirical observation in Section 2 that the absolute and relative impact of the GSP program on imports of textiles, consumer goods, and agricultural products into the United States from Latin American countries is generally negative or insignificant.

However, there is a fairly direct first step that one should take in assessing what, if any, effective role domestic special interests might have had in tailoring preferential trade agreements to protect themselves. One ought to read the documents to determine what, if any, exceptions and escape clauses are contained in the agreements since the naive hypotheses would lead one to expect exceptions to be few and inconsequential. Key sections of the GSP, the Lomé Convention (the Common Market's equivalent of the GSP), and the CBI are contained in an appendix that is available from the author upon request.

As indicated in Section 503(c)(1) of the GSP

> The President may not designate any article as an eligible article ... if such article is within one of the following categories of import-sensitive articles—(A) textile and apparel articles which are subject to textile agreements, (B) watches, (C) import-sensitive electronic articles, (D) import-sensitive steel articles, (E) footwear articles, (F) import-sensitive semimanufactured and manufactured glass products and (G) any other articles which the President determines to be import-sensitive in the context of the Generalized System of Preferences. (U.S. Statutes at Large, 1974, pp. 2069–2070)

Clearly, these and other provisions of the GSP were shaped by domestic economic and political considerations in the United States and served to blunt the marginal value of the GSP to developing nations.

While we do not have data for developing country exports to Europe under the conditions of the Lomé Convention, it is instructive to review how internal economic and political concerns within the European Community narrowed the scope for duty-free imports from developing nations in Africa, the Caribbean, and Pacific areas (ACP) into the European Community:

Article 3
If the offers made by firms of the ACP states are likely to be detrimental to the functioning of the Common Market and if any such detriment is attributable to a difference in the conditions of competition as regards prices, Member States may take appropriate measures, such as withdrawing concessions. (EEC, 1975, p. 603)

Article 10
1. If, as a result of applying the provisions of this Chapter, serious disturbances occur in a sector of the economy of the Community or of one or more of its Member States, or jeopardize their external financial stability, or if difficulties arise which may result in a deterioration in a sector of the economy of a region of the Community, the latter may take,

or may authorize the Member State concerned to take, the necessary safeguard measures. These measures and the methods of applying them shall be notified immediately to the Council of Ministers. (EEC, 1975, p. 608)

Finally, the CBI contains many of the same eligibility exceptions as the GSP and also requires annual reports to Congress by the International Trade Commission monitoring the impact of imports of eligible goods in the U.S. industries involved:

SEC. 213. ELIGIBLE ARTICLES

(b) The duty-free treatment provided under this title shall not apply to—

(1) textile and apparel articles which are subject to textile agreements;

(2) footwear, handbags, luggage, flat goods, work gloves, and leather wearing apparel not designated at the time of the effective date of this title as eligible articles for the purpose of the generalized system of preferences under title V of the Trade Act of 1974;

(3) tuna, prepared or preserved in any manner, in airtight containers;

(4) petroleum, or any product derived from petroleum, provided for in part 10 of schedule 4 of the TSUS; or

(5) watches and watch parts. ... (U.S. Statutes, 1983, p. 5064)

(2) In preparing the assessments required under paragraph (1), the Commission shall, to the extent practicable:

(A) analyze the production, trade and consumption of United States products affected by this Act, taking into consideration employment, profit levels, and use of productive facilities with respect to the domestic industries concerned, and such other economic factors in such industries as it considers relevant, including prices, wages, sales, inventories, patterns of demand, capital investment, obsolescence of equipment, and diversification of production; and

(B) describe the nature and extent of any significant change in employment, profit levels, and use of productive facilities, and such other conditions as it deems relevant in the domestic industries concerned, which it believes are attributable to this Act. (U.S. Statutes, 1983, p. 5070)

Each of the three examples of exceptions to preferential trade agreements with developing countries reflects the imprint of effective lobbying to mold the final document in ways that are much more protective of domestic industry interests than the naive view would suggest. Therefore, it seems quite reasonable to ask whether or not the preferential trade agreements finally adopted succeeded at all in moderating the adverse effects of tariffs and NTBs on industrialized country imports from developing nations.

4. Preferential Agreements and U.S. Protectionism

Tables 13.6 to 13.9 are direct estimates of equations (1) and (2) in Section 3. Each table contains four regressions to permit us to represent tariff protection by either nominal tariffs or effective protection rates in the United States.

With respect to the Caribbean Basin we find that GSP imports into the United States are not biased toward the high-tariff, NTB end of the commodity spectrum as the naive hypothesis would suggest. And, to the extent that the GSP has had any relative impact on the structure of U.S. imports from the Caribbean region, it has been to bias trade away from industries that enjoy NTB protection in the United States. This is significant in light of earlier work by Ray (1981a, 1981b), Marvel and Ray (1983), and Ray and Marvel (1984) indicating that U.S. NTBs have been used to substitute for the loss of tariff protection in some industries and to supplement tariff protection in others as world trade agreements reduced overall tariff rates. In effect, the GSP apparently re-enforces the distorting effect of U.S. NTBs on Caribbean exports of manufactured goods to the United States. Tables 13.7 to 13.9 indicate that GSP imports and relative imports are either neutral with respect to U.S. tariffs and/or NTBs or actually magnify the distorting effects of U.S. protectionist measures on exports of manufactures from South America, Brazil, and Mexico to the United States. Not one of the 32 protection coefficients in Tables 13.6 to 13.9 is positive and significant. And, in terms of relative import shares, the GSP systematically distorts U.S. imports of manufactured products from the Caribbean Basin, South America, Brazil, and Mexico away from product lines protected by NTBs in the United States.

Table 13.10 summarizes information with respect to the determinants of eligibility of imports into the United States from the Caribbean region under the terms of the CBI.[10] Eligibility is biased away from textiles and from concentrated industries, which would be expected to have relatively low lobbying costs. The CBI initiative appears to provide no significant incentive for imports of either consumer goods or agricultural-based manufactures into the United States from the Caribbean. As indicated in equations (10.2) and (10.3) in Table 13.10, which are the estimates of equation (3) in Section 3, the CBI does not offset the distorting effects of

Table 13.6 U.S. Protection and Imports from the Caribbean Basin under the GSP, 1983

Independent variables	Dependent variables			
	GSP imports from the Caribbean Basin	GSP imports from the Caribbean Basin	Percent of GSP imports in U.S. imports from the Caribbean Basin	Percent of GSP imports in U.S. imports from the Caribbean Basin
Constant	1.021 (1.95)	1.064 (1.86)	0.502 (4.071)	0.583 (4.330)
U.S. nominal tariffs	—	0.032 (0.56)	—	−0.017 (1.298)
U.S. effective protection	0.024 (0.82)	—	−0.003 (0.505)	—
U.S. nontariff trade barriers	−0.531 (0.64)	−0.513 (0.62)	−0.359 (2.023)	−0.332 (1.859)
R^2	0.0047	0.0030	0.019	0.020
Number of observations	201	201	201	201

Note: The first two regressions were estimated using OLS and the last two using Tobit to address limited dependent-variable estimation problems. Absolute t-statistics appear in parentheses.

270

Table 13.7 U.S. Protection and Imports from South America under the GSP, 1983

		Dependent variables		
Independent variables	GSP imports from South America	GSP imports from South America	Percent of GSP imports in U.S. imports from South America	Percent of GSP imports in U.S. imports from South America
Constant	5.537 (4.97)	6.081 (4.99)	1.444 (11.29)	1.497 (10.924)
U.S. nominal tariffs	—	−0.274 (2.17)	—	−0.028 (2.28)
U.S. effective protection	−0.123 (1.88)	—	−0.013 (2.039)	—
U.S. nontariff trade barriers	−0.918 (0.52)	−0.710 (0.40)	−0.702 (4.246)	−0.683 (4.106)
R^2	0.018	0.023	0.085	0.085
Number of observations	228	228	228	228

Note: The first two regressions were estimated using OLS and the last two using Tobit to address limited dependent-variable estimation problems. Absolute t-statistics appear in parentheses.

271

Table 13.8 U.S. Protection and Imports from Brazil under the GSP, 1983

			Dependent variables	
Independent variables	GSP imports from Brazil	GSP imports from Brazil	Percent of GSP imports in U.S. imports from Brazil	Percent of GSP imports in U.S. imports from Brazil
Constant	3.288 (4.87)	3.689 (4.80)	1.464 (10.68)	1.482 (9.911)
U.S. nominal tariffs	—	−0.169 (2.01)	—	−0.033 (2.29)
U.S. effective protection	−0.067 (1.71)	—	−0.018 (2.63)	—
U.S. nontariff trade barriers	−1.378 (1.30)	−1.134 (1.05)	−0.918 (5.25)	−0.886 (4.995)
R^2	0.025	0.030	0.130	0.125
Number of observations	211	211	211	211

Note: The first two regressions were estimated using OLS and the last two using Tobit to address limited dependent-variable estimation problems. Absolute t-statistics appear in parentheses.

Table 13.9 U.S. Protection and Imports from Mexico under the GSP, 1983

Independent variables	Dependent variables			
	GSP imports from Mexico	GSP imports from Mexico	Percent of GSP imports in U.S. imports from Mexico	Percent of GSP imports in U.S. imports from Mexico
Constant	2.574 (5.52)	2.705 (5.31)	0.917 (8.17)	0.940 (7.76)
U.S. nominal tariffs	—	−0.063 (1.18)	—	−0.018 (1.45)
U.S. effective protection	−0.027 (0.99)	—	−0.009 (1.41)	—
U.S. nontariff trade barriers	0.437 (0.57)	0.507 (0.66)	−0.513 (3.14)	−0.498 (3.02)
R²	0.005	0.007	0.031	0.029
Number of observations	238	238	238	238

Note: The first two regressions were estimated using OLS and the last two using Tobit to address limited dependent-variable estimation problems. Absolute t-statistics appear in parentheses.

273

Table 13.10 Probability of U.S. Authorization for Manufactured Products to Be Imported from the Caribbean Basin Area under the Provisions of the Caribbean Basin Initiative

Independent variables	(6.1) Probable U.S. approval of CBI imports from the Caribbean Basin	(6.2) Probable U.S. approval of CBI imports from the Caribbean Basin	(6.3) Probable U.S. approval of CBI imports from the Caribbean Basin	(6.4) Probable U.S. approval of CBI imports from the Caribbean Basin	(6.5) Probable U.S. approval of CBI imports from the Caribbean Basin
Constant	0.556 (1.415)	−0.235 (2.51)	−0.358 (2.518	−0.479 (2.94)	−0.543 (3.09)
Consumer goods	0.338 (1.428)	—	—	—	—
Manufactured agricultural goods	0.484 (1.69)	—	—	—	—
Manufactured textiles	−0.797 (2.06)	—	—	—	—
Skill intensity of production	−0.943 (1.25)	—	—	—	—

	(1)	(2)	(3)	(4)	(5)
Average output/plant	0.001 (0.82)	—	—	—	—
Capital-labor ratio	0.002 (2.66)	—	—	—	—
Industrial concentration	−0.014 (2.66)	—	—	—	—
Percent of GSP imports in U.S. from the Caribbean Basin 1983	—	—	—	0.005 (2.36)	0.005 (2.43)
U.S. effective protection	—	0.008 (1.17)	—	0.008 (1.07)	—
U.S. nominal tariff	—	—	0.018 (1.26)	—	0.021 (1.44)
U.S. nontariff trade barriers	—	0.032 (0.16)	0.019 (0.09)	0.041 (0.19)	0.022 (0.10)
R^2	0.087	0.006	0.008	0.032	0.037
Number of observations	201	201	201	201	201

Note: The regressions were estimated using Probit to address the estimation problems associated with dummy dependent variables. Absolute t-statistics appear in parentheses.

275

U.S. tariffs and NTBs on imports from the Caribbean. In fact, the CBI apears to be positively related to relative GSP imports into the United States from the Caribbean and therefore to generally re-enforce the distorting effects of the GSP already discussed.

5. Concluding Remarks

The evidence assembled in this study indicates that U.S. preferential trade agreements with developing countries in the Western Hemisphere fail to compensate for the discriminatory effects of U.S. tariffs and NTBs on the structure of imports from these countries. In fact, the GSP and CBI may actually magnify some trade-flow distortions associated with U.S. trade restrictions on imports from those countries. These results are less surprising when we realize that preferential trade agreements are molded by the same domestic political and economic interest group pressures that gave rise to the structure of post–Kennedy Round tariffs and NTBs in the United States.

In addition, if intra-industry trade is a force for trade liberalization, the force is not with the developing nations. Commodities that are involved in U.S. intra-industry trade can be characterized as producer goods not consumer goods, and they are neither capital-intensive nor subject to scale economics. Furthermore, U.S. intra-industry trade is not significant in either manufactured agricultural products or manufactured textiles.

As matters stand, neither U.S. preferential trade agreements nor the rapid growth of intra-industry trade appear to be promising vehicles for providing Latin American countries with access to the U.S. market for exports of manufactured goods in which they have a comparative advantage in production. While preferential agreements have promoted an expansion of Latin American exports of manufactures to the United States, they also may have contributed to inefficient distortions in the pattern of those exports.

Notes

[1]Data sources are indicated in the Appendix, which is available from the author upon request.

[2]Variable definitions and sources of data appear in the Appendix.

[3]See Table 1(c) in the Appendix.

[4]Tables 2(b)–2(e) in the Appendix list major and minor U.S. imports from the Caribbean, South America, Brazil, and Mexico.

[5]Excerpts from both documents appear in the Appendix.

[6]Excerpts from the CBI appear in the Appendix.

[7]Major U.S. imports from each of the four regions appear in Tables 3(b)–3(e) in the Appendix.

[8]Variable definitions and sources appear in the Appendix.

[9]Variable definitions and sources appear in the Appendix.

[10]Unfortunately, full-year data for 1984 U.S. imports from the Carribean under the CBI were not available at the time that this chapter was prepared.

References

Balassa, Bela (1967a). "The Impact of the Industrial Countries' Tariff Structure on Their Imports of Manufactures from Less Developed Areas." *Economica* 34 (November): 372–83.

————— (1976b). *Trade Liberalization Among Industrial Countries: Objectives and Alternatives*. New York: McGraw-Hill.

Balassa, Bela and Associates (1971). *The Structure of Protection in Developing Countries*. Baltimore: Johns Hopkins University Press.

Baldwin, Robert E. (1976). "The Political Economy of Postwar U.S. Trade Policy." *The Bulletin* 4 (N.Y.U. Graduate School of Business).

Becker, Gary S. (1983). "A Theory of Competition among Pressure Groups for Political Influence." *Quarterly Journal of Economics* 98 (3) (August): 371–400.

Bhagwati, Jagdish (1969). "On the Equivalence of Tariffs and Quotas." In *Trade, Tariffs and Growth*, edited by J. Bhagwati, pp. 248–65. Cambridge, Mass.: M.I.T. Press.

————— (1982). "Shifting Comparative Advantage, Protectionist Demands, and Policy Response." In *Import Competition and Response*, edited by J. Bhagwati, pp. 153–84. Chicago: National Bureau of Economic Research.

Brander, James A. (1981). "Intra-Industry Trade in Identical Commodities." *Journal of International Economics* 12 (1) (February): 1–14.

Caves, Richard E. (1976). "Economics Models of Political Choice: Canada's Tariff Structure." *Canadian Journal of Economics* 9 (May): 278–300.

Cheh, John H. (1974). "United States Concessions in the Kennedy Round and Short-run Labor-Adjustment Costs." *Journal of International Economics* 4 (November): 323–40.

European Economic Community (1975). "Africa-Caribbean-Pacific." *The Courier* no. 31 (Special Issue), March, pp. 596–622.

Falvey, Rodney E. (1983). "Protection and Import-Competing Product Selection in a Multi-Product Industry." *International Economic Review* 23, 4 (October): 735–49.

Grossman, Gene (1982). "Import Competition from Developed and Developing Countries." *Review of Economics and Statistics* 64, 2 (May): 271–81.

Grubel, Herbert G., and P. J. Lloyd (1975). *The Theory and Measurement of International Trade in Differential Products*. New York: Halsted Press.

Helpman, Elhanan (1981). "International Trade in the Presence of Product Differentiation, Economies of Scale and Monopolistic Competition: A Chamberlin-Hickscher-Ohlin Approach." *Journal of International Economics* 11 (3) (August): 305–40.

Keesing, Donald B. (1983). "Linking up to Distant Markets: South to North Exports of Manufactured Consumer Goods." *American Economic Review Papers and Proceedings* 73 (May): 338–32.

Kravis, Irving B. (1971). "The Current Case for Import Limitations." In *United States Economic Policy in an Interdependent World*. Washington, D.C.: Government Printing Office.

Krugman, Paul (1979). "Increasing Returns, Monopolistic Competition, and International Trade." *Journal of International Economics* 9 (4) (November): 469–79.

——— (1980). "Scale Economies, Product Differentiation, and the Pattern of Trade." *American Economic Review* 70 (5) (December): 950–59.

——— (1981). "Intraindustry Specialization and the Gains from Trade." *Journal of Political Economy* 89 (5) (October): 959–73.

——— (1983). "New Theories of Trade among Industrial Countries." *American Economic Association Papers and Proceedings* 73 (2) (May): 343–47.

Lancaster, Kelvin (1980). "Intra-Industry Trade under Perfect Monopolistic Competition." *Journal of International Economics* 10 (2) (May): 151–76.

Marvel, Howard P., and Edward J. Ray (1983). "The Kennedy Round: Evidence on the Regulation of International Trade in the United States." *American Economic Review* 73 (March): 190–97.

—— (1984). "Intra-Industry Trade: Sources and Effects on Protection." (Manuscript.) Ohio State University (July).

Peltzman, Sam (1976). "Toward a More General Theory of Regulation." *Journal of Law and Economics* 9 (August): 211 40.

Pincus, J. J. (1975). "Pressure Groups and the Pattern of Tariffs." *Journal of Political Economy* 83 (August): 757–78.

Ray, Edward J. (1981a). "The Determinants of Tariffs and Nontariff Trade Restrictions in the U.S." *Journal of Political Economy* 89 (February): 105–21.

—— (1981b). "Tariff and Nontariff Barriers to Trade in the United States and Abroad." *Review of Economics and Statistics* 63 (May): 161–68.

Ray, Edward J., and Howard P. Marvel (1984). "The Pattern of Protection in the Industrialized World." *Review of Economics and Statistics* (August): 452–58.

Stigler, George J. (1971). "The Economic Theory of Regulation." *Bell Journal of Economics and Management Science* 2 (Spring): 3–21.

United States Statutes at Large (1974). Vol. 88, Part 2, pp. 1363–2545, "Public Laws," 93rd Congress, Second Session.

—— (1983). Volume "Unbound," pp. 5060–71, "Public Laws," 98th Congress, First Session.

Verreydt, Eric, and Jean Waelbroeck (1982). "European Community Protection against Manufactured Imports from Developing Countries: A Case Study in the Political Economy of Protection." In *Import Competition and Response*, edited by J. Bhagwati, pp. 369–93. Chicago: National Bureau of Economic Research.

VII

INTEREST RATE POLICY

14

Financial Reform in a Small Open Economy with a Flexible Exchange Rate

Andrés Dauhajre

1. Introduction

To increase the interest rate on savings deposits is one of the recommendations that international financial institutions, particularly the World Bank and the International Monetary Fund, usually make to less developed countries with insufficient domestic savings levels to finance the necessary investment for maintaining adequate economic growth. The experts who work at those institutions consider, following the models of McKinnon (1973), Shaw (1973), and Kapur (1976), that the increased interest rates on time deposits would raise the level of savings in the economy and close the gap that exists between savings and investment. The increase in savings would increase the real volume of funds in the banking system and, consequently, the net flow of banking credit necessary to finance investment. Kapur argues that this larger flow of banking credit to finance investment projects would cause an increase in domestic production in the long run. This, in turn, would reduce inflationary pressures. These considerations might be correct in theoretical frameworks for developed economies. However, these arguments are not necessarily valid in

Research for this chapter was partially supported by the Rural Savings Mobilization Project in the Dominican Republic, sponsored by USAID, the Ohio State University, and the Central Bank of the Dominican Republic.

theoretical frameworks that would be adequate for small underdeveloped open economies.

The results obtained by McKinnon and by Kapur essentially depend on a hidden assumption concerning the structure of the assets market. All these authors assume that the portfolio shift into savings deposits comes out of an "unproductive" asset such as gold, cash, and so forth. This is a too-drastic simplication of the financial structure of most less developed countries. These countries, including the Dominican Republic, are characterized by the existence of informal money markets where the public and nonregulated finance companies lend directly to firms and farmers. The existence of this alternative asset, which provides more intermediation than the formal banking system itself, may change McKinnon's and Kapur's conclusions radically.

Van Wijnbergen (1983) has analyzed a macroeconomic portfolio model that contains a formal and informal credit sector using the guidelines of Tobin's (1969) general equilibrium model for the analysis of monetary theory. In his model, Van Wijnbergen takes into consideration the existence of three financial assets: money (M1), which does not bear interest; time deposits that bear a fixed interest rate (r_{td}); and credits on the informal market at a flexible rate (i). Van Wijnbergen analyzes the potential impact that an increase in the formal interest rate would have on economic activity. The impact on the latter will depend on the behavior of the financial assets portfolio.

The objective of this chapter is to translate Van Wijnbergen's model into a flexible exchange rate framework with perfect capital mobility. Flexibility of the exchange rate has accelerated in recent years due to the adjustment programs implemented by several Latin American countries as a result of negotiations with the IMF. Costa Rica and the Dominican Republic are clear evidence of this flexibilization process of the exchange rate.

2.   Flexible Output and Fixed Prices

In this section we will present a simplified model that focuses mainly on the asset markets and on the substitution effects generated by changes in the interest rate on savings deposits. In order to specify the real sector we have assumed a simple Keynesian demand-determined output mechanism.

We assume that the public distributes its financial wealth among money, time deposits in the formal market, time loans and/or deposits in the informal market, and certificates of deposit abroad, taking into account the real rates of return of these four financial assets[1] (minus the inflation rate $\dot{p}$, the real interest rate on time deposits $r_{td} - \dot{p}$, the real interest rate of the informal market $i - \dot{p}$, and the real interest rate in the international market $i^* - p^* = i^*$, if we assume that $p^* = 0$), real income y, and real wealth R/p.

The distribution of the real financial wealth is specified following a Tobin-like portfolio model in which, for the sake of simplicity, unitary wealth elasticities have been assumed:

$$C^d = \theta^c(\underset{-}{\dot{p}}, \underset{-}{r_{td}}, \underset{--}{i}, \underset{+}{i^*}, y) \frac{R}{p} \tag{1a}$$

$$TD = \theta^{td}(\underset{-}{\dot{p}}, \underset{+}{r_{td}}, \underset{--}{i}, \underset{+}{i^*}, y) \frac{R}{p} \tag{1b}$$

$$L_{im} = \theta^{im}(\underset{-}{\dot{p}}, \underset{-}{r_{td}}, \underset{+}{i}, \underset{-}{i^*}, \underset{-}{y}) \frac{R}{p} \tag{1c}$$

$$eCD^* = \theta^*(\underset{+}{\dot{p}}, \underset{-}{i}, \underset{+}{i^*}, \underset{+}{y}) \frac{R}{p} \tag{1d}$$

where C^d, TD, L_{im}, eCD^* represent the real demand for money, time deposits, time loans and/or deposits in the informal market, and certificates of deposit in the international market (in local currency), respectively. The demand equations for financial assets are accompanied by the usual adding-up conditions:

$$\sum_k \theta_j^k = 0 \qquad \sum_k \theta^k = 1 \tag{1e}$$

where subindex j indicates the partial derivative in relation to argument j. In addition, we impose the assumption of gross substitutes; so the demand functions have positive derivatives with respect to their own rate of return, and negative ones with respect to the rates of return of the three alternative assets.[2] Finally, we assume that the demands for C^d, TD, and CD^* are positively associated with real income; this implies that, by means of the consistency conditions (1e), the supply of loans in the informal market depends negatively on real income:

$$\theta_y^{im} < 0 \tag{1f}$$

We assume that the only source of funds for commercial banks are private time deposits (TD) for which reserves have to be maintained at rate ρ. Banks distribute the rest of their assets among free reserves and loans,[3] depending on the rate of inflation and the interest rate that banks charge on loans (r_L), so that the supply of loans (in real terms) is equal to:

$$L_b^s = b(\dot{p}, r_L)(1 - \rho)TD \qquad 0 < b < 1 \tag{2}$$

We have also assumed that firms absorb all loans that commercial banks are willing to offer, as these are offered at an interest rate (r_L) which is below the informal market interest rate. The rest of credit required by firms is supplied by the informal market at rate i. Firms need credit to finance working capital. The latter depends positively on the real wage and product:[4]

$$Df = Df (w/p, y) \tag{3}$$
$$+ \quad +$$

where Df is the demand for working capital by firms in real terms. If we put all these specifications in a Tobin-style accounting structure, we obtain Table 14.1, where MB is the monetary based and TD^s is the supply of time deposits by domestic commercial banks (also in real terms). The monetary base is defined as follows:

$$MB = NFA + NDC_g^{cb} \tag{4}$$

where NFA represents net international reserves in local currency and NDC_g^{cb} the net domestic credit of the central bank to the government. Under flexible exchange rates, the central bank does not intervene on the foreign currency market and net international reserves cannot vary:

$$NFA = \overline{NFA} \tag{5}$$

Consequently, the monetary base can only vary if the authorities modify the volume of credit channeled by the central bank to the government. The monetary base is an exogenous variable that can be modified at discretion by the monetary authorities. For the time being we will assume that $NDC_c^{cd} = 0$. Table 14.1 incorporates into line TD the assumption that the ceiling on the interest rate for time deposits implies that the latter are determined by demand. Likewise, the small country assumption enables us to assume that the supply of deposits abroad is also demand determined, where eCD^{*s} represents the supply of certificates of deposit by foreign banks. Given that TD and CD^* are determined by demand, we finally obtain the

Table 14.1

		Supply			
		Assets Holders			
Assets		Public	National commercial banks	Firms	Foreign commercial banks	Supply
---	---	---	---	---	---	---
(C^d)	Money	$\theta^c(\dot{p}, r_{td}, i, i^*, y)\frac{R}{P}$	$+ eTD + (1 - b(\dot{p}, r))(1-\rho)TD$			$=MB/P$
(TD)	Time deposits in the Formal market	$\theta^{td}(\dot{p}, r_{td}, i, i^*,y)\frac{R}{P}$	$-TD^s$			< 0
(L$_{im}$)	Time loans and/or deposits in the Informal market	$\theta^{im}(\dot{p}, r_{td}, i, i^*, y)\frac{R}{P}$	$+ b(\dot{p}, r_L)(1-\rho)TD$	$-D_f(\frac{w}{p}, y)$		$= 0$
(eCD*)	Certificates of deposit abroad (in the local currency)	$\theta(\dot{p}, i, i^*, y)\frac{R}{P}$			$-eCD^{*s}$	< 0

equilibrium conditions for the money market and the informal financial market. However, these conditions are not independent, which means that the equilibrium condition of the informal market implies equality of real demand and supply of money. We will hereinafter use the equilibrium condition of the informal market:

$$\theta^{im}(\dot{p}, r_{td}, i, i^*, y)\frac{R}{p} = Df(w/p, y) - b(\dot{p}, r_L)(1 - \rho)TD \qquad (6)$$

In a standard model with perfect capital mobility, the nominal interest rate will differ from the international nominal interest rate $(i\star)$ by the expected rate of depreciation of the exchange rate $(\dot{e}^e)$. In our model, the capital flows equilibrium condition is similar to that of the standard model once we replace the nominal domestic interest rate by the nominal interest rate of the informal market. Equation (7) specifies this equilibrium condition of capital flows under the assumption that expectations are formed rationally

$$i = i^* + \dot{e} \qquad (7)$$

The goods markets will remain at a very simple level, mainly in order to emphasize the portfolio aspects of the model. We set forth a simple Keynesian fixed-price mechanism where output adjusts to excess demand:

$$\dot{y} = \pi[A(e/p, i - \dot{p}, y) - y] \qquad A_e > 0 \qquad A_i < 0 \qquad 0 < A_y < 1 \quad (8)$$

The domestic good demand function states that the demand for this good increases when the exchange rate and real income increase, and decreases when the informal market real interest rate increases. Given that we have assumed that the price of the domestic good is fixed, we may rewrite the three equilibrium conditions (6)–(8) as follows:

$$\theta^{im} \underset{-\quad +-\ -}{(r_{td}, i, i^*, y)}\frac{R}{p}$$

$$= \underset{+\quad +}{Df(w/p, y)} - b(r_L)(1 - \rho)\theta^{td} \underset{+\quad --\ +}{(r_{td}, i, i^*, y)}\frac{R}{p} \qquad (6')$$

$$i = i^* + \dot{e} \qquad (7')$$

$$\dot{y} = \pi[A(e/p, i, y) - y] \qquad (8')$$

where we have substituted TD by its equivalent in equation (1b). The three equilibrium conditions are plotted in Figure 14.1. The LM, IS, and KF curves contain the combinations of real output (y) and informal market interest rate (i) that guarantee equilibrium in the informal credit market (and money market), the goods market, and the capital flow market, respectively. The system of equations (6')–(8') can also be plotted in the plane y,e. Figure 14.1 depicts the equilibrium conditions in both planes.

Let us assume that monetary authorities want to implement a financial reform and that one of the policies to adopt is an increase in the interest rate on time deposits paid by domestic commercial banks (r_{td}). The increase in the interest rate on time deposits in the formal market alters the portfolio equilibrium that individuals wish to maintain; assets holders will move their funds from the informal market and reduce their demand for money. However, given that capital flows are ruled by the condition i = i* + ė, when the increase in r_{td} occurs people do not change their holdings of certificates of deposit in foreign banks. The impact of an increase in r_{td} on the informal market interest rate is given by:

$$\frac{di}{dr_{td}}\bigg|_{LM}^{y=\bar{y}} = \frac{(1 - b + \rho b)\, \theta^{im}_{r_{td}} - b(1 - \rho)\, \theta^{c}_{r_{td}}}{\theta^{c}_i + \theta^{*}_i + (1 - b + \rho b)\theta^{td}_i} \gtrless 0 \qquad (9)$$

where the denominator is negative and the numerator may have any sign. If we analyze the result shown in (9), we observe that the shift of the LM curve will depend on the relative sensitivity of the demand for money and

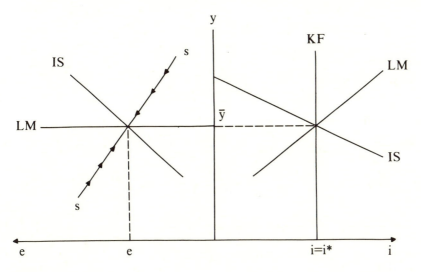

Figure 14.1

the demand for loans in the informal market to changes in the interest rate on time deposits. From the numerator in (9) we note that:

$$\frac{\theta^{im}_{r_{td}}}{\theta^{c}_{r_{td}}} \gtrless \frac{b(1-\rho)}{1-b(1-\rho)} \implies \left.\frac{di}{dr_{td}}\right|^{y=\bar{y}}_{LM} \gtrless 0 \tag{10}$$

The explanation is as follows. Let us consider the case where asset holders increase their time deposits using a larger proportion of funds that were located in the informal market: $\theta^{im}_{r_{td}}/\theta^{c}_{r_{td}} > b(1-\rho)/[1-b(1-\rho)]$.

In this case, the total supply of funds available for firms will be reduced to the extent in which funds are shifted from the informal market, which provides total intermediation (as they are not subject to legal reserves), toward the banking system that only provides partial intermediation (as a proportion of these funds is absorbed by free and required reserves). Consequently, the increase in r_{td} generates an excess demand for loanable funds available in the informal market, which leads to a rise in the informal market interest rate (i). The LM curve in Figure 14.2 moves toward the right.

However, the rise in the informal market interest rate implies that savings deposits and/or loans in the informal market constitute a financial asset with a higher return than certificates of deposit abroad, as $i > i\star + \dot{e}$. Consequently, the increase in the informal market interest rate produces a capital inflow that generates an appreciation of the exchange rate. The

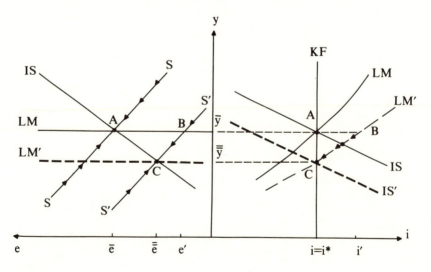

Figure 14.2

exchange rate appreciates from ē to e′ in Figure 14.2. However, the informal market interest rate can rise beyond the interest rate on certificates of deposit abroad if and only if there exist expectations of depreciation of the exchange rate (ė > 0). Therefore, after its initial appreciation, the exchange rate will experience a slow depreciation till it reaches its new equilibrium at point C.

The informal market interest rate increases and the economy moves toward point B in Figure 14.2. The increase in i reduces aggregate demand, and consequently the level of output starts to decline.

On the other hand, the appreciation of the exchange rate reduces aggregate demand as the relative price of the domestic good increases, and thus output declines even more. The IS curve (ẏ = 0) moves toward the left. The decline in output generates an excess supply of loanable funds in the informal market, which in turn leads to a slow reduction in i. Consequently, in this first case, a financial reform (increase in r_{td}) produces a capital inflow, appreciates the exchange rate, and reduces the level of output. The informal market interest rate, although it rises initially, returns to its previous equilibrium level (i = i*).

Let us now consider the case where assets holders increase their time deposits in the banking system mainly by reducing their money stocks $\{\theta^{im}_{r_{td}}/\theta^{c}_{r_{td}} < b(1 - \rho)/[1 - b(1 - \rho)]\}$. Given the fact that money is an unproductive asset, any reduction of the latter in order to increase time deposits leads to a larger supply of loanable funds available for firms, and, consequently, equilibrium in the informal market demands a lower informal market interest rate. The LM curve shifts to the left in Figure 14.3.

However, the reduction in the informal market interest rate makes savings deposits and/or loans in the informal market less attractive as financial assets with respect to certificates of deposit abroad, because i < i* + ė. Consequently, the reduction in i generates a capital outflow that induces a depreciation of the exchange rate. The exchange rate depreciates from ē to e′ in Figure 14.3. However the informal market interest rate may fall below the interest rate on certificates of deposit abroad if and only if there exist expectations of appreciation of the exchange rate (ė < 0). Therefore, the exchange rate initially overshoots; afterwards, it appreciates until it reaches its new equilibrium level ē̄.

The decline in the informal market interest rate stimulates aggregate demand, and the economy starts shifting toward point C as the level of output increases.

To this we should add the fact that the depreciation of the exchange rate lowers the relative price of domestic goods, which shifts the IS to the right up to IS′ in plane i,y.

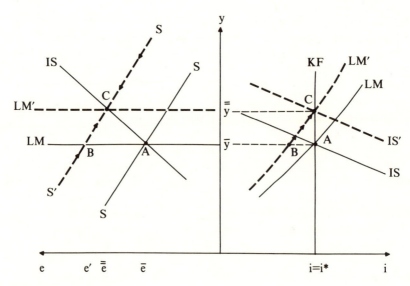

Figure 14.3

The increase in y creates an excess demand for funds in the informal market, which puts pressure on the informal market interest rate to rise to the point where the latter reaches its previous equilibrium level (i = i*).

In sum, in this second case, the financial reform produces a capital outflow, depreciates the exchange rate, and increases the level of output. The informal market interest rate, although it declines at the beginning, returns to its previous equilibrium level (i = i*).

Let us now analyze the impact on this particular kind of economy of an increase in the interest rate charged by local commercial banks on loans channeled toward firms (r_L). An increase in the loan interest rate in the formal financial system will induce banks to reduce the volume of their free reserves and consequently will increase the volume of credit channeled to the firms by means of the formal banking system. There is no doubt that this will expand economic activity. Formally, from (6') on, we note that the LM curve will shift to the left in the plane y,i of Figure 14.3 as:

$$\frac{di}{dr_L}\bigg|_{LM}^{y=\bar{y}} = \frac{b_{r_L}(1 - \rho)\theta_i^{td}}{\theta_i^c + \theta_i^* + (1 - b + \rho b)\theta_i^{td}} < 0 \tag{11}$$

The reduction in the informal market interest rate is due to the fact that the demand for credit on this market has now been reduced because the increase in r_L enables commercial banks to channel part of their free reserves and, consequently, increases the availability of formal credit at a rate below that of the informal market.

The drop in i stimulates capital flight as certificates of deposit abroad are paying a higher rate than that payed in the informal market ($i < i^*$). This capital outflow implies a depreciation of the exchange rate. The exchange rate depreciation will provoke a shift in demand from the imported good toward the domestic good.

On the other hand, the reduction in i allows for a decrease in the informal market real interest rate, which constitutes an additional factor of expansion of the demand for the domestic good. The excess demand will put pressure on domestic output, and consequently the level of output will increase.

The exchange rate will initially overshoot and the real exchange rate will depreciate, which will tend to improve the current account of the balance of payments.[5] In summary, the increase in r_L increases output and investment, improves the current account of the balance of payments and induces a capital flight via the decline in the informal market interest rate. Figures 14.3 shows these results.

Let us finally consider the impact on the economy of a reduction in the legal reserve rate (ρ). A reduction in the reserve rate has the same qualitative impact as an increase in the loan interest rate. Formally,

$$\frac{di}{dr_L}\bigg|_{LM}^{\bar{y}=\bar{y}} = \frac{b\theta^{td}}{-\theta_i^c + \theta_i^* + (1 - b + \rho b)\theta_i^{td}} > 0 \tag{12}$$

The reduction in ρ enables the formal commercial bank to channel more loans toward firms at a rate below that of the informal market. In other words, the reduction in ρ generates more intermediation in the formal market. Firms will take more loans and reduce their demand for credit in the informal market, which in turn causes a reduction in the informal market interest rate. The dynamic process and results are equivalent to the case of the increase in r_L. The reduction in the legal reserve rate will expand economic activity and investment. Figure 14.3 also depicts the impact of a reduction in ρ on the main macroeconomic variables.

3. Fixed Output and Flexible Prices

In this section we will modify the model presented in the previous section in order to allow for a certain flexibility in the price of the domestic good and, at the same time, maintain domestic output fixed at its full employment level. The model will pay attention to the asset markets and the substitution effects generated by changes in the interest rate on savings deposits in the formal market. For specification of the real sector we assume an ad-hoc inflation equation whose economic justification has been given by Barro (1972) and Sheshinsky and Weiss (1977). As we will see further, this equation is similar to the one used by Dornbusch (1976) and Dauhajre (1983).

The specification of the assets market is similar to the one presented in Section 2, after eliminating the level of income y as a determinant of the distribution of wealth among the different assets. The specification is modified as follows:

$$C^d = \theta^c(\dot{p}, r_{td}, i, i^*) \frac{R}{p} \qquad \qquad (13a)$$
$${-}\ \ {-}\ \ \ {-}\ {-} \phantom{\frac{R}{p}}$$

$$TD = \theta^{td}(\dot{p}, r_{td}, i, i^*) \frac{R}{p} \qquad \qquad (13b)$$
$$\phantom{TD = \theta^{td}(}{-}\ {+}\ \ \ {-}\ {-} \phantom{\frac{R}{p}}$$

$$L_{im} = \theta^{im}(\dot{p}, r_{td}, i, i^*) \frac{R}{p} \qquad \qquad (13c)$$
$$\phantom{L_{im} = \theta^{im}(}{-}\ {-}\ \ {+}\ {-} \phantom{\frac{R}{p}}$$

$$eCD^* = \theta^*(\dot{p}, i, i^*) \frac{R}{p} \qquad \qquad (13d)$$
$${+}\ {-}\ {+} \phantom{\frac{R}{p}}$$

where C^d, TD, L_{im}, and eCD^* maintain their previous definitions. These demands for financial assets equations are also accompanied by the summation conditions (1e) of Section 2.

For analytical tractability, we will assume that banks will increase the supply of loanable funds only when the interest rate that commercial banks charge on loans rises, so that the supply of loans (in real terms) is equal to:[6]

$$L_b^s = b(r_L)(1 - \rho)TD \qquad 0 < b < 1 \qquad \qquad (14)$$
$${+}$$

Real demand for credit to finance working-capital requirements will only depend on the real wage, given that output cannot vary in the short term:

$$D_f = D_f(w/p) \qquad \qquad (15)$$
$${+}$$

Table 14.2

	Assets	Demand — Assets Holders — Public	Domestic commercial banks	Firms	Foreign commercial banks	Supply
(C^d)	Money	$\theta^c(p, r_{td}, i, i^*)\dfrac{R}{P}+$	$\rho TD + [1 - b(r_L)](1 - \rho)TD$			$= MB/P$
(TD)	Time deposits in the Formal market	$\theta^{td}(p, r_{td}, i, i^*)\dfrac{R}{P}-$	TD^s			< 0
(L_{im})	Loans and/or time deposits in the Informal market	$\theta^{im}(p, r_{td}, i, i^*)\dfrac{R}{P}+$	$b(r_L)(1 - \rho)TD$	$-D_f(w/p)$		$= 0$
(eCD^*)	Certificates of deposit abroad (in the local currency)	$\theta^*(p, i, i^*)\dfrac{R}{P}$			$-eCD^{*s}$	< 0

295

Table 14.2 summarizes the specification of the assets market and its respective equilibrium conditions. The explanation offered in the previous section is also valid for Table 14.2. The equilibrium condition of the informal market is given by:

$$\theta^{im}(\dot{p}, r_{td}, i, i^{*})\frac{R}{p} = D_f(w/p) - b(r_L)(1 - \rho)TD \tag{16}$$

The assumptions of perfect capital mobility and rational expectations (here, perfect foresight) are maintained. The capital flows equilibrium condition is, hence, similar to that of the previous section, $i = i^{*} + e$.

The goods market will follow a very simple behavior pattern; portfolio aspects will remain predominant. We set forth an ad-hoc inflation equation similar to Dornbusch (1976):[7]

$$\dot{p} = \pi[A(e/p, i - \dot{p}) - \bar{y}] \qquad A_e > 0 \qquad A_i < 0 \tag{17}$$

in which prices change according to disequilibrium in the goods market. In view of an excess demand of the domestic good and given the impossibility of altering output in the short run, the price of the domestic good will increase slowly until it eliminates the initial excess demand. It is important to point out that the adjustment of domestic prices is gradual.

The three equilibrium conditions of this new scenario are summarized as follows:

$$\theta^{im}\ \underset{-\ -\ \ +-}{(\dot{p}, r_{td}, i, i^{*})}\frac{R}{p}$$

$$= D_f(w/p) \underset{+}{-} b(r_L)(1 - \rho)\theta^{td}\underset{-\ +\ \ --}{(\dot{p}, r_{td}, i, i^{*})}\frac{R}{p} \tag{18}$$

$$i = i^{*} + \dot{e} \tag{19}$$

$$p = \pi[A(e/p, i - \dot{p}) - \bar{y}] \tag{20}$$

The three equilibrium conditions are shown in Figure 14.4. The IS, LM, and KF curves contain the combinations of the rate of inflation ($\dot{p}$) and informal market interest rate (i) that guarantee equilibrium in the goods market, in the informal financial market (also, in the money market), and for capital flow, respectively. Figure 14.4 also depicts the resulting phase diagram in the plane $\hat{e}, \dot{p}$.[8]

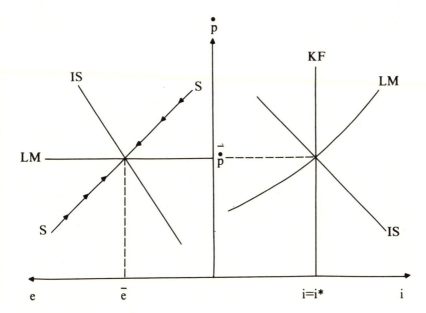

Figure 14.4

Let us assume that the monetary authorities proceed with the implementation of a financial reform characterized by an increase in the interest rate on time deposits paid by local commercial banks (r_{td}).

The increase in the interest rate on time deposits in the formal market will alter the portfolio equilibrium of assets holders; they will shift funds from the informal market and will reduce their stock of the "unproductive" asset (money).

As in the previous case, the variation in r_{td} will not have a direct impact on the holdings of certificates of deposit abroad. The impact of a rise in the time-deposit rate is similar to the one in the previous section:

$$\left. \frac{di}{dr_{td}} \right|_{LM}^{p=\bar{p}} = \frac{(1 - b + \rho b) \, \theta^{im}_{r_{td}} - b(1 - \rho) \, \theta^{c}_{r_{td}}}{\theta^{c}_{i} + \theta^{\star}_{i} + (1 - b + \rho b)\theta^{td}_{i}} \gtrless 0 \qquad (21)$$

where the denominator is negative and the numerator can have any sign. Just as in the model with the fixed prices and flexible output, we may note that the direction of the shift of the LM curve will depend on the sensitivity of the demand for money, and of the demand for loans in the informal market with respect to changes in the interest rate on time deposits in the formal market.

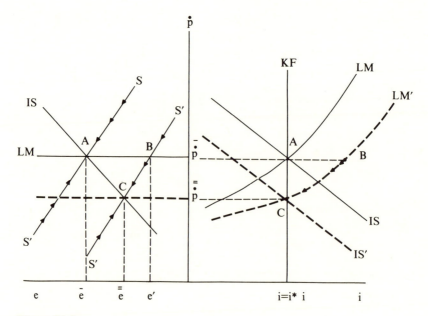

Figure 14.5

We may verify that:

$$\frac{\theta^{im}_{r_{td}}}{\theta^{c}_{r_{td}}} \gtreqless \frac{b(1-\rho)}{1-b(1-\rho)} \Rightarrow \left.\frac{di}{dr_{td}}\right|_{LM}^{\dot{p}=\bar{p}} \gtreqless 0 \tag{22}$$

Let us analyze the case where the asset holders increase their time deposits by shifting a large proportion of funds that were deposited in the informal market. As we saw previously, the total supply of funds available for firms will be reduced to the extent in which funds shift from the informal market, which provides total intermediation, to the banking system, which only provides partial intermediation. Consequently, the increase in r_{td} creates an excess demand for loanable funds in the informal market that induces an increase in the informal market interest (i). The LM curve shifts toward the right in Figure 14.5.

The increase in the informal market interest rate makes time deposits and/or loans on the informal market more profitable than certificates of deposit abroad, because $i < i^*$. Consequently, the increase in i produces a capital inflow that generates an appreciation of the exchange rate.

However, given the condition that $i = i^* + \dot{e}$, the interest rate of the informal market would exceed the interest rate abroad (i^*) if and only if there exist expectations of depreciation of the exchange rate ($\dot{e} < 0$). Consequently, although the exchange rate appreciates at the beginning, it will undergo depreciation further ahead. Nevertheless, the final result will be an appreciation of the exchange rate. The exchange rate appreciates from $\bar{e}$ to e' in Figure 14.5, and then depreciates from e' to $\bar{e}$.

The appreciation of the exchange rate implies that the relative price of the domestic good deteriorates due to the decline in the price of the imported good. Consequently, the decrease in i generates a reduction in the demand for domestic goods. This effect will reduce the rate of inflation. On the other hand, the increase in the informal market interest rate leads to an increase in $i - \dot{p}$, the real interest rate of that market, and consequently to an additional reduction in the demand for domestic goods. Both forces, operating in the same direction, produce a decline in the rate of inflation. In this case a financial reform would imply a reduction of inflationary pressures. The IS curve shifts toward the origin in Figure 14.5.

To the extent to which the informal market real interest rate increases due to the reduction in $\dot{p}$, the excess demand for loanable funds in the informal market is eliminated slowly and the nominal interest rate of that market returns to its initial equilibrium position $i = i^*$. However, the real rate, $i - \dot{p}$, will be larger. The real exchange rate (e/p) will experience a real appreciation and, consequently, will worsen the current account. The rate of inflation, however, will be lower.

Let us now analyze the case where asset holders increase their time deposits in the banking system by reducing in a larger proportion their stocks of money.

As money is an "unproductive" asset, any reduction of the latter to increase time deposits will generate a larger volume of funds available for firms and, hence, will create an excess supply of loanable funds in the informal market. The major availability of funds in the formal market at an interest rate of $r_L > i$ will cause firms to reduce their demand for loans in the informal market and to increase their demand for loanable funds in the formal market. The equilibrium in the informal market demands a reduction in the interest rate of this market. The LM curve shifts toward the left in Figure 14.6.

However, the reduction in the informal interest rate makes savings deposits and/or loans in the informal market less attractive as financial assets than certificates of deposit abroad, as $i > i^*$. Consequently, asset holders react to this divergence and start substituting local deposits by deposits abroad. This capital outflow generates a depreciation of the exchange rate, represented by the jump of $\bar{e}$ to e' in Figure 14.6. On the other hand, the interest rate of the informal market may fall below the interest rate abroad if and only if there exist expectations of appreciation in the exchange rate ($\dot{e} > 0$). It is for this reason that the exchange rate initially experiences an overshooting and then appreciates until it reaches its new equilibrium level $\bar{\bar{e}}$.

The depreciation of the exchange rate makes imported goods more expensive and improves the relative price of the domestic goods. The real exchange rate depreciation stimulates the demand for domestic goods. Moreover, the reduction in the informal market interest rate implies a decline in the real rate, $i - \dot{p}$, and therefore an additional expansion of the demand for domestic goods. Given that output does not respond in the short term, the aggregate excess demand will generate a higher rate of inflation. In this case, the financial reform feeds inflationary pressures. The IS curve shifts toward the right in Figure 14.6.

The increase in $\dot{p}$ reduces the informal market real interest rate, $i - \dot{p}$, which tends to eliminate the excess supply of loanable funds that existed initially on that market.

The nominal interest rate i will return to its initial equilibrium $i^* = i$, but the real rate $i - \dot{p}$ will definitely be lower. The real exchange rate (e/p) will experience a real depreciation in the short run and, consequently, might improve the current account on the balance of payments, depending on how fast prices react. The economy's rate of inflation will be higher. Figure 14.6 summarizes these results.

Let us now consider the impact an increase in the active interest rate (r_L) would have on this new macroeconomic scenario. It can be shown that

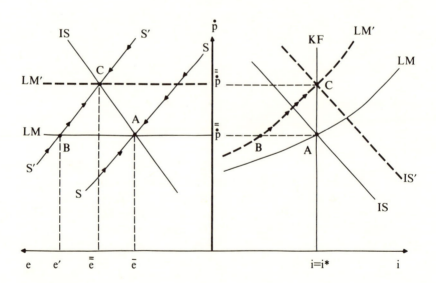

Figure 14.6

the results presented in Section 2 are maintained, and that, consequently, the informal market interest rate will decline. However, whereas in the model of Section 2 this had an expansive impact on output, in this new scheme the rise in r_L generates major inflationary pressures.

The reduction in i implies a capital flight and, consequently, a depreciation of the exchange rate. Both factors generate an aggregate excess demand that accelerates the inflation rate as output does not respond in the short run. Figure 14.6 illustrates these results.

A reduction in the legal reserve rate in this scenario has the same impact as a raise in r_L. The result shown in equation (12) also remains valid in this new model.

4. Conclusions and Policy Recommendations

In this chapter we have analyzed the potential impact of a financial reform in a small open economy with a flexible exchange rate, characterized by the existence of informal financial markets. The effect of this policy was examined in two different scenarios. In the first model, with fixed prices and flexible output, we found that if the sensitivity of the demand for loans in the informal market was greater than the sensitivity of the demand for money, the financial reform would have a recessive effect on the economy. On the other hand, if assets holders replaced money by time deposits in greater proportion, the financial reform would have an expansionary effect on economic activity. In the first case, the exchange rate appreciates and the current account deteriorates, while in the second case the exchange rate depreciates and the current account improves. In the second model, with flexible prices and fixed output, we showed that when the informal market interest rate increases, the financial reform has a deflationary impact on the economy and the appreciation of the exchange rate deteriorates the current account. When asset holders replace money by time deposits in a larger proportion, the financial reform provokes inflationary pressures and the depreciation of the exchange rate improves the current account.[9]

The message for policymakers of a small open economy is clear: a financial reform may have very diverse effects. Consequently, one has to be very careful in such an important aspect of economy policy.

The policymakers possess, however, some instruments that may be used to prevent possible negative effects of a necessary financial reform. As we observed in the previous models, policymakers can modify the legal reserve rate of the formal banking system and the loan interest rate that commercial banks charge on loans channeled toward firms in order to cushion the potentially negative effects of an increase in the interest rate on time deposits.

For instance, if the monetary authorities consider that an increase in interest rate on time deposits would have a recessionary effect on the economy, the reserve rate might be reduced to counteract this negative effect of the financial reform in economic activity. However, authorities should consider the fact that a reduction in the legal reserve rate would accelerate the process of money creation and, consequently, would provoke inflationary pressures. On the other hand, the authorities could increase the loan interest rate that commercial banks charge on loans. This would cause a reduction in free reserves of commercial banks and would, consequently, channel more loanable funds to firms at a rate below that of the informal market.

On the side of the informal market, financial policy should also be designed carefully. Implementation of policies tending to regulate that market in the absence of modifications in the operation of these institutions might increase the comparative advantage of the informal sector. In January 1985, for instance, the Monetary Board of the Dominican Republic issued a resolution aimed at regulating the operation of the informal market. This policy tends to reduce considerably the risk for assets holders who make loans on this market. The possible intervention by monetary authorities on the informal market in view of crisis situations and possible bankruptcies reduces the risk and, consequently, tends to raise the effective interest rate of the informal market. This policy, beside widening the gap that exists between the formal and informal sectors, may have adverse macroeconomic effects. Assets holders might feel motivated to transfer resources from the formal market to the informal one, reducing the availability for loanable funds for firms at lower rates, which might depress economic activity. However, it should be pointed out that this policy, by increasing the real profitability of assets of the informal market, stimulates capital inflow and/or discourages their drain abroad.

Again, the monetary authorities should systematically follow-up on the impact of these policies on both markets, formal and the informal, so that the formal market, which channels credit to firms at lower rates, is not harmed. If regulation of the informal market elevates the effective interest rate of this market via a reduction of the risk, the authorities should find mechanisms to raise also the effective interest rate of the formal sector or to reduce the informal market interest rate, as would result from a reduction in the legal reserve rate of the formal sector.

A policy that is usually recommended for reducing the gap between both markets is to establish a legal reserve rate for deposits received by institutions of the informal market. However, this policy would raise the interest rate of this market and provoke a recessionary effect on the economy. We must remember that the implementation of this legal reserve rate would reduce intermediation of the informal market so that informal financial institutions would now supply partial intermediation.[10] Given that the interest rate on that market is flexible, the lesser availability of loanable funds to satisfy a given demand would cause a rise in the interest rate on that market. However, the increase in the informal market interest rate, although it would have a recessionary impact in the short run, would stimulate asset holders to reduce their stocks of financial certificates abroad and to increase their loans in the informal financial market.

Consequently, financial reforms may have adverse effects on the economic activity of a small open economy with a flexible exchange rate. However, policymakers possess instruments that can eliminate these adverse effects and guarantee that the financial reform generates the desired effects.

Notes

[1]We assume that the domestic inflation rate is equal to the inflation rate of domestic goods and that the deflator of nominal variables is the price index for domestic goods. However, the correct specification is to set forth an inflation index that takes into account the prices of the domestic and imported goods and the weights of these goods in total expenditure. In this case, the deflator of nominal variables would be $\alpha p + (1 - \alpha)e$, where e is the exchange rate, and α and $1 - \alpha$ are the weights of domestic and imported goods in expenditure. Inflation would be $\alpha \dot{p} + (1 - \alpha)\dot{e}$.

[2]We assume that demand for certificates of deposit abroad does not depend on the interest rate on time deposits (r_{td}). Given that $i > r_{td}$, the assumption of perfect capital mobility implies that $i = i^* + e > r_{td}$, and consequently, to the extent to which $i > r_{td}$, the level of r_{td} does not alter the demand for certificates of deposit abroad.

[3]We assume that banks cannot use funds to buy certificates of deposit abroad (CD^*).

[4]The model could be extended by introducing the real exchange rate as a determinant of the demand for working capital. If imported raw materials requirements are important, the real exchange rate should be included as an argument.

[5]If the relative price effect dominates the income effect on the current account.

[6]The results do not change if $b = b(r_L, \dot{p})$.

[7]The IS curve is negatively sloped if $1 + \pi A_i > 0$, as in Dornbusch (1976). Let us suppose that an alteration occurs on the goods market so that $\dot{p} > 0$. The real interest rate will suffer a reduction equal to $\dot{p}$. However, the reduction in the real interest rate will stimulate the demand for the domestic goods, which would imply an additional increase in the price of the domestic good equivalent to $-\pi A_i$. Consequently, to have a stable domestic goods market, which means that the price of the domestic good converges toward a stable equilibrium value, it is required that the change induced in $\dot{p}$ be smaller than the initial change generated by the alteration. This implies that $1 + \pi A_i > 0$.

[8]Again, the existence of a stable path toward equilibrium requires that $1 + \pi A_i > 0$.

[9]If we allow for flexibility of both prices and output we would find that if the informal market rate rises initially, the financial reform would be stagflationary. If the informal rate declines as a result of a rise in r_{td}, the financial reform would stimulate economic activity and reduce inflationary pressures. These results differ from those of McKinnon and van Wijnbergen. On the other hand, if the economy is characterized by the currency substitution phenomenon, the probability of an increase in the informal market interest rate when the financial reform is implemented declines, given that the assets holders could also shift part of their financial wealth from foreign currency (also an "unproductive" asset) to savings deposits in the formal financial market.

[10]We must point out that some of the informal financial institutions in the Dominican Republic behave as if they had to maintain legal reserves. However, their self-imposed reserve rate is generally lower than that of the formal institutions.

References

Barro, R. (1972). "A Theory of Monopolistic Price Adjustment." *Review of Economic Studies* 39 (January): 17–26.

Dauhajre, A. (1983). "Dual Exchange Rate Dynamics with Incomplete Segmentation and Rational Expectations." Unpublished Ph.D. Dissertation, Columbia University, New York.

Dornbusch, R. (1976). "Expectations and Exchange Rate Dynamics." *Journal of Political Economy* 84 (6) (December): 1161–76.

Kapur, B. (1976). "Alternative Stabilization Policies for Less Developed Economies." *Journal of Political Economy* 84 (4, pt. 1) (August): 777–95.

McKinnon, R. (1973). *Money and Capital in Economic Development.* Washington, D.C.: Brookings Institution.

Shaw, E. (1973). *Financial Deepening in Economic Development.* Oxford: Oxford University Press.

Sheshinsky, E., and Y. Weiss (1977). "Inflation and Costs of Price Adjustment." *Review of Economic Studies* 44: 287–309.

Tobin, J. (1969). "A General Equilibrium Approach to Monetary Theory." *Journal of Money, Credit, and Banking* 1 (February): 15–29.

van Wijnbergen, S. (1983). "Interest Rate Management in LDC's." *Journal of Monetary Economics* 12 (3) (September): 433–52.

15

Microeconomic Foundations of Financial Liberalization: Interest Rates, Transactions Costs, and Financial Savings

Paul Burkett & Robert C. Vogel

1. Introduction

During the past decade, development theorists have shown increasing interest in the financial prerequisites for economic growth and stability in market-oriented developing countries (see, for example, McKinnon, 1973; Shaw, 1973; Kapur, 1976; Galbis, 1977; Mathieson, 1980). Macroeconomic analyses along these lines have emphasized the important benefits of financial liberalization, especially in the form of uncontrolled and/or positive real rates of interest, in facilitating the efficient mobilization and allocation of funds. Conversely, the impacts of interest rate controls and other policies of financial repression common in many developing countries have been strongly criticized. Policies attempting to fix interest rates below equilibrium levels are said to impede savings mobilization, distort credit allocation, worsen income distribution, and put upward pressure on the rate of inflation relative to a financially liberal regime of market-determined interest rates.

In the development of the microeconomic foundations of financial liberalization, attention has been focused predominantly on credit allocation—almost to the exclusion of savings mobilization. The theory has been well developed that financial repression, especially in the form of interest rates controlled below equilibrium levels, results in credit rationing that distorts the allocation of credit away from optimal patterns (González-Vega, 1984)[1] Transaction costs have been identified as a primary element in this credit rationing (Adams and Nehman, 1979). Lenders respond to interest rate ceilings by shifting transaction costs to borrowers, and even by imposing additional unnecessary costs (that is, implicit interest) to restrict the demand for credit. Meanwhile, borrowers are willing to pay added transaction costs until the entire gap if filled between the controlled low rates and what would have to be paid in the form of explicit interest in the absence of interest rate ceilings (Cuevas and Graham, 1982).

In contrast, development theorists have provided few insights into the microeconomic foundations of financial liberalization from the perspective of saving mobilization—with one notable exception to be discussed in detail below. In fact, discussions of savings in the development literature have often been plagued by confusion between two different concepts: (1) saving as a flow, or that part of income which is not consumed, and (2) savings as a stock of financial assets that have been accumulated over time. It is also important (as initially emphasized by Porter, 1966) to distinguish carefully between currency, on the one hand, and bank deposits, on the other, so that the benefits from an expanded demand for and use of currency are not confused with an expansion of financial intermediaries and their services. In developing some microeconomic foundations of savings mobilization to assess more clearly the benefits of financial liberalization, the model in this chapter takes the division of income between saving and consumption as given and deals with the allocation of wealth among four categories of assets. In addition, one of these assets is money (that is, currency) which can be exchanged directly for all other goods and services, while another is a financial asset (for example, bank deposits) which cannot be used directly as a medium of exchange but first must be traded for money at some (transaction) cost to the holder.

Despite the continuing controversy concerning the responsiveness of saving (versus consuming) to a change in interest rates, it is reasonably well established that the demand for financial assets does respond significantly to changes in the expected real returns on these assets (see, for example, Adams, 1978). However, such a result does not, by itself, provide an adequate basis for a microeconomic theory of savings and financial liberalization, nor does it fully explain the experience with successful savings mobilization in Peru that prompted the research underlying this chapter. In the late 1970s, the Peruvian Government initiated some tentative steps toward financial liberalization, especially by raising controlled interest rates to substantially higher levels (although they remained negative in real terms). At the same time, a Peruvian cooperative bank undertook a savings mobilization project (assisted by the U.S. Agency for International Development) that far surpassed its original objectives.[2] Deposit holdings at this cooperative bank not only increased significantly in response to higher (though still negative) real rates of interest, but also increased substantially relative to deposits at Peruvian commercial banks that were paying the same rates of interest.

The notable success of this cooperative bank in mobilizing savings, especially relative to Peruvian commercial banks, could not be explained solely as a response to higher interest rates. Many observers, even including some officials of the cooperative bank itself, attributed this success to promotional campaigns that included publicity and prizes and were skeptical that deposits would be maintained when campaigns were ended. Nonetheless, deposits at the cooperative bank continued to grow both in real terms and relative to commercial bank deposits even during noncampaign periods, albeit at a somewhat slower rate. The microeconomic foundations of financial liberalization and credit allocation have indicated the importance of transaction costs, and there have also been some interesting but unrigorous discussions of the importance of transaction costs for depositors in explaining savings behavior (see, for example, Adams, 1978; Elegalam, 1978; and Von Pischke, 1978). Analysis of the Peruvian cooperative bank supported these views by revealing that "good service for depositors" (that is, lower transaction costs and increased liquidity for deposits) was a crucial element in successful savings mobilization during a period of tentative financial liberalization.[3]

As mentioned above, there is one model that has explored the benefits of financial liberalization from the perspective of the microeconomic foundations of household savings behavior in developing countries—the model articulated by McKinnon (1973, especially Chapter 6) a decade ago. In contrast to the neoclassical position that money balances and physical capital are substitutes (see, for example, Levhari and Patinkin, 1968), McKinnon stresses the "complementarity of money and physical capital" in the wealth portfolios of household firms in developing countries. In contrast to the neoclassical assumptions that financial markets are perfect and physical capital is perfectly divisible, McKinnon assumes that household firms in developing countries must rely on self-finance (credit is unavailable) and that outlays for productive investment projects loom large relative to the current income flows of most of these household firms. Consequently, under McKinnon's assumptions, to undertake investment projects with high returns—a crucial element in economic development— often requires the prior accumulation of stocks of assets.

Under financially repressive conditions, when rates of return on money balances are so low that the value of these balances is continuously eroded by inflation, it may be difficult or even impossible for household firms to accumulate the stocks of assets required to undertake productive investment projects. Accumulating inflation hedges may be the only alternative, even though inflation hedges may have high costs for their holders (for example, deterioration in storage and high transaction costs when exchanged for money) and for society in general (for example, excessive production of goods that serve as inflation hedges).[4] Under conditions of financial liberalization, with positive real rates of return on money balances, household firms will have the incentive and the ability to accumulate money balances in order to undertake larger-scale and more productive investment projects and, at the same time, to reduce their holdings of unproductive and costly inflation hedges.

This chapter extends McKinnon's results by dropping the restrictive assumption that indivisibilities in physical capital are significant for household firms in developing countries. Even without such indivisibilities, the benefits of financial liberalization can be shown through the complementarity of financial assets and physical capital in the portfolios of household firms.[5] The model in the present chapter integrates more fully the portfolio and inventory approaches to the demand for money and applies them to a case of four assets: money, physical capital, inflation hedges, and financial assets (where, as mentioned above, financial assets, which may include bank deposits, cannot be used directly as a medium of exchange but must first be converted to money by incurring some transaction costs). This integration of the asset-selection and cash-management decisions of household firms not only confirms the crucial role of interest rates in financial liberalization but also reveals the equally important role of transaction costs—the costs for household firms in developing countries of making exchanges between money and financial assets and between money and inflation hedges.

2. A Model of the Savings Behavior of Household Firms in Developing Countries

Household firms in developing countries must, in general, make four simultaneous choices: (1) the choice between consumption and saving (that is, between present and future consumption), (2) the choice between labor and leisure, (3) the choice of a bundle of income-generating assets, and (4) the choice of a set of liquidity sources for funding cash flows associated with consumption and/or productive activity. The present chapter is concerned with the factors determining the forms in which the *stock* of household savings are held (for example, financial versus nonfinancial) rather than the *flow* of savings as determined by the gap between income and consumption. The focus here is therefore on choices (3) and (4), while choices (1) and (2) will be taken as given.

The interaction between the choice of income-generating assets and the choice of cash-flow sources has received virtually no analytical treatment in the literature on household savings in developing countries, even though the methodological tools for such an analysis are known from the theory of money demand. In particular, analysis of the wealth-allocation decision corresponds to portfolio theories of money demand (for example, Tobin, 1958), while analysis of cash-flow management corresponds to inventory theories (Baumol, 1952; Tobin, 1956; Miller and Orr, 1966). A synthesis of these two views is required for an adequate understanding of the savings behavior of household firms, especially in developing countries undergoing financial liberalization. Some theorists have attempted to achieve such a synthesis by inserting money directly into utility and/or production functions (for example, Levhari and Patinkin, 1968; for a review of these models, see Joyce, 1981). However, such an approach is unable to deal explicitly with transaction costs or the crucial distinction between cash and financial assets such as savings deposits, because it subsumes the liquidity of assets into their "marginal utilities" or "marginal products." Thus, "the sources of the productivity of money [and financial assets] are not clearly enough exposed" (Moroney, 1972; see also Feige and Parkin, 1971, and Claasen, 1975, for similar views).[6]

The present chapter attempts a direct synthesis of the portfolio and inventory approaches to financial decision making, one which maintains the independence of both views, yet shows their interaction.[7] This is necessary in order to confront the interaction of wealth allocation and cash-flow management in determining the forms in which savings are held.

Consider a household firm whose labor/leisure and consumption/saving tradeoffs are given. This household knows all variables in the model below with complete certainty and has no access to credit.[8] It is assumed that the household's decisions are based on the criterion of wealth maximization. Assuming constant capital values for the household's assets (see below) this criterion reduces to that of maximizing a flow of income over a certain period, which will be referred to as the production period.

The household is constrained to an initial endowment of real wealth (W) which it costlessly allocates among four assets at the start of the production period. These assets are physical capital (K), cash (M), hedges (H), and a financial asset (A).[9] The financial asset should be thought of as a (noncheckable) savings deposit. The real yield to physical capital is $r(K)$, and this yield is only collected at the end of the production period (for example, via the revenue obtained from the sale of a crop after harvest). Furthermore, $r'(K) < 0$, indicating that the real yield to physical capital decreases with the amount held, due to the fixed technology and limited managerial resources available to the typical household firm in the short run.

The household must fund operating costs associated with investment in physical capital. (A small farmer must obtain gasoline and incur maintenance costs on a tractor, for example.) For simplicity, assume that these operating costs occur in a continuous, constant flow over the production period, a flow adding up to a total outlay of gK, where $g > 0$. It is also assumed that operating costs are required to obtain, but do not affect, the magnitude of r(K). In other words, g is fixed because of zero substitutability between physical capital and the inputs covered by operating costs.[10]

Since M is simply cash, on which no interest is paid, its real yield is $-p$, where p is the rate of inflation. The real yields to hedges and the financial asset are $h - p$ and $d - p$, respectively. All three of these yields are given for the household firm.[11]

The household can use withdrawals from M, H, and/or A as a liquidity source for funding operating costs (gK). For simplicity, assume that any withdrawals from A occur in a continuous, constant flow (at the same rate as gK), a flow adding up to W_A.[12] Similarly, withdrawals from H occur in a continuous, constant flow adding up to W_H. The transaction costs incurred when these two liquidity sources are used are $C_A(W_A)$ and $C_H(W_H)$,[13] such that:

$$C'_A(W_A) > 0 \qquad C'_H(W_H) > 0$$

$$C''_A(W_A) > 0 \qquad C''_H(W_H) > 0$$

(1)

indicating that marginal transaction costs are positive and increasing, for both hedges and the financial asset.

At this point two things can be noted about the household's problem. First, cash will be held strictly as a liquidity source for funding gK. The usefulness of cash for the household firm stems solely from the fact that cash balances can be tapped (to cover operating costs) without incurring any transaction costs. Cash will never be held for its own ability to generate income, since its yield is less than the yields to H and A. Second, if the yields to hedges and the financial asset differ, the one with the lower yield will be held (if at all) solely as a source of liquidity.[14] To clarify these two points, consider the case in which $d - p > h - p$. In this case, $H = W_H$, since hedges will be held (if at all) solely in order to fund operating costs. This is also the case most relevant for comparison with McKinnon's complementarity hypothesis, since the financial asset and physical capital are competing assets.

During the initial part of the production period, M will be used to fund operating costs, so as to avoid unnecessary foregone income from H and/or A. Since $gK = M + H + W_A$, the fraction of the production period during which M is used as a liquidity source is M/gK. Furthermore, the average amount of cash held during this portion of the production period is M/2 (since cash flow occurs at a constant rate). Thus, the yield to holding money is $-p(M/2)(M/gk)$, or more simply $-(p/2)(M^2/gK)$.

The next liquidity source used will be H, so as to avoid any unnecessary losses of income due to the excess of $d - p$ over $h - p$. The yield to H occurs on the full amount of hedges during the fraction of the production period in which cash is used as the liquidity source. In addition, the fraction of the period in which H is tapped for operating costs is H/gk, and the average amount of hedges held during this fraction of the period is $H/2$. The total yield to H is thus $(h - p)[H(M/gK) + (1/2)(H^2/gK)]$.

The financial asset will be used as the liquidity source during the remaining fraction of the production period, W_A/gK. The average amount of A withdrawn during this fraction of the period is $W_A/2$. The foregone interest due to financial asset withdrawals is thus $-(1/2)(d - p)(W_A^2/gK)$.

Thus, in the case where $d - p > h - p$, the net income earned by the household firm can be expressed as follows:

$$y = r(K)K + (d - p)A - (p/2)(M^2/gK)$$
$$+ (h - p)[H(M/gK) + (1/2)(H^2/gK)]$$
$$- (1/2)(d - p)(W_A^2/gK) - C_A(W_A) - C_H(H) - gK \qquad (2)$$

The household's task is to maximize y, subject to the following constraints:

$$gK = M + H + W_A \qquad (3)$$

$$A \geqslant W_A \qquad (4)$$

$$W = K + A + H + M \qquad (5)$$

$$(K, A, M, H, W_A) \geqslant 0 \qquad (6)$$

Even under our simplifying assumptions, the efficient running of a household firm is clearly a difficult task. The household firm must not only allocate wealth between the income generators (K and A), but must also decide the extent to which cash or withdrawals from H and/or A will be used to fund operating costs. For the latter problem, the use of M economizes on transactions costs but allows a portion of the wealth portfolio to be directly eroded by inflation during a portion of the production period. Use of A or H as the liquidity source causes higher transaction costs but allows the household—unlike for M—to collect a yield on a liquidity source during part of the production period.

The Lagrangian for this problem is:

$$Z = y + L_1(W - K - A - H - M)$$
$$+ L_2(gK - M - H - W_A) + L_3(A - W_A) \qquad (7)$$

where y is defined as in equation (2) above. Differentiation of (7) with respect to the choice variables and the assumption of interior solutions yields the constraints and the following first-order conditions:

$$Z_K = r(K) + Kr'(K)$$
$$+ (1/K^2)(1/g)[(1/2)pM^2$$
$$+ (1/2)(d - p)W_A^2 - (h - p)(HM + (1/2)H^2)]$$
$$- g - L_1 + L_2g = 0 \qquad (8)$$

$$Z_A = (d - p) - L_1 + L_3 = 0 \qquad (9)$$

$$Z_M = -p(M/gK) + (h - p)(H/gK) - L_1 - L_2 = 0 \qquad (10)$$

$$Z_H = (h - p)[M + H](1/gK) - C'_H(W_H) - L_1 - L_2 = 0 \qquad (11)$$

$$Z_{W_A} = -(d - p)(W_A/gK) - C'_A(W_A) - L_2 - L_3 = 0 \qquad (12)$$

Let us first investigate the conditions for optimal cash management. Consider the case in which $A > W_A$, that is, the case in which the financial asset is used both as an income generator and as a liquidity source. Via the slack condition $L_3 Z_{L_3} = 0$, $A > W_A$ implies that $L_3 = 0$. (The asset constraint on W_A is nonbinding.) Using equation (9), this implies that $L_1 = d - p$. This makes sense, because equation (8) tells us that L_1 is the yield to physical capital adjusted for cash flow and operating costs. Thus the fact that $L_1 = d - p$ is just another way of denoting that K and A are competing assets.

Inserting $L_1 = d - p$ into (10) and (11), then equating (10), (11), and (12), yields the following results:

$$W_A/gK = 1 - \{[C'_A(W_A) - C'_H(H)]/(d - h)\} \qquad (13)$$

$$M/gK = C'_H(H)/h \qquad (14)$$

Using the fact that $H/gK = 1 - [(M + H)/gK]$, (13) and (14) imply that:

$$H/gK = \{[C'_A(W_A) - C'_H(H)]/(d - h)\} - [C'_H(H)/h] \qquad (15)$$

Equation (13) indicates that use of the financial asset as a liquidity source (for funding operating costs associated with a given investment in physical capital) is positively related to the financial asset's yield and liquidity (the latter being defined as the inverse of marginal transaction costs) relative to hedges. The opposite is true for hedges, as shown by equation (15). Equations (13) and (15) also indicate that the use of H as a liquidity source implies that financial assets are illiquid relative to hedges over at least part of the range of W_A defined by the value $gK - M$. Inflation hedges will tend to be displaced by financial assets as a source of liquidity as financial development causes the yield and liquidity of the latter to increase over time. Interest rates and transaction costs are both crucial determinants of financial asset holdings, as well as the extent to which the option of holding financial assets facilitates the productive activities of household firms.

The use of money balances as a liquidity source is negatively related to the yield of, and positively related to the marginal transaction cost of withdrawing from, inflation hedges [see equation (14)]. Furthermore, if the value of $C'_H(H)/h$ in (15) is substituted into (14), we obtain the following result:

$$M/gK = \{[C'_A(W_A) - C'_H(H)]/(d - h)\} - (H/gK) \qquad (14')$$

indicating that use of M as a liquidity source is also negatively related to the yield and liquidity of the financial asset. Equations (14) and (14') embody an important result: that hedges can be displaced by either cash or financial assets. If the goal is to decrease the use of costly (to society) inflation hedges as stores of value, this can be achieved via increased monetization of the economy (for example, via a decreased inflation rate). This monetization effect must be distinguished from the further displacement of hedges (and of cash balances) by financial assets, which occurs as financial development reaches the stage where secure deposits of reasonable yield and liquidity become available to household firms. This latter development not only decreases the resource costs associated with inflation hedging, but also increases the availability of investment funds via the lending operations of financial intermediaries. Thus, the model's distinction between cash and financial assets allows us to conceptualize more clearly the differences between the monetization and intermediation stages of financial development.[15]

The above conditions for optimal cash management are the same if $A = W_A$, that is, if A is used solely as a liquidity source. This is easily verified by noting that $A = W_A$ implies $L_3 > 0$, via the slack condition $L_3 Z_{L_3} = 0$. This further implies, via (9), that $L_3 = L_1 - (d - p)$. If this equality is substituted into (12), and (10) through (12) are equated, conditions (13) through (15) once again result. Financial deepening can occur even if physical capital dominates the financial asset as an income generator for the household firm, that is, even if the yield to K (adjusted for cash flow and operating costs) never falls to $d - p$ over the range of K defined by the household's wealth endowment (W).

The other part of the household's problem is the choice of income generating assets. In the present case, in which $d - p > h - p$, the relevant assets are K and A. To obtain the portfolio balance condition, we note again that $L_3 = 0$ if A is used as an income generator on the margin (that is, if $A > W_a$). If this equality is substituted into (12), and (12) in turn substituted into (8), the result may be written as follows:

$$L_1 = [r(K) + Kr'(K)]$$
$$+ (M/gK)[(p/2)(M/K)] + (W_A/gK)(1/2)(d - p)(W_A/K)$$
$$- (H/gK)\{(h - p)[(1/2)(H/K) + (M/K)]\}$$
$$- g[1 + C'_A(W_A) + (W_A/gK)] \tag{16}$$

Equation (16) indicates the presence of complementarity of financial assets and physical capital in two ways: (1) the third term in (16) shows that an increase in $d - p$ causes an increase in the interest collected from A (during the fraction of the period W_A/gK), due to any increased holdings of K resulting in a larger cash-flow requirement; and (2) the direct effect of decreased financial transaction costs is to increase the effective yield to physical capital.

Let us now consider the case where the yield to hedges exceeds the yield to the financial asset, or $h - p > d - p$. This situation will be characteristic of a financially repressive regime of below-equilibrium interest rates, in which K and A are not competing assets for the household firms. The yield to physical capital (adjusted for cash flow and operating costs) will be driven down to $h - p$ via increased investment in K. Since the actual portfolio balance condition contains no additional insights beyond those just mentioned, it will not be presented here.

Methodologically, the present case is symmetrical to the one considered previously, in that it involves a straightforward switch of the roles played by H and A in the household's cash-management problem. In this case, since $h - p > d - p$, the financial asset will be used (if at all) solely as a liquidity source; hence $W_A = A$. Via a procedure analogous to that used for the previous case, the following conditions for optimal cash management can be derived:

$$W_H/gK = 1 - \{[C'_H(W_H) - C'_A(A)]/(h - d)\} \tag{17}$$

$$M/gK = C'_A(A)/d \tag{18}$$

$$A/gK = \{[C'_H(W_H) - C'_A(A)]/(h - d)\} - C'_A(A)/d \tag{19}$$

Conditions (17) and (19) show that use of A as a liquidity source presumes that it is liquid relative to H over some portion of the range of W_H defined by $gK - M$. (This marginal transaction cost differential is necessary to offset the lost income due to the fact that $h - p > d - p$.) Given this requirement, the demand for A varies positively with its yield and liquidity relative to hedges. Furthermore, the use of cash (M) to fund operating costs is negatively related to the yield and liquidity of the financial asset. These results thus indicate that increased mobilization of financial resources from household firms is feasible even if hedges dominate financial assets as income generators. Clearly, both the yield and the liquidity of financial assets are crucial determinants of the extent to which savings are held in financial form, even under conditions of complete certainty.

A program of financial liberalization would involve a transition from the case of $h - p > d - p$ to that in which $d - p > h - p$. This entails a transition from a situation in which financial assets are held (if at all) solely as liquidity sources, to one in which financial assets are held as income-generating assets *and* liquidity sources. For household firms in developing countries, financial liberalization involves: (1) displacement of both hedges and cash balances by financial assets as a source of funding cash flows, and (2) displacement of hedges by bank deposits as income-generating assets. These changes are likely to be particularly beneficial for nonwealthy household firms in inflationary environments, as such households' inflation hedges often feature higher storage costs (hence lower yields) and higher transaction costs than those of wealthier households, and a movement into cash balances in response to these higher hedging costs causes rapid erosion of household wealth.

Lastly, consider the case in which the yields to A and H are equal. In this case, the household will be indifferent between hedges and the financial asset as income generators, and the effective yield to physical capital will be driven down to $d - p = h - p$.

The cash-management aspect of this case is more interesting. Since the yields to A an H are equal, the household is indifferent about the order in which these two assets are used as liquidity sources, and the only factor affecting the choice between A and H is their relative liquidity. In other words, the household firm will equate the marginal transaction costs of withdrawing from the two assets. The extent to which cash (M) is used as a liquidity source is determined by the same factors as previously, so that the following optimal cash management conditions are obtained:

$$C'_H(W_H) = C'_A(W_A) \tag{20}$$

$$M/gK = C'_H(W_H)/h = C'_A(W_A)/d \tag{21}$$

Equation (21) indicates that the demand for cash is negatively related to the yield and liquidity of both hedges and the financial asset. From (20), we see that use of A as a liquidity source depends solely on its liquidity relative to H. However, it must be remembered that any increase of $d - p$ will create a situation in which $d - p > h - p$. Thus, even in the present case, increases in the liquidity or yield of A cause decreased demand for both cash and hedges.

The model indicates that recognition of cash-flow constraints associated with physical capital enriches the analysis of "complementarity of money and capital" by pinpointing the crucial distinction between money as means of purchase (cash balances) and money as store of value (financial assets). The use of stocks of assets for funding cash flows implies that the yield and liquidity of these assets are crucial determinants of both financial asset demand and the ability of household firms to utilize physical capital efficiently. The effects pointed out above do not depend on technical characteristics of capital, as in McKinnon's model, but on the realities of working capital and cash-flow costs (transaction costs and foregone interest), especially for household firms in developing countries.

3.   Conclusion

The foregoing analysis has shown the usefulness of integrating the portfolio and inventory approaches to the demand for money in order to explain the financial savings behavior of household firms in developing countries and thereby to strengthen the microeconomic foundations of financial liberalization. It is not necessary to make the restrictive assumption that physical capital has significant indivisibilities in order to show that financial assets and physical capital can be complements. Moreover, the benefits of financial liberalization are shown to flow not only from higher returns on financial assets but also from lower transaction costs in making exchanges between financial assets and the medium of exchange. Higher yields and improved liquidity (lower transaction costs) for financial assets facilitate increased savings mobilization and a better allocation of capital to higher yielding projects. Financial assets of reasonable yield and liquidity are particularly crucial for nonwealthy households in developing countries, as the inflation-hedging opportunities of such households are likely to be more costly than those of wealthier households (see Vogel, 1984).

Household firms in developing countries face a formidable task as they confront the joint problems of asset selection and cash management, and the magnitude of this task is reflected in the restrictive nature of some of the assumptions used in the present model. The possibility of relaxing some of these assumptions has already been noted and provides some interesting avenues for future research. For example, without the assumption of indivisibilities in physical capital, it is also possible to drop the assumption of no access to external credit for household firms in developing countries. Dropping this assumption could not only highlight the importance of differentials between borrowing and lending rates of interest, but could also lead toward a unified analysis of the role of transaction costs in both borrowing and deposit operations. In addition, it should be possible to extend the model to cases of uncertainty (as already done by Vogel and Buser, 1976, for the McKinnon model) and perhaps to include the risks of loss (other than from inflation) inherent in holding cash balances or deposits at financial institutions.

The model in this chapter also has significant implications for empirical work on financial liberalization. Those who have found that increased interest rates do not lead to increased holdings of financial assets have sometimes been criticized for failing to take inflation (and inflationary expectations) properly into account, but the failure to take transaction costs into account may be even more important. Transaction costs for depositors can be expected to vary inversely with interest rates paid on deposits, as financial institutions substitute implicit interest for explicit interest when interest rates are held below equilibrium, thereby leading to estimated coefficients for interest rates that are significantly biased when transaction costs are ignored. The importance of interactions between interest rates and transaction costs for financial institutions as well as for household firms indicates the usefulness of additional research on the behavior of financial institutions under different regimes of interest rate restrictions (see Burkett, 1985).

Notes

[1]Furthermore, despite arguments that low interest rates together with credit controls can assist the poor and promote production in priority sectors, the costs and risks of dealing with different classes of borrowers cause subsidies to flow away from the poor, while the fungibility of credit minimizes any stimulation of production in priority sectors (Von Pishke and Adams, 1980).

[2]See Burkett (1984) and Vogel (1984) for a detailed description of the Peruvian financial liberalization experience and especially for a detailed description and analysis of the cooperative bank's savings mobilization project.

[3]See Burkett (1985) for a detailed analysis of the behavior of financial intermediaries with respect to the deposit opportunities offered to savers under different regimes of controlled and uncontrolled interest rates. This analysis goes considerably beyond earlier analyses of deposit rate ceilings (such as Regulation Q) in the developed countries.

[4]In a world of uncertainty, household firms may also hold inflation hedges rather than money balances in order to reduce the risks from unexpected future inflation. See Vogel and Buser (1976) for an extension of McKinnon's model to include such uncertainty, and a demonstration that reduced uncertainty about future inflation is another aspect of financial liberalization that can contribute to the complementarity of money and capital.

[5]The assumption of no access to credit can also be dropped, although this is not done here.

[6]Ben-Zion (1974) attempts to overcome this problem by including an inventory-theoretic component in a money-demand model where money already appears in the firm's production function, but this leads to the conceptual problem of defining a "productive service" for money apart from its role as medium of exchange.

[7]Feige and Parkin (1971) develop a synthesis of portfolio and inventory analyses which is similar to that formulated here, but their work differs from the present model in that: (1) their concern is with the demand for cash rather than financial assets, (2) they do not include a cash-flow constraint on physical capital, and (3) they include commodity market *and* financial transaction costs in their model, whereas the present analysis focuses on the latter.

[8]The assumption of no access to credit is not made because of any claim to empirical validity, but rather for purposes of simplification.

[9]Empirically it may be quite difficult to distinguish between H and K, since inefficient additions to physical capital are one of the forms in which inflation hedging often occurs (see McKinnon, 1973, Chapter 6).

[10]In reality, some operating costs (for example, maintenance) can be delayed. We assume that g is fixed for mathematical tractability.

[11]One requirement of an inflation hedge is that its nominal yield (h) must show a positive response to the rate of inflation (p). In most developing countries, nominal yields to financial assets are fixed by administrative decree. Hence the increased popularity of hedges as p increases.

[12]The reason why financial-asset withdrawals occur at the same rate as the flow of operating costs is that the household firm will never use more than one liquidity source simultaneously, for reasons discussed below in the text.

[13]Both $C_A(W_A)$ and $C_H(W_H)$ include the time costs of withdrawals for the household firm, although the continuous flow framework (and the assumption of a given choice between labor and leisure) prevents us from explicitly isolating these costs. For a model of money demand which explicitly treats the time costs of withdrawals from financial assets, see Karni (1973).

[14]Of course, in reality liquidity sources are also held for precautionary purposes (for example, for unexpected consumption outlays due to emergencies or unforeseen bargains).

Indeed, all consumption expenditures (whether unforeseen or not) can be viewed as an additional cash-flow constraint for the household firm. The present analysis abstracts from these factors, due to its focus on the forms in which savings are held, rather than the choice between flows of consumption and saving. Furthermore, any concrete analysis would have to treat the relative security of cash, hedges, and financial assets as a determinant of the forms in which savings are held. Also, if d is fixed by government decree, then the high (hence highly variable) inflation rates common in developing countries can cause d − p to be more uncertain than h − p. If household firms are risk-averse, this will depress the demand for financial assets and increase the demand for hedges. See Vogel and Buser (1976).

[15]Of course in any concrete case the monetarization and intermediation stages of financial development are likely to overlap. Nonetheless, the conceptual distinction between the two stages can be useful in evaluating the benefits and costs of financial policy alternatives (for example, expansion of branch offices of banks into rural areas) in developing countries. See, for example, the classic article by Porter (1966).

References

Adams, Dale W (1978). "Mobilizing Household Savings through Rural Financial Markets." *Economic Development and Cultural Change* 26 (April): 547–60.

Adams, Dale W, and G. I. Nehman (1979). "Borrowing Costs and the Demand for Rural Credit." *Journal of Development Studies* 15 (January): 165–76.

Baumol, William J. (1952). "The Transactions Demand for Cash: An Inventory Theoretic Approach." *Quarterly Journal of Economics* 66 (November): 545–56.

Ben-Zion, Uri (1974). "The Cost of Capital and the Demand for Money by Firms." *Journal of Money, Credit and Banking* 6 (May): 263–69.

Burkett, Paul (1984). "Savings Mobilization in the Third World: Theory and Evidence from Peru." Ph.D. Thesis, Syracuse University. (January).

_____ (1985). "Interest Rate Restrictions and Deposit Opportunities for Small Savers in Developing Countries: An Analytical View." Unpublished Manuscript, University of Miami.

Claasen, Emil-Maria (1975). "On the Indirect Productivity of Money." *Journal of Political Economy* 83 (April): 431–36.

Cuevas, Carlos, and Douglas H. Graham (1982). "Interest Rate Policies and Borrowing Costs in Rural Financial Markets." Unpublished Manuscript, Dept. of Agricultural Economics, Ohio State University.

Elegalam, P. O. (1978). "The Queueing Cost of Banking in Lagos." *Nigerian Journal of Economic and Social Studies* 20 (November): 437–50.

Feige, Edgar L., and Michael Parkin (1971). "The Optimal Quantity of Money Bonds, Commodity Inventories, and Capital." *American Economic Review* 61 (June): 335–49.

Galbis, Vicente (1977). "Financial Intermediation and Economic Growth in Less Developed Countries: A Theoretical Approach." *Journal of Development Studies* 13 (January): 58–72.

González-Vega, Claudio (1984). "Credit Rationing Behavior of Agricultural Lenders: The Iron Law of Interest Rate Restrictions." In *Undermining Rural Development with Cheap Credit*, edited by Dale W Adams, Douglas H. Graham, and J. D. Von Pischke. Boulder: Westview Press.

Joyce, Joseph (1981). "Money and Production in the Developing Economies: An Analytical Survey of the Issues." *Journal of Economic Development* 6 (December): 41–70.

Kapur, Basant (1976). "Alternative Stabilization Plans for Less Developed Economies." *Journal of Political Economy* 84 (August): 777–95.

Karni, Edi (1973). "The Transactions Demand for Cash: Incorporation of the Value of Time into the Inventory Theoretic Approach." *Journal of Political Economy* 81 (September–October): 1216–25.

Levhari, David, and Don Patinkin (1968). "The Role of Money in a Simple Growth Model." *American Economic Review* 58 (September): 713–53.

Mathieson, Donald (1980). "Financial Reform and Stabilization Policy in a Developing Economy." *Journal of Development Economics* 7: 359–95.

McKinnon, Ronald I (1973). *Money and Capital in Economic Development*. Washington, D.C.: Brookings Institution.

Miller, Merton, and Daniel Orr (1966). "A Model of the Demand for Money by Firms." *Quarterly Journal of Economics* 80 (August): 413–35.

Moroney, John R. (1972). "The Current State of Money and Production Theory." *American Economic Review* 62 (May): 335–43.

Porter, Richard C. (1966). "The Promotion of the 'Banking Habit' and Economic Development." *Journal of Development Studies* 2 (July): 346–66.

Shaw, Edward S. (1973). *Financial Deepening in Economic Development*. New York: Oxford University Press.

Tobin, James (1956). "The Interest Elasticity of Transactions Demand for Cash." *Review of Economics and Statistics* 38 (August): 241–47.

———— (1958). "Liquidity Preference as Behavior Towards Risk." *Review of Economic Studies* 25: 65–86.

Vogel, Robert C. (1984). "Savings Mobilization: The Forgotten Half of Rural Finance." In *Undermining Rural Development with Cheap Credit*, edited by Dale W Adams, Douglas H. Graham, and J. D. Von Pischke. Boulder: Westview Press.

Vogel, Robert C., and Stephen Buser (1976). "Inflation, Financial Repression, and Capital Formation in Latin America." In *Money and Finance in Economic Growth and Development*, edited by Ronald I. McKinnon. New York: Dekker.

Von Pischke, J. D. (1978). "Towards an Operational Approach to Savings for Rural Developers." *Savings and Development* 2: 43–55.

Von Pischke, J. D., and Dale W Adams (1980). "Fungibility and the Design and Evaluation of Agricultural Credit Projects." *American Journal of Agricultural Economics* 62 (November): 719–26.

VIII

THE FINANCIALLY SUPPRESSED ECONOMY

16

Employment in a Controlled, Open Economy

John McDermott

Despite the adverse effect on employment, most developing countries, including those in the Caribbean, set minimum wages and institute various other controls over many areas of economic activity.[1] In this chapter we wish to consider the consequence, mainly on employment, of foreign exchange control combined with the minimum wage. We shall focus on the difficulty that exists in securing imported inputs that are complementary to labor. Not only is it at times impossible to obtain all the input that may be desired at prevailing prices, but the *future* availability of the input is uncertain as well. That is of little interest if firms cannot store the input. Yet, it is well known that controls create tremendous incentives for such storing and that abnormally high inventories of scarce inputs are bound to exist whenever uncertainty is generated or enhanced by interventions into markets.[2] Our focus will be on the relationship between the hoarding of inputs and employment when firms face two constraints: a minimum wage, and a rationed quantity of foreign exchange.

Normally, in a one-sector model with a minimum wage, the amount of employment would rise with increases in the price of the output, or with declines in the prices of any complementary inputs. We shall see that in the present model this is no longer strictly true: due to the possibility of future shortfalls of input allotments, firms *may* respond to *permanent* reductions in complementary input prices, (and *will* respond to *expected* reductions) by reducing their current demand for labor. Similar results hold for changes in output price, risk perception, and interest rates and for devaluation. Thus, rationing of foreign exchange will compound the employment problems generated by minimum wages. This chapter details another reason, if any more are necessary, to liberalize the mechanisms of international trade.

The plan of the chapter is as follows. Section 1 describes the model; Section 2 considers the response to several disturbances; and Section 3 offers some concluding observations.

1. The Model

1.1. The Minimum Wage

We shall assume a very simple structural model to make the basic points with as much clarity as possible. First, we assume that the economy is completely specialized in producing a commodity for export and home consumption. Imports consist of both consumer items and inputs which cooperate with labor to produce the single good.

Output of the home good is given by:

$$y = F(L, Z) \tag{1}$$

where L is the amount of labor employed and Z is the amount used of the imported input. The production function is assumed to possess *decreasing returns* to scale, reflecting the existence of at least one other input (capital, land, etc.) whose quantity is being held fixed.[3] We shall also assume that labor and imported materials are *complements* in production. Thus: F_L, F_Z > 0; $F_{LZ} = F_{ZL}$ > 0; F_{LL}, F_{ZZ} < 0. The results below would, of course, be affected considerably if the inputs were substitutes. The substitute case, however, would appear to be rare in the LDC context.

Let p^* and q^* be the world currency prices of output and of the input, respectively. Given the small country assumption, home currency prices are $p = ep^*$ and $q = eq^*$ (e is the home-money price of foreign exchange) and the *nominal* wage, w, is *fixed* at $\hat{w}$.[4] In the absence of both storability of Z (the imported input) and rationing of foreign exchange, L and Z could be thought of as demand-determined through the following profit-maximizing conditions:

$$F_L = \hat{w}/p \equiv \bar{w} \tag{2}$$

$$F_Z = q/p \equiv \bar{q} \tag{3}$$

where F_L and F_Z are the marginal products of labor and materials,

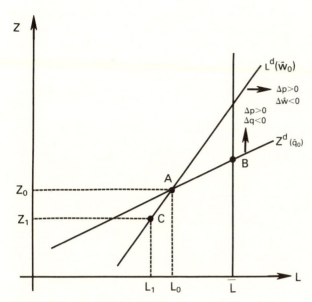

Figure 16.1 Factor demands.

respectively, and both depend on the amounts of L and Z currently in use. Figure 16.1 illustrates this. The curve labeled $L^d(\tilde{w}_0)$ shows the demand for labor as a function of Z, given the real wage $\tilde{w}_0$. Similarly, $Z^d(\tilde{q}_0)$ shows the demand for the imported input as a function of L, given $\tilde{q} = \tilde{q}_0$. Only at point A are both demands satisfied simultaneously. Full employment is $\bar{L}$; an effective minimum wage keeps the actual employment level below the full-employment level. Employment will rise toward full employment if either p^* rises, q^* falls, $\hat{w}$ falls, or e rises (the last works exactly like a fall in $\hat{w}$ since $\tilde{q}$ would not be affected). As employment rises, imports of the input also rise if, as we assume, the two factors are complements. Without a minimum wage and assuming other prices do not adjust, wages would fall until equilibrium occurred at point B.

1.2. Foreign Exchange Rationing

The amount of Z that a firm can purchase will depend upon the amount of foreign exchange that it can obtain from the central bank. If we assume that these funds are rationed randomly to each firm, independently of any action the firm might take, then we allow the possibility, at least, that A will fall short of Z_0 in Figure 16.1 and, therefore, that L will fall short of L_0.

In particular, if the firm were *constrained* in the present period to purchase no more than Z_1 units of the input, then it would hire only L_1 workers: unemployment is even worse than it has to be.

The possibility of holding inventories of Z may add still another layer to the unemployment, since in certain circumstances (these are explored below) increased demand for inventories will be satisfied by reducing current use of Z and, inevitably, current employment.

We are bypassing some interesting and important questions about interfirm and interindustry allocation of the scarce foreign exchange allotments, about the degree of transferability of quotas, questions of corruption, and of under- or overinvoicing of current-account transactions. The basic nature of these problems is dealt with in Bhagwati (1978). We are, in effect, assuming that all firms are alike, and that each may be currently constrained below its notional demand for the input, and that each faces *some* uncertainty about the future availability. In other words, there is no parallel market for foreign exchange, no re-sale of scarce inputs at market-clearing prices, and no smuggling, at least not in sufficient amounts to thoroughly eliminate the uncertainty surrounding future quantities.[5]

1.3. The Formal Problem

Let S_t be the amount of the input with which the firm begins period t. Let B_t be the amount of the input bought in t. It follows immediately that

$$S_{t+1} = S_t + B_t - Z_t \tag{4}$$

Let X_t be the total amount of foreign exchange (expressed in units of the imported input: $X = eX^*/q$) available to the firm due to rationing. It must be the case that

$$B_t \leq X_t \tag{5}$$

It will be convenient to define b as the fraction of the foreign currency ration actually used:

$$B_t = b_t X_t \qquad 0 \leq b_t \leq 1 \tag{6}$$

The current value of X is known in each t, but future values of X are not. We assume that X is a random variable, independently and identically distributed (iid) through time with density $\theta(X)$. The firm has full knowledge of this density.

The rational firm will pick values for b_t, S_{t+1}, and L_t in every period in order to maximize the discounted expected value of the sum of future profits. Formally, the problem is to maximize

$$J = \sum_{t=0}^{T} \alpha^t E[p_t F(L_t, Z_t) - q_t b_t X_t - \hat{w} L_t] \tag{7}$$

by choice of b_t, S_{t+1}, and L_t, where $\alpha \equiv 1/(1 + r)$ is the discount factor and r is the exogenous rate of interest. The maximization is subject to:

$$Z_t = b_t X_t - S_{t+1} + S_t \tag{8}$$

$$b_t, S_{t+1}, L_t \geq 0 \tag{9}$$

$$S_{T+1} = 0 \tag{10}$$

Equation (10), the transversality condition, says that at the end of the planning horizon (date T) the firm does not want to hold any of the input. T may be interpreted as the date at which the firm goes out of business. This may be infinity; but whether it is or not, the firm would not wish to be holding any stock with market value. As a final piece of notation, let W_{t+1} be the *expected profit* in period $t + 1$ as of t, and let $W'_{t+1} = \partial W_{t+1}/\partial S_{t+1}$.

The firm's choices will have to satisfy the following Euler equations:

$$\partial J/\partial L_t \equiv QL = pF_L - \hat{w} = 0 \tag{11}$$

$$\partial J/\partial b_t \equiv Qb = pF_Z - q \geq 0 \tag{12}$$

$$\partial J/\partial S_{t+1} \equiv QS = -pF_Z + \alpha W'_{t+1} \leq 0 \tag{13}$$

Equation (11) can always be satisfied with equality, since we have assumed that employment is demand-determined. Qb will be zero only if $0 < b < 1$; that is, only if the firm is currently unconstrained in its purchases of foreign exchange. If it is constrained ($b = 1$), then Qb < 0. Equation (13) will be zero if $S_{t+1} < 0$. If the firm does not hoard any of the input, then QS < 0 and $S_{t+1} = 0$.

The last of the above conditions, equation (13), represents the novelty of our approach to the problem of quotas and static efficiency. Alone, it is quite sensible and states that the firm should equate the current marginal value-in-production of a unit of the input to its marginal value-in-storage, the latter given by the discounted value of *expected* marginal profit (W'_{t+1})

in the next period. We shall see that events that influence the marginal storage value may have important repercussions upon current input use and employment.

1.4. The One-Period Solution

Although of little interest in itself, the problem in which $t = T$ is important to solve in order to be able to solve the multiperiod version. If there is a single period, there is no uncertainty: X_T and S_T are known, given by, respectively, the central bank and history; S_{T+1} is known to be zero by equation (10). Picking b_T and L_T to maximize profits boils down to selecting point A in Figure 16.1, if possible, and, if it is not, picking $b_T = 1$ and hiring labor according to the demand curve. Point C in Figure 16.1 is such a point of constraint: even buying all the available foreign exchange will not allow the firm to reach its notional, profit-maximizing point. It still, however, may choose the amount of labor to employ in accordance with its notional demand, given the amount of Z exogenously.

We conclude this subsection by deriving an expression for $\bar{X}_T$, the necessary foreign exchange ration in order that the firm *not* be constrained in period T. First, note that equation (11) establishes L as a function of Z and $\tilde{w}$ (the real wage). Write this:

$$L = l(\overset{+}{Z}, \overset{-}{\tilde{w}}) \tag{14}$$

where the signs posted over the arguments refer to signs of partial derivatives. Next, substitute (14) into (12), so that if the firm is *unconstrained*,

$$pF_Z[l(Z, \tilde{w})] - q = 0 \tag{12'}$$

that is, equation (12) holds with equality, and L is picked notionally. The minimum X_T that will satisfy (12') is clearly that for which $b = 1$. Thus, letting $b = 1$ and $S_{t+1} = 0$ in (8), substituting into (12'), and rearranging slightly, yields:

$$F_Z[l(\bar{X}_T + S_T, \tilde{w}), \bar{X}_T + S_T] = \tilde{q}_T \tag{12''}$$

This defines $\bar{X}_T$ implicitly. We see that $\bar{X}_T$ depends on both real factor prices, $\tilde{w}$ and $\tilde{q}$, and on the quantity of the input with which period T begins, S_T.

1.5. The Two-Period Solution

Now consider the situation of the same firm in period $T - 1$ (we shall not go beyond two periods in this chapter) so that X_T is unknown. Now, both (12) and (13) must be satisfied: the former depends only on current variables, but the latter depends critically on the expectation of X_T and the marginal profit it will elicit.

Let us define

$$f(\bar{Z}, \bar{w}) = F_Z[l(\bar{Z}, \bar{w}), \bar{Z}] \tag{15}$$

to be the marginal product of Z under the assumption that the firm's labor demand is always satisfied; that is, it is F_Z for movements along a given L^d curve in Figure 16.1, for fixed $\bar{w}$, and for movements to new L^d curves for fixed levels of Z. The amount of L in use has been endogenized.

Equation (12) may now be written as follows, having substituted for Z from (8):

$$f(b_{T-1}X_{T-1} - S_T + S_{T-1}, \bar{w}) = \bar{q}_{T-1} \tag{16}$$

This equation establishes b_{T-1} as a function of S_t. In Figure 16.2 the relationship appears as the curve ABC and is to be interpreted as the set of points which satisfies the first and second of our three necessary conditions. It becomes horizontal at 1: any increase in storing when $b = 1$ will cause $f > \bar{q}$ and $Qb > 0$, since no more of the input is available under the rationing scheme. In its upward-sloping range its slope is $1/X_{T-1}$: an increase in S_T of 1 unit requires b_{T-1} to rise by $1/X_{T-1}$ units to keep f equal to the constant $\bar{q}$. This is clearly implied by Equation (16).

The third condition will be fulfilled (along with the first) if

$$-p_{T-1}f(b_{T-1}X_{T-1} - S_T + S_{T-1}, \bar{w}) + \alpha W'_T = 0 \tag{17}$$

where the expected value of marginal profit, W'_T, can be written as:

$$W'_T = \int_0^{\bar{X}^T} p_T f(X_T + S_T, \bar{w}_T)\theta(X_T)dX_T + \int_{\bar{X}_T}^\infty q_T\theta(X_T)dX_T \tag{18}$$

This expectation[6] depends upon S_T, $\bar{w}_T$, p_T, and q_T, both directly and through $\bar{X}_T$ which is defined implicitly in (12''). The important thing to note at this point is that W'_T *rises* with p_T and q_T (future money prices), as well as with $\bar{w}_T$ (the future real wage), and *falls* with increases in S_T, the amount actually stored. Although less obvious, W'_T *also rises* if either the mean of

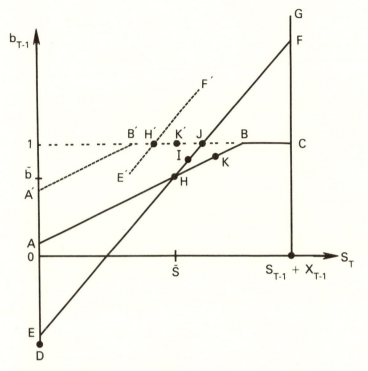

Figure 16.2   Purchase and storage.

$\theta(X_T)$ *falls*, or the density becomes more "risky" in the Rothschild–Stiglitz (1970) sense.[7]

Equation (17) also establishes a relationship between b_{T-1} and S_T. In Figure 16.2 the DEFG curve represents this implicit function: it shows the set of b_{T-1} and S_T such that the third and first of the necessary conditions are satisfied. This locus is also upward sloping and must be steeper than ABC where they cross since $\partial W'/\partial S_T < 0$.

If the two cross along the upward-sloping segment AB then we say that the firm is "currently unconstrained" since the optimal value, $\tilde{b}$, is less than 1. In Figure 16.2, point H shows such an unconstrained optimum: $\tilde{b}$ and $\tilde{S}$ are the optimal values of the two choice variables. For a different set of exogenous variables the loci might be A'B'C and E' F', in which case the firm would be "currently constrained." The equilibrium is now H' in Figure 16.2: b = 1 and storage is positive. In terms of Figure 16.1, the constrained situation corresponds to a point like C.

In sum, if the firm does not have enough foreign exchange to purchase all it desires for both current use *and* inventory holding (for example, point

H′ in Figure 16.2), it will cut back on *both* to some extent, in the process reducing employment.

The idea is both simple and important, and deserves emphasis. When quantity controls on imports create the need for strategic inventories, employment ceases to be a simple function of real factor prices and becomes dependent on both the current available quantity of the input (if it is less than the notional amount) and upon the expected future availability of the input.[8] The latter influence becomes most important when the former is operative. That is, when the firm is constrained (which is presumably the normal situation if there is a need for foreign exchange control), any impetus to increase inventory stock (the reasons for which are given below) will decrease its current labor demand. This happens because the firm must use less of the imported input currently, in order to store more, and this reduces labor's marginal product. The existence of the minimum wage guarantees that unemployment will rise. It is clear that, if there were no minimum wage regulations, in place of increased unemployment workers would experience a decline in their real wage.

2.   Comparative Statistics

Changes in prices may be classified as "temporary" (only p_{T-1}, q_{T-1}, $\bar{w}_{T-1}$, or e_{T-1} change), as "expected" (only p_T, q_T, etc. change), or as "permanent" (both p_{T-1} and p_T, q_{T-1} and q_T, etc. change). In addition, we can consider changes in the rate of interest (r), and in the characteristics of the probability density. To begin with, consider changes in q, the price of the imported input.

2.1.   Input Price

Temporary changes in q shift AB in Figure 16.2; expected changes shift EF; and permanent changes shift both. To see how these shifts occur, refer to equations (16) and (17).

In this subsection, we will consider a *fall* in q, a disturbance which always raises employment in the absence of the kind of foreign exchange rationing we are analyzing. A *temporary* fall in q raises AB and, if the firm is *currently unconstrained*, moves the equilibrium point to I in Figure 16.2. It is obvious that this raises both purchases (b rises) and inventories (S rises), but current use, Z, also increases. We know this because Z is constant along any given AB line, by construction, so movements upwards along the EF segment raise use and employment. Therefore, falling input prices will improve employment, as in the standard case, provided that the firm is not currently constrained.

It is clear that falling input prices (temporary, still) will eventually lead to the firm's being constrained. After this occurs (that is, after point J is reached) further decreases in q have *no effect on employment*, or indeed on any other variable. The segment AB keeps shifting to the left (for example, A'B'), but the horizontal portion is now relevant and it, of course, does not move.

An *expected* fall in q (that is, only q_T changes) will not affect AB but, since the perception of lower input prices in the future raises expected future marginal profit, W'_T [see equation (18)], this will move EF out to the right. If the firm is *unconstrained* there is no employment effect at all. The new equilibrium is point K, and the use of Z is unchanged: the firm increases its purchases only in order to increase inventory stock. If however, the firm began at the constrained point H', the *perceived reduction in future input prices would reduce current employment*. The reasoning is as follows: if the firm is currently buying all of the input it is allowed to, any increase in inventory must be met by reducing current use. As Z falls, L^d falls since the marginal product of labor is positively related to the amount of Z in use. In Figure 16.2, E'F' moves to the right, establishing a new equilibrium at K'. The rise in S_T requires a fall in current demand for both inputs.

A permanent fall in q is a blend of the above: both curves move. It is easy to verify that *employment falls if the firm is constrained, but rises if it is unconstrained*. It never remains unaffected.

A paradoxical implication is that permanently *higher* input prices may *raise* employment by discouraging firms from holding inventories.

2.2. *News about Foreign Exchange Rationing*

The firm will react currently to any news about the probability of securing foreign exchange in the future. Bad news [a fall in the mean or an increase in the riskiness of $\theta(X_T)$] will move EF out, while good news would move it back. The AB line is never affected. What this means for employment follows directly from our past results. Bad news either has no effect (if the firm is currently unconstrained) or will reduce employment (firm is constrained). Of course, in both cases inventories will rise. Conversely, good news either has no effect or raises employment. This suggests that a liberalization effort which is firmly stated and credibly executed will have a potentially important once-and for-all beneficial effect on employment (or real wages if there is no minimum wage). People will react to this "good news" by reducing inventories, and raising current input use, which increases labor's marginal product.

2.3. Interest paid

Interest rates behave like news in that only EF is affected. Another paradoxical effect arises here. Falling interest rates raise QS, enhancing the value of storing, and EF moves right as it does with bad news. As with bad news, employment will fall if the firm is currently under constraint. At best, employment is unchanged.

2.4. Output Price

A temporary increase in p (due to a world price change, say) will affect both AB and EF. It raises AB and moves EF back. This disturbance is different from the others in two respects. First, $P_{t-1}F_Z$ increases both because p_{T-1} rises and because the real wage falls, leading to greater employment at a fixed amount of input use [see equation (17)]. Second, the rise in p, though temporary, does affect EF since the *opportunity cost* of storing, $p_{T-1}F_Z$, has increased [see equation (18)], even though the discounted expected benefit is unchanged.

This means that *temporary output price increases always improve employment*. Even if the firm is constrained, by raising the opportunity cost of storage, firms hoard less of the input, use more of it, and hire more labor. In Figure 16.2, E'F' would move back: b_{T-1} stays equal to unity, and S_T falls, raising Z_{T-1}.

Expected future price increases, unfortunately, may reduce employment. When p_T rises, EF moves out (W'$_T$ goes up; $p_{T-1}F_Z$ is unchanged) and AB stays in place. So again, the best that can happen is that employment is left unchanged. At worst (if the firm is currently buying its full allotment of foreign exchange) employment must fall.

A permanent price change clearly raises AB. The employment consequences in the constrained case, however, hinge entirely upon whether EF moves out or back. Fortunately, it must move back. The existence of discounting ($\alpha < 1$) and the possibility of no future constraint ($X_T < \bar{X}_T$) ensure that the rise in current opportunity cost ($p_{T-1}F_Z$) outweighs the rise in expected marginal profit of hoarding (W'$_T$). Therefore, employment must rise regardless of the firm's current position when the output price rises, and that rise is expected to be permanent.

2.5. Devaluation and Fall in Minimum Wage

Since the money price of the input is set on world markets, a devaluation leaves the real input price unchanged and acts just like a fall in the minimum wage. Both reduce $\tilde{w}$, the real wage. The effects of these are virtually indistinguishable from an increase in the output price, since temporary devaluations raise F_Z, and expected future devaluations raise W'_T. Permanent devaluations, then, are helpful in raising employment levels, just as higher output prices are.

Unfortunately, *expected* devaluation alone *reduces* employment, at least if the firm is currently constrained (otherwise, there is no effect). The reasoning is by now familiar: a future devaluation increases the value of hoarding Z because the future marginal productivity of Z is increased when the real wage falls. Inventory rises; current use and employment diminish. Expectations of future devaluation would, in fact, be quite likely, since the central bank has already been forced into a rationing scheme, indicating a declining (or, at least, historically low) stock of international reserves. Devaluation may be the next step; and the greater it is expected to be, the smaller will be current employment. Our analysis suggests, therefore, that lingering expectations of devaluation are much worse than the actual devaluation, and that countries would be well advised to eliminate as expeditiously as possible the exchange disequilibrium, whether or not they can actually fully liberalize the market for foreign currency.

3. Conclusions

One lesson of this chapter is that combining controls over economic activity may enhance the negative consequences of each. Specifically, exchange rationing will contribute to the unemployment due to a minimum wage in two related ways. First, it may cause the firm to be constrained currently, unable to purchase enough of the imported input and thus forced to reduce its employment level to maximize profit. Second, it causes expectations about the future state of rationing (and of other variables) to affect current employment since, if the firm is currently constrained, any disturbance that enhances the desirability of hoarding the input will cause reductions in both current input use and employment.

Although we have chosen to emphasize the employment effects, which are probably of primary concern to the Caribbean nations, the implications for output, inventory accumulation, and purchasing are straightforward.

Several extensions of this analysis come to mind. One is to increase the number of periods to N or to infinity. This would make the model richer, but it would probably not change the main conclusions. More interesting would be to integrate this essentially supply-side analysis into a model of balance-of-payments determination. This would entail adding a household sector and describing its behavior with respect to the foreign exchange constraint. Also, the money supply and demand functions would have to be specified. A final extension would be an explicit modeling of the government's objectives with regard to its foreign exchange reserves. If a "rationing function" could be learned by households, then the randomness would shift away from its allotment over to the exogenous variables that would be determining that allotment.

The political and social dimensions of minimum wage laws make it unlikely that they will ever be eliminated or "devalued away" in real terms for any length of time. This chapter suggests that it then becomes important to liberalize the foreign exchange market as a method of reducing, if not eliminating, unemployment.

Notes

[1]For a survey and some case histories of minimum wage policy, see Starr (1981) and International Labor Organization (1968). Krueger (1983) presents a comprehensive study of employment policy and liberalization in 12 LDCs.

[2]For some evidence on this point see Bhagwati (1978), pp. 110–112, which provides an excellent exposition of the overall effects of tariffs and quantitative restrictions on the efficiency and welfare of developing economies.

[3]The standard work on the open, minimum-wage economy is that by Brecher (1947a, 1974b). He concentrates on constant-returns-to-scale technology in a two-sector model and shows that the quantities of inputs demanded are indeterminate from the supply side. To pin down the production point, he requires a less-than-perfectly elastic foreign offer curve. To avoid that problem, we assume decreasing returns. As shown below, real factor prices are sufficient to determine factor demands and output.

[4]We choose to work with fixed nominal wages since governments typically set minimum wages in money terms. Some countries, notably Chile, have indexed minimum wages, to disastrous effect. Brecher (1974a, 1974b) deals with wages fixed in units of one of the two produced goods.

[5]There is literature on input uncertainty and the theory of the firm, but most of it concentrates on input *price* uncertainty, not quantity uncertainty (for example, Blair, 1974; Martin, 1981; Scheinkman and Schechtman, 1983; Turnovsky, 1971). In the context of quotas in an open economy see Young (1982). For some macroeconomic implications of exchange control, see McKinnon and Mathieson (1981).

[6]The form of equation (18) comes from the fact that X_T can end up either below $\bar{X}_T$ [in which case *actual* marginal profit in period T is $p_T f(\cdot)$] or above $\bar{X}_T$ (in which case the firm gains only q_T, in a marginal sense, since it need not actually purchase as much of the input in period T). These two possibilities are weighted by the known density function, $\theta(X_T)$.

[7]If the mean of $\theta(X_T)$ falls, the weight is shifted to the first integral in equation (18), and away from the second. Since $p_T f < q_T$ for $X_T > \bar{X}_T$, W'_T must increase. "More risky" means more probability weight in the tails and less in the center. Increasing the variance of a normal density will increase its "riskiness" by this definition. When riskiness rises W'_T rises, even if the mean remains unchanged, because $f(\cdot)$ is a downward-sloping function of X.

[8]The idea that firms and individuals cease to respond exclusively to price signals when they face constraints on sales of products or services originated with Clower (1965) and Patinkin (1965) in the modern era. Barro and Grossman (1976) analyze situations of general excess demand, as well as general excess supply.

References

Barro, R. J., and H. I. Grossman (1976). *Money, Employment and Inflation*. New York: Cambridge University Press.

Bhagwati, J. N. (1978). *Anatomy and Consequences of Exchange Control Regimes*. New York: NBER (Ballinger, Cambridge).

Blair, R. D. (1974). "Random Input Prices and the Theory of the Firm." *Economic Inquiry* (June): 214–26.

Brecher, R. A. (1974a). "Minimum Wage Rates and the Pure Theory of International Trade." *Quarterly Journal of Economics*: 98–116.

―――― (1974b). "Optimal Commercial Policy for a Minimum-Wage Economy." *Journal of International Economics*: 139–49.

Clower, R. W. (1965). "The Keynesian Counter-Revolution: A Theoretical Appraisal." In *The Theory of Interest Rates*, edited by F. H. Hahn and F. Brechling. New York: Macmillan.

International Labor Organization (1968). "Minimum Wage Fixing and Economic Development." *ILO Studies and Reports*, New Series, No. 72, Geneva: ILO.

Krueger, A. O. (1983). *Trade and Employment in Developing Countries: Volume 3, Synthesis and Conclusions*. Chicago and London: National Bureau of Economic Research; University of Chicago Press.

Martin, R. E. (1981). "Stochastic Input Deliveries." *Economic Inquiry* (October): 640–49.

McKinnon, R. I., and D. J. Mathieson (1981). "How to Manage a Repressed Economy." *Princeton Essays in International Finance* 145 (December).

Patinkin, D. (1965). *Money, Interest and Prices*. New York: Harper & Row.

Rothschild, M. and J. E. Stiglitz (1970). "Increasing Risk: I. A Definition." *Journal of Economic Theory*: 225–43.

Scheinkman, J. A. and J. Schechtman (1983). "A Simple Competitive Model with Production and Storage." *Review of Economic Studies* (July): 427–41.

Starr, G. (1981). *Minimum Wage Fixing*. Geneva: International Labor Organization.

Turnovsky, S. J. (1971). "The Theory of Production under Conditions of Stochastic Input Supply." *Metroeconomics*: 51–65.

Young, L. (1982). "Quantity Controls vs. Expenditure Controls in International Trade under Uncertainty." *Journal of International Economics* (February): 143–64.

17

Government Revenue from Money Creation in Latin America: 1977–81

Lynn McFadden

Governments can obtain revenues through taxation or by borrowing or issuing money. Whether this last occurs as a printing-press operation or more formally through increases in central bank credit to the government, money issue can be, at least temporarily, a powerful and attractive means of financing government expenditures.

This chapter estimates government revenue from money creation in Latin America. Specifically, the seigniorage revenues that Latin American countries obtained during a recent five-year period from 1977 to 1981 are measured, and seigniorage as a percentage of GNP and total government expenditure is calculated. In Section 1, the topic of seigniorage is introduced by a comparison of its nature under commodity-based money systems and fiat money systems, and the relationship of seigniorage with inflation and with government finance is briefly discussed. Section 2 presents data on the use of seigniorage by 18 Latin American countries and the United States for the period 1977–81. We find that money creation (or equivalently, central bank credit extended to the government), measured as the annual change in high-powered money, has been an important source of revenue for many Latin American countries. Section 3, which is divided into two parts, compares the results of this research with work by Fischer (1982) and Connolly (1983) and briefly relates seigniorage rates to inflation rates.

Helpful comments were provided by Niso Abuaf and Michael Connolly.

1. An Introduction to Seigniorage

The term seigniorage, as originally applied to commodity money, refers to the difference between the value of the metal content of a coin and its value as money, the latter being represented by the value of the goods and services for which the government or individuals were willing to exchange it. The difference between the value as money and the mint costs represents net revenue to the issuer.

Under commodity-based money systems, seigniorage was relatively low, since a government had to buy metal and mint it to issue money. Extraction costs placed limits on the profitability of the issuance of money.

Under the fiat money systems of modern economies, possible seigniorage revenue is relatively high, since printing paper money (and the associated administrative costs, of course) is cheaper than acquiring and minting precious metal. Increasing the issue of money, and hence seigniorage, requires no immediate government or central bank purchase of gold, silver, or other metallic commodity.[1]

There is another difference in the nature of revenue from money creation under a fiat money system that has to do with the fact that fiat money is a liability of the issuer. When a government issued commodity money, it was simply swapping assets in a transaction that was essentially once and for all complete at the time of money issue. However, under the present fiat money systems, money is a liability of the government. When a government resorts to the overissue of fiat money and both inflation and a decline in the public's demand for cash balances ensue, then the government may gain through a reduction in the real value of its total outstanding monetary liabilities.

Thus, it is with the predominance of fiat money systems that the terms "inflation tax" and "inflation tax revenue" have become significant in discussions of seigniorage. While seigniorage and inflation tax revenue are not synonymous, they are both measurements of the gains that may be achieved when a government uses central bank credit, rather than taxes or borrowing, to finance its operations. Seigniorage measures the current resources a government receives from money issue and is simply the annual increase (if there is one) in high-powered money. The revenue from what Cagan (1956) called "the tax on cash balances," or the inflation tax revenue, includes the real value of the new money issued and any reduction in the real value of the government's total monetary liabilities.

As suggested above, the formula for seigniorage revenue is simply dH/dt or ΔH, where H stands for high-powered money. It is seigniorage that is measured in this study, because the intent is to pinpoint the current revenues that the governments of Latin American countries have recently obtained through money creation.

All governments that issue their own money earn seigniorage, and some portion of monetary expansion that maintains a stable price level thus serves to finance government spending. However, excessive reliance on money issue to finance government expenditures results in inflation.

Several Latin American countries have had historically high inflation rates. For example, the average inflation rate in Argentina for the period 1960–75 was 57%; the average inflation rate for Chile for the period 1960–77 was 89% (Fischer, 1982). The inflation rates experienced in many of the other Latin American countries are much higher than those experienced by the industrialized countries and, on the whole, are as high or higher than those experienced even in other less developed nations. Consequently, it is likely that seigniorage rates would be high in some Latin American countries.

2. Research Methods

For each of the 18 Latin American countries included in this study and for the United States, the annual change in high-powered money during the period 1977–81 was calculated. The level of the monetary base (H) is found in Line 14, Reserve Money, of the country pages of the International Monetary Fund (IMF) *International Financial Statistics Yearbook 1982*.

The annual change in high-powered money (ΔH), or annual seigniorage, was expressed as a percentage of the gross national product (GNP) in current prices for each year, which is found in Line 99a of the IMF *Yearbook*. The change in high-powered money as a percentage of GNP is designated the seigniorage/GNP rate for the purposes of this chapter. The individual annual seigniorage/GNP rates for each country for the period 1977–81, or for as many years of this period for which data were available, were summed and averaged. The average seigniorage/GNP rates are found in Table 17.1.

Annual seigniorage for each country for each year was also expressed as a percentage of the government revenue (R) plus seigniorage (ΔH) for the year in question. Government revenue is found in Line 81 of the IMF *Yearbook*. The change in high-powered money as a percentage of government revenue plus the change in high-powered money (that is, $\Delta H/[R + \Delta H]$) is designated the seigniorage/total revenue rate for the purposes of this chapter. The average rates for each country for the period 1977 to 1981, or for as many years of this period for which data were available, are also found in Table 17.1.

The average inflation rates for some countries for the period 1977–81 were also calculated, using data from Line 64, Consumer Prices, of the IMF *Yearbook*. The average inflation rates appear in Table 17.2.

Table 17.1 Average Seignorage Rates

	Average of ΔH/GNP	Average of ΔH/(R + ΔH)
Argentina	0.062	0.237
Bolivia	0.016	0.156
Brazil	0.024	0.203
Chile	0.037	0.097
Colombia	0.033	–
Costa Rica	0.029	–
Ecuador	0.020	0.137
El Salvador	0.011	0.067
Guatemala	0.010	0.081
Guyana	0.011	–
Honduras	0.009	0.052
Mexico	0.056	0.271
Nicaragua	0.002	0.098
Paraquay	0.028	0.198
Peru	0.057	0.235
Suriname	0.015	0.062
Uruguay	0.038	0.137
Venezuela	0.014	0.049
United States	0.005	0.023

3. Discussion of Results

3.1. *Seigniorage Revenue Rates*

The data presented in Table 17.1 indicate that for many Latin American countries, seigniorage has been a significant source of revenue. With the exception of Nicaragua, seigniorage revenues are equal to at least 1% of GNP for all the Latin American countries included in this study, and the seigniorage/GNP rates for these countries are at least twice as high as the rate experienced in the United States. For all countries for which data were available, seigniorage revenues are equal to at least 5% of total revenue (that is, government revenue plus seigniorage), and the seigniorage/total revenue rates are at least twice as high as the rate experienced in the United States.

An arbitrary classification is assumed for the sake of discussion, as follows: countries with average seigniorage/GNP rates (that is, ΔH/GNP) above 3.5% are designated "very high" seigniorage-use countries: countries with rates between 1.6 and 3.4% are designated "moderate/high" seigniorage-use countries, and countries with rates of 1.5% and below are designated "low" seigniorage-use countries. Five countries, then, had very high average seigniorage/GNP rates during the period 1977–81; these are Argentina, Chile, Mexico, Peru, and Uruguay.

Six countries were found to have moderate/high average seigniorage rates during the period 1977–81; these are Bolivia, Brazil, Colombia, Costa Rica, Ecuador, and Paraguay.

Seven of the 18 Latin American countries (along with the United States) fell into the low seigniorage-rate class; these are El Salvador, Guatemala, Guyana, Honduras, Nicaragua, Suriname, and Venezuela.

Comparing the results of this study with the seigniorage rates reported by Fischer (1982) for the period 1960–75 reveals that patterns of seigniorage usage in Latin America are, on the whole, consistent between this study and Fischer's, indicating that countries that relied most heavily on seigniorage throughout the 1960s and the first half of the 1970s have continued this practice through the end of the 1970s and the beginning of the 1980s. This same pattern of trends established in the earlier period continuing in the later period is found for the moderate/high and low seigniorage-rate countries. An important exception to these trends is the case of Mexico and Peru. These two countries have "moved up" into the

Table 17.2 Average Inflation Rates for Very High Seigniorage-rate and Low Seigniorage-rate Countries

	Average of $\Delta H/GNP$	Average inflation rate
Very high seigniorage-rate countries		
Argentina	0.062	1.433
Peru	0.057	0.594
Mexico	0.056	0.238
Chile	0.037	0.440
Low seigniorage-rate countries		
United States	0.005	0.098
Honduras	0.009	0.106
Guatemala	0.010	0.108
El Salvador	0.011	0.146
Guyana	0.011	0.160

very high seigniorage-rate class since the earlier period addressed by Fischer, when they were in the moderate/high class.

Some of the highest individual annual seigniorage/GNP rates found while calculating the data presented in this study are a rate of 9.1% for Mexico in 1977; rates of 7.5% and 7.9% for Peru in 1979 and 1980, respectively; and a rate of 6.9% for Argentina in 1978.

A comparison of the present results on seigniorage/total revenue rates with the work of Fischer can be made for only 11 of the 19 countries addressed in this study, since data were missing for the others. For 6 of these 11 countries (Ecuador, El Salvador, Guatemala, Honduras, Venezuela, and the United States), seigniorage/total revenue rates for the period 1977–81 are similar to those that existed during the period 1960–75. For 3 of the 11 countries (Argentina, Chile, and Uruguay), the seigniorage/total revenue rate dropped by roughly 50% from the earlier period to the later, while the seigniorage/GNP rate remained similar. For 2 of the 11 countries (Paraguay and Peru), both types of seigniorage rates are found to have roughly doubled from their values in the earlier period.

Some of the highest individual seigniorage/total revenue rates found while calculating the data presented in this study are a rate of 41% for Mexico in 1977, a rate of 30% for Argentina in 1978, and a rate of 29% for Peru in 1979.

Connolly (1983) studied inflation, the variability of inflation rates, and currency pegging in Latin American countries. Of the 6 countries he identified as having strong dollar pegs during the period 1973–81, 4 (El Salvador, Guatemala, Honduras, and Venezuela) are found to be in the low seigniorage-rate class in this study. The other 2 of the 6 countries (Ecuador and Paraguay) are found to be in the moderate/high class.

This result agrees with the fact that countries that peg their currency, and cannot independently determine the amount of seigniorage they collect, create the smallest relative amount of high-powered money.

All 5 of the Latin American countries for which similarity between both types of seigniorage rates in the earlier and later period was found are nations that pegged their currency to the U.S. dollar for at least part of the two periods. Of the 4 countries that exhibited significant change in relative seigniorage revenues between the earlier and later periods, only 1 (Paraguay) employed a currency peg. This casual observance on currency pegging and the temporal stability of seigniorage rates is noted in light of other evidence that Latin American countries that have maintained currency pegs have evidenced monetary stability (Connolly, 1983).

In Argentina, Mexico, and Peru, average seigniorage was over 5% of GNP and over 20% of total revenue during the period addressed by this study, representing a significant source of funds. Seigniorage revenues in other Latin American countries are relatively high compared to the United

States or to a selection of other countries, both industrialized and developing. As both Fischer (1982) and Connolly (1983) point out, the size of a country's seigniorage revenue may influence a country's use of a currency peg or a foreign money. In the first of these two cases of means of monetary discipline, a country would not be able to determine the size of its seigniorage revenue; this would be dependent on monetary policy in the nation whose currency is being pegged to. In the second case of use of a foreign money, seigniorage revenue would be lost entirely. This loss of control over seigniorage or total loss of seigniorage revenue may be a major obstacle to currency pegging, the use of a common money, or other possible means of increasing economic stability in many Latin American countries.

3.2. Seigniorage Rates and Inflation

The reliance of Latin American countries on seigniorage must also be considered in light of the high inflation rates that countries with high seigniorage rates have experienced. Table 17.2 presents the average seigniorage/GNP rate and the average inflation rate for the period 1977–81 for five countries found to have seigniorage/GNP rates in the very high class, and for five countries with rates in the low class. There is a close relationship between seigniorage and inflation rates, at least for the particular countries and time period represented in Table 17.2. The high rates of inflation that the countries with high seigniorage rates have experienced signal a game of lessening returns, as the inflation that results from one round of money issue may force a government to expand the monetary base even more the next time around to achieve the same amount of real revenue, as the demand for money in real terms declines (Cagan, 1956).

Note

[1] If governments are backing the new money they issue with additional international reserves, then the supposition that there are minimal financial barriers to producing seigniorage revenues may be questioned.

References

Cagan, Phillip (1956). "The Monetary Dynamics of Hyper-inflation." In *Studies in the Quantity Theory of Money*, edited by Milton Friedman. Chicago: University of Chicago Press.

Connolly, Michael (1983). "The Case for Monetary Integration in Latin America." In *Stochastic Approaches to the Open Economy*, edited by J. Bhandari. Cambridge: M.I.T. Press.

Fischer, Stanley (1982). "Seigniorage and the Case for a National Money." *Journal of Political Economy*. 90 (April): 295–313.

International Monetary Fund (1982). *International Financial Statistics Yearbook 1982*. Washington, D.C.: International Monetary Fund.

List of Contributors

Michael Connolly is Professor of Economics at the University of South Carolina. He has held previous positions at Harvard University and the University of Florida. He has a B.A. degree from the University of California at Berkeley and a Ph.D. in Economics from the University of Chicago. Dr. Connolly has published articles on international economics in the major journals and has served as an economic consultant in Latin America, the Caribbean, and Africa.

Claudio González-Vega is Professor of Agricultural Economics and of Economics at the Ohio State University. Previously, he was Dean of Economic Science at the Universidad de Costa Rica. His undergraduate work was completed in Costa Rica, and he received his M.Sc. from the London School of Economics and his Ph.D. from Stanford University. Dr. González-Vega specializes in finance and development and has contributed a number of articles to academic journals on these subjects. He has served as an economic consultant in Latin America and the Caribbean, Asia, and Africa.

Mario Blejer is Senior Economist in the Fiscal Affairs Department of the International Monetary Fund. He has a Ph.D. degree in Economics from the University of Chicago. Dr. Blejer has held previous appointments at the Centro de Estudios Monetarios Latinoamericanos in Mexico City, New York University, Boston University, and the Hebrew University of Jerusalem. He has published widely in the area of international monetary economics, including key articles on Argentina, Brazil, and Mexico.

Philip Brock is Assistant Professor of Economics at Duke University. He holds a Ph.D. degree in Economics from Stanford University, specializes in international economics, and has done research as a Fulbright Scholar in Santiago, Chile.

Paul Burkett is Assistant Professor of Economics at the University of Miami, Miami. He has a Ph.D. degree in Economics from Syracuse University and specializes in development economics.

Guillermo A. Calvo is Professor of Economics at Columbia University. He holds a Ph.D. degree in Economics from Yale University. Dr. Calvo specializes in international economics and has published in the major journals. He has also served as an economic consultant in various countries in Latin America.

Víctor Canto is Associate Professor of Business and Finance at the University of Southern California. He has a Ph.D. in Economics from the University of Chicago and a B.S. degree from the Massachusetts Institute of Technology. Dr. Canto specializes in monetary issues in developing countries, has contributed in particular to the theory of currency substitution, and has served as an advisor to the Central Bank and Finance Ministry of the Dominican Republic.

Vittorio Corbo is Professor of Economics at the Pontificia Universidad Católica de Chile and is currently on leave at the World Bank as a participant in the Southern Cone Research Group. He has a Ph.D. degree in Economics from the Massachusetts Institute of Technology. Dr. Corbo specializes in international monetary economics and has published widely in major academic journals.

Sergio de la Cuadra is Professor of Economics at the Pontificia Universidad Católica de Chile. He has an advanced degree in Economics from the University of Chicago and has served as Minister of Finance and Governor of the Central Bank of Chile.

Andrés Dauhajre is Professor of Economics at the Universidad Católica Madre y Maestra. He has a Ph.D. degree in Economics from Columbia University. Dr. Dauhajre's specialty is international economics, and he is a consultant to the Central Bank of the Dominican Republic.

Sebastian Edwards is Assistant Professor of Economics at the University of California at Los Angeles. He received his Ph.D. degree in Economics from the University of Chicago. Dr. Edwards specializes in stabilization policies in Latin America and has published articles in major academic journals. He has also been Visiting Researcher at the World Bank as a participant in the Southern Cone Research Group.

Arturo Fernández-Pérez is Professor of Economics and Chairperson at the Instituto Tecnológico Autónomo de México in Mexico City. He holds a graduate degree from the University of Chicago and specializes in public finance and international economics. He is also a consultant to the Ministry of Finance of Mexico.

Hugo Guiliani Cury is Governor of the Central Bank of the Dominican Republic. He holds an advanced degree from the University of Miami and is a Professor at the Universidad Católica Madre y Maestra.

Arnold Harberger is Distinguished Professor of Economics at the University of Chicago and Professor of Economics at the University of California at Los Angeles. He received his doctorate from the University of Chicago. Dr. Harberger has made major contributions to the theory of taxation, welfare, international economics, and development economics. He has been a consultant to many governments internationally, particularly in Latin America.

Mohsin S. Khan is currently in the Research Department of the World Bank. He is a graduate of the London School of Economics and has published many articles on international economics and monetary subjects. His work has appeared regularly in the *IMF Staff Papers*.

John McDermott is Associate Professor of Economics at the University of South Carolina. He has a Ph.D. degree from Brown University. Dr. McDermott has held previous positions at the University of Delaware and at the Economic Commission for Latin America in Santiago, Chile. His field is international economics, with specialization in Brazil.

Lynn McFadden is Staff Economist with the Economics Group, Chase Manhattan Bank, New York. She has a Master's degree in Economics from the University of South Carolina.

Jaime de Melo is Research Economist of the Development Research Department of the World Bank. He has a Ph.D. degree from Johns Hopkins University and codirected the Southern Cone Research Group. He has worked extensively on the case of Uruguay.

Edward J. Ray is Professor of Economics and Chairperson of the Economics Department at the Ohio State University. Dr. Ray's specialty is trade and tariff restrictions, and he has published numerous journal articles on these topics.

Silvia Sagari is Assistant Professor of Economics at New York University. Dr. Sagari's specialty is international monetary economics.

Edward Tower is Professor of Economics at Duke University. He has a B.A. and a Ph.D. degree from Harvard University. Dr. Tower's specialty is international economics. He has published many articles in major journals and is an economic consultant in Africa, particularly the Sudan.

Robert C. Vogel is on leave from the University of Miami, Miami. He has a Ph.D. degree in Economics from Stanford University. Dr. Vogel specializes in money and finance in developing countries. He has served as an economic consultant in Chile, Costa Rica, and Ecuador and on the Staff of the Council of Economic Advisors.

Summer 1985 International Economics Students of ITAM (Instituto Tecnológico Autónomo México): Alejandra Alvarado-Ham, Miguel Angel Díaz-Ayala, Felipe Gerardo Figueroa-Muñoz, Gerardo Freire-Alvarado, Eugenio González-Luna, Juan Antonio Laguna-Guerrero, Ander Legorreta-Molina, Antonio Martínez-Mendoza, Diana Mier y Concha, José Pacheco-Meyer, Gabriela Quesada-Lastiri, Antonia Ruíz-Suarez, Jaime Villaseñor-Zertudie, Juan Salles-Vincourt, Ricardo Weihmann-Illades, and Martín Werner-Wainfeld.

Sweder van Wijnbergen is Staff Economist at the World Bank. Dr. Wijnbergen's specialty is international monetary economics and the exchange rate. He has published numerous articles in major U.S. and European journals.

Roberto Zahler is Economist at the Economic Commission for Latin America in Santiago, Chile. He holds a Ph.D. degree from the University of Chicago and specializes in money and exchange rate questions in Latin America.

James E. Zinser is Professor of Economics at Oberlin College. He has a Ph.D. degree in Economics from the University of Oregon. Dr. Zinser specializes in financial intermediation in Latin America, about which he has published several articles, and has carried out research in Buenos Aires.